GOVERNING EUROPE

Governing the European Union

Contributors to this volume

Simon Bromley, Faculty of Social Sciences, The Open University.

Laura Cram, Department of Government, University of Strathclyde.

Richard Heffernan, Faculty of Social Sciences, The Open University.

Brigid Laffan, Dublin European Institute, University College Dublin.

Paul Lewis, Faculty of Social Sciences, The Open University.

Christopher Lord, Institute for Politics and International Studies, University of Leeds.

David Scott Bell, Institute for Politics and International Studies, University of Leeds.

Michael Smith, Department of European Studies, Loughborough University.

Daniel Wincott, Department of Politics and International Studies, University of Birmingham.

GOVERNING EUROPE

Governing the European Union

edited by Simon Bromley

SAGE Publications
London • Thousand Oaks • New Delhi

in association with

The Open University

This publication forms part of the Open University course DD200 *Governing Europe*. The other books that make up the *Governing Europe* series are listed on the back cover. Details of this and other Open University courses can be obtained from the Call Centre, PO Box 724, The Open University, Milton Keynes MK7 6ZS, United Kingdom: tel. +44 (0)1908 653231, e-mail ces-gen@open.ac.uk

Alternatively, you may visit the Open University website at http://www.open.ac.uk where you can learn more about the wide range of courses and packs offered at all levels by The Open University.

For availability of other course components, contact Open University Worldwide Ltd, The Berrill Building, Walton Hall, Milton Keynes MK7 6AA, United Kingdom: tel. +44 (0)1908 858785; fax +44 (0)1908 858787; e-mail ouwenq@open.ac.uk; website http://www.ouw.co.uk

SAGE Publications Ltd
6 Bonhill Street
London EC2A 4PU

SAGE Publications Inc.
2455 Teller Road
Thousand Oaks
California 91320

SAGE Publications India Pvt Ltd
32, M-Block Market
Greater Kailash - I
New Delhi 110 048

British Library Cataloguing in Publication Data
A catalogue record for this book is available from The British Library.

Library of Congress catalog record 133449.

Edited, designed and typeset by The Open University.

Printed and bound in the United Kingdom by The Bath Press, Bath.

ISBN 0 7619 5460 0 (hbk)
ISBN 0 7619 5461 9 (pbk)

1.1

Contents

PREFACES   ix

**CHAPTER 1   INTRODUCTION: GOVERNANCE AND
                    THE EUROPEAN UNION**   **1**
Simon Bromley

1   Introduction   1

2   Politics and government   5

3   Models of the EU   13

4   Looking forward   17

References   25

Further reading   26

CHAPTER 2   BUILDING THE EUROPEAN UNION   **27**
Richard Heffernan

1   Introduction   27

2   The history of the EU   29

3   Exploring European interdependence   36

4   Issues of formation and development   40

5   The EU from a historical perspective   46

6   Conclusion   51

References   52

Further reading   52

**CHAPTER 3   THE NATION STATE IN THE
                    EUROPEAN UNION**   **53**
Simon Bromley

1   Introduction   53

2   Europe and the modern states system   54

3   The pattern of integration in Western Europe   61

4   The governance of the EU   66

5   Beyond the sovereign state?   72

6   Conclusion   78

References   80

Further reading   80

**CHAPTER 4 LAW, ORDER AND ADMINISTRATION
IN THE EUROPEAN UNION   81**
Daniel Wincott

1   Introduction   81

2   Law, the European Court of Justice and the European
    Community   83

3   Europe and the administration of 'law and order'   99

4   Conclusion   108

References   110

Further reading   112

**CHAPTER 5 THE RE-FORGING OF EUROPEAN
POLITICAL TRADITIONS   113**
David Scott Bell

1   Introduction   113

2   European political culture and the party traditions   116

3   The party traditions   121

4   Party traditions in the European Parliament   136

5   Conclusion   140

References   141

Further reading   142

**CHAPTER 6 INTEGRATION AND POLICY
PROCESSES IN THE EUROPEAN UNION   143**
Laura Cram

1   Introduction   143

2   What is European integration?   144

3   Integration and the EU as a system of governance   151

4   Conclusion   161

References   162

Further reading   164

CHAPTER 7 DEMOCRACY AND DEMOCRATIZATION IN THE EUROPEAN UNION 165

Christopher Lord

1	Introduction	165
2	What is democracy?	166
3	Democratization of the EU through national institutions	170
4	A democratic political system at the European level?	174
5	The further democratization of the EU	183
6	Conclusion	187
	References	187
	Further reading	190

CHAPTER 8 FINANCE AND BUDGETARY PROCESSES IN THE EUROPEAN UNION 191

Brigid Laffan

1	Introduction	191
2	Why study the EU budget?	192
3	A short history of the EU budget	195
4	Making and managing the EU budget	202
5	The future of the budget – Agenda 2000	212
6	Finance and governance	216
7	Conclusion	219
	References	220
	Further reading	220

CHAPTER 9 THE ENLARGEMENT OF THE EUROPEAN UNION 221

Paul Lewis

1	Introduction	221
2	Enlargement and the contemporary EU	222
3	The history of EU enlargement	228
4	The contemporary process of enlargement	236

5 Enlargement: facing new challenges 246

6 Conclusion 252

References 253

Further reading 254

CHAPTER 10 EUROPEAN FOREIGN AND SECURITY POLICY 255

Michael Smith

1 Introduction 255

2 Statehood, security and foreign policy 258

3 From political co-operation to a foreign and defence policy 262

4 The EU and the architecture of European foreign and security policy 272

5 The EU and the management of European security 276

6 Conclusion 282

References 285

Further reading 286

CHAPTER 11 CONCLUSION: WHAT IS THE EUROPEAN UNION? 287

Simon Bromley

1 Introduction 287

2 The EU: intergovernmental or supranational? 288

3 Is the EU a regulatory state? 293

4 Questions of governance, authority and legitimacy 299

References 302

Further reading 303

APPENDIX A CHRONOLOGY OF THE BUILDING OF THE EUROPEAN UNION 304

INDEX 311

ACKNOWLEDGEMENTS 326

Series preface

The three volumes that appear in this series are part of the course *Governing Europe* from the Faculty of Social Sciences at The Open University. The course is, in the main, the product of the Politics Discipline within the Faculty, but it has benefited from the participation of a number of academic colleagues from other areas of the University, notably from the Economics, Sociology, Social Policy and Geography Disciplines and from the Arts Faculty. The interdisciplinary approach fostered by this co-operation carries on a long tradition of courses originating within the Faculty of Social Sciences that have tried to preserve a broadly based academic output across the social sciences. The Open University remains almost unique in its ability to foster and preserve such an approach, despite moves toward strict discipline lines across the academic world more generally. The three books in this series, while specializing in particular aspects of the issue of governing Europe, maintain an interdisciplinary style throughout. The fact that the books still stand together as a coherent series, and work for the course as a whole, is testament to the ability, enthusiasm and sheer hard work of my colleagues on the Course Team. I thank them all.

To mention all of the people associated with the project by name would create an impossibly long list, but I must record my special thanks to a number of individuals. First, without the other two editors of the books, Simon Bromley and Montserrat Guibernau, life would have been impossible in the three years that it took to prepare the course. Their role has been central to the successful outcome of the project. With clear and penetrating analytical skills and patient attention to detail, they have accomplished the successive drafting and redrafting of chapters with cheery good humour, even while working under impossibly tight schedules. I would also like to extend very special thanks to the course manager for *Governing Europe*, Eileen Potterton. Seldom has someone so new to the OU grasped the tasks at hand so quickly, so firmly and to such good effect. Her expert managerial skills and unflappable manner have calmed the nerves and smoothed the brows of many a fraught academic. Other key members of the Course Team – Paul Lewis, Richard Heffernan, Mark Smith, Will Brown, Chris Brook and Mark Pittaway – made their own invaluable contribution to the collective discussions that helped frame the books and establish their content. Rob Clifton and Bob Kelly, ably assisted by two OU Associate Lecturers, Brenda Martin and Graham Venters, added the final touches as they constantly reminded us of the primary teaching objectives of these texts. Dianne Cook, Anne Hunt and June Ayres typed and formatted three drafts of each chapter with their usual good-natured efficiency.

Added to this have been the meticulous editorial skills of Mark Goodwin and Lynne Slocombe, the graphic design skills of Caroline Husher, who designed the striking covers for the books, and Jonathan Hunt and Gill Gowans from the Copublishing Department, who helped to launch the series with Sage. And in this respect I would like to thank Lucy Robinson of Sage, both for her early enthusiasm for the project and for her later support and guidance as the books moved through the production process and into the public domain.

The Open University could not operate as successfully as it does without contributions from academics and others from outside the institution. The *Governing Europe* series has relied upon a wide range of academic input from specialists in European politics and economics from a number of universities in the UK and mainland Europe. This refreshing additional scholarship has only added to the quality of the product. Special mention must also be made of the External Assessor of *Governing Europe*, Mike Smith of the University of Loughborough. As one of the UK's ablest and wisest European Studies academics, his careful and thoughtful assessment of the chapter drafts and his expert advice more generally on matters European have been warmly appreciated.

Finally, two colleagues who have now left The Open University, David Held and Anthony McGrew, were instrumental in getting the course up and running, along with the then Head of the Discipline, Richard Maidment. The fact that I inherited a course structure and a set of book proposals from these colleagues that did not change to any great extent after they had left the project is a testament to the originality and robustness of their early proposals.

Grahame Thompson
Chair, *Governing Europe*
Milton Keynes, August 2000

Book preface

I would like to thank all the contributors to this volume for the generosity with which they have given of their time, skills and effort. In the midst of many other concerns, they have all responded admirably, and often at short notice, to produce work of high quality. The Course Team on *Governing Europe*, especially our Chair, Grahame Thompson, made a great contribution in steadily improving successive drafts as the book began to take shape. I would also like to record my appreciation of David Held and Anthony McGrew, who did so much work to give shape to this book before I took over as editor. Their initial thinking made my job much easier. Anne Hunt, June Ayres and Dianne Cook worked on successive drafts with great professionalism and unfailing good humour. Mark Goodwin and Lynne Slocombe edited the book with such skill and calm that my role was made easier than I had either reason or right to expect. And lastly, but by no means least, I would like to say a special word of thanks to our External Assessor on *Governing Europe*, Mike Smith, who not only contributed to this volume above and beyond the call of duty but was also an indispensable source of wise counsel and helpful advice.

Simon Bromley
Editor, *Governing the European Union*
Milton Keynes, August 2000

Chapter 1
Introduction: Governance and the European Union

Simon Bromley

1 Introduction

As the European Union (EU) moves into the twenty-first century it is worth pausing to note the dramatic change in Europe's fortunes over the course of the last hundred years or so. For the first half of the twentieth century Europe was an arena of political conflict and violence, both within and between states, and the focus of two world-wide wars that left millions of people dead. Yet in the next 50 years Europe was transformed dramatically as nation states that had once been rivals, even military enemies, came together to form an apparently permanent, open-ended, expanding and unified political system to govern an ever increasing amount of their common affairs. The transformation began with the Treaty of Paris (1951), which established the European Coal and Steel Community, and continued through the Treaty of Rome (1957), which set up the European Economic Community (EEC), to the Treaty on European Union (TEU) (1992). The TEU brought into being the EU itself and consolidated moves toward greater co-operation in a Common Foreign and Security Policy, Justice and Home Affairs and Economic and Monetary Union. The development of the EU represents a remarkable political departure for Europe (see Box 1.1 overleaf). At first the experiment was confined to the liberal-democratic states of Western Europe, as the Cold War division of the continent into 'East' and 'West' had brought Central and Eastern Europe under communist and Soviet control. But given the dissolution of communism and the end of the Cold War at the start of the 1990s, the membership of the EU now looks set to expand.

There are many questions that can be asked about this remarkable development. To begin with, there is a range of historical questions about the origins of European integration. We might ask about the reasons for European integration and the development of the EU. Why did a limited agreement between six war-ravaged states – West Germany, France, Italy, Belgium, the Netherlands and Luxembourg – to create a means of administering and reconstructing their coal and steel industries evolve

Box 1.1 The development of the European Union

1951 The Treaty of Paris, signed by Belgium, France, West Germany, Italy, Luxembourg and the Netherlands (the 'Six'), establishes the European Coal and Steel Community (ECSC), which comes into operation in 1952.

1957 The Treaties of Rome, signed by the Six, establish the European Economic Community (EEC) and European Atomic Energy Community (Euratom), which come into operation in 1958.

1965 The Brussels (Merger) Treaty is signed, bringing the ECSC, Euratom and the EEC into a common institutional format, the European Communities, which takes effect in 1967.

1973 The first 'enlargement': Denmark, Ireland and the United Kingdom join the Community.

1981 Greece joins the Community.

1986 Spain and Portugal join the Community.

The Single European Act is passed to speed up and complete the creation of the Common Market outlined in the Treaty of Rome that established the EEC.

1990 The unification of East and West Germany (the territory of the former East Germany becomes part of the Community).

1992 The Treaty on European Union is signed at Maastricht, establishing the three 'pillars' of the renamed European Union. The first pillar is the European Communities; the second pillar is a Common Foreign and Security Policy; and the third pillar is co-operation in the field of Justice and Home Affairs. The Maastricht Treaty also establishes a timetable and framework for Economic and Monetary Union and the introduction of a single currency.

1995 Austria, Finland and Sweden join the EU.

1997 The Treaty of Amsterdam strengthens the basis for co-operation in the second and third pillars and increases the power of the European Parliament.

into a political system that includes all the major states of Western Europe? Moreover, why did this political system develop its own bureaucracy, parliament and courts, with at least some responsibility for nearly all aspects of government and public policy? Next, we might be interested in the way the political system thus created works. How does a Union of (currently) fifteen separate nation states, each with its own government, operate as a political system? How is the EU organized, politically speaking, what are its principal institutions and what do they do? How are decisions taken, and how are political demands and needs registered in the system, translated into policy and administered or executed as outcomes? And finally, what *is* the European Union? What is it for, and what has become of the member states that have made it, and are continuing to make it, as it takes on an ever deeper role and wider membership? What kind of institution or organization does the EU represent? Is it unique? How do the member states within it relate to one another and to the Union itself, and in what ways have they been transformed as a result of building the Union?

In May 1950 Robert Schuman (right), the French Foreign Minister, and Jean Monnet (left), France's Planning Commissioner, put forward the Schuman Plan, which led to the formation of the ECSC.

In short, why did the EU develop, how does it work and what type of political system does it represent? These questions are closely related to one another and represent three different approaches to the EU. In this book we are concerned with all three questions to some extent, but our principal focus is the third question. What kind of political system is the EU, how does it relate to the political systems of its member states, and how do these systems interact and evolve over time? We have put these kinds of questions at the front of our investigation because we believe that the EU represents a novel kind of political entity. We are primarily concerned to understand the nature of this entity and the ways in which its member states seek to use it to govern Europe. Thus this is not a book about the history or theory of European integration as such, nor is it primarily concerned with the detail of politics and policy within the EU. (See Dinan (1999) for a comprehensive account of the processes and history of European integration; Rosamond (2000) for a survey of theories of integration; and Hix (1999) and Nugent (1999) for analyses of the EU political system.) This book does not ignore the history of European integration and the development of the EU or neglect the politics and policy of the EU. It is simply that its emphasis lies elsewhere, on investigating the nature of the EU and its relations with its member states as a way of examining the significance of its history and the relevance of its policies for the governance of Europe.

Our focus on the 'what' questions – what is the EU, what is it for and what are the relations between the EU and its member states? – also represents an attempt to investigate something that has become, if anything, harder to comprehend over time. Somewhat paradoxically, the nature of the EU is in some respects less clear now than it was in the 1950s. We know a great deal about the historical origins of European integration and the subsequent development of the EU, and the reasons for its formation are by now understood fairly well. But whatever the reasons for the formation of the Union, it has continued to evolve in unforeseen ways in radically changing circumstances. The EU of the 1990s is not simply the Community of the 1950s writ large. There is thus a limit to how far an understanding of the EU's past can assist our comprehension of it in the present. What we need to grasp is just what the EU does for its member states, or what they are able to do by means of it, such that they continue to give it their support. We also know a great deal about how politics and policy operate within the EU. As a result of painstaking research by a generation of scholars, the details of how the EU works, politically speaking, are well understood. But what is all this policy *for*, and what difference does it make to the governance of the member states, either domestically or in terms of their relations with one another?

The answers to these questions – what does the EU do for its members, what difference does it make? – remain something of a puzzle. In fact, as suggested above, they may be more difficult to answer now than they were 50 years ago. When six states signed the Treaty of Rome to establish a common market in the EEC it was relatively straightforward to say what they were doing. But when fifteen states collectively call themselves a Union, when the citizens of the member states are also (to some extent) legally and politically citizens of the Union, and when the Union has growing responsibilities in all the core areas traditionally associated with the government of sovereign states, it is by no means clear what is going on. This book is above all an attempt to unravel this paradox.

In the rest of this chapter I shall introduce some of the main themes developed in more detail in the book. Our aim is to explore the idea that the EU represents a novel kind of political system but this is not as straightforward as it appears: it is much easier to say what the EU is not than to give a convincing account of it in positive terms. There are perhaps two main reasons for this, which must be borne in mind as you read this book. First, there is the obvious but important point that the EU is a 'moving target', constantly evolving and developing as its membership changes, as it is called upon to perform new tasks in new ways and as the external environment in which it operates changes. This more or less constant change means that any characterization of the EU is liable to be superseded by subsequent developments. It also means that any attempt to capture the nature of the EU, if it is to prove of more than momentary relevance, is duty bound to offer an account of the process of change itself, to interpret a pattern of integration for which we cannot know the end point.

The fact that the EU is developing, in an as yet unknown direction, is another way of saying, second, that it is *new*: it is neither a conventional state nor a normal intergovernmental organization, yet it operates as a political system of some kind. In this respect, the difficulty raised by the EU is that we are accustomed to thinking about and analysing politics in the context of the nation state. But there is no necessary connection between the two. Or, to state matters rather more precisely, one can certainly have politics and a political system without a state, even if one cannot have a state without politics. The nation state is only one way of configuring the generic activity of politics and governance. To make this point clearly, I must, first, say something about what we mean by the general activity of 'politics' and the idea of 'governance', and second, demonstrate that the government of the nation state is only one way of organizing political life.

2   Politics and government

The word 'politics' is typically associated with the business of governments and states, the sphere of public policy and questions of authority. We shall see that politics is all these things, but it is useful to start by drawing a few distinctions for the sake of clarity. In the most general sense of the term, politics is a particular kind of social activity concerned with the authoritative control of social interaction, that is, a form of control in which some have the power of command over others. As such, political activity can be distinguished from other types of social interaction (say, cultural or economic) not by reason of its subject matter, nor even primarily by its distinctive methods, but rather by the kinds of circumstances that call for political action, by the predicament that gives rise to the need for politics. Politics cannot be defined by its subject matter, since this is potentially limitless: there is a politics of death and taxes, a politics of the economy and welfare, a politics of the arts, a politics of religion, sex and so forth. Nor can politics be characterized by its methods or means as, say, the exercise of power, since power is itself multifaceted and not all relations of power are political ones – see Mann (1986) and Runciman (1989). Politics is certainly related to the exercise of power but only in a special sense. It is about the exercise of power in relation to a particular kind of predicament: namely, a situation in which a group or association or society of people require a common course of action or policy or rule to govern their conduct. If all members of the population had identical interests and beliefs, a common policy could emerge on the basis of consensus without the need for authoritative control. But in reality social interaction is typically characterized by differences of interest and belief, and some means must be found to formulate and give effect to collectively binding rules. That is to say, some must have the power of command (authority) over others. Political activity in its most general sense is a response to this predicament and, when it is successful, it results in authoritative social control for the population.

Politics, then, is the field of collectively binding, authoritative decision making. In this most general sense, political activity is ubiquitous in, as well as across and between, modern societies, operating in many different places and at many different levels. Wherever a group or association requires a common policy, and whenever there is disagreement about what that policy should be, there is scope for politics. Many such groups – families, churches, multinational firms, trades unions, non-governmental organizations, universities and so on – exist in modern societies, and each may be said to give rise to politics in the most general sense of the term. Moreover, most such organized groups develop specific procedures and, on occasion, specialized institutions for arriving at and giving effect to the common policy of the group. These arrangements are often and rightly called structures of 'governance', since they involve attempts at rule making, social co-ordination and steering based on collective action for common purposes. In its most general sense, then, 'governance' refers to the arrangements by which groups arrive at and give effect to a common policy: that is, governance is the relatively standardized processes and institutions by which purposeful outcomes are produced for any political system. Thus we may speak of corporate governance, university govern-ance, the governance of international non-governmental organizations, and so forth.

In *Governing the European Union*, however, we are primarily interested in politics and governance in a more singular but also more encompassing sense: namely, with the kind of political activity that occurs at the level of society as a whole. Politics in this respect refers to the realm of collectively binding decision making for society as a whole, the sphere of *public* policy in its broadest sense. This kind of politics is about the making, implementing and enforcing of rules for the collective, public aspects of social life, that is, politics at the level of government and the state. This is reflected in our everyday usage of the word 'government'. Consider the following definitions.

> The [governance] of units like the family, the Church, the trade union or the firm may properly be called 'private' government. It is, however, to what might by contrast be called 'public' government, that is to say, the government of the territorial state, that the term 'government' is commonly applied.
>
> (Finer, 1970, p.37)

> For any given population, a government exists for them to the degree that one of the groups exercising authority over them exercises authority over all the others or claims, without challenge from a rival claimant, a generalized authority for its orders over those of every other organization. It may not make effective its claimed priority in case of conflict, and in some

cases may not even wish to enforce a priority. But the generality
and uniqueness of its claim to priority distinguish it.

(Lindblom, 1977, pp.21–2)

What is explicit in Finer, and implied by Lindblom, is that in modern
societies when we speak of 'the government' we are concerned with
political activity at the level of the state, since states exercise rule over a
fixed territory and its population and so define the scope and limits of a
society. The need for government in this more singular but encompassing
sense arises when a state requires a common policy and rival structures of
governance (Finer's 'private' governments) within the population advocate policies that are mutually exclusive: 'government and politics come
into contact at the point where a course of action has to be selected for
the whole of the society' (Finer, 1970, p.6).

In summary, within the state politics can be studied as the social activity
concerned with the formation and implementation of collectively binding public policy, that is, the realm of authoritative decision making.
Political governance can be analysed in terms of the institutions, rules
and actors involved in collective decision making, that is, the ways and
means by which the members of a society seek to realize their political
objectives. Thus while politics is an ever present feature of social
interaction, nation states are compulsory, territorial associations claiming
to exercise exclusive rule through a government. A 'government' is a set
of institutions and procedures for taking and giving effect to political
decisions at the level of the state: it is the public authority concerned with
rule making (the legislature), implementing policy (the executive) and
adjudicating disputes (the judiciary).

2.1   The nation state

In this context, it is important to note that the member states of the EU
are highly distinctive kinds of political entity, representing only one form
of politics and governance for society as a whole. There is a vast academic
literature about the concept of the state and the different historical types
of state, but for our purposes here it is sufficient simply to list some of the
key features of the European 'nation state'. Sam Finer (1997, pp.2–3) has
described these features as follows.

1   They are territorially defined populations, each recognizing a common
paramount organ of government.

2   This organ is served by specialized personnel: a civil service to carry out
decisions and a military service to back these by force where necessary
and to protect the association from similarly constituted associations.

3   The state so characterized is recognized by other similarly constituted
states as independent in its action on its territorially defined – and
hence confined – population, that is, on its subjects. This recognition
constitutes what we would today call its international 'sovereignty'.

4   Ideally at least, but to a large extent in practice also, the population of the state forms a community of feeling – a *Gemeinschaft* [a community of identity] based on self-consciousness of a common nationality.

5   Ideally at least, and again to a large extent in practice, the population forms a community in the sense that its members mutually participate in distributing and sharing duties and benefits.

In the case of the constitutional nation states that developed in Europe, especially in the nineteenth century, the kinds of states that are now the norm within the EU, three further features are worth noting (see Finer, 1997, pp.1298–303). To begin with, relations between people, as well as between individuals and groups and the government, are subject to legal regulation. Next, the members of these states are citizens capable of participating in the process of government, not merely objects to be administered as subjects of absolute authority. And finally, significant aspects of social interaction – especially, the economy and the domestic realm of family life – are respected as in some ways 'private' and beyond the direct control of the public authorities.

This combination of features – legality, citizenship and respect for the private sphere – within constitutional nation states implies that the governance exercised by the state does not extend to all aspects of social interaction. Significant areas of social life are either ungoverned or left to govern themselves through whatever 'private' or self-governance they can fashion. How does society, the myriad forms of ungoverned and privately or self-governed social interaction, relate to the more formal apparatus of the government and the state? There is no simple answer to this question. It is likely that patterns of power and influence flow in both directions: upwards, from the ungoverned and privately governed processes located in society to the formal institutions of government and the state; and downwards, from the public activity of the government and the state, that is, the law and public policy, to the workings of 'private' arenas. Two main generalizations may be added to this model.

First, nation states make *claims* to an exclusive and compulsory form of rule across fixed territories. The rule of the state is exclusive in that it recognizes no competitors within its territory, and it is compulsory in so far as it is, in the last instance, coercively imposed by an effective monopoly of the organized means of violence. Nation states assert the supremacy of top-down government over the claims of other forms of 'private' governance within their societies. But these claims are always *conditional* and imperfectly realized, as a claim to supremacy on behalf of a government requires a reciprocal recognition of its validity by the people and their 'private' governance structures. To see the importance of this we need only note that, in principle, the political rules of a society can be established and upheld in different ways. Collectively binding decisions that involve the power of some to command others can be made through the threat or use of force, by means of material inducements of one kind or another, or because the rules are regarded as appropriate or right by those who have to follow them. In short, force, bribery and legitimacy.

The last of these, that is, political rule and the power to command that are regarded as rightful, is termed 'legitimate political authority'. For the most part, politics in liberal-democratic states is based on legitimate authority; the political rule has a normative foundation and does not operate simply on the basis of force and bribery. Governments operate mainly by means of governmental authority. If governments lack authority they must resort to other bases of rule, namely coercion or bribery, and these are generally less effective as they involve the deployment of costly resources. As Charles Lindblom points out: 'The efficiency of authority – specifically, the low marginal cost of any single exercise of authoritative control – explains its central role in government. Governmental control through *ad hoc* deployment of rewards and penalties ... is hopelessly expensive and time consuming for the vast tasks of government' (1977, p.22).

But what makes the exercise of power legitimate? David Beetham argues that that power is legitimate 'to the extent that: (i) it conforms to established rules; (ii) the rules can be justified by reference to beliefs shared by both dominant and subordinate, and (iii) there is evidence of consent by the subordinate to the particular power relation' (1991, pp.15–16). In the case of political authority in liberal-democratic states, the legitimacy of the government depends on a specific set of criteria of legality, justifiability and legitimation. These are:

> ... the constitutional rule of law as the distinctive liberal-democratic mode of legality; the principle of popular sovereignty as the source of its political authority, and a broadly construed rights defence (freedom, welfare, security) as the purpose of government; consent subsumed under electoral authorization; and external recognition and support for its distinctive political arrangements.
>
> (Beetham and Lord, 1998, p.9)

The second generalization is that nation states also assert their independence from external structures of governance based outside their territories. Nation states have, or at least claim, what Finer referred to above as international 'sovereignty'. Whereas a claim to internal or domestic supremacy must be matched by a reciprocal recognition by the population, a claim for independence *vis-à-vis* other similarly constituted states must be matched by other states. And where such a claim is not recognized as legitimate it too must be defended by force and bribery. In fact, it has been conventional to distinguish domestic from international politics precisely on the basis of this issue. Domestic politics, governance within the territory of the state, has been seen as the potential site of legitimate politics, the realm where authority may rule. This is not to say that all governments govern by means of legitimate authority, merely that it is possible. Relations *between* states, in contrast, have been seen as inherently ungovernable, since there is no form of legitimate authority beyond or above the nation state at the level of the inter-state system, nor even one with a monopoly over the means of coercion of the kind that is available to governments operating within a nation state. For this reason the relations between states have traditionally been described as *anarchic*, not to signal chaos but more precisely to indicate the absence of any superordinate authority within the international system. To establish collectively binding rules for the relations between states there is only force, or the threat of force, and bribery – there is no legitimacy. As it has been traditionally understood, the inter-state system is not really a *political* system at all. Such rules as may apply are either followed as a result of the self-interested calculations of states or are imposed by coercion.

Box 1.2   Some key terms

Politics. The activity of arriving at and giving effect to a common policy in circumstances where one is needed but there are alternative courses of action. It involves some having the power of command over others.

Governance. The relatively standardized processes and institutions by which purposeful outcomes are produced in any political system.

Government. The specialized, formal governance structure of a state.

State. The organization of exclusive and compulsory rule over a territory and people.

Nation state. A territorially organized people, with a government that successfully claims domestic supremacy and external independence, a monopoly over the organized means of violence and a degree of mass or popular legitimacy.

Authority. The power of command of a ruler or an office over subordinates.

Legitimacy. A complex of normative rules, justifications and consent that can underpin an exercise of power.

Anarchy. A condition in which politics, governance and government based on authority are not possible.

International or *inter-state system*. The external relations between states, characterized by anarchy.

Let me summarize the discussion thus far (see Box 1.2). Within nation states the government is the principal agency and site of governance, the way in which political power is organized and directed, at least for the collective, public decisions of society as a whole. Governments govern through authority, which in liberal democracies is law-bound and derives from the people. In the international system of relations between states, in contrast, there is no authoritative governance. Each state rules itself and nothing rules the collectivity of states, even though the latter might call itself an 'international community'. This does not mean that the international system lacks order, merely that any order is not the result of purposive, collectively binding decision making.

2.2 Some questions of governance

In addition to the relations between states, two other realms *within* society are often said to be anarchic, that is, lacking in superordinate, binding relations of authority. The most obvious is the market economy; the other is civil society, the realm of interaction among individuals, families, groups and organizations that is neither part of the economy nor part of the state. Let us consider the example of the economy. If the principal means of government is authority, the basic feature of the economy is 'allocation', understood as the production and exchange of goods and services. Allocation involves processes that transform goods and services of one kind into another, as well as the transfer of control or ownership of those goods and services from one set of people to another. In market economies, the system of allocation is highly decentralized, in so far as there are many different producers of goods and services, each specializing in different ways and to different degrees. Co-ordination between different producers and between producers and consumers is brought about by prices set by the interaction of supply and demand in competitive markets. Whereas the authoritative co-ordination of govern-ment involves collective choice, market allocation is the realm of individual choice, or at least choices by small groups.

In a market economy, what the Scottish economist Adam Smith (1723–90) called the 'invisible hand', that is, the self-interested interaction of producers and consumers responding to prices in competitive markets, determines the overall outcome in a decentralized system of allocation. Hugely complicated feats of co-ordination are achieved without anyone consciously willing the outcome. In both the economy and civil society there may be islands of private governance, even limited forms of authority (as of bosses over workers, or of parents over children), but there is no overarching, purposive, binding authority other than that provided from without by the government and the state. (In this latter respect, therefore, these realms are also distinct from the international system, which cannot be governed from the outside, since there is neither authority nor a coercive monopoly beyond the state.)

The political order, ruled by a set of permanent, centralized and authoritatively co-ordinated institutions of government – what the seventeenth-century English political philosopher Thomas Hobbes (1588–1679) christened the 'Leviathan', stands over and against the 'natural' social orders of the market and civil society. (The 'Leviathan' is a sea monster from the Book of Job in the Bible.) These institutions are natural in the sense that order arises spontaneously by the interaction of uncoordinated private actions. And as Jack Lively and Andrew Reeve have pointed out, 'questions of the relationship between the state and these alternative orders and of the modes of mediation between them have determined in important ways the modern political agenda' (1997, p.65). On closer inspection, however, the image of a Leviathan state ruling the natural orders of the economy and society from without, standing guard over and against these orders, and protecting them from other states outside the territory, may be somewhat misleading. There are two dimensions to consider in this regard.

First, since the rule of constitutional nation states is conditional and limited, the relation of governance between governors and governed is best understood not simply as one of 'rulers' and 'ruled', but rather as one in which each conditions and mutually controls the other, and in which both parties are subjected to the pattern of legitimation founded in the rule of law and democratic politics. In this context, the *de facto*, informal, self-governing activities of the governed may regulate (that is, govern) the *de jure*, formal rulers of the state just as much as the latter govern the former. That is, the laws that the state can make may be constrained by the interests and activities of the governed just as much as those activities are regulated by the law. (Although this point has been much emphasized in the recent literature on questions of governance in complex, contemporary societies, it was in fact formulated as early as the seventeenth century by John Locke (1632–1704) in his criticism of Hobbes's theory of the state. Since then it has been a persistent, if submerged, theme of liberal political theory.)

Second, while it is true that there is no authority above and beyond that of the nation state in the inter-state system, it does not follow that states acting together cannot accord one another respect and develop 'principles, norms, rules and decision-making procedures'(Krasner, 1983, p.1), in short, institutions, to regulate their common affairs and interaction. Moreover, if a degree of consensus among states emerged, perhaps through extensive participation in shared institutions, they might come to regard the principles and so forth as legitimate. In this case, while the international system would not have a *government*, it would still be formally anarchic; it would have developed a degree of informal *governance*. (Once again, this idea has been recently emphasized in the idea of international 'governance without government', but it was anticipated by the eighteenth-century moral and political philosopher Immanuel Kant (1724–1804).) The likelihood of this happening is reinforced once we recognize that the natural orders of the economy and society are not necessarily territorially constrained by the scope of governmental authority. Economic and social interactions often cross national borders in ways that escape the effective control of the state. And just as governments may share the governance of 'their' societies with the self-governing processes of, say, the economy, so they may also share in the governance of international or transnational economic processes with other states.

3 Models of the EU

The study of the EU is important and challenging precisely because it raises these kinds of questions about governance. The EU undermines any sharp distinction between the governance that governments are responsible for within the state, and the ungoverned, anarchical nature of their relations with one another. The EU is a political system, a structure of governance, that spans the domestic or national level, on the one side, and the intergovernmental or international level, on the other. In so doing it challenges us to rethink our conventional ideas about governance. As Helen Wallace writes, 'the EU is an "in between" phenomenon, both a transformation of country politics and a new form of relationships between countries' (2000, p.100). The EU undermines the idea that governance in a member state is the sole responsibility of the government of that state, since much of what happens politically within the territories of the member states now depends on decisions taken by the Union. By the same token, the relations between the member states of the Union are no longer ungoverned, since much of their 'inter-state' interaction with one another is also structured by decisions taken at the level of the EU. In addition, while it is clear that the EU has been constructed by states – it is the result of a succession of international treaties – much of the impetus for the ongoing development of the EU has come from the essentially ungoverned processes of the international economy and from the 'private' forms of governance located within and across the economies and civil societies of the member states – see Guibernau (2001) and Thompson (2001).

How, then, can we characterize the governance of the EU? To make a start I shall begin with two deliberately oversimplified models.

3.1 An intergovernmental model

The first model regards the EU as a particularly extensive as well as intensive form of *intergovernmental organization*. There are a number of intergovernmental organizations in the contemporary international system, ranging from general institutions such as the United Nations, through major single-purpose but multilateral bodies like the World Trade Organization (WTO) and the International Monetary Fund (IMF), and regional associations such as the North American Free Trade Association (NAFTA) and the Association of South East Asian Nations (ASEAN), to specialist forums such as the International Energy Agency (IEA) and the International Telecommunications Satellite (Intelsat). These are organizations formed by states to pursue the common interests of the membership, in which specific powers may be delegated to the organization and where decision making on some issues may be shared or 'pooled' between the member states, especially when those states are unable to achieve their objectives by acting alone. The organization may have its own permanent staff, institutions and resources to carry out its delegated tasks, and there may be systems of weighted majority voting in some areas of decision making, although unanimity and one-state-one-vote is the norm for important matters. The organization may also encompass some quasi-judicial mechanism for resolving disputes between member states. In the contemporary international system there are hundreds of intergovernmental organizations. Is the EU just one more to add to an ever-expanding list?

Even those analysts who argue that the EU is an intergovernmental organization concede that it is a very special one. To begin with, the range of issues for which the EU has some responsibility is quite unlike that of any other such organization. According to Simon Hix (1999), the political system of the EU produces five types of 'policy output'.

- *Regulatory policies*, concerning the workings of the single market, environmental and social policies and aspects of industrial policy.

- *Redistributive policies*, involving transfers of resources from one group to another through the EU budget (for example, the Common Agricultural Policy).

- *Macroeconomic stabilization policies*, including the role of the European Central Bank and its management of Economic and Monetary Union (EMU) and the common currency, the euro.

- *Citizen policies*, relating to the civil, political, economic and social rights of the citizens of the EU.

- *Global policies*, concerned with the EU's role as an actor in the wider international system; for example, trade and foreign aid policies, the Common Foreign and Security Policy and defence co-operation.

In addition, the powers that have been delegated to the EU by its member states are considerably more extensive than those found in other intergovernmental organizations. The EU has its own legislative body, the European Parliament, which on some matters has the power of co-decision with the governments of the member states. The permanent bureaucracy of the EU, the Commission, has significant powers of policy initiative and implementation. The Commission forms one part of the EU's executive, the other being the Council of Ministers. Most strikingly of all, the EU has its own legal order organized around the European Court of Justice (ECJ) and the corpus of Community law, although this applies mainly to the first pillar of the Union. The European legal order has supremacy over the national laws of member states in cases of conflict and can be directly invoked by the citizens of the member states, against their own governments if necessary.

And finally, the EU has developed and is continuing to develop responsibilities in areas of public policy that have traditionally been regarded as the core of modern statehood: law, money, taxation, security, the rights of citizens, and the right to represent the population in the wider international system. I have already noted that the Community legal order has supremacy over national law. In addition, EMU has resulted in most members of the EU relinquishing their national currencies and pooling decision making around a common currency, the euro. National policies on taxation are also constrained by EU-wide decisions, and the getting and spending of the EU's own budget is now a highly institutionalized process. The EU is also developing competence in the field of the Common Foreign and Security Policy (the second pillar of the EU) as well as in defence co-operation and even a common defence. EU-wide co-operation on citizen policies in the field of Justice and Home Affairs (the third pillar) is also developing. And on some matters, trade for example, the EU represents the population of the Union in the wider international community.

Given the range of EU policies, the competence and powers of its institutions and its encroachment on the core aspects of modern statehood, what does it mean to say that the EU is a special type of intergovernmental organization? This question raises issues about the nature of statehood within the nation state, the character of international law, and the relation of European law to international law as well as to the national legal systems of the member states. It also depends on what kinds of monetary and budgetary competence the EU has in relation to the member states and the nature of its responsibilities in the areas of a Common Foreign and Security Policy and Justice and Home Affairs. In essence, intergovernmental interpretations of the EU argue that the pooling of decisions related to statehood and the exercise of powers delegated to EU-wide institutions – the European Parliament, the Commission, the budget, the European Court of Justice and Community law – remain under the collective control of the governments of the member states. In this view, the decisions of the Union and the authority of the EU's 'policy outputs' are derived directly from the joint authority of the member states and their governments.

3.2   A supranational model

The second model of the governance of the EU argues that the delegation of powers and the competence of the EU-wide institutions have gone so far as to have created a form of *supranational* governance. Two leading theorists of the EU as a form of supranational governance, Alec Stone Sweet and James Caporaso (1998, p.92), put the argument as follows.

> Whereas intergovernmentalists argue that integration is produced by joint decisions taken by member state governments, we claim that transnational interactions, as shaped by [EU] organizations, are the crucial catalysts. Whereas intergovernmentalists conceptualize the Commission and the ECJ as more or less faithful agents of the member states, and by extension of the Council of Ministers, we see them working in the service of transnational society.

And as Caporaso (1998, p.335) has also pointed out, it may be helpful to consider EU governance as a hybrid form.

> The central conceptual device is not the isolated ideal type but rather a continuum running from pure intergovernmental politics ... to a supranational polity in which [EU] institutions possess jurisdiction and authority over the individual member states in specified policy areas. The form of the supranational polity is an open question. It could be organized along federal lines ... it could take the form of islands of regulatory authority corresponding to discrete tasks ... or it could take the form of a strongly member state-driven process where delegated authority is carefully circumscribed, monitored and controlled.

To the extent that the EU is a supranational form of governance, we are entitled to ask about the source of its authority. If a supranational political system is making, implementing and enforcing collectively binding decisions for the citizens of the Union as a whole, then on what basis is this rule exercised, and how does it relate to the authority claimed by the member states? This raises fundamental issues about the location of authority in the multinational, multi-level governance of the EU. For example, as the supranational elements of the EU expand and intensify – if indeed that is what has been happening – will the EU need to develop its own source of authority, independent of that supplied by the member states? How might it do so? This raises another set of issues: is there a shared family of European political traditions (liberalism, conservatism, social democracy and so forth) that cuts across the various national patterns of politics and could feed into an EU-wide political process? Has political action within the EU been restructured around the governance of the EU, or does it remain stubbornly national in focus? And can the EU acquire a democratic legitimacy of its own? If the EU develops an independent source of authority, will it also embrace its own state-like monopoly over the organized means of violence? In short, will the EU become more state-like itself? Or will a new form of polity emerge 'beyond' the sovereign state, a form of post-sovereign and post-national political order?

Moreover, the project of European integration has been as much economic and social or cultural as it has been political. Much of the impetus behind the political building of the EU and the policies developed within it has come from, and been aimed toward, widening and deepening the economic and social integration of the *economies* and *societies* of the member states. I have already noted that the combination of legality, citizenship and respect for the private spheres of the economy and society implied that the rule of liberal-democratic states is con-ditional and limited, that significant areas of economic and social life are either ungoverned or privately governed. This point applies not only to interaction within the territory of the state but also to economic and social processes that cross national borders. We have also seen that the relative autonomy of the economic and social spheres means that the relation of governance between the political authorities and private citizens cannot be understood simply as one of 'rulers' and 'ruled', since each shapes the activities of the others within a common framework of liberal-democratic legality and politics. The relation of governance is a two-way street. As the process of European integration advances, so the relation of governance becomes not just one between the political authorities of a given member state and its 'own' economy and society but also one between that state and the economies and societies of all the member states. Thus not only is governance shared between the member states of the EU, it is also negotiated between these states and their increasingly *transnational* economies and societies.

These questions of the intergovernmental versus the supranational characteristics of the EU, together with the relations between the formal governance of the state and the informal governance of economies and societies, have never been more important. Developments after the Single European Act (1986) and the Treaty on European Union (1992) have not only considerably extended the role of the EU in the governance of the member states, but also deepened the EU's involvement in questions of economic and social regulation. At the same time, the end of the Cold War and the fall of communism in Eastern Europe foreshadow a major expansion of EU membership. Enlargement poses a direct challenge to the current delicate balance of intergovernmental and supranational governance, for new members can be accommodated only through significant institutional change to the governance of the EU or by allowing different groups of member states to proceed with integration at different speeds. Enlargement will also alter the character of economic and social integration in Europe. The EU always has been, and looks set to continue to be, a moving target.

4 Looking forward

In Chapter 2, 'Building the European Union', Richard Heffernan looks at the forging of 'an ever closer union of the peoples of Europe' and offers a primarily intergovernmental reading of the process. Starting from the formation of the European Coal and Steel Community (ECSC), Heffernan points out that the institutions of the EU are distinctive in that they embody two different principles of political authority: the intergovernmental and the supranational. The ECSC set the pattern of an intergovernmental treaty establishing an organization with some supranational powers. Heffernan then traces the historical development of the EU, from the ECSC through to the Treaties of Maastricht and Amsterdam in the 1990s and the launching of the project of Economic and Monetary Union. Throughout this process, which has involved widening the EU from six to fifteen states, the balance between these two principles has altered: 'The shift away from pure intergovernmentalism toward a degree of supranationalism lies at the heart of European integration and is a key feature of a growing Europeanization.'

Heffernan also argues that mapping out 'when' things happened also involves asking 'how' and 'why' they did so. From the historical record he identifies four main historical experiences that predisposed the states of Western Europe to co-operate after the Second World War. First, there was the legacy of war itself and the desire to avoid future wars in Europe. Second, and related to conflict and destruction, there was a widespread belief that economic reconstruction and post-war prosperity would be strengthened if states co-operated. Third, the Cold War division of Europe encouraged the states of Western Europe to see themselves as part of a single political community. Fourth, and finally, this sense of political community was reinforced by the spread of liberal-democratic political values throughout Western Europe.

Notwithstanding these powerful historical experiences in favour of integration of some kind, the member states have faced two conflicting objectives: to pool, share and even delegate sovereignty in pursuit of economic gains, and to hold on to sovereignty at the national level. In this context, Heffernan emphasizes that the supranational elements of the EU are the result of intergovernmental agreement by treaty, but he also notes that the governance of the EU is increasingly pursued in the interests of 'Europe' as well as those of its member states. On balance, however, he feels that there is no remorseless logic behind the widening, deepening EU. Nothing is inevitable; the EU has no predetermined destination. The extent of shared 'European' traditions and values cannot be assumed and, while the peoples of Europe have become more 'European', they remain national citizens first, and European citizens second. Thus while he recognizes the role of internationalization and globalization in increasing national interdependence and the self-reinforcing dynamic of integration itself, Heffernan concludes that, in the specific regional context of post-war Western Europe, inter-governmentalism has been and remains the key feature of the building of the EU.

In Chapter 3, 'The nation state in the European Union', I take a closer look at the nature of the states that have been building the EU and at whether the process of integration is questioning their sovereignty. The European nation state is a form of political organization that became widespread only in the nineteenth century, although its origins can be traced back considerably further. The development of these states was associated with the formulation of the principle or doctrine of sovereignty: namely, the idea that the continuous public power of the state should be the supreme source of authority within the territory of the state, and that states should formally recognize one another as equals. Especially in the constitutional and national form that emerged in the late eighteenth and nineteenth centuries, this doctrine of sovereignty was linked to the principles of the liberal rule of law, the popular authorization of government and democratic mechanisms of representation and accountability. It has been these liberal, constitutional nation states that have built the EU.

The development of the European nation state went hand in hand with the development of a European states system based on the balance of power, in which any threatening increase in the power of one state was matched by a counterbalancing alliance of other states. This power-balancing often led to war, but it did preserve the system of states as a *states system*: that is, a political system whose members were states and in which supreme political authority, or what was now called *sovereignty*, was located at the level of the state. I go on, however, to argue that, first, the development of the nation state in a liberal-democratic direction was by no means guaranteed, and second, that this balance of power broke down twice to produce catastrophic world wars. The first half of the twentieth century provided little evidence for the viability of either liberal democracy or the European states system. Only after the Second World War, and under the shadow of the Cold War division of Europe, was liberal democracy consolidated in Western Europe. And only with the direct intervention of the superpowers, the Soviet Union and the USA, was the security dimension of the European states system stabilized.

In this context, I argue that Western European integration was able to proceed and the EU was able to develop as a form of 'civilian power' alongside the other institutions of Western integration, especially the North Atlantic Treaty Organization. Specifying the character of that integration is complex as it involves elements of intergovernmental authority and aspects of supranationalism, as well as forms of confederal and even federal authority. Finally, I look at what has happened to the sovereignty of the nation state as post-war integration has replaced pre-war rivalry and the EU has developed an increasingly complex political dynamic. What is the relation between the sovereignty of the nation state, the character of European law and the supranational aspects of the EU? What questions are raised for the democratic legitimacy of the EU by the increasingly tangled picture of shared, divided and delegated authority?

In Chapter 4, 'Law, order and administration in the European Union', Daniel Wincott examines the character of the European or Community legal order to explore the question: What is the EU? He considers the role of Community law, the part played by the European Court of Justice (ECJ) in the process of European integration and the contribution of the resulting European legal order to the development of European regulatory policies. Wincott argues that the Community legal system is the single most novel feature of the EU, and that a full understanding of the nature of the EU must include the nature of its legal system. At the same time, he points out that focusing on the character and scope of Community law helps us to distinguish between the 'supranational' aspects of the EU and the 'intergovernmental' aspects, since it is largely true that the ECJ has jurisdiction over supranational policies but not intergovernmental ones. Community law applies fully to the first pillar (the Communities) but not to the second (Common Foreign and Security Policy) or the third (Justice and Home Affairs).

Wincott shows that the Community legal order developed dramatically as the ECJ became able to promulgate the doctrines of direct effect and the supremacy of European law in relation to the national laws of member states. In the process, not only did the ECJ develop Community law but national courts and legal systems became 'Europeanized'. Wincott stresses, however, that this process can be understood only by seeing the development of Community law in the wider context of the roles played by member states, other EU institutions, national legal systems and the societies and actors operating in the EU. The increasingly robust character of the European legal order and its growing legitimacy in the eyes of both member states and societal actors are sometimes referred to as the 'constitutionalization' of the Community legal system. Wincott argues that this process has played a central role in the development of the regulatory policies in the Community pillar of the EU, which rely on a workable legal system.

EU policy on Justice and Home Affairs (the third pillar) developed intergovernmentally, outside the Community pillar and the jurisdiction of the ECJ. However, a number of developments have recently increased the pressure for aspects of JHA to move into the Community pillar. In turn, this migration of JHA issues from the third to the first pillar has had the effect of incorporating stronger elements of intergovernmentalism into what had previously been the most supranational aspect of the EU.

Wincott concludes that, considered as a legal system, the EU has long had federal characteristics but that EU institutions, as such, have little or no ability to use violence to enforce legislation and so must rely on the resources of member states. Given that the Community legal order is a central resource for the regulatory policies of the EU, this poses a conundrum. The Community legal system may evolve into something quite novel: a new, non-coercive but binding form of law. Or it may, ultimately, come to rely on the coercive capacities of the national legal systems with which it is entwined.

The future direction of the EU will depend partly on the degree to which its development can draw upon common political traditions across the European scene, patterns of political aspiration and action that cut across national boundaries. The nature of the major political traditions in Europe, their attitude to the project of European integration and their alignment in the European Parliament are explored by David Bell in Chapter 5, 'The re-forging of European political traditions'. Focusing on the families of party political traditions as the main institutional embodiment of political culture, Bell argues that the political cultures of modern Europe have many elements in common, notwithstanding the rise of the nation state and nationalism in the nineteenth and twentieth centuries. Thus although the major political traditions found in modern European politics are shaped by the diverse national experiences in which they are located, there is a common family of traditions operating in and across Europe.

Bell argues that the main political traditions in Europe are derived from the dual 'revolutions' of nation building and industrialization in the nineteenth and twentieth centuries. These major transitions associated with the development of the modern nation state and capitalist, industrial economies created a series of social and political cleavages that formed the basis for different political ideologies and party traditions. Bell surveys the key features of secular conservatism, Christian democracy, liberalism, the extreme right, socialism and social democracy, communism, and the more recent additions of the Greens and regional parties.

That these traditions are indeed common across Europe, despite national differences, is illustrated by the fact that national parties cohere into identifiable blocs within the European Parliament. While the pattern of party activity within the European Parliament does not simply aggregate the various parties representing each tradition, the broad party groupings are recognizably similar to the traditions surveyed by Bell. He therefore concludes that, while the building of European institutions has been an issue that has divided party families because of the intrusion of distinctive *national* outlooks, the question of 'Europe' and European integration does not itself constitute a new 'revolution' to add to the historical cleavages. To the extent that this is so, the party traditions might be expected to support, or at least not hinder, the process of integration.

This focus on party traditions is complemented by Laura Cram's discussion of politics and policy making in the EU in Chapter 6, 'Integration and policy processes in the European Union'. The original grand debates focused on the character of European *integration*. Cram points out that 'integration' can mean different things, from a constitutional end-state through a set of social and cultural background conditions to a dynamic process leading to a new kind of political community. The first round of discussions was structured by a contrast between supranational analyses, which saw integration as a movement beyond the nation state, and intergovernmental views, which argued that co-operative integration can strengthen the state in some respects. While the supranational view appeared to characterize the early phases of European integration, the intergovernmental view seemed more in tune with the apparent stalling of momentum between the mid-1960s and the 1980s.

Cram notes that this debate was revived by the increased pace of integration after the passing of the Single European Act (1986), but the focus of scholarly attention shifted from bargaining among member states and supranational and intergovernmental elements to day-to-day politics and policy making within the institutions of the EU. This approach sees the EU as a political system that, in the field of regulatory policy in particular, produces outputs comparable to those of national governments. To the extent that this is so, to the degree that the EU functions in a shared system of governance, it is perhaps less important to ask where the EU is heading than to ask what it actually does. In this respect, Cram proposes the idea of the EU as a 'regulatory state'.

In conclusion, Cram suggests that, as the network of actors involved in the EU policy process widens and the reach of the EU regulatory state extends, politics at the national level is increasingly affected by developments at the EU level. This Europeanization of political actors, loyalties and organizations might serve to develop 'European' identities among the EU's citizens and hence become the basis for a new political community beyond the nation state.

The question of the nature of the political community in the EU is taken up by Chris Lord in Chapter 7, 'Democracy and democratization in the European Union'. Lord argues that there is likely to be a strong – but problematic – relationship between the democratization of the Union and its acceptability to citizens because significant aspects of the EU are now supranational and its policy outputs increasingly raise the question of who benefits from the process of integration. Nevertheless, thinking about a democratic route to legitimacy for the EU is by no means simple, since the EU is not a state and does not yet form a fully developed political community. The institutions of the EU do not comprise a government in the normal sense of the term. There are general features of democratic governance relating to public control and political equality, as well as principles by which these can be realized, such as popular authorization, representation and accountability, but applying them to a complex, multi-level polity, a non-state political system made up of many nationalities, is a difficult undertaking.

Lord considers two complementary ways in which the EU can be seen as democratic to a greater or lesser extent. One route is to consider EU democracy through the use of national institutions, applying the notion of consociational democracy to the intergovernmental aspects of the Union. He identifies several strengths of this approach, not least its fit with the continuing strength of national political identities, but argues that it does not really serve to legitimate the supranational elements of the EU. The second route seeks to provide the EU with its own, purpose-built democratic institutions. In this context, Lord takes a close look at the role of the European Parliament (EP). He finds that, although the outcomes of elections to the European Parliament reflect primarily the national or domestic concerns of voters rather than European issues as such, party groups in the EP are organized along familiar lines and perform an important representative function. Moreover, while the powers of the EP are still limited in relation to the EU's executive – the Commission and the Council – they have increased over time and are approaching full legislative co-decision in relation to many first-pillar matters.

Finally, Lord asks how the EU might be further democratized. Three options have attracted significant attention: first, strengthening the powers of the EP; second, directly electing the President of the Commission; and third, introducing Europe-wide referendums. These proposals have strengths and weaknesses from the point of view of democracy, and Lord suggests that striking a balance between the maintenance of democratic procedures at the national level and extending democracy at the European level is a complex process in which trade-offs may apply. He concludes that the EU is currently better at representation than accountability: its very success in allowing so many perspectives to be represented creates a complex form of consensus politics in which it can be difficult to determine who should be accountable for what.

In Chapter 8, 'Finance and budgetary processes in the European Union', Brigid Laffan takes a close look at the finances of the EU. Although the EU's power to spend public money is small compared with the national budgets of member states, Laffan argues that it forms an important part of the EU, complementing and supplementing the regulatory order of market integration. The political forces and institutional actors driving the process of integration wanted more than a free-trade area from the beginning. They gave priority to market integration and hence regulation, but they also wanted to create a social space that was not dominated by market outcomes.

Laffan traces the evolution of the budget through three phases: a formative period, 1952–1969, in which the foundations of the EU budget were established; a period of crisis, 1970–1986, involving continuous conflict; and a period of consolidation and institutionalization, 1987–1999, characterized by an expansion in the size of the budget and the adoption of new rules and institutions for making and managing it. She shows how the EU budgetary process – both the big multi-annual package deals struck between the member states and the detailed annual budget cycle – has been stabilized and institutionalized. The making and management of the budget have become more consensual and predict-able. Laffan also describes how the new rules survived a strong test in the negotiations over the 1999 deal (Agenda 2000) arising from significant conflicts between coalitions of member states over the net gains and losses of enlargement in the context of a limited expansion of the budget.

Laffan concludes that, although the budget has become an essential part of the EU political system, the EU is not going to replicate the public finances of a nation state. Rather it will continue to deploy public finance as a complement to national budgetary resources, as a support for political integration and as a supplement to market integration. According to Laffan, the budget is a small but nevertheless vital addition to the EU's role as a regulatory state.

I have already noted that understanding the EU is difficult because it presents a 'moving target'. There are many reasons for this but one of the most important is that a major process of enlargement is underway. In Chapter 9, 'The enlargement of the European Union', Paul Lewis argues that this is one of the most demanding tasks to be grappled with at the outset of a new century. How it will be tackled and the success of the outcome are matters of critical importance for the development and future success of the EU. The Union has always maintained that any European state may apply to become a member, but what 'European' means in this context and what the criteria of membership are have not always been clear. The latter now include the stability of the institutions guaranteeing democracy, the rule of law, human rights, and respect for and protection of minorities; the existence of a market economy, as well as the capacity to cope with competitive pressures and market forces within the EU; and an ability to take on the obligations of membership, including adherence to the aims of political, economic and monetary union.

The enlargements so far have brought in other members of the Western European system and have been relatively unproblematic, although by no means straightforward or quick. Lewis argues that accommodating the states of Eastern Europe presents challenges of an altogether different kind because of the sheer number of applicants, the economic gap between applicants and existing members, the distinctive political backgrounds of the applicants and uncertainty about their political status, and the degree of institutional change that would be required of existing EU arrangements.

In the light of these issues, Lewis notes that the negotiations over enlargement will be protracted and conflict-ridden, as member states disagree about the acceptability of new members, as the existing members bargain with the applicants and as both contend over the future institutional shape of the EU. He concludes that enlargement is a challenge the EU simply cannot afford not to meet: it will make or break the existing Union. It seems inevitable that, to produce an EU that is not just larger but more effective, the next enlargement will have to be accompanied by significant institutional reforms. So successful enlargement is likely to strengthen supranational tendencies over the existing and well-established patterns of EU intergovernmentalism.

For much of its history the EU has been regarded as a 'civilian' power, a process of economic and political integration among and between nation states that did not encroach on the core state responsibilities of foreign and security policy or on questions of defence. The military and security interests of many Western European states were addressed at the national level and by the North Atlantic Treaty Organization led by the USA. But as Michael Smith shows in Chapter 10, 'European foreign and security policy', this picture is changing in unexpected ways. By the end of the 1990s an accelerating process of institutionalization and policy making in the foreign and security arena was underway in response to the EU's growing role in areas previously defined as 'high politics' and the prerogative of member states and the North Atlantic Treaty Organization.

The new project of EU co-operation in a Common Foreign and Security Policy (CFSP: the second pillar) raises fundamental questions about the ways in which Europe is 'governed'. Can the EU be an independent actor in security and foreign policy? How far do the member states retain control over what the EU might do, and over their own national security and foreign policies? What happens when the EU comes into collision with other institutions, such as NATO? And to what extent can the EU hope to 'manage' European security when confronted by the kinds of crisis and conflict that have erupted in the post-Cold War era?

In addressing these questions, Smith explores the extent to which foreign and security policy can be governed in an inherently unpredictable and uncontrolled environment, and examines how the institutionalization of EU policy making relates to the wider security 'architecture' of Europe, which is shaped by competing national priorities, other security institutions such as NATO and the rapidly changing external environment produced by the end of the Cold War. Using the EU's role in the crises and conflicts in the former Yugoslavia as a case study, he evaluates the EU's capacity to manage its security environment. Smith concludes that the degree to which the CFSP can be managed at the level of the EU is one of the most dynamic and exciting issues of 'governing the Union' in the early twenty-first century.

In short summary, these are some of the themes explored in the rest of the book. In the final chapter, Chapter 11, I shall return to my starting point to review what we have learned and what more we might say in answer to the question: 'What is the EU?'

References

Beetham, D. (1991) *The Legitimation of Power*, London, Macmillan.

Beetham, D. and Lord, C. (1998) *Legitimacy and the European Union*, London, Longman.

Caporaso, J. (1998) 'Regional integration theory' in Sandholtz, W. and Stone Sweet, A. (eds) *European Integration and Supranational Governance*, Oxford, Oxford University Press.

Dinan, D. (1999) *Ever Closer Union*, London, Macmillan (second edition).

Finer, S. (1970) *Comparative Government*, Harmondsworth, Penguin.

Finer, S. (1997) *The History of Government*, Oxford, Oxford University Press.

Guibernau, M. (ed.) (2001) *Governing European Diversity*, London, Sage/The Open University.

Hix, S. (1999) *The Political System of the European Union*, London, Macmillan.

Krasner, S. (1983) 'Structural causes and regime consequences: regimes as intervening variables' in Krasner, S. (ed.) *International Regimes*, Ithaca, NY, Cornell University Press.

Lindblom, C. (1977) *Politics and Markets*, New York, Basic Books.

Lively, J. and Reeve, A. (1997) 'The emergence of the idea of civil society: the artificial political order and the natural social orders' in Fine, R. and Rai, S. (eds) *Civil Society*, London, Frank Cass.

Mann, M. (1986) *The Sources of Social Power*, Cambridge, Cambridge University Press.

Nugent, N. (1999) *The Government and Politics of the European Union*, London, Macmillan (fourth edition).

Rosamond, B. (2000) *Theories of European Integration*, London, Macmillan.

Runciman, W. (1989) *A Treatise on Social Theory*, Cambridge, Cambridge University Press.

Stone Sweet, A. and Caporaso, J. (1998) 'From free trade to supranational polity: the European Court and integration' in Sandholtz, W. and Stone Sweet, A. (eds) *European Integration and Supranational Governance*, Oxford, Oxford University Press.

Thompson, G. (ed.) (2001) *Governing the European Economy*, London, Sage/ The Open University.

Wallace, H. (2000) 'Studying contemporary Europe', *British Journal of Politics and International Relations*, vol.2, no.1, pp.95–113.

Further reading

Chapters 3 and 4 of Barry, N. (2000) *An Introduction to Modern Political Theory*, London, Macmillan (fourth edition).

Chapters 1 and 2 of Finer, S. (1970) *Comparative Government*, Harmondsworth, Penguin.

Lindblom, C. (1977) *Politics and Markets*, New York, Basic Books.

Chapter 2
Building the European Union

Richard Heffernan

1 Introduction

In the gradual transformation of the European Coal and Steel Community (ECSC) into the contemporary European Union (henceforth the EU), an increasing number of European states have embraced the objective of forging 'an ever closer union among the peoples of Europe'. While smaller in geographical terms than North or South America, Asia or Africa (the European continent would fit into the continental USA twice), the fifteen member states of the EU form the world's largest trading bloc. In 1996 the member states had a combined population of 372 million, much larger than the 260 million of the USA, and the EU had a population density four times that of the USA. In addition, the EU's combined gross domestic product (GDP) is larger than that of the USA. The Europe that has been built over the past 50 years symbolizes the co-operation of a number of European nation states prepared to work with each other in the common pursuit of prosperity and security, encouraged by self-interest and an expanded sense of a European identity.

No other international organization has anything like the policy responsibilities of the EU. To some extent, it provides for the supranational regulation of the production, distribution and exchange of goods, services, capital and labour, thus ensuring the free movement of each across the borders of member states. It helps to regulate the single market, harmonize standards of production and exchange at both the national and the European level, provide member states with a single voice on trade policy, and transfer resources across regions and production sectors by devices such as the Common Agricultural Policy (CAP) and regional aid.

Over time the membership of the EU has expanded from the six states of the 1952 ECSC to fifteen states. This 'widening' of the EU has been accompanied by a 'deepening': the increased responsibilities granted the EU by member states through international treaties. This deepening has seen Europe gradually extend its policy responsibilities, from co-operation in the production of coal and steel to the establishment of a customs union, the encouragement of a single market, the adoption of Europe-wide regulatory policies and the development of a common monetary policy in the form of a single currency. Ever closer ties of association have prompted these shifts, and these developments have, in turn, led to ever closer ties of association.

Deepening and widening illustrate a European economic and political integration in which 'ever closer union' is defined as 'forming, co-ordinating and blending national economies and polities into unified and functioning wholes' (Peterson, 1999, p.255). Yet the substance, form and timing of integrationist objectives within the EU are a matter of considerable debate. The building of the EU in the last half of the twentieth century raises many pressing and urgent questions of national sovereignty and autonomy in an age of increasing national interdependence. The EU has developed as a regional network of nation states that have agreed a series of international treaties – 'three aimed at trade liberalization and two at monetary co-operation' (Moravcsik, 1998, p.2) – designed to pool their sovereignty in a number of instances governing direct relations between them.

The deepening of the EU is most tellingly illustrated by the key historical stages of European integration (Box 2.1).

Box 2.1   Historical stages in European integration

1   Free trade area: no visible trade restriction between members.

2   Customs union: free trade area plus common external tariff.

3   Single market: customs union plus free movement of goods (no non-tariff barriers or other state-imposed restrictions).

4   Common market: single market plus free movement of capital, labour and services.

5   Monetary union: a common market plus a common currency.

6   Economic union: monetary union plus a common economic policy.

The EU reached stage 4 in 1999/2000, and is currently embarking on stage 5. In January 1999 eleven of the fifteen member states participated in the launch of European monetary union (the exceptions being the UK, Denmark and Sweden, which have opted not to join for the time being, and Greece, which has not yet met the economic criteria for entry). In the first half of 2002 the currencies of these fifteen states – banknotes and coinage – will be replaced by a European single currency. Of course, this does not of itself make economic union (stage 6) inevitable, but it certainly makes it more likely and brings it a stage closer. An additional stage, political union (stage 7), would be effected through the establishment of a 'United States of Europe'. However, as of January 2000 the historical process marking a movement from stage 1 to stage 4 underpins the emergence of what may best be described as 'Europeanization', the process of 'ever closer union' between EU member states. It does not yet represent economic or political union.

The historical process toward ever greater and closer co-operation (if not political union) is best illuminated by an investigation of how the Europe of yesterday became the EU of today. The piecemeal, gradual 'Europeanization' of contemporary European politics tells us a great deal about the changing nature, status and function of the EU. Of course, understanding the historical development of the EU by understanding 'when' events took place leads us into debates about 'why' the events happened. A 'nuts and bolts' institutional account of the building of the EU therefore means dealing with 'when' and 'where' as well as 'how' and 'why'.

2 The history of the EU

Applicants for EU membership have to be not only physically located in Europe but also well-established liberal democracies with stable and well-functioning market economies. The principle of *acquis communautaire* requires entrants to agree in advance to existing European treaties, laws, policies and objectives, and enlargement requires unanimous consent on the part of existing members. (The *acquis* is the extensive body of EU legislation, treaties and case law.) Over time the widening of the EU has seen membership expand from the original six members of the ECSC to fifteen members at the time of writing.

- Founder members: France, Germany, Italy, the Netherlands, Belgium and Luxembourg.
- The first enlargement: Denmark, the Republic of Ireland and the UK join in 1973.
- The second enlargement: Greece joins in 1981, and Portugal and Spain join in 1986.
- The third enlargement: Austria, Sweden and Finland join in 1995.

Norway was accepted into membership as part of the third enlargement, but voted against entry in a referendum. Switzerland applied for membership in 1992 but its application was suspended indefinitely the same year. In March 1998 accession negotiations were formally opened with Poland, Hungary, the Czech Republic, Cyprus, Slovenia and Estonia, and at the Helsinki European Council in December 1999 accession negotiations were opened with Slovakia, Romania, Bulgaria, Latvia, Lithuania and Malta. At the same meeting, Turkey, which had had its application suspended in 1997, found itself restored to 'candidate status'. So it is possible that the EU will come to embrace as many as 27 member states in the next ten years.

2.1 The functions and characteristics of the EU

The EU of today has two principal functions. First, it seeks to secure economic and political benefits for its member states by intergovernmental co-operation and supranational management (and, some suspect, through federal aspirations). Second, it fosters co-operation by requiring member states to pool their sovereignty in the pursuit of common objectives, which in turn bring individual advantages. As a result, the EU has developed two unique characteristics: it has a complex institutional structure, more complex than that found in other international bodies, and it operates through a combination of intergovernmental and supranational activities. Over time the EU has been transformed from a strongly intergovernmental organization with a supranational element to a less strong intergovernmental organization with supranational overtones and clear ambitions. The terms 'intergovernmental' and 'supranational' may be defined as follows.

- Intergovernmental organizations enable each member state to pursue its own national interests and exercise a veto on developments it does not favour.

- Supranational organizations limit the ability of member states to exercise a national veto and obliges them to follow decisions supported by a majority or a qualified majority of their fellow member states.

The development of the EU from the ECSC through the European Economic Community (the EEC) and the European Community (the EC) has been enacted by treaty and member state negotiation. The six most significant negotiations are the Treaty of Paris (1951), the Treaty of Rome (1956), the establishment of the Common Agricultural Policy (1966), the establishment of the European Monetary System (1978 to 1979), the Single European Act (1986) and the Maastricht Treaty (1992). All marked significant changes in the EU's focus and function and prompted the establishment and/or the further empowering of supranational European institutions by intergovernmental arrangement. The shift away from pure intergovernmentalism toward a degree of supranationalism lies at the heart of European integration and is a key feature of a growing Europeanization. EU member states accept that the decisions they reach have to be binding decisions. Yet member states have chosen to participate in the EU and, having joined, no EU member has ever left.

Post-1945 European integration has been encouraged by states pursuing their individual self-interest in co-operating one with another. In terms of a deepening international co-operation, the post-1945 world witnessed a flowering of international organizations such as the United Nations and international financial institutions such as the World Bank and the IMF. This trend encouraged Europeans to pursue the idea of a specifically European organization. The earliest European institutions included the European Recovery Programme of 1947 (another name for the Marshall

Plan, in which the USA provided over $13 billion to promote the economic reconstruction of Western Europe), the Council of Europe and the Organization for European Economic Co-operation (OEEC), an organization set up to monitor economic recovery. They explored issues of common interest via intergovernmental links designed to build understanding through dialogue and discussion.

In May 1949 ten states signed the Statute of the Council of Europe to achieve greater unity, an aim that was to be 'pursued through the organs of the Council by discussions of questions of common concern and by agreements and common action in economic, social, cultural, scientific, legal and administrative matters and in the maintenance and further realization of human rights and fundamental freedoms' (quoted in Nugent, 1999, p.13). The Council was primarily an intergovernmental institution and, with the important exception of entrenching human rights in the European Convention of Human Rights (1950), it has pursued mostly inconclusive discussions of issues of common concern to its member states. Although the ten founder states had grown to encompass 38 states by 1998, the Council of Europe for many proved nothing more than a 'talking shop', even if it discharged the useful purpose of enabling member states to exchange information and engage in political dialogue.

2.2   From the ECSC to Maastricht

Disappointed in the weak, wholly intergovernmental structures of the Council of Europe, European integrationists turned their attention away from diplomatic alliances toward attempts to foster a common European identity through economic co-operation. In May 1950 the Schuman Plan proposed that European countries pool their coal and steel resources and establish a new international authority for the purpose of jointly managing the coal and steel market. Inspired by a number of keen Euro-federalists, such as Jean Monnet, this proposal was negotiated in advance by France and West Germany, two states keen to co-operate with each other (and prepared to proceed by themselves if need be). The proposal was warmly received by Italy, the Netherlands, Belgium and Luxembourg (although it was opposed by the UK, which declined to join). In April 1951 the six founding nations signed the Treaty of Paris, which established the European Coal and Steel Community (ECSC) in July 1952. Thus was today's EU born, although its growth and subsequent development have been a product of the years since 1952.

The ECSC was an extremely ambitious undertaking. Not only did it establish the foundation of a common market in coal, steel and related products, but it was also 'the first of the inter-state organizations to possess significant supranational characteristics' (Nugent, 1999, p.37). From the very beginning, the ECSC was a quasi-supranational institution established by intergovernmental treaty, the two competing developments that were to lie at the heart of subsequent European developments. The ECSC was administered by a High Authority, a supranational executive composed of nine members appointed by the member states (with at least one appointed by each member and two from both France and West Germany), which was obliged to act independently of any national interest. The High Authority was under the overall direction of a Council of Ministers drawn from all six member states, all of which had the power of veto with regard to High Authority initiatives. In addition, a purely advisory Common Assembly composed of nominated members from national legislatures met periodically to make non-binding recommendations and pass comment on ECSC activities, and a Court of Justice was charged with the responsibility of settling disputes between member states and between member states and ECSC institutions.

The ECSC was essentially a confederation of its member states through the integration of one functional economic sector: the production and distribution of coal and steel. While able collectively to exert influence on the High Authority, all six members none the less did cede a degree of sovereignty to a supranational institution, which had the power to prohibit the use of coal and steel subsidies, take action against restrictive practices, promote research and development, and control prices under certain conditions.

The ECSC was deemed a considerable success by its member states, and it was agreed in principle at the Messina Conference of June 1955 that their association should be deepened. Following the deliberations of the intergovernmental committee chaired by Paul-Henri Spaak, and the publication of its report in May 1956, further intergovernmental negotiations between the six member states led to the signing of the two Treaties of Rome establishing the European Economic Community (EEC) in March 1957. The principal Treaty of Rome created a customs union by abolishing tariffs and quotas and imposing a common external tariff protecting the six from external trade. The second treaty set up the European Atomic Energy Community (Euratom), an intergovernmental agency to promote co-operation in the development of nuclear technology. Both the EEC and Euratom came into being in January 1958, and their political institutions closely reflected the established ECSC model. While the ECSC, EEC and Euratom remained separate institutions, with some overlap, the Brussels Treaty of April 1965 merged all three in July 1967 under one set of institutions known as the EC or the 'Common Market'.

The UK was strongly in favour of a European free-trade area but against joining the EEC. In 1958 the UK helped to establish the European Free Trade Association (EFTA). The UK was keen to establish a free-trade area separate from the EEC that would abolish tariffs and quotas without imposing a common external tariff, which it believed would hinder its own trade. EFTA was an explicitly intergovernmental, trade-based organization. Its seven members – the UK, Austria, Denmark, Norway, Portugal, Sweden and Switzerland – became known as the 'outer seven', as opposed to the 'inner six' of the EEC. But EFTA never really took off and was hamstrung by its failure to negotiate a free-trade agreement with the EEC. This left the EEC as the principal economic forum for European co-

The signing of the Treaty of Rome in the Capitol, Rome on 25 March 1957.

operation. In the early 1960s efforts to join the EEC by three states – the UK, the Republic of Ireland and Denmark – were unsuccessful due to France's veto of British membership in 1961 to 1963 and 1967. Ever keen to promote French interests within the EEC, de Gaulle considered Britain to be far too close to a USA he distrusted, and as a political and economic rival whose entry would considerably diminish France's influence in a French-dominated, six-member EEC. When the French President departed the political scene in 1969 the stage was set for the re-opening of entry negotiations, and the UK, Ireland and Denmark became members in January 1973.

The Treaty of Rome was an enabling agreement, and it was in the period between 1958 and 1969 that the then EEC was consolidated as a viable international community. After the admission of the UK, the Republic of Ireland and Denmark in 1973, and the second accession that saw Greece join in 1981 and Spain and Portugal join in 1986, the period from 1973 to 1985 represented something of a hiatus in the development of the EU. This was despite occasional, never realized, declarations in favour of 'monetary union' by 1980, such as the 1970 Werner Report. The establishment of the European Monetary System in March 1979 was intended to create a zone of monetary stability in Europe and promote financial co-operation among member states, but it was not designed as a deliberate step toward monetary union. The EMS was created to oversee an Exchange Rate Mechanism (the ERM), which set limits on the fluctuations of exchange rates, and a new European currency unit, the ECU, was formed from a 'basket' or weighted average of the currencies of member states. But this was a non-treaty-based agreement and members were free to opt in or out. States were not required to join the ERM;

Greece has never been a member, and Britain joined in October 1990 before withdrawing in September 1992, when currency speculation made British membership at the exchange rate at which it had entered no longer tenable. This period also saw the institutionalization of summitry in 1974 in the form of the European Council: meetings of the heads of government (plus foreign ministers) organized by the member state holding the European Presidency, which rotates between the member states every six months.

After this hiatus the pace of European integration quickened. In 1986 EU member states agreed to establish a genuinely single market, one that would eliminate non-tariff barriers inside the community in addition to the general tariffs eliminated in 1968. The Treaty of Rome's objective of building a common market was partly achieved in the abolition of customs duties and quantitative limits on trade, but other rules and regulations still obstructed the free movement of capital, labour, goods and services. The 1986 Single European Act (SEA) swept away the regulatory and fiscal restrictions still hampering the establishment of a genuine, completely unified, single European market. By 1992 all non-tariff barriers were to be dismantled and all physical barriers in the form of internal border controls removed. It was also envisaged that fiscal barriers in the form of value-added taxes and sales taxes would eventually be harmonized. This form of re-regulation established common policies within the single market and was intended to set in place a set of common standards, a 'level playing field', and so fashion a genuinely 'border-less' internal market.

Following on from the SEA, extensive discussions within the EU resulted in the negotiation of the Maastricht Treaty by the European Council in December 1991. Maastricht marked a significant step forward in the integrationist process and the Treaty, correctly entitled the Treaty on European Union (TEU), was a huge stride in the direction of economic, if not political, union. It agreed a series of harmonization measures within the single market, particularly in regard to the labour market, and set out both the principle of the single currency in the form of European Monetary Union and a framework for its introduction from 1999 to 2002. Maastricht also increased the competencies of the EU and redefined Europe as three distinct pillars (see Box 2.2 opposite).

In June 1997 the European Council agreed the Treaty of Amsterdam, the product of an Intergovernmental Conference (ICG) convened after Maastricht to consider further proposals for European integration. Yet the Treaty of Amsterdam steered well away from wide-ranging institutional changes to the EU. It did not make significant changes to the EU's policy-making procedures, take significant steps toward preparing the EU for further enlargement or concern the issue of monetary union. It was, to all extents and purposes, an attempt to revise, simplify, clarify and consolidate the Maastricht Treaty (and other European Treaties), and in that sense it was not a dramatic or ground-breaking initiative. Amsterdam did, however, inch the integrationist project forward in improving the

> ## Box 2.2   The pillars of the EU (after Maastricht)
>
> 1 The Community pillar, made up of the European Economic Community (EEC), the European Coal and Steel Community (ECSC) and the European Atomic Energy Community (Euratom).
>
> 2 Common Foreign and Security Policy (CFSP).
>
> 3 Justice and Home Affairs (JHA).
>
> The three pillars are bound together as the European Union, but the second and third pillars are not supranational to the same extent as the first pillar. The second and third pillars are more strictly inter-governmental in character. The obligations they impose are binding on the member states but, unlike the provisions of the first pillar, they do not constitute Community law.

effectiveness and efficiency of the Common Foreign and Security Policy, enhancing the notion of European citizenship, streamlining existing EU decision-making procedures and providing for a degree of flexibility in regard to 'ever closer union'.

At Maastricht, support for a single currency was encouraged by the belief that EU national currencies remained a key impediment to the harmonization of trade and the establishment of a truly single market. European Monetary Union (EMU), the adoption of a single currency managed by an independent Central European Bank, with European responsibility for overseeing national economic policies, was now represented as a logical and unavoidable extension of the 1986 Single European Act. As a consequence, should it succeed, '[m]onetary union represents the most visible, potentially irreversible, move away from the traditional functions of the nation state currently on the European agenda' (Wallace, 1999, p.516).

The single currency came into being in January 1999, although it is not scheduled to replace existing currencies until 2002. Eleven of the fifteen member states of the EU signed up; Greece did not meet the economic criteria to join, and the UK, Sweden and Denmark stayed out. While the pace and direction of European integration have been fiercely contested, the establishment of a genuinely single market and the adoption of a single currency represent considerable advances for European integration. Of course, the attitudes of individual member states have, on occasion, differed considerably and continue to do so. Some states – notably Belgium, the Netherlands, Luxembourg, Italy and Germany – are far more integrationist than others. The willingness of the Danish and British to be Europe's 'awkward partners' is also well known. The introduction of the Single European Act saw the integrationist tide, which had ebbed for most of the period from 1965 to 1985, begin to flow stronger, a phenomenon considerably reinforced by the 1992 Treaty on European Union signed at Maastricht.

Summary

- The EU was born as the ECSC in 1952, but its subsequent development through the EEC and the EC has been a product of a period that has seen the integrationist process flow, then ebb, then flow again. (See the Appendix to this book for a chronology of key dates and events.)

- The widening of the EU has seen membership expand from the original six members of the ECSC to fifteen members at the time of writing.

- Tired of intergovernmental structures such as the Council of Europe, European integrationists turned their attention away from diplomatic alliances toward attempts to foster a common European identity through economic co-operation.

3   Exploring European interdependence

What explains the development of the EU? For what reasons has the number of EU member states increased; first to nine, then ten, then twelve and now to fifteen, with three likely to join in the immediate future? How and why have the policy arenas in which the EU is involved increased over time? Mapping out 'when' the ECSC developed into the EU requires answers to the questions 'how' and 'why'. It is important to understand that the contemporary EU did not simply emerge, but has been constructed as the product of intended and unintended actions taken over time by actors and institutions operating at the level of member states and the European institutions themselves. The ever widening and deepening EU can therefore be understood by reference to the EU of yesterday. Its development is part of a historical chronology by which the EU was constructed as its member states recognized their interdependence and sought to build up ties of collective interest, reciprocal co-operation, solidarity and mutual esteem. At root, the EU reflects an increasing awareness on the part of its member states (and would-be member states) of a need to supplement their national rule-making and decision-taking capacities through international co-operation.

3.1 War and the process of European integration

The twentieth century has undoubtedly played a significant role in prompting European integration: in particular, the experience of inter-necine rivalry from 1900 to 1918 and 1933 to 1945 and the remaking of Europe after 1945. Europe is composed of a number of different states, with distinct and ever changing political systems and regimes, and European conflict rather than co-operation was the pre-1945 norm. National rivalries provoked divisions and tensions born of competing economic and political interests. Germany invaded France three times between 1870 and 1945, and the European continent was the crucible for the two destructive world wars of the twentieth century. And in time of war – 1870 to 1871, 1914 to 1918 and 1939 to 1945 – the boundaries of Europe were dramatically redrawn, only to be redrawn again by the victors once hostilities were concluded.

The post-1945 remaking of Europe is in large part a legacy of the First World War, the inter-war period and the Second World War. Before 1945 Europe was a divided continent, rent by the political legacy of the First World War and its unsatisfactory conclusion at the Treaty of Versailles. European nations were organized in one of three broad forms.

- Liberal-democratic regimes were governed by the rule of law and the selection of governing élites through periodic free and fair elections.

- Authoritarian regimes were governed by ruling oligarchies that abided by a set of rules prescribed by an imposed legal code.

- Totalitarian regimes, such as Hitler's Third Reich and Stalin's USSR, governed through force, accepting no limit to the authority of the state, which could do whatever it chose without limit.

The emergence of these different political regimes served to exacerbate European tensions during years disfigured by opposed political ideologies and incompatible, dangerous and in many cases detestable regimes. European divisions cast great shadows over the continent, dividing states into competitive blocs for defensive and offensive purposes, each seques-tered in its hatred for the others.

The impact of the Second World War on Europe cannot be overstated in terms of the physical, economic and political reconstruction needed to repair the very fabric of the continent. Only one Western European combatant, Britain, came out of the war with its political system intact. In 1945 Europe was divided into three distinct categories. First, states that had not been invaded: democracies such as Britain, non-combatants such as Switzerland and the Republic of Ireland, and authoritarian regimes such as Spain and Portugal. Second, states that had been occupied such as France, Belgium, the Netherlands, Luxembourg, Denmark and Norway. Once liberated, these states had to restore pre-war constitutions or devise new constitutions and compose new governments to revitalize their political systems. Third, states that had been defeated and occupied by the allies such as Germany, Austria, Italy, Greece and Finland. The discredited political regimes of these states were torn up by the roots and replaced by entirely new constitutions, institutions and political systems.

Having to rebuild and start anew encouraged some states to pursue a specifically European identity, one in which Europe was a definable and specific place. As a result, European co-operation was prompted by European security concerns, political stability, socio-economic reconstruction and the political symbolism associated with a club of Western European liberal democracies (Wallace, 1996, pp.19–20). These factors help explain why the European states co-operated as Europeans after the end of the Second World War, and why they have continued to do so ever since. Shared interests encouraged regional co-operation, and three key issues may be identified.

- The growing belief on the part of key European actors that a future war in Europe could be prevented if European states co-operated with one another.

- A recognition of Western Europe as a geographically specific region, in terms of political and economic similarities and as common participants in the Cold War, in which states had common and reciprocal political and economic interests.

- An acknowledgement that the economic reconstruction and post-war prosperity of individual European states would be enhanced by mutually beneficial, collective economic and political co-operation.

After 1945 the notion of Western Europe as an interdependent, specific region was strengthened as its constituent nations became more and more co-operative, not only in the diplomatic sphere but also, gradually, in the economic and political spheres as well. European interdependence was significantly underlined by the desire to integrate West Germany into Western Europe (and the desire of West German élites to be integrated), a desire prompted by the belief that uncontrolled nationalism could lead to another European war.

Post-war Europe was divided into East and West following the defeat of Hitler's Germany. Western Europe lay firmly within an Anglo-American sphere of influence, while the Soviet Union laid physical claim to the great swathe of Eastern and Central Europe, an area stretching from the Baltic Sea to the Black Sea. Symbolized by the division of Germany, this process created two spheres of influence that persisted from 1947 to 1990: the Cold War. Western European states were obliged to recognize the need for diplomatic co-operation to ensure their individual and collective security. In addition, European states (and the USA) were increasingly keen to ensure that West Germany would be bound firmly into Western Europe to protect the West from the Soviet 'threat' and ensure that Germany itself would not repeat its past aggression.

While not a direct product of the Cold War, European co-operation was certainly encouraged by it. Western European states' recognition of their common interests as liberal democracies and market economies prompted a need to promote a common association. After 1947 East–West security concerns helped to create a sense of political solidarity in Western Europe, the key symbolic moments being the Berlin Crisis and fall of Czechoslovakia in 1948. The USA acknowledged that the defence of Western Europe was necessary to contain the USSR and prevent it, by diplomatic and (if necessary) military means, from advancing beyond its pre-existing sphere of influence. In April 1949 a European–Atlanticist alliance, the North Atlantic Treaty Organization (NATO), was agreed to by ten Western European states plus the USA and Canada. In addition, the perception of Western Europe as of the 'West' rather than the 'East', a result of Cold War realities, was underlined by distinguishing the region from south-western Europe and the countries of the Iberian peninsula, specifically the then authoritarian political regimes of Spain and Portugal.

Curiously, the division of Europe helped solidify the co-operation of Western European states in ways not seen before. As control over the initial remaking of Europe passed from European nations to non-European superpowers, Western European nations individually and collectively resolved to try to enhance their reputations, rebuild their economies and develop their political systems. Many suggested that this would be best achieved by economic and political co-operation in addition to diplomatic and military alliance. From 1946 the European states began to exert a collective identity as a collegial set of nation states. (The exception was the UK, which maintained a distance from the continent, emphasizing its world role, its continuing imperial ties and its 'special relationship' with the USA.)

An ill-fated attempt to set up a proto-European defence force, the European Defence Community (EDC), had been agreed to by the six members of the ECSC but was vetoed by France in 1954. Support for some form of European defence initiative briefly re-emerged in the form of the Western European Union (WEU), an intergovernmental institution that oversaw the rearmament of West Germany and its military integration into Western Europe. But the failure of the EDC reinforced the belief of enthusiastic Europeans that co-operation was best encouraged by economic rather than diplomatic or other means. This acknowledgement that economic reconstruction by individual European states would be enhanced by their economic and political co-operation was encouraged by the USA's support for Western Europe through the introduction of Marshall Aid in 1948. The economic reconstruction of Europe encouraged a sense of Western European identity. In this way the rebuilding of West Germany and its economic integration into Western Europe became part of the promotion of European co-operation in the face of the West's deepening stand-off with the Soviet Union and its eastern European satellites. Marshall Aid also encouraged European economic growth, which in time facilitated the creation of a dynamic European market from which co-operating Western European nations (as well as the USA) would reap considerable economic benefits.

Finally, a deepening Western European identity was encouraged by the spread of liberal democracy following the defeat of the Axis powers. In 1939 only nine European nation states out of 29 could claim to be democratic by a contemporary definition; excepting totalitarian and authoritarian regimes, only Denmark, Finland, Norway, Sweden, Czechoslovakia, Ireland, Luxembourg, the Netherlands and the UK allowed men and women the equal right to vote. After 1945 Western European states were for the first time all market economies and liberal democracies, a fact that made co-operation and association more feasible. The exceptions were Spain and Portugal, which remained non-democratic authoritarian regimes until the mid-1970s, whereupon that impediment to their joining the EU was lifted and both states acceded as part of the second enlargement in 1986. Gradual and piecemeal Europeanization was heavily dependent upon this common identity. Shared political and economic ideals encouraged the formation of European institutions, a development that in turn fostered ever closer trans-governmental co-operation within an increasingly integrated and regionalized economy.

Summary

A number of perspectives encouraged the post-war desire of European states for geopolitical stability and collective security.

- The idea that future wars in Europe would be prevented if European states co-operated with each other.

- The belief that the economic reconstruction and post-war prosperity of individual European states would be enhanced by mutually beneficial economic and political co-operation.

- Cold War East–West security concerns, which helped create a sense of political solidarity in Western Europe, one reinforced by collective efforts at economic and institutional reconstruction (such as the European Recovery Programme).

- A sense of a Western European identity, which was greatly assisted by the post-war spread of liberal democracy and the dissemination of the common political values of the centre-left and centre-right.

4 Issues of formation and development

EU states supportive and sceptical of the integration project have contested both its pace and direction and continue to do so. The key issue dividing them has been: When the 'economic benefits which the Community was bringing ... were recognized and welcomed', to what extent should they 'be paid for with a transfer of national sovereignty to the likes of the Commission, the European Parliament, or a Council of Ministers taking its decision by majority vote'? (Nugent, 1999, p.25). The making of the EU has been an uneasy compromise between intergovernmentalism and supranationalism. Member states have had two competing objectives.

- Pooling or surrendering sovereignty through political and economic integration in order to secure national prosperity.
- Retaining sovereignty in order to maintain their autonomy, even in the face of encroaching global pressures and economic interdependence.

Intergovernmentalism

Intergovernmentalism enables member states to pursue their own national interests and exercise a veto on developments they do not favour. Supranationalism limits their ability to exercise a national veto and obliges them to follow decisions supported by a majority or qualified majority of their fellow member states. Internal tensions between member states and between member states and European institutions over this intergovernmental versus supranational question have been a key and recurring issue in the building of the EU. The more supranational its procedures, the more integrated the EU becomes (Sandholtz and Stone Sweet, 1998). Efforts to introduce a number of proposed supranational developments after 1958 were stymied by French intransigence during the 'empty chair dispute' of July 1965 to January 1966, when France boycotted EU institutions in protest at pressures to abandon unanimity and consensus in the decision-making process. The Luxembourg Compromise of 1966 re-established unanimity rather than qualified majority voting as the rule.

Supranationalism

Although the EU does 'exert considerable "supranational" powers, or powers which transcend national boundaries, authorities or interests' (Peterson, 1999, p.255), this involves the implementation of existing international treaties. In determining treaties, intergovernmentalism has been the European norm, a fact underpinned by the enlargement of the community from six members to nine members in January 1973. This was particularly marked by the accession of the UK, then, as mostly since, a keen advocate of intergovernmental methods. None the less there has been a gradual, if incremental, increase in the supranational nature of the EU since the Luxembourg Compromise and in the wake of the Single European Act and the Treaty on European Union. Today the EU continues to embrace intergovernmentalism, but it has adopted a number of supranational characteristics as it has become 'wider' and 'deeper'. Of course, the EU has had no definable centre. It primarily exists in the form of its institutions, especially the European Council, the Council of Ministers, the Commission, the Parliament and the Court of Justice: '[T]he real essence of EU politics [is] the constant interactions within and between EU institutions in Brussels, between national governments and Brussels, within the various departments in national government, in bilateral meetings between governments, and between private interests and government officials in Brussels and at the national level' (Hix, 1999, p.4). EU institutions remain both intergovernmental and supranational in character.

4.1 How is the EU governed?

Historically, the *formation* of major legislation has been by intergovernmental means but, once agreed to by member states, the *implementation* and *enforcement* of treaties has been by supranational means.

- The main supranational institutions are the Commission, the Parliament and the Court of Justice.
- The main intergovernmental institutions are the European Council and the Council of Ministers.

Today the intergovernmental European Council, which is composed of heads of government and their foreign affairs ministers, is the most important European institution in determining the pace, direction and, indeed, feasibility of integration. It decides strategic direction, the accession of new members, the agreement to new treaties and the determination of policy priorities. It is responsible for forging the Europe of tomorrow. The European Council and the Council of Ministers have had the power of decision making as both executive and legislature. They set out EU objectives, co-ordinate international policies, resolve differences among member states and resolve differences between European institutions.

The European Commission, which is composed of twenty Commissioners with responsibility for particular policy areas (all of whom are nominated by national governments but obliged to act as 'Europeans'), is headed by the President of the Commission, who is appointed for a five-year term by the European Council. It makes legislative proposals that the European Council/Council of Ministers may accept, amend or reject. It also guards and enforces existing treaties and legislation agreed to by the European Council/Council of Ministers, administers and manages the EU, and executes EU policies. In contrast with the European Council and the Council of Ministers, the European Commission is essentially a secondary executive. It makes proposals to the Council and/or the Council of Ministers and implements Council decisions, but has only the power of recommendation, not decision.

The day-to-day work of the Commission is carried out by the twenty-strong College of Commissioners, their personal staffs and the 28,000-strong Commission bureaucracy, which is organized into 24 Directorate Generals with responsibility for specific policy areas such as External Relations, Economic and Financial Affairs, Agriculture, Internal Market and Financial Services, and Personnel and Administration. Generally speaking, the Commission's formal powers have been confined to influencing the deliberations of the Council and discharging its will. Yet at particular times and under particular circumstances, especially through its right to comment on Council proposals and make recommendations to the Council, the Commission can exercise considerable informal power. A proactive Commission can significantly shape EU deliberations and decisions. Under the presidency of Jacques Delors from 1985 to 1995, the Commission encouraged member states to sign up to the 1986 Single

European Act and played an influential role in the deliberations leading to the signing of the 1992 Treaty on European Union. On both occasions the Commission found that it was knocking on an open door.

The European Parliament has been directly elected since 1979 and comprises 626 Members of the European Parliament (MEPs) drawn from each member state based on population. In contrast with the Councils and the Commission, it has strictly limited powers and is permitted to advise and occasionally (in limited areas) to co-decide matters. It is consulted on the appointment of the Commission and, through the power of censure, can dismiss the Commission by a two-thirds majority vote. While the Parliament's role has grown in recent years, it remains advisory and supervisory.

The European Court of Justice (the ECJ) is responsible for the enforcement of the EU's supranational legal system and interprets, applies and adjudicates EU laws that are binding on all member states.

For a great deal of the history of the EU these interactive institutions have worked together: the Commission proposing and recommending, the Parliament advising, the European Council and the Council of Ministers deciding (with some participation from the Parliament and the Commission), and the European Court enforcing. Within the European Council unanimity is the rule, compromise the method and, as with the British opt-out from monetary union and the Social Chapter at Maastricht, the negotiation of opt-outs regarding future treaties is permissible.

Intergovernmentalism, QMV and moves toward supranationalism

The day-to-day legislative and executive work of the EU is enacted by the Commission together with the Council of Ministers meeting in its various functional policy forums (agriculture, finance, trade and so on). Yet, while national governments act on an intergovernmental basis within the European Council, meetings of the Council of Ministers have become more supranational and less intergovernmental since the Single European Act. When the Commission makes a recommendation to the Council of Ministers, the decision to adapt, amend or reject it is usually taken on the basis of unanimity. But with respect to policies on the single market, trade, agriculture and fisheries, qualified majority voting (QMV) can apply. In introducing QMV into the previously wholly intergovernmental Council of Ministers the EU took another step away from intergovernmentalism. Each state holds a weighed vote related to its size, with the four largest states – Germany, Britain, France and Italy – holding ten votes each, and the smallest – Luxembourg – holding two votes. Of the total 84 votes in the Council of Ministers, 27 votes are needed to block a proposal.

Although the Council continues to operate on the basis of unanimity wherever possible, the introduction of a qualified majority qualifies the national veto. This marks a shift away from the intergovernmental procedures of 1952 to 1986. In areas where QMV applies the Council is committed to seek consensus rather than pursue a majority by virtue of an informal agreement not to pursue a vote where fundamental disagreement exists between member states. However, despite considerable (and continuing) supranational encroachment in the form of an occasionally proactive Commission, the introduction of QMV the gradual enhancement of the powers of the European Parliament, the interactions between national governments as well as between national governments and Brussels remain key to understanding how decisions are made regarding the future development of the EU.

4.2   Negative and positive integration

The building of the EU is explained by nation states engaging in *joint* actions to formulate *common* policies and make *binding* decisions for *individual* and *collective* advantage. Naturally, there are periodic tensions between competing interests at the national level, most notably the desire to secure economic benefits from ever closer union and concerns about surrendering national autonomy. However, while the building of the EU has been largely prompted by inter-state bargaining, a form of 'negative integration' involving states interacting for their own advantage, it has also been accompanied by a degree of 'positive integration'. As states have become more European the EU has taken on its own identity and its own policy responsibilities, and the governance of the EU is increasingly pursued in the interests of 'Europe' as well as those of its member states.

Hence there is both a formal and an informal aspect to European integration: formally, through intergovernmental bargaining for specific objectives, member states willingly transfer power and authority to European institutions; informally, power and authority are increasingly ceded by member states as a result of ever increasing and deepening economic and political integration. Formal integration has been encouraged by informal integration. In enacting and enforcing decisions the EU exerts a wider influence that enhances its supranational character at the expense of its intergovernmental past.

But while a historical pattern can be discerned with regard to economic integration, it is not the case that Europe has automatically and inexorably moved from being a free-trade area to a customs union, to an internal commodity market, to a single common market. Nor is it inevitable that it will subsequently become a single economic unit through the adoption of monetary union. It is also not guaranteed that monetary union will result in economic union or political union. There is no remorseless logic behind the widening, deepening EU. Nothing is inevitable. Despite the best claims of supporters of a federal Europe, the EU has no predetermined destination. It has been built over time through the combined efforts of its member states, the logic of the international treaties they have agreed, and the efforts of the European institutions they have fashioned and within which they participate.

It is worth noting that it has taken the EU 43 years to increase its membership from six to fifteen and to move from co-ordinating the production of iron and steel to embracing monetary union. While it is hotly debated whether this represents sudden or sluggish progress, early hopes that integration would be fast and direct were misplaced. The process of integration has certainly been erratic. The declared intention of the 1969 Hague Convention that the EEC would establish economic and political union by 1980 is only one illustration that European aspirations can run way ahead of political realities. The development of the EU has at times been halting, if not faltering, and at other times it has taken great leaps forward. There have been both fast and slow periods in the 'deepening' of the EU.

- Fast periods of integration include: 1950 to 1958 (the establishment of the ECSC and its transformation into the EEC), 1970 to 1973 (the first enlargement), 1977 to 1979 (the establishment of the European Monetary System and the Exchange Rate Mechanism) and, quite dramatically, 1985 to 1997 (the second and third enlargements, the signing of the Single European Act, the Treaty on European Union and the Treaty of Amsterdam, and the establishment of monetary union).

- Slow periods of integration include: 1958 to 1970 (the consolidation of the Treaty of Rome and the building of the EEC), 1973 to 1977 (bedding down the first enlargement, the adoption of summitry), and 1979 to 1985 (budgetary disputes). These were periods in which the EU appeared content to consolidate rather than advance. They were characterized by internal tensions and disagreements, most notably during the French opposition to enlargement, the CAP and QMV negotiations in 1961 to 1965 and the budgetary disputes of 1980 to 1984.

The slow and contentious pace of European integration is reflected in the historical emergence of the EU. The desire of national governments to co-operate internationally for reasons of self-interest conflicts with their eagerness to retain national sovereignty and autonomy. The historical trade-offs between these demands lie at the heart of the integrationist process. None the less, the widening and deepening of the EU is now a historical fact.

Yet while the EU does reflect accommodated national interests, the extent to which this has been the product of shared European traditions, histories and values must be explored, it cannot be assumed. The idea that a common European identity now coexists with, and may well replace, pre-existing national identities is a very large supposition, despite the dramatic 'Europeanization' that has taken place since 1950. While the peoples of Europe may now be more 'European' (and are legally citizens of the EU), they remain national citizens first and European citizens second. After 50 years the EU is far from being a finished product and in no way resembles a United States of Europe.

Although 'political ideals and utopian visions of a united Europe may have had at least some part to play in the early post-war years, more recently they have counted for little and it has been hard-headed national calculations of economic and political advantages and disadvantages that have been the principal determinants of the nature and pace of the integration process' (Nugent, 1999, p.9). The continuing significance of national self-interest has been central to the integration process. If, according to Alan Milward, '[t]he strength of the European Community ... lies in the weakness of the nation state' (Milward, 1992, p.446), William Wallace is also correct to suggest that 'the weakness of the European Community lies in the strength of national and sub-national identities. Economic integration, driven by technological change and global competition, is counterbalanced by political disintegration' (Wallace, 1997, p.46).

Summary

- The making of the EU has been an uneasy compromise between intergovernmentalism and supranationalism.

- Member states willingly transfer power and authority to EU institutions through intergovernmental bargaining. Informally, power and authority are increasingly ceded by member states as a result of widening and deepening economic and political integration.

- However, while the EU in no way resembles a United States of Europe, significant supranational developments have taken place, although these do not necessarily detract from the role of intergovernmentalism in determining the future direction of the EU.

- The pace of European integration has been variable: at times faltering, at other times able to take great leaps forward.

5   The EU from a historical perspective

While institutions such as the Council of Europe and NATO 'all remained recognizably international institutions. The European Community [has been] something else: less than a federation, certainly, but much more than an institutional intergovernmental regime' (Wallace, 1999, p.511). The EU now represents an international political system in which member states have ceded some constitutional independence, their 'sovereign equality modified, economic autonomy long since deeply compromised, security managed through an integrated alliance, internal borders opened and external borders managed through a common regime, monetary sovereignty shortly to yield to a single currency' (ibid.).

In identifying the explanations that illuminate how and why the EU was built, four free-standing but complementary historical and theoretical perspectives can be identified.

- The specificity of Western Europe.

- The impact of economic, political and cultural globalization and the internationalization of decision taking, which increases interdependence and encourages regional forms of governance.

- The pursuit of national interests and preferences through inter-state bargaining conducted within European institutions.

- The self-reinforcing dynamic of a 'wider' and 'deeper' EU, which encourages 'ever closer union' among EU members. In addition, would-be member states have become more and more eager to pool their sovereignty in exchange for the economic benefits and international status EU membership is perceived to confer.

5.1 The specificity of Western Europe

In inhabiting the same small continent, European nations have long been interdependent, and interdependence is not born of the modern age, nor is it the automatic or unthinking result of newly fashioned global forms of industry, finance or culture. The autonomy of all states has always been affected by the actions of other states and by the economic, political and military decisions other states take as they pursue their own goals. The invasion of Belgium twice this century is perhaps testimony to that. The idea of Europe as a distinct and important entity has grown significantly over the past 50 years. While Europe is 'a region with long, albeit interrupted, traditions of transnational interaction and co-operation, both formal and informal, going back centuries' (Wallace, 1996, p.17), it was only after 1945, as European nations began to draw back in on themselves, that a Western European specificity was encouraged.

As has already been noted, the collective memory of two world wars promoted the belief that transnational conflict within Europe would be mitigated by transnational co-operation; that, put crudely, war would be unlikely should states 'hang together, for fear of hanging separately'. The post-1945 preoccupation with collective security in the wake of past conflicts was further entrenched by the emergent Cold War from 1947 and made Western European efforts at geopolitical stabilization seem ever more necessary. As increasingly economically co-operative liberal democracies with advanced welfare states and high levels of collective state provision began to perceive their common interests, European nations rejected the ever narrowing differences that had previously divided them.

This Europeanization was also assisted by the fact that states with overseas territories such as Belgium, France, the Netherlands, Portugal and the UK began to divest themselves, and be divested, of their colonial holdings. The UK achieved a relatively peaceful disengagement in, say, India and Central Africa, if not in Egypt; France violently attempted to forestall disengagement in Vietnam and Algeria. Whatever the process, European de-colonization prompted continental powers, and in time the UK, to draw back from the world beyond Europe. Taken together, these processes led to European states becoming more willing to consider themselves European, which in turn promoted the possibilities of wider and deeper European co-operation.

5.2   Globalization and the internationalization of decision making

In the post-Cold War world this Western European specificity is in the process of being broadened out to embrace a Europe-wide form of co-operation. From the perspective of a globalization thesis, economic globalization promotes an internationalization of decision making, reflecting 'the stretching of political relations across space and time; the extension of political power and political activity across the boundaries of the modern nation state' (Held et al., 1999, p.49). This leads to a degree of internationalization of decision making in the form of internal regimes and quasi-supranational institutions, such as the EU, and fashions a multi-layered system of governance.

There are six steps by which interdependence encourages the growth of intergovernmental and/or supranational organizations.

1   The growth of global interconnectedness and economic globalization ...

2   results in national borders become increasingly permeable.

3   This facilitates a diminution of states' capacities,

4   which in turn requires states to co-operate one with another in order to mitigate the effects by combining with others.

5   This naturally encourages the growth of international agencies, and, inevitably, supranational institutions; and ...

6   encourages internationalized, if regionalized, systems of governance.

(adapted from Held et al., 1999, pp.74–7)

As has already been argued, globalization may deepen the interdependence of nations by strengthening the market and civil society at the expense of the individual state. But it doesn't create that interdependence. In 'a distinctly west European effort to contain the consequences of globalization ... west Europeans invented a form of regional governance to extend the state and to harden the boundaries between them and the rest of the world' (Wallace, 1996, p.17).

But if economic interdependence requires states to co-operate, it may be encouraged by the *belief* that the boundaries of nation states have become more brittle and that nation states are less independent as a result. If globalization is *perceived* to weaken the autonomy of the nation state, as national borders become more and more permeable to global capital flows and the internationalization of industry, co-operation and integration through regional governance offers the nation state an opportunity to reassert some degree of autonomy. States may co-operate voluntarily and need not be coerced into doing so: internationalization born of globalization is a factor encouraging European co-operation, but it does not explain the EU, nor can it *of itself* explain European integration.

5.3   Intergovernmental bargaining

European integration since 1945 has been a historical process, it is not something that took place over night. Integration has proceeded by fits and starts in a process of 'punctuated equilibrium', in which the pace and direction of European integration has been largely determined by national preferences and by inter-state bargains cut within European institutions. Andrew Moravcsik argues that 'European integration resulted from a series of rational choices made by national leaders who consistently pursued economic interests ... in response to structural changes in the global economy. When such interests converged, integration advanced' (Moravcsik, 1998, p.3). He suggests that the substance of EU integration 'did not supersede or circumvent the political will of national leaders; it reflected their will' (ibid., p.4).

Although influenced by the bargaining strengths of member states and, to a lesser extent, supranational demands, the pace and direction of integration reflect the national preferences of member states. Britain's role as what Stephen George (1999) has termed the 'awkward partner' illustrates this point. Its present decision to stand aloof from monetary union indicates the freedom of manoeuvre that the governments of member states continue to enjoy, even if the gradual Europeanization of the UK indicates how states and societies adapt to the wider process of European integration. The UK is a well-established European power, but it has always couched its interests in a wider, international perspective that lies beyond the continent of Europe. Britain looked to the four corners of the globe during its imperial heyday, and felt itself to be far closer to the USA than to Europe in the middle third of the twentieth century. It is only in the past 30 years or so that it has slowly, and not necessarily smoothly, adjusted itself to its new identity as a European nation state, as its imperial interests have dwindled and economic rationales have dictated a rapprochement with its European neighbours.

Britain's post-1957 rapprochement with its European neighbours is an instructive case study of the growing economic (and therefore political) significance of the EU. Having continued to define itself as a world power *of* Europe but not necessarily *in* Europe from 1945 to 1955, Britain was obliged to come to terms with its somewhat straitened circumstances. Acknowledging its junior status to the USA within the Western Alliance and its post-imperial status served to strengthen Britain's European credentials, even if its participation in Europe has largely remained hesitant and on occasion perhaps even half-hearted.

Federalist readings of the history of the EU suggest that federal ideals are encouraged by the pre-existing and ever deepening forms of co-operation already embedded at the European level. Yet, beyond promoting its initial beginnings, the ideals of a federal Europe, one governed by a supra-national élite concerned with non-national issues, have played only a marginal part in the integrationist process. While co-operative, the member states of the EU are not homogeneous. The members are all liberal-democratic, market economies, but the EU remains a collection of distinct, interdependent states that have enjoyed different, if intertwined, historical trajectories. EU member states continue to be characterized by distinct political, economic, cultural, linguistic and religious traditions and identities. It is true that ever closer political and economic union will itself be encouraged by closer political and economic union, but the dynamic of European integration has largely resulted from the fact that '[g]overnments co-operated when induced or constrained to do so by economic self-interest ... European integration exemplifies a distinctly modern form of power politics, peacefully pursued by democratic states for largely economic reasons' (Moravcsik, 1998, p.5).

This in no way invalidates other explanations of integration, such as the specificity of Europe or the impact of globalization and the deepened interdependence it prompts. It only emphasizes the role that national preferences have played in the building of the EU and the contribution that member states who chose to delegate and pool their sovereignty have made to this ongoing process. There is no definitive, predetermined end-game with regard to a federal Europe, only a deepening co-operation between nation states engaged in inter-state bargains struck at a European level. Although significantly influenced by other factors, EU develop-ments are ultimately determined by national preferences played out against the backdrop of these other explanations.

If European decisions restrict the freedom of the nation state to take decisions autonomously in some areas, it is because the nation state has willed it that way. The motivation born of national interest is important in explaining the development over time of the EU and is worth emphasizing. Thus although it is the case that to a degree 'within the Union, sovereignty is now ... clearly divided; any conception of sover-eignty which assumes it is an indivisible, illimitable, exclusive and perpetual form of public power – embodied within an individual state – is outmoded' (Held et al., 1999, p.74), it is 'the member states [that] have limited their sovereign rights' (Mancini, 1991, p.180) and so taken the lead in building the EU over the past 50 years.

Summary

- There are a number of free-standing and complementary explanations of ever closer European integration: the specificity of Western Europe; economic, political and cultural globalization encouraging the internationalization of decision taking; and the pursuit of national interests and preferences through inter-state bargaining conducted within European institutions.

- Of course, the 'wider' and 'deeper' the EU becomes, the more likely 'ever closer union' among the members states becomes. In addition, would-be member states become more and more eager to join the EU in pursuit of the economic benefits and international status that EU membership is perceived to confer. None the less, national preferences pursued through inter-state bargaining have lain at the heart of the building of the EU since 1952.

6   Conclusion

The building of the EU has been a historical process, prompted by both accident and design, through deliberate initiatives and unintended consequences. There has been no predetermined path, no automatic transition from sovereign states to constituent parts of a European federation. The expansion of the EU has involved both a widening of the membership and a deepening pattern of institutionalization. This has led to an increase in membership from the original six ECSC states in 1952 to the present-day fifteen members and the EU's accumulation of policy responsibilities, which help provide a degree of internationalized governance at the European level.

In historical terms the self-definition of Western Europe as a geographically specific region was encouraged by the fact that states had political and economic similarities and were common participants in the Cold War. This helped foster a sense of shared political and economic interests. In addition, Europeanization was encouraged by the belief that a future conflict in Europe would be prevented if European states co-operated politically and economically, and that the prosperity of individual European states would be enhanced by this mutually beneficial co-operation.

Finally, to a considerable degree global interdependence and Europeanization have fostered a deepening desire on the part of European states to pursue co-dependence with each other in combination with the geographical and political specificity of post-war Western Europe. Together these factors illuminate the emergence over time of the 'ever closer union' of the EU. The gradual, piecemeal, but unmistakable, shift in the EU away from pure intergovernmentalism toward a degree of supranationalism lies at the heart of European integration. But while this is an important facet of a growing Europeanization, intergovernmentalism has been and remains the key feature of the building of the EU.

References

George, S. (1999) *An Awkward Partner: Britain in the European Community*, Oxford, Oxford University Press (third edition).

Held, D., McGrew, A., Goldblatt, D. and Perraton, J. (1999) *Global Transformations*, Cambridge, Polity Press.

Hix, S. (1999) *The Political System of the European Union*, London, Macmillan.

Mancini, F.G. (1991) 'The making of a new constitution for Europe' in Keohane, R. and Hoffman, S. *The New European Community*, Boulder, CO, Westview Press.

Milward, A. (1992) *The European Rescue of the Nation State*, London, Routledge.

Moravcsik, A. (1998) *The Choice for Europe: Social Purpose and State Power from Messina to Maastricht*, London, UCL Press.

Nugent, N. (1999) *The Government and Politics of the European Union*, London, Macmillan.

Peterson, J. (1999) 'Sovereignty and independence' in Holliday, I., Gamble, A. and Parry, G. (eds) *Fundamentals in British Politics*, London, Macmillan.

Sandholtz, W. and Stone Sweet, A. (eds) (1998) *European Integration and Supranational Governance*, Oxford, Oxford University Press.

Wallace, H. (1996) 'Politics and policy in the EU: the challenge of governance' in Wallace, H. and Wallace, W. (eds) *Policy Making in the European Union*, Oxford, Oxford University Press.

Wallace, W. (1997) 'The nation state – rescue or retreat' in Gowan, P. and Anderson, P. (eds) *The Question of Europe*, London, Verso.

Wallace, W. (1999) 'The sharing of sovereignty: the European paradox', *Political Studies*, vol.47, pp.503–21.

Further reading

Parts 1 and 2 of Dinan, D. (1999) *Ever Closer Community*, London, Macmillan.

Moravcsik, A. (1998) *The Choice for Europe: Social Purpose and State Power from Messina to Maastricht*, London, UCL Press (especially Chapters 1 and 7).

Wallace, W. (1994) *Regional Integration: The West European Experience*, Washington, DC, Brookings Institution.

Chapter 3
The nation state in the European Union

Simon Bromley

1   Introduction

What are the roles of the member states in the European Union? And is the Union itself in the process of becoming a federal state?

These apparently straightforward questions are extremely difficult to answer, for the development of the European Union raises questions that go to the very centre of politics and political analysis. The complex relations between the member states and the key institutions of the Union – the Commission, the Parliament and the European Court of Justice (ECJ) – force us to think about what we understand political authority to be. Who has it, and where and how is it exercised? It is no easy task to describe how we are governed and how we govern ourselves in the European Union. This is why arguments about the character of the European Union and about how its member states and citizens relate to it are never far from the centre of political debate.

Compared with the rivalries and conflicts that produced two world wars in the first half of the twentieth century, the degree of co-operation achieved among the liberal-democratic, market-oriented, capitalist states of Western Europe has been a remarkable achievement. To some extent the pattern mirrors that found more generally among the major Western states (including Japan). Yet only in Western Europe has this co-operation taken the form of a new kind of political entity (the Union) involving elements of genuine and apparently durable supranational, or even proto-federal, authority. Elsewhere in the West co-operation has been primarily intergovernmental in nature. What is unique is the duration, extent and depth of the integration in Europe, as well as the commitment to the development of that integration. Moreover, European integration has evolved steadily in a rapidly changing international context, surviving major shifts in the international economy in the 1970s and the reshaping of the continental states system after the end of the Cold War. Why did the member states of the European Union embark on such a peculiar enterprise, and how have they been transformed as a result? What kind of political order have they been building, and how does it relate to the politics of the member states?

This chapter will explore these questions. Sections 2 and 3 take an essentially historical look at the crisis-ridden development of the nation state and the states system in Europe, examining the eventual stabilization of both and the distinctive pattern of integration in Western Europe that followed the Second World War. Co-operation emerged as a response to half a century of warfare and political chaos. There is no historical or geographical parallel to the intensity and extent of the political conflict and violence experienced by Europe in the first half of the twentieth century. We need to understand why this was so, and how and why the conflict came to an end. When the relevant geopolitical and political context has been described, we shall move on to examine the pattern of integration in Western Europe after the Second World War and the place of the European Union within it. What has been the relationship between the military and security integration expressed in the Atlantic framework of NATO, the general pattern of multilateral economic integration in the West as a whole, and the particular forms of integration found within the European Union?

Sections 4 and 5 turn from history to analysis. One of the striking features of the European Union is the way it has evolved over time, steadily expanding its membership, its competences and its powers. We shall see that the European Union is unique in many respects, although other international organizations have elements in common with it. Whatever else it might be, the European Union is certainly a special kind of international organization. How can we account for this? Section 4 attempts to answer this question by looking at several models of the political organization of the Union, each offering a different perspective on how it is governed. Section 5 looks to the future. Is the Union destined to become a federal state, progressively eclipsing the sovereignty of its member states as it takes on more and more supranational authority? Or is it essentially an unusually wide-ranging and deep form of intergovernmental co-operation between what remain sovereign nation states? To answer these questions we shall have to consider what is meant by the sovereignty of the state, and examine the complexities of the location of authority within member states and of the ways they have shared and delegated authority in the institutions of the European Union.

2 Europe and the modern states system

Most of us take it for granted that we live in a state with clear borders, with one currency and a single language for public communication, governed more or less effectively by a government that enacts binding laws for the whole territory and conducts a range of public policy. To pay for its activities the state has the power to levy compulsory taxes. The state also maintains a monopoly of control over the means of organized violence – the police and the armed forces. Some states are multinational and multilingual, and some have constitutions that delegate or reserve certain functions and powers to lower levels of government. But if they are states they will have one currency, one set of laws (or at least a final legislative authority), and one central government controlling one set of armed forces, all paid for out of a central budget.

Political activity – that is, the making and implementing of collectively binding policies – is aimed primarily at controlling and directing the affairs of the state. Political parties are organized on this basis, as is the formation of public opinion through the mass media. In fact, we take these things for granted because we can do little else. Try living without a state: it is not just illegal, it is also very difficult. Political life in the modern world is organized on the basis of states.

These things are not just questions of political organization. Many citizens identify with their state and with their fellow citizens, assuming that other peoples in other states do likewise. Historically speaking, a common sense of national identity has often been forged by the development of the modern state: unifying the economy through transport and communications infrastructures and a common legal system; extracting resources from the population and mobilizing it for defence and war; and educating the population in a national language and ministering to its health and social welfare. All of these processes bind 'nationals' together in all sorts of ways. In other cases, nationalism – that is, the political programme in which a people demand a state of their own – has become the focus of élites and then of mass movements within multinational states or empires. Thus defined, nations come to demand their own state. In short, states create nations and nationalism builds states: statehood and national identity have co-evolved in complex ways.

2.1   The rise of the modern European state

It wasn't always like this. Indeed, when the great German sociologist Max Weber defined 'state' in his textbook *Economy and Society* (written shortly before the First World War) he noted that the concept had reached its full development only 'in modern times'. Weber defined a (modern) state as follows.

> A 'ruling organization' will be called 'political' insofar as its existence and order is continuously safeguarded within a given *territorial* area by the threat and application of physical force on the part of the administrative staff. A compulsory political organization with continuous operation will be called a 'state'

insofar as its administrative staff successfully upholds the claim
to the *monopoly* of the *legitimate* use of physical force in the
enforcement of its order.

(Weber, 1978, p.54)

Prior to the emergence and consolidation of modern states in a protracted
process lasting from the seventeenth to the nineteenth century, political
authority and power were distributed among units with overlapping
jurisdictions and ill-defined and shifting boundaries. Empires, kingdoms,
city states and the like competed with lords, city leagues, peasant
communities and the Church for political authority. Moreover, these
political units often served the private interests of rulers rather than any
general public functions; as a result, their hold on most people's lives was
extremely rudimentary. There was no regular taxation, no system of
uniform law and no public coercive forces. In addition, these political
units competed for power and influence with the Church, which then
performed some of the functions that we now associate with the state:
collecting taxes, making laws and even maintaining coercive forces. Most
people would have identified themselves in religious or regional terms,
not national terms.

Gradually, however, a new form of political unit emerged and came to
dominate and then monopolize the political scene: the modern state.
Quentin Skinner characterized this shift in the following terms.

The decisive shift was made from the idea of the ruler
'maintaining his state' – where this simply meant upholding
his own position – to the idea that there is a separate legal and
constitutional order, that of the State, which the ruler has a
duty to maintain. One effect of this transformation was that
the power of the State, not that of the ruler, came to be
envisaged as the basis of government. And this in turn enabled
the State to be conceptualized in distinctively modern terms –
as the sole source of law and legitimate force within its own
territory, and as the sole appropriate object of its citizens'
allegiances.

(Skinner, 1978, pp.ix–x)

According to Skinner, this idea of the modern state emerged gradually in
the Europe of the Renaissance and the Reformation, particularly in the
England and France of the sixteenth century. Skinner also points out that,
at the same time, a new doctrine emerged that these states should be the
supreme source of political authority within their territories – the
'doctrine of sovereignty'. In other words, states not only became more
powerful, increasing their capacity to act, but they also gained authority,
developing a socially recognized *right* to rule their societies.

The emergence of the modern state claiming sovereignty posed several
new questions. How should this new sovereign power be regulated? On

what basis was sovereignty justified, and what purposes should it serve? And how should the relation between the rulers and the ruled be organized? There are many answers to these questions, but roughly speaking we can say that the main conflicts concerned the following issues.

- The struggle between the tradition of *raison d'etat* (the reason or interests of the state) and the constitutional rule of law (state action is subordinate to the law) as the means of regulating state power.

- The contest between an hereditary principle of authority (the rule of kings, queens and the aristocracy) and the idea that the people are the ultimate source of authority and government should serve their ends.

- The battle between authoritarian and democratic ways of ordering the relations between the rulers and the ruled.

From the eighteenth century onwards, the form of the modern state was increasingly defined in *liberal-constitutional* and *national* terms. In the constitution of a liberal state, both the executive and the legislative branches of the state – which, respectively, control and legitimate its coercive powers – are themselves subject to judicial judgement, such that the rule of law applies equally to private citizens and to public officials. States became national to the extent that the justification for liberal-constitutional rule was derived from the people through the principle of popular sovereignty, as espoused in the American and French Revolutions, and to the degree that the purpose of the state was to uphold the freedoms, welfare and security of its citizens. From the nineteenth century onwards these increasingly liberal-constitutional and national states faced growing pressures to become *democratic*, to seek consent to their rule through open and competitive electoral arrangements involving the entire adult population, propertied and property-less, male and female.

These three principles – the rule of law, popular sovereignty and democracy – had to be fought for. The passage from seeing the state as the property of an hereditary ruler to a state based on law, legitimated on the basis of the rights of a self-governing people and founded on democratically expressed consent, was a tortuous one. It looked as if these battles were on the way to being won by the late nineteenth and early twentieth century, but the First World War and its aftermath swept away any confidence that liberal democracy was the only viable political form for the modern European state. This conclusion was amply confirmed by the rise of soviet communism in Russia after 1917, and the emergence of fascism in Italy and Germany and other forms of authoritarian rule across much of southern, central and eastern Europe in the inter-war years. In fact, liberal democracy did not become the norm in Europe, and then only in Western Europe, until after the end of the Second World War in 1945.

2.2   The rise and fall of the European states system

Whatever the character of their internal or domestic political arrangements, one important consequence of the development of a number of these increasingly modern states in Europe was that, despite various attempts at empire building, no one state was ever able to achieve political dominance of the continent. After the religious, civil and national wars of the seventeenth century, especially after the Thirty Years War ended in 1648, a multiplicity of competing states became a permanent feature of the European landscape. Whether by accident or design, a 'balance of power' came to operate in the European system of states whereby any threatening increase in the power of one state was matched by a counterbalancing alliance of other states, in a process of perpetual motion. The balance of power did not produce peace. On the contrary, its very operation often led to war. But it did preserve the system of states as a *states system*: that is, a political system whose members were states and in which supreme political authority, or what was now called *sovereignty*, was located at the level of the state. Sovereign states came to recognize and legitimate one another as formal equals. That is to say, modern European states came to be accorded legitimacy not only by their citizens but also by each other. Collectively, the system of states refused to recognize other forms of political authority organized along different lines from the modern state – empires, city states, urban leagues and stateless areas gradually fell off the map of Europe. Most competitors for political power lost, and most of those that disappeared did so as a result of war and conquest. In Volume 1 of *Das Kapital* (first published in 1867), Karl Marx wrote that capitalism came into the world 'dripping from head to toe, from every pore, with blood and dirt' (Marx, 1976, p.926). That is no doubt so; it is certainly true of the modern European state and states system.

The new European states system soon outgrew its European origins by virtue of the political and military power generated by the new states, especially when harnessed to the resources provided by an industrial and capitalist economic system. European states carved out empires in the non-European world. Indeed, perhaps the most important fact about international relations at the beginning of the twentieth century was the European dominance of the rest of the world: European settlers developed the Americas and subsequently achieved independence from the old colonial powers, forming new states in the Western Hemisphere; the Slav peoples of European Russia migrated eastwards into the Tsarist empire's Asian lands; and from 1880 to 1914 formal European colonial rule was extended to much of Asia and Africa. This expansion of people, trade and capital laid the basis for the creation of an interdependent world, with Europe and the areas of European settlement (especially North America) at the centre.

Towards the end of the nineteenth century, especially from the 1890s onwards, the domination of the world by European states started to be undermined. The principal reason for this was that recognizably modern states presiding over industrialized, capitalist economies began to emerge in other parts of the world. Economic and military power thus gradually spread to other parts of the international system. After the end of the Civil War in the USA (1865), an increasingly powerful federal state was constructed and the North American economy entered a phase of rapid industrialization. In Japan, after the Meiji Restoration (1868), a modern state and economy were also developed. Russia, a Eurasian power rather than simply a European one, also moved forward rapidly. Within Europe, the newly unified Imperial German state (1871) entered a period of rapid and broadly based industrialization.

As far as the European balance of power was concerned, it was this conjunction of the rise of German power within Europe and the strengthening of Russia and the USA outside it that was critical. Prior to the First World War, rising German power in Europe posed a threat to the interests of Britain, France and Russia. For France and Britain, limiting German power on the continent was the primary aim, but they were also concerned to hold on to their imperial possessions in the non-European world. Russia supported the Slav populations in both the Ottoman and Austro-Hungarian empires, while Germany guaranteed the position of the latter. The USA was concerned that no single power should dominate the Eurasian world, since that would enable such a state to achieve world-wide preponderance, threatening its own position in the Western Hemisphere and its interests in the Far East. And whereas the economic interests of Germany and Britain were in conflict, since both exported manufactured goods and needed to import food and raw materials, the interests of the USA largely complemented those of Britain. Thus when the First World War broke out in 1914, Russia, France, Britain and the USA were all ranged against Germany (although the USA did not enter the war until 1917).

2.3   The decline of the European order

The outcome of the First World War radically altered the geopolitics of Europe, changing the balance of power. The Ottoman and Austro-Hungarian empires collapsed, thereby creating many new states, united only by their weakness and smallness; the power of Germany and Russia were (temporarily) weakened; and the international power and status of Japan and the USA were strengthened. European states were no longer the sole arbiters of world affairs, or even of European affairs. The Russian Revolution in 1917 also altered the political situation. The communist or state-socialist challenge to the capitalist states of Europe was now no longer a theoretical possibility, a vague aspiration of working-class parties and trade unions, but a practical reality in the shape of the new Soviet state. From 1917 to 1928 the Soviet state was preoccupied with civil war, reconstruction and laying the foundations of an industrial economy, but between 1928 and 1941 industrial and military development raced ahead at unprecedented speed. Stalin's Soviet Union was increasingly a geopolitical and political force to be reckoned with.

The First World War and the peace making that followed it failed to stabilize the European states system, despite the continuing illusion of British and French domination. After its late but crucial role in the Allied victory and the peace making at Versailles, the USA withdrew from direct involvement in European affairs. The new Soviet state in Russia was preoccupied with internal affairs, and politically and ideologically hostile to the rest of capitalist Europe, a posture that was reciprocated by the West. Britain and France were unable to contain the renewed growth of German power, which could not be accommodated within a merely European states system. The inter-war years saw deep economic crisis and a breakdown of the international economic order. In many capitalist countries, more or less constitutional governments were replaced by authoritarian and fascist regimes, most notably in Nazi Germany after Hitler's rise to power in 1933. Stalin's Soviet Union was a brutal dictatorship.

The Second World War began with Germany's invasion of Poland in 1939, and became truly global in 1941 with the Nazi invasion of the Soviet Union in June and the Japanese attack on the US fleet at Pearl Harbour in December. In their European aspects, the alignments of the Second World War were similar to those of the First World War. Germany overran France on this occasion, but Britain, the USA and Russia were ranged against Germany. (Italy attempted to remain neutral during the First World War, despite being an ally of Germany and Austria–Hungary, but was attacked by the latter in 1916. In the Second World War Italy joined the Axis powers, but the overthrow of Mussolini in 1943, shortly after a successful Allied invasion of Sicily, left the new regime fighting with the Allies against the Germans, who controlled much of northern and central Italy.)

The outcome of the Second World War fundamentally reshaped the balance of power in world politics. It undermined the empires of Britain, France, Belgium, Italy and the Netherlands; it (temporarily) reduced the power of the main Axis states – Germany, Italy and Japan; it massively increased the power of the main military rivals to Hitler's Germany – Stalin's Soviet Union and, above all, Roosevelt's USA; and it thereby helped to create the bipolar international system of the post-war period. The new balance of power came to be organized around military and political competition between the two new superpowers – the Communist Soviet Union and the liberal-democratic, capitalist USA. The Allies – Britain, the USA and Russia – fell apart and the Cold War took a grip on world politics. This bipolarity was reinforced by the superpowers' possession of an effective monopoly of nuclear weapons and their delivery systems.

The outcome of the Second World War also dramatically altered the nature of politics within the capitalist states of Europe. In the crisis years of the inter-war period a fear of socialism and communism persuaded much of Europe's ruling classes and élites to support authoritarian, even fascist, forms of politics, such that the liberal democracies were more or less confined to the north-western tip of the continent. The Second World War discredited authoritarian and fascist rule across the whole of what became Western Europe, even if democracy was not consolidated in Greece, Spain and Portugal until the 1970s and 1980s. In Greece post-war democratic rule was interrupted by a military coup and subsequent army rule between 1967 and 1974. The Salazar dictatorship in Portugal fell in 1974, and a fully democratic constitution was adopted in 1982. After the death of General Franco in 1975 Spain began a transition to democracy that was also concluded in 1982. In what became Eastern Europe, by contrast, authoritarian rule remained the norm, although it took a communist form after the defeat of fascism. The transition to liberal democracy in Eastern Europe did not begin until the collapse of communist rule in 1989.

Summary

- The development and consolidation of the modern state is a relatively recent phenomenon, taking place in Europe between the seventeenth and nineteenth centuries. The development of a number of nation states in Europe also produced a European states system regulated by the balance of power.

- European states expanded into the rest of the world, spreading the modern nation state and the associated states system on a global basis.

- Both the development of the modern state and the expansion of the states system were conflict-ridden processes that produced two world wars. Only after the Second World War did the European states system stabilize in the context of the new bipolar, super-power-dominated international system.

3 The pattern of integration in Western Europe

As far as integration in Western Europe was concerned, the radically different outcomes of the First World War and Second World War were particularly important. Crudely speaking, the First World War solved nothing. After the Second World War, however, the German state no longer existed and authoritarian forms of the capitalist state were utterly discredited. (It was no accident that the only remaining dictatorships in Western Europe – Spain and Portugal – had not been involved in the Second World War.) Germany was occupied by the victorious Allied powers (as was Japan). In Italy, as Allied military power pushed north after 1943, sovereignty was steadily regained by the new anti-fascist government, but the Allies, especially the USA, remained a strong influence on the post-war reconstruction of Italian politics. Moreover, Britain and

France were no longer first-rank, global powers, as their empires were in terminal decline and they were economically exhausted by the war. The Soviet Union was now fully engaged in European affairs, if still ideologically opposed to the capitalist West, and despite immense losses of people and materials it commanded a huge military force. The USA emerged from the Second World War as the most powerful state, economically and militarily, that the world has ever seen, producing nearly as much economic output as the rest of the major powers combined and with a (short-lived) monopoly on nuclear weapons. Any new political arrangements among the European states would have to come to terms with the immense influence of the superpowers.

3.1   The superpowers and integration in Western Europe

The consolidation of the Cold War between the USA and the Soviet Union divided Europe into two mutually hostile camps, geopolitically and politically. Eastern Europe came under Soviet domination, largely through the presence of the Red Army and the forcible imposition of pro-Moscow, communist regimes. In Western Europe, the USA exercised considerable influence through its occupying role in West Germany and through the economic and military assistance it was able to offer the states of Western Europe. If Soviet dominance in the East was largely unwanted and maintained by coercion, the USA's influence in the West was largely welcomed and consensual. One crucial outcome of this Cold War division of Europe was that Germany was divided into two states, East and West: the German Democratic Republic in the east and the Federal Republic of Germany in the west.

After the defeat of German (and Italian) fascism in Europe, Soviet power in the East and the ensuing ideological rivalry between the communist and capitalist camps changed the geopolitical and political calculations of the states of Western Europe, making the containment of Soviet and communist power the main priority. The USA was keen to encourage integration in Western Europe, but as the USA was now a global power this integration had to be 'fitted into a wider Atlantic framework' (Lundestad, 1998, p.4). The wider Atlantic framework was defined by the United Nations (UN) and its multilateral economic organizations: the General Agreement on Tariffs and Trade (GATT), the International Monetary Fund (IMF) and the World Bank; the policies of post-war economic reconstruction launched by the USA under the European Recovery Programme (the Marshall Plan) in 1948; and, most importantly, the military alliance of the North Atlantic Treaty Organization (NATO), which was established in 1949. In so far as European integration was consistent with this wider network, policy-makers in the USA believed that it would serve a range of purposes: it would provide a means of promoting the American model of political and economic organization; over time a stronger and more integrated Western Europe would reduce the economic and military burden on the USA of containing Soviet power; and it would limit and channel West German power in a stabilizing manner.

Although German power had been drastically reduced by defeat in the Second World War and its subsequent Cold War division, the question of how to integrate the new West Germany into the states system of Western European and the wider Atlantic order still remained. France was particularly concerned about the future power of West Germany, and the USA was fearful that a desire for reunification might lead West Germany to accept a neutral role, thereby effectively strengthening the Soviet position in Europe. In fact, after the outbreak of the Korean War in 1950, the USA was insistent that West Germany should be allowed to re-arm. On the economic front, it was also clear that there could be no recovery in Western Europe without the revival of the West German economy. France was initially suspicious about the rebuilding of West German power and wanted to act in co-operation with Britain on defence matters to contain any future threat from Germany. For its part, Britain still saw itself as a world power and was reluctant to commit military resources that could be used globally to the defence of Western Europe. The British therefore sought the direct involvement of the USA in rebuilding and securing Western Europe. Finally, for the new West German state (established in 1949) security depended on the guarantees provided by the USA within the Atlantic order. The recovery of its economy and a legitimate international role required a rapprochement with France and Britain.

The role of NATO was crucial in the context of external security. NATO was formed in 1949 as a collective military security arrangement, with an integrated military command structure in which an attack on any one member state was to be treated as an attack against all. It was organized under the political and military dominance of the USA. NATO linked states in Western Europe (Britain, France, Iceland, Norway, Denmark, Belgium, the Netherlands, Luxembourg, Portugal and Italy) to the USA and Canada. Greece and Turkey joined NATO in 1952 and Spain in 1982. It was an alliance directed against the Soviet Union and its European presence. The USA also maintained a formal military security arrangement with Japan. Together, these states formed the core of the wider intergovernmental arrangements through which the West organized its affairs – the GATT, the IMF, the World Bank and the Organization for Economic Co-operation and Development (OECD).

The most contentious question for NATO was the potential membership of West Germany. Between 1946 and 1948 the USA and Britain unified the parts of Germany they occupied, introduced a common currency to the entire Allied area, including the French zone, and incorporated the western areas into the Marshall Plan. The American and the British together convened the arrangements to set up a new West German state in September 1948. In April 1949 NATO was formed and in May 1949 the Federal Republic of (West) Germany was established, thereafter becoming a powerful actor in its own right. As has already been noted, US pressure for West German rearmament grew after the outbreak of the

Korean War (in June 1950). In August 1949 the Soviet Union had successfully tested a nuclear bomb, and in October of the same year the communists proclaimed the People's Republic of China. The Cold War was warming up.

West German Chancellor Konrad Adenauer meets the foreign ministers of France, the UK and the USA in Paris in 1954. Adenauer agreed to re-arm West Germany in return for concessions on sovereignty and membership of NATO.

The French proposed a European Defence Union that would accommodate some West German rearmament within the context of a European framework. Although the USA came to support this proposal, it did not pass the French National Assembly. A British compromise saw West Germany join NATO via the West European Union in May 1955. The Allies then ended their military occupation of West Germany, although Britain and the USA promised to maintain a strong military presence in the Federal Republic.

3.2   The nation state and integration in Western Europe

Because the USA guaranteed the West's security against the Soviet Union and the communist world, other Western states could concentrate their attention on essentially economic co-operation. If NATO and the wider Atlantic framework in which the West organized itself in the Cold War provided for external security, then essentially economic integration in Western Europe might help to recover the domestic authority of nation states. The 'civilian' power of the European Union was created against the background of the geopolitical stabilization of Western Europe and its insertion into the US-led Atlantic order.

As far as the domestic authority of Western European states was concerned, it is important to recall that most of them (including all the original members of the Union) had failed in their primary task: to guarantee the security of their populations. Germany had been fought to unconditional surrender and occupied by the victorious armies; France had surrendered and recovered its territory only by force of Soviet and American arms; Italy had been invaded by the Allies in the south and occupied by the Germans in the north; Denmark, Norway, Holland, Belgium and Luxembourg had all been overrun by the Nazis; and Greece had been invaded by Italy and Germany. Only Spain, Portugal, Sweden, Switzerland and Ireland were able to remain neutral. Britain had not been invaded and had emerged victorious, but its economy was severely weakened by the war effort. Its empire was crumbling and its overall contribution to the Allied victory, while strategically crucial, had been small in comparison with the Soviet and American efforts. The Western European states, therefore, desperately needed to find a means of not only regaining their external security but also recovering their domestic authority.

The key question was: How could they co-operate with one another? For the most part Britain and the USA assumed that Western European integration and Atlantic integration pointed in the same direction. But they differed as to the form that integration should take. The USA was keen to encourage a sharing or pooling of sovereignty by the European states in the direction of supranational, proto-federal arrangements, thereby overcoming old national differences and rivalries. Britain, by contrast, wanted co-operation to take an intergovernmental form in which nation states retained their identities and their sovereign rights. In contrast to the British and US view that Atlantic and Western European integration were entirely consistent, France believed that European and US interests might be different, and particularly resented the US military dominance of NATO and Western European security. But France shared Britain's emphasis on intergovernmental forms of co-operation that would maintain national sovereignty. West Germany was itself a federal state and, in any case, was not fully sovereign as a result of the political and military restraints placed upon it by the victorious Allies. West Germany thus felt less threatened by supranational arrangements than either Britain or France. West Germany was also closely linked to the USA by virtue of their shared security concerns.

The major motivations behind the formation of the European Coal and Steel Community (ECSC) in 1951 and the signing of the Treaties of Rome in 1957 are difficult to determine. Andrew Moravcsik (1998) has argued that economic concerns were uppermost. Alan Milward (1992) has suggested that integration was as much about recovering and re-legitimating the authority of states discredited by war, in an attempt to rescue the nation state. Milward is undoubtedly right to say that economic co-operation would have counted for nothing without a solution to the problem of Germany's future in Europe. 'What, after all, was personal security for Europeans in 1945 without personal security against Germany?' (Milward, 1992, p.45). And no country felt that need more clearly than France, at war with Germany in 1871, from 1914 to 1918, and from 1939 to 1945. For France, the Union provided a framework in which a new relationship with West Germany could be forged. For West Germany, it served as a vehicle to legitimate the new state and reconstruct the economy. The Franco-German relationship was to dominate the politics of the Union until the 1980s, and perhaps beyond. France attempted to strengthen the Franco-German relationship at the expense of US influence over integration in Western Europe, especially after General de Gaulle's return to power in 1958. But when confronted with such a choice, West Germany opted for an Atlantic priority in security matters, in that it joined NATO's newly established Nuclear Planning Group in the mid-1960s, while France withdrew from the organization's integrated military command. Still, France was able to veto British membership of the European Union until the end of the 1960s, despite West German and American preferences for early British entry.

Summary

- Integration in Western Europe and the development of the European Union took place in the context of the Cold War division of Europe and of the German state.

- The European Union developed as an attempt to integrate the liberal-democratic states of Western Europe after half a century of political conflict and warfare.

- The military security of the West European states was assured by the US-led framework of NATO. Within this context, the European Union developed as a 'civilian power'.

4   The governance of the EU

Given the different interests of the founding member states – West Germany, France, Italy, Belgium, the Netherlands and Luxembourg – it is perhaps not surprising that the establishment of the European Coal and Steel Community and the European Communities appeared to offer something for all. But how were the ECSC and the European Communities organized in political terms? The Treaty establishing the ECSC (1951) and the Treaties of Rome (1957), which established the Community pillar of what eventually became the European Union, represented a distinctive model of international organization. Consider, first, the case of the ECSC. This had an executive branch of government, the High Authority, which was to act independently of the member states but did not derive authority from being elected – its members were appointed by the member states. This was justified on the basis that the Treaty defined its functions, so it was primarily an executive body created for a specific purpose by what remained sovereign states. It was not a government, although it performed certain executive or administrative functions. But since the High Authority was to be operationally independent of member states once established, and since it was not to be accountable to a legislature or an electorate, the Treaty also created a Court of Justice to ensure that the law of the Treaty was observed throughout the Community. The Treaty also provided for a Council of Ministers, representing the member states, and for an appointed Assembly, although both were intended to play a role secondary to that of the High Authority.

The European Union was intended to have a much broader remit than the ECSC and its operation was intended to be both open-ended and continuous (for example, it provided for 'ever closer union of the peoples of Europe' and stated that any European state may apply for membership). But its political structure was essentially the same as that of the ECSC, with one important difference. The Treaty establishing the European Economic Community 'provided for legislation to be adopted by the Council on a proposal from the Commission', whereas 'in the ECSC the High Authority was the main law-making organ' (Hartley, 1999, p.10). The Council of Ministers was, at least to begin with, in essence an intergovernmental forum. At some stage, and on some issues, the Treaty laid down that the Council would legislate on the basis of qualified majority voting (QMV). Finally, the European Court of Justice (ECJ) was empowered not only 'to rule on the validity of Community acts in issue before national courts' but also 'to rule on the *interpretation* both of Community acts and of the Treaty itself' (Hartley, 1999, p.13).

The Treaty provided for the Council to legislate through *regulations* and *directives*. Article 189(249) of the Treaty asserts that:

> A regulation shall have general application, it shall be binding in its entirety and directly applicable in all member States.

> A directive shall be binding, as to the result to be achieved, upon each member State to which it is addressed, but shall leave to the national authorities the choice of form and methods.

So the European Union was a product of the Treaties signed by sovereign states, but in building the Union its members constructed a political edifice with some genuinely supranational features. Four of these would seem to be particularly important. To begin with, there is the Commission (the successor to the High Authority of the ECSC); its members are appointed by national governments but they are required to act independently of those governments. Next, there is the European Parliament; this was originally an appointed body like the Assembly in the ECSC, but since 1979 it has been directly elected. Then there is the European Court of Justice, with the powers noted above. All of these institutions have a Union-wide role. Finally, the activities and programmes of these bodies are paid for out of the Union's own budget, drawn from tariff revenues, levies on agricultural imports, an element of the standard Union-wide value-added tax and a levy on national governments related to their share of the Union's gross domestic product (GDP). (Remember that it was also envisaged that the Council of Ministers would in some areas come to operate, including by enacting regulations, on the basis of QMV.)

4.1 Confederation, supranationalism and federation

What are states doing when the Treaties they sign establish an open-ended and continuous, if limited, legislative and judicial authority for some common purposes? The answer depends on the nature of the authority they establish and the purposes for which it is established.

It was originally intended that the main business of the Community would be the 'low' politics of economic and social regulation and, in particular, the creation of a common market based on the 'four freedoms': the free movement of goods, people, capital and services. It was envisaged that this would be a form of 'negative' integration, focusing on removing national barriers between member states. Over time, it became clear that the creation of a common market would also involve elements of positive integration – the creation of Union-wide rules, standards and policies.

If the limited authority established by states can act only on the basis of the unanimous support of the members, the organization is called a 'confederation' of states. In a confederation each state counts equally and has a right of veto, or at least any state that does not agree is not bound by the decisions of the others.

If there are decision-making mechanisms that can override the objections of one or more member states *and the rulings of the common authority have direct effect in the legal systems of the members*, the organization is said to be 'supranational'. In forming a supranational authority, states collectively use their general rights of sovereignty to limit the future exercise of their individual rights in some areas, handing over jurisdiction in those areas to another body. Ultimate sovereignty is not compromised, since the state can always leave the organization and repatriate the specific competences involved. But as long as the supranational organization persists, its provisions go beyond the collective exercise of sovereignty that is pooled and delegated for specific executive and administrative purposes, as a state and its citizens could be bound by genuine and enforceable legislation made by a relatively autonomous authority that claims jurisdiction for the entire body in its designated areas of competence.

A final model of political co-operation is 'federation'. In this case the federating states explicitly surrender their sovereignty to the federal structure. When states join together to form a federation, they create a federal legislature to represent all the people of the federation and make laws, as well as a federal executive, either drawn from the legislature or directly elected by the people. The constitution of such a federation will typically specify some division of power between the (old) states and the (new) federal government. There will also be a 'supreme' constitutional court to rule on the interpretation of the constitution as well as on other matters. Typically, the federal level of government is charged with a minimum of defence and foreign policy, on the one hand, and control over the currency and taxation, on the other hand. Many other aspects of government, especially much of the detail of economic and social policy, may be reserved for the states. Whatever the details, the previously separate sovereignties of the states are done away with and the new federation becomes sovereign in its own right. The parts of a federal state do *not* have a unilateral right to leave the federation.

Thus when states confederate they retain their sovereignty, since the confederation can act only on the basis of unanimity, or members are free not to be bound by the decisions of the majority. States can surrender their sovereignty to a wider federation, which then becomes a new sovereign state. And, somewhere between retaining and losing sovereignty, states can establish supranational organizations.

4.2   The complexities of governing the European Union

One of the reasons why the European Union is so difficult to understand is that it does not conform easily to any of these models, or rather it combines bits of all of them in a unique manner. The major developments of the Union – the founding Treaties and the subsequent evolution by means of new Treaties (for example, Maastricht and Amsterdam) – are intergovernmental agreements of an essentially confederal kind. Decision making in the European Council and much of the work of the Council of Ministers are also intergovernmental or confederal, notwithstanding the growth of QMV in the Council of Ministers. The Community's own institutions are, of course, supranational – the Commission, the European Parliament, the European Court of Justice (ECJ), and its own budgetary resources. However, the European Commission is in no way equivalent to the executive branch of a properly federal system such as the USA. Nor is the European Parliament equivalent to a federal legislature, despite the steady if limited growth of its powers. The Union does have its own budget but it is tiny (a little over 1 per cent of the Union's combined GDP) compared with the budgets of federal governments in, say, the USA or Canada or the budgets of the member states (typically 40 per cent of GDP or more). And prior to the Treaty of Maastricht the Union had only extremely limited powers in the areas traditionally reserved to federal governments or even confederal arrangements – defence and security, and currency and taxation.

However, the Economic and Monetary Union (EMU), agreed at the Treaty of Maastricht, and the creation of an independent European Central Bank (ECB) represent an important departure in this respect. Equally, the growth of co-operation in the second and third pillars of the Union, agreed at the Treaty of Amsterdam (1997), represent a further evolution in a confederal as well as a federal direction. The second pillar is the Common Foreign and Security Policy (CFSP), which the Treaty of Maastricht envisaged as primarily intergovernmental. The Treaty of Amsterdam confirms that arrangements in this area are to be essentially confederal, and that co-operation in the area of defence should be strengthened by closer relations with the West European Union. The third pillar is Justice and Home Affairs (JHA), and Amsterdam agreed that significant parts of the co-operation in this area are to come under the supranational workings of the Union. The Treaty of Amsterdam also gave the citizens of the Union important new legal and political rights (for example, the right to take the institutions of the Union to the European Court of Justice, and the right to vote and stand as a candidate in local and European elections in a member state of which the person is not a national but in which they reside).

Notwithstanding these important innovations, at present the Union is best characterized as a particularly intense form of intergovernmental co-operation, with some pooling and delegating of sovereignty to facilitate common aims and objectives. This might be described as the supra-national exercise of pooled sovereignty, in so far as QMV applies to genuinely legislative acts, with some aspects of implementation and administration delegated to supranational institutions. The view that the Union is essentially intergovernmental is apparently confirmed by the fact that political systems in Europe – the patterns of party organization, voting and the like – are still nationally organized. There is no European government answerable to a European electorate or European public opinion.

4.3   The political dynamics of European integration

So, the Union does not appear to be an embryo federal state. It looks rather like a special experiment in the collective exercise of sovereignty, organized along both confederal and supranational lines.

But is this conclusion too hasty? Is it derived from too static a picture of the institutions that govern the Union? And what about the dynamic processes of the Union's development? After all, many people think of the European Union as an embryo federation. The language of an 'ever closer union of the peoples of Europe' suggests that something more than mere intergovernmentalism is going on. (For all its formal similarities with other intergovernmental arrangements, there isn't really anything else like the Union in the modern world.) It seems clear enough that the decision making of the supranational institutions of the Union, and those aspects of the decision making of the Council of Ministers that operate according to QMV, amount to genuinely legislative activity. The Council is empowered to make regulations (which have direct effect in member states) on the basis of QMV. Moreover, since the Treaty of Maastricht the citizens of the member states are now also citizens of the Union. Maastricht also marked the decisive step towards a common currency for most of the members (something common in earlier processes of federation). As we have seen, the Treaty of Amsterdam reinforced these developments, as well as making important changes to the second and third pillars of the Union.

Even if it is agreed that the Union does not constitute an independent legal order with its own independent legal powers (see Section 5), that it is not presently a federation, might it not still have a *political* dynamic that tends towards ever greater supranationalism, with federation as the logical end point? The argument here comes in many different forms but at its core are two sets of considerations. The first is that member states have accepted the supranational aspects of the Union, and especially the growing role of the European Court of Justice (ECJ), as a way of making credible commitments to one another, primarily to achieve the economic integration inherent in the 'four freedoms'. If the working of the Union has to rely on traditional intergovernmental agreements followed by national incorporation for all of its activities, this would presuppose a very high degree of trust in one another's willingness to implement what had been agreed, and a similarly demanding degree of confidence in the integrity and efficiency of one another's legal systems. Since this trust and confidence are lacking, states have found it better to go along with an expanded role for the supranational elements in general, and for the ECJ in particular. The second consideration is that it is only by means of QMV that the Council has been able to 'sustain a central role in Union decision making, in spite of a widening membership and a growing agenda' (Beetham and Lord, 1998, p.74). Strict intergovernmentalism, with its need for unanimity, could not cope with the complex demands of European decision making. In both cases, the political necessities of operating in the Union progressively expand its supranational components. To me this argument seems undeniable.

But, in my view, to see this in terms of states losing power to the Union would be misleading. One must not assume that the relations between the member states and the Union are 'zero sum': that is, one must not assume that if the Union gains power, then the member states have lost some. It is possible that by acting collectively, and sharing decision making in supranational institutions, the member states are creating powers that are greater than 'that held in aggregate by each state acting alone, in which each state then shares' (Weatherill, 1995, p.3). In contrast to its sovereignty, the power of a state does not concern its rights of final jurisdiction but rather its practical ability to pursue a given course of action and to achieve its objectives. States acting collectively can presumably achieve more than they can when they act alone. Individual states, therefore, have to assess whether what they gain by acting collectively under QMV in the Council and by committing to one another through the role of the ECJ is more or less than what they lose by curtailing their unilateral freedom of political decision making. If one assumes that states can make this assessment – that they are sufficiently unified and rational for the various trade-offs to be knowable, measurable and comparable – then one must conclude that the use of supranational devices such as QMV and the ECJ does not involve surrendering national power to other bodies, but is a means of creating power at a higher level, power the states then share. Only if one believes that states lack the necessary unity and rationality to make such assessments might one reasonably conclude that they are surrendering power.

Summary

- The European Union represents a highly distinctive form of international organization with confederal, supranational and federal features. This makes debates about its character very complex.

- The European Union has developed a political dynamic that has widened and deepened the pattern of integration among the member states.

5   Beyond the sovereign state?

In the view of many, the Treaties of Maastricht and Amsterdam have confirmed a process that has been present in embryo since the founding Treaties, namely the transfer to the supranational authorities of the Union of some of the key responsibilities historically associated with modern statehood: control over the currency, decisions on public spending and the national debt, aspects of the administration of justice, and the co-ordination and implementation of foreign policy. Did the member states surrender some of their national sovereignty when they established these supranational aspects of the Union? If they did, were they beginning a process that would eventually transfer sovereignty from the national to the European level, thereby creating a federal European state? And if they did not, what is the status of the supranational components of the Union? To address these questions we must, first, define a little more clearly what we mean by the sovereignty of the state and, second, investigate the status of supranational organizations under international law.

5.1   National sovereignty defined

Sovereignty, in the sense that I use it here, is essentially a legal concept, relating to the right to make, apply and enforce laws. The member states of the European Union all have liberal-democratic constitutions under the rule of law (it is a condition of membership). This means that the actions of their governments and their citizens are bound by law. In this context, to say that a state is sovereign is to say that it has the right, within its own territory, to determine the extent of its own jurisdiction. If a state can determine the extent of its own jurisdiction, and is not subject to the jurisdiction of another inside or outside its territory, then it is sovereign. Sovereignty, in short, is the ability to have the final say on legal matters within the territory of the state. In a liberal-democratic state, sovereignty resides in the people as politically organized under the constitution. The constitution (which may be written or unwritten) will determine where the various powers of sovereignty – legislative, executive and judicial – reside and how they are to be exercised. The ultimate justification of liberal-democratic sovereignty comes from the individual and collective rights of a self-governing people.

5.2   National sovereignty and international law

What happens, legally speaking, when a sovereign state signs a treaty with other states? This question takes us into the realm of international law, that is, the law that pertains to relations between sovereign states. Within international law, it is generally accepted that 'the effect of an international treaty in the domestic legal system of a State that is a party to it is a matter for the constitutional law of the State in question' (Hartley, 1999, p.24). Some states have constitutions that assert that the provisions of an international treaty signed by the state are to count as part of the domestic law of the state. These states are called 'monist' states (an example is the Netherlands): the constitution provides that international treaties are directly effective, or 'self-executing', in the domestic legal system. So once the Netherlands has concluded an international treaty the Dutch courts will enforce its provisions as if they were part of the domestic law. Other countries (the UK, for example) are known as 'dualist' states: in these states, national legislation must be passed to give domestic effect to any treaty signed by the state. In the absence of such legislation the courts will not enforce the provisions of an international treaty.

Whether a country is monist or dualist is a matter for its own constitution, not a matter for international law. Moreover, it is a widely accepted principle that countries may have national legislation that conflicts with the provisions of an international treaty to which they are a signatory. (Of course, this means that international law is a less than perfect system. But that is just a feature of international law, a result of the fact that it is law made between sovereign states.) On this understanding, states retain their sovereignty, indeed they exercise or use it, when they sign treaties.

Let us consider a concrete example. In 1949 ten West European states (the UK, France, the Benelux countries, Italy, Norway, Sweden, Denmark and Ireland) signed the Treaty of Westminster. This established the Council of Europe (not to be confused with the European Council of the European Union, which was established in 1974) and the European Commission for Human Rights and its Court (again not to be confused with the Commission and Court of the European Union). The signatories agreed to uphold the decisions of the Court. For a monist country such as the Netherlands this was quite straightforward. The provisions of the European Convention on Human Rights and Fundamental Freedoms will have direct effect in national law and will be enforced as such by the Dutch courts. In dualist Britain, by contrast, the provisions were not self-executing. By signing the Treaty of Westminster the British government did, however, give its citizens the right to appeal to the European Court of Human Rights, and on many occasions it has ruled in their favour. On these occasions UK law was only made consistent with the rulings of the Court through Parliament enacting new legislation. The resulting political embarrassment led to political pressure to incorporate the Convention directly into UK law.

The incorporation was done by the new Labour government in 1998. But the form in which it was accomplished is very revealing. Under the UK Human Rights Act (1998, came into force in 2000):

> The [UK] Courts are charged with the task of so interpreting the domestic laws of the United Kingdom that they avoid, so far as possible, conflicts with Convention rights (as British Courts interpret these in light of the jurisprudence of the European Court of Human Rights). In the case of any Act of the UK Parliament that the Courts find impossible to interpret as compatible with Convention rights, they are to issue a 'declaration of incompatibility'. It will then be for Government and parliament to decide how, if at all, to amend domestic law to eliminate the incompatibility, and a simplified legislative process is available to this end.
>
> (MacCormick, 1999, p.107)

Thus no loss of sovereignty, no erosion of final legislative and judicial authority, has taken place. This example illustrates the general point that signing international treaties does not involve surrendering national sovereignty. It merely involves agreeing to do something.

5.3   The European Union and international law

It is important to remember that the European Union was founded by Treaties concluded by sovereign states, and that all of its subsequent expansion and development has taken the form of new Treaties. We have also seen that these Treaties created supranational institutions – notably the Council, operating under QMV, and the European Court of Justice – capable of producing directly effective European legislation and judicial judgements. What, then, is the status of the founding Treaties and the subsequent body of European law? Roughly speaking, there are two contrasting views.

On the one hand, it can be argued that the relevant Treaties have the same status under international law as any others (for example, the Treaty of Westminster) and that the member states retain their full sovereign rights. In this view, the status of European law is doubly derivative: it is based on the authority of the institutions created by the founding Treaties and they, in turn, derive their authority from the sovereignty of the states that signed them (and have subsequently agreed to them).

On the other hand, it has been argued that European law represents a new kind of law, separate from both national law and the general body of international law, under which the member states do not retain their full sovereign rights. Perhaps most importantly, some have argued that there has been a constitutionalization of the Treaties that established the Union, brought about by the European Court of Justice exercising its right to interpret their meaning. In short, the ECJ claims that:

> *By contrast with ordinary international treaties, the EEC Treaty has created its own legal system* which, on the entry into force of the Treaty, became an integral part of the legal system of the Member States and which their own courts are bound to apply. By creating a Community of unlimited duration, having its own institutions, its own personality, its own legal capacity of representation on the international plane and, more particularly, real powers stemming from a limitation of sovereignty or a transfer of powers from the States to the Community, the Member States have limited their sovereign rights, albeit within limited fields, and have thus created a body of law that binds both their nationals and themselves.

> (The European Court, *Costa v. ENEL*, 1964; quoted in Hartley, 1999, pp.123, 136)

The ECJ has long maintained that European laws have *direct effect* and *supremacy* in the national legal systems of the member states. These are the defining features of law in a federal system. The ECJ takes the view that Treaty provisions and directives are directly effective, as well as regulations, and that in cases of conflict European law has supremacy over national law. That is to say, the ECJ argues that the Union's legal system is distinct not only from the national legal systems of the member states, which like international law it clearly is, but also from the more general body of international law between states. If this were so, it would mean that the member states have subordinated their national legislative and judicial competence to the jurisdiction of the ECJ, albeit only in some areas. They would no longer be fully sovereign in those areas where the ECJ claimed competence; they would have created elements of a federal order.

This interpretation is at odds with that expressed in the national legal systems of several member states. Remember that according to international law the status of a treaty in the domestic legal system of a signatory is a matter for the constitution of the signatory. The Treaties also assert that *regulations* are to be directly effective within the Community but that directives are to require national implementation. Consider the case of the UK. The UK is a dualist country, that is, treaty provisions have to be incorporated into domestic law for the UK courts to recognize them. Yet the Treaty itself says that regulations made by the Union are to be directly effective. How can this be so? Hartley explains the apparent paradox as follows.

> The innovation introduced by the Community Treaties is ... that, while self-executing provisions of ordinary international treaties have direct effect in the courts of contracting States only if their constitutions so provide, EC regulations have such effect irrespective of the constitutional law of the country concerned (i.e. whether monist or dualist). In the case of a dualist country such as the United Kingdom, the difference is that a provision in an ordinary international treaty will be applied by British courts only if British legislation so provides; directly effective Community law, on the other hand, will be applied even if there is no British legislation specially so providing.
>
> (Hartley, 1999, p.135)

This is certainly a departure from the previously understood relation between national law and international law for a dualist country. However, and this is the crucial point, 'Community law as a whole applies in the United Kingdom only because a British statute, the European Communities Act 1972, so provides' (Hartley, 1999, p.135). That is to say, there is a *UK* law stating that European law is to be treated by the UK courts as if it were part of domestic law on an ongoing basis. The UK Parliament at Westminster retains the full legislative authority to repeal that Act, or any part of it. If it ever were to do so, the UK courts have made it clear that they would rule accordingly. The same, or a similar, position applies in the other countries of the Union. That is to say, European law can be directly effective or self-executing only because, and for as long as, national legislatures or constitutions say so. National courts in member states recognize this law as binding because their national legislatures or constitutions have told them to do so. Specific legislative and judicial competences have been pooled and delegated to the institutions of the Union but no member state has thereby compromised its sovereign rights to final legislative and judicial competence in its own territory.

Moreover, according to this view, if the ECJ tried to give itself, or any other institution of the Union, 'powers that are not conferred by the Treaties, the resultant judgements and legal acts would be inapplicable' in 'most, if not all, of the ... Member States' (Hartley, 1999, p.160). Furthermore, the ECJ has no power to prevent member states amending the Treaties as they see fit, including abolishing the Court or even the Union as a whole. Finally, although the Treaties do not provide for it, it is clear under international law and the law of member states that a member state is free to leave the Union if it wishes. It follows, therefore, that the Union has no legal authority to create power for itself at the expense of the member states, either individually or collectively. Only the member states acting *unanimously* can do this (treaty revision requires unanimity). Worse still from the point of view of the ECJ, member states retain the right to legislate contrary to European law in the eyes of their own national courts. (This is expressly provided for in the UK Human Rights Act (1998) in relation to the rulings of the European Court of Human Rights.)

In this view, Union institutions do not have ultimate authority or even an authority that is independent from that of member states, at least not according to the legal systems of the member states. In this sense, the member states of the Union remain sovereign because neither the Union as a whole nor any of its institutions, such as the ECJ, have the jurisdiction to determine the extent of their own jurisdiction. This principle was explicitly reaffirmed by the highest constitutional courts of Germany and Denmark during the ratification of the Treaty of Maastricht, and similar views have been expressed by the highest courts in Italy, France, the UK and other states. A new legal system, such as the body of European law, can become independent only if it can find a means of enforcing its judgements independently of the authorities that created it. The legal system based on the ECJ does not have these means: it has no territory, no coercive forces, no source of popular authorization and no revenues to speak of that it can call its own – these all belong to the member states. It operates through the agency of the national legal systems of the member states and they continue to recognize the ultimate authority of their national legislatures or constitutions. And under what circumstances might national courts transfer their primary allegiance to the ECJ?

Summary

- Sovereign states are characterized by an exclusive and final right to jurisdiction within their territories. When sovereign states sign treaties and make international agreements with one another they retain this sovereignty under international law.

- The European Union is distinctive in so far as its member states have agreed to recognize the jurisdiction of a supranational authority in some areas.

- There is a debate about status of the sovereignty of the member states of the Union, between those who see European law as a kind of international law in which states remain sovereign and those who argue that the European legal order is distinct and that states have (in some areas) subordinated their sovereignty to the supranational authority of the Union.

6   Conclusion

Can member states go on pooling and delegating specific legislative competences to supranational institutions and still remain sovereign? At some point doesn't the growth of supranationalism tip over into proto-federalism and then to outright federation? Won't the legal and constitutional position catch up with the realities of political power? If the realities of political decision making are increasingly supranational, and not just intergovernmental, can law and sovereignty remain national? In my view this is a line of thought that deserves to be taken seriously, and one that is reinforced by the Treaty of Maastricht, specifically its provisions on Economic and Monetary Union (EMU) and the role of the European Central Bank. It is also reinforced by the Treaty of Amsterdam (1997), which provided for an expansion of supranational decision making in the new pillars of Common Foreign and Security Policy and Justice and Home Affairs.

The fear that a state might lose its sovereignty by stealth, somehow unnoticed, is groundless. A transfer of final legislative and judicial competence could happen only by an explicit mechanism that commanded widespread popular assent. It would, almost certainly, presuppose the writing of a constitution for the European Union, another Treaty between the member states explicitly authorizing the transfer, and the endorsement of both by whatever constitutional means apply in the member states and, perhaps, by the new 'people' of the European Union. None of this could happen without the citizens of the member states knowing about it! No, the danger is somewhat different. States have agreed to pool and delegate sovereignty in the Council, and the decisions taken by governments in Europe are very hard to keep track of in national parliaments and assemblies, as indeed are the rulings of the ECJ. States certainly know what they have been doing, but citizens and national political representatives are often poorly informed, not only about what has been done but also about the implications. The real problem is not one of sovereignty but one of democracy, or rather a problem produced by the growing tension between these two principles.

We have seen that the ultimate justification for the sovereignty of liberal-democratic states under the rule of law lies in the rights of a self-governing people. National courts recognize national legislation as binding because that legislation represents the will of the people as articulated through the political process defined by the constitution. But if the member states are increasingly making laws collectively, and through the supranational aegis of the Union, what happens to the democratic component of the justification for sovereignty and the rule of law? What is the role of the people (now citizens) of Europe in the process of European law making, and is it sufficient for the purposes of democratic accountability? If there is to be European legislation and a European judicial system, should there not also be a Constitution for the people (not peoples) of Europe?

William Wallace has suggested that the process of sharing and delegating sovereignty in the particular circumstances of integration in Western Europe has created a paradox. 'The central paradox of the European political system in the 1990s is that governance is becoming increasingly a multi-level, intricately institutionalized activity, while representation, loyalty and identity remain stubbornly rooted in the traditional institutions of the nation state' (Wallace, 1999, p.521).

As the gap widens between the practical location of political decision making at the European level and the theory of national peoples forming self-governing communities, will there be a need to establish the legitimacy of the European institutions in their own right in the eyes of the people of Europe? In short, will the Union become sovereign? Or will the national character of politics continue to place limits on – perhaps in some respects reverse – the extent of supranational and proto-federal organization? Or will the present balance or stand-off between the claims of national and Union jurisdictions continue to evolve harmoniously?

These questions are far from abstract, if only because the context within which the Union and its member states must now operate is so different from that which shaped most of its development. The Cold War has ended, and with it the geopolitical and political division of Europe. This not only puts the expansion of the Union to the East on the agenda but has also changed the nature of the USA's military and strategic interest in Europe, putting more pressure on European states to organize their own foreign and defence policies in a co-operative manner. Germany is now unified again and dominates the continent's economy. Taken together, the end of the Cold War, the reunification of Germany and the partial disengagement of the USA pose a new set of challenges to the member states, one quite unlike anything they have had to face since the Union was founded after the Second World War.

The modern nation state, ruled by law, justified by the authority of the people (or the nation) and governed as a liberal democracy, started life in Europe. But so did national rivalries, modern warfare and mass killing. Perhaps Europe will be the birthplace of the first post-sovereign, post-national political order that is still ruled by law and respects the rights of self-governing individuals. After centuries of war, perhaps the Union will, as some of its founders hoped, find a way of binding people together in new and peaceful ways, rather than balancing the power of separate nation states against each another. The modern nation state began in Europe, perhaps its successor(s) will appear there first as well.

References

Beetham, D. and Lord, C. (1998) *Legitimacy and the European Union*, London, Longman.

Hartley, T. (1999) *Constitutional Problems of the European Union*, Oxford, Hart Publishing.

Lundestad, G. (1998) *'Empire' by Integration: The United States and European Integration, 1945–1977*, Oxford, Oxford University Press.

MacCormick, N. (1999) *Questioning Sovereignty: Law, State and Nation in the European Commonwealth*, Oxford, Oxford University Press.

Marx, K. (1976) *Das Kapital: Volume 1*, Harmondsworth, Penguin Books.

Milward, A. (1992) *The European Rescue of the Nation State*, London, Routledge.

Moravcsik, A. (1998) *The Choice for Europe: Social Purpose and State Power from Messina to Maastricht*, London, UCL Press.

Skinner, Q. (1978) *The Foundations of Modern Political Thought: Volume 1 – The Renaissance*, Cambridge, Cambridge University Press.

Wallace, W. (1999) 'The sharing of sovereignty: the European paradox', *Political Studies*, vol.47, pp.503–21.

Weatherill, S. (1995) *Law and Integration in the European Union*, Oxford, Clarendon Press.

Weber, M. (1978) *Economy and Society Volume 1*, Berkeley, CA, University of California Press.

Further reading

Hartley, T. (1999) *Constitutional Problems of the European Union*, Oxford, Hart Publishing.

Milward, A. (1992) *The European Rescue of the Nation State*, London, Routledge.

Spruyt, H. (1994) *The Sovereign State and its Competitors*, Ithaca, NY, Cornell University Press.

Chapter 4
Law, order and administration in the European Union

Daniel Wincott

1 Introduction

What is the European Union? Is it an international organization, a state, or something in between? Might it be a new form of 'post-sovereign' polity, the cutting edge of political development in an era of globalization? Are we witnessing the emergence of the EU as a regulatory state, displacing the traditional national Keynesian welfare states of Western Europe? These are big questions about the future of the state in Europe. In this chapter I will argue that they can only be answered in a satisfactory way by looking at the character and role of the EU's legal system. Thus, this chapter will explore some of the complexities of the EU's legal order. In it we will be mainly concerned with the 'Community' pillar, on the one hand, and with policies concerned with Justice and Home Affairs (the third pillar), on the other. The nature of the 'Community' legal system and the impact of the European Court of Justice (ECJ) on the process of European integration will receive particular scrutiny. An understanding of Community law is also essential if we are to make sense of the day-to-day operation of the EU. For example, without a legal system it would be impossible for the European internal market to exist, since the smooth operation of economic activities across borders presupposes a common framework of commercial law to regulate the single market.

Studying the character and scope of Community law also helps us to distinguish between the 'supranational' aspects of the EU and the 'intergovernmental' ones over which the member states retain greater control. Roughly speaking, the ECJ has jurisdiction over supranational policies, but not over intergovernmental ones. This distinction is closely connected to the three 'pillars' of the EU that have existed since the Maastricht Treaty. The first pillar is the European Communities, often called simply the 'Community pillar', and covers the areas of co-operation and integration associated with the founding policies of the EU on economic integration. The second pillar covers co-operation on the Common Foreign and Security Policy (CFSP). Finally, the third pillar refers to co-operation in the field of Justice and Home Affairs (JHA). Together, these three pillars make up the European Union. The Union has a more strongly 'supranational' character in the Community pillar, where Community law applies and where the ECJ has an important role to play. By contrast, the more intergovernmental second and third pillars, in which member states retain greater control over policy, fall beyond the scope of the ECJ.

Some people might find it ironic that the European Court of Justice does not have full authority – and 'Community' law does not apply fully – in relation to the 'law and order' issues of 'internal' security, and in relation to policies on justice and home affairs. We will see that this apparent disjuncture tells us a great deal about the character of European law and about the state-like character (or rather lack of it) of the EU. We will see that any adequate characterization of the EU must take an overall view, covering both the 'Community' and the intergovernmental pillars.

What follows is therefore divided into two broad sections. In Section 2 we consider the role of Community law and the part played by the ECJ in the process of European integration. Here we will focus on the Community pillar, rather than on the EU as a whole, since the 'European' legal system (Community law) only operates fully in the first pillar. In this context, we will examine the role of the ECJ in the development of Community law, and the contributions of both that law and the Court to wider processes of integration (and disintegration) in Europe. We will consider the importance of Community law for the development of European regulatory policies, which some see as creating a European regulatory state (Majone, 1996). I will argue that the Community legal system is the most novel feature of the EU. Focusing on its legal system casts considerable light on the character of the EU as a whole, which is neither a typical international organization nor a conventional state.

In Section 3 we will evaluate the development of policies related to Justice and Home Affairs (JHA). While JHA is distinct from the Community, it is also important to stress the connections between these two 'pillars'. In the first place, part of the impetus behind the development of co-operation over JHA came from attempts to deal with some consequences of economic liberalization carried out under first-pillar policies. In this context, JHA seems set to develop rapidly over the next few years, but how will it do so? Will it continue to be a separate intergovernmental pillar, largely outside the framework of Community law and the ambit of the ECJ, or will it migrate in whole or part into the more supranational Community pillar? And if it does move in the latter direction, what will the development of JHA imply for the character of the Community pillar and the need of the EU for state-like capacities of its own? Will the EU need to develop a coercive capacity of the kind that states have traditionally maintained to sanction their national legal systems? Does JHA signal that the EU will develop its own coercive capacity, or will it instead simply give national police (and other agencies concerned with internal security) even more autonomy from democratic control or accountability at the national level? Will the migration of JHA policy into the Community pillar undermine the latter's supranational elements? These are the issues we will explore in Section 3.

In the Conclusion (Section 4) we will bring our discussions of the development of Community law and JHA policy together in order to see what general light these considerations cast on the overall character of the EU.

2 Law, the European Court of Justice and the European Community

To appreciate the issues and debates surrounding the development of Community law it is important to have some understanding of the Community legal system, so this section begins with a brief outline of the operation of the courts and processing of cases in what is a very complex legal system.

2.1 The Community legal system: a brief review

There are two main 'Community' Courts: the Court of Justice (ECJ), with which we are mainly concerned; and the Court of First Instance (CFI). The CFI was created to reduce the burden on the ECJ (especially in connection to cases concerning the EU's own staff) and all its decisions are subject to appeal to the higher court. The ECJ itself has been designed to protect the judges against pressure from their state of origin and is made up of one judge from each of the member states. Judges are appointed for a fixed term, although an appointment can be renewed. Once appointed a judge can be removed only by a collective decision of the other judges. No dissenting opinions are published – decisions of the ECJ appear as the collective will of the whole Court.

In addition to the judges, the ECJ is served by 'Advocates-General'. An Advocate-General provides a summary – or 'opinion' – of the relevant case law, and this is published some time before the Court actually comes to a decision. Although these summaries are not binding, they usually provide a good indication of the judgement that the judges eventually make. Given that the actual decisions are often overly concise and obscure, these opinions are an extremely valuable guide to the 'thinking' of the Court.

The European Court of Justice

Cases can come before the ECJ in a number of ways. In the first broad category of cases, either a Community institution or a member state takes another institution or state to Court. It is, however, worth noting that in general the member states do not take one another to Court. The initial Treaty of Rome seems to have envisaged that the main mechanism for enforcing Community law would involve the Commission taking member states to Court. In all these cases, the Court's decision is directly binding on the state or institution in question. Since the Maastricht Treaty the Court has been able to impose fines where its decisions have not been respected. That said, the ECJ does not have an 'ultimate' sanction against a state determined to flout its authority. Moreover, as a single court, judging cases brought by a small group of 'central' institutions, it is difficult to see how its rulings could have had much effective reach into the detail – the nooks and crannies – of economic and social life across Europe.

In fact, the operation of the ECJ has been more subtle and complex than this suggests. An initially little noticed provision of the Treaty of Rome has hugely increased the reach of the Court. Article 234 (formerly 177) allowed national courts in the member states to make a 'preliminary reference' to the ECJ if an issue before them involved the interpretation or applicability of Community law. This procedure allowed individuals, lawyers and national courts to use Community law much more effectively as part of the overall body of law regulating economic and social life. And today more than half the cases considered by the ECJ are preliminary references. Strictly speaking, the ECJ does not make a binding decision in these cases; it simply helps the national court with the interpretation of Community law. In practice, however, the ECJ's 'decisions' have carried considerable authority. The procedure has thus blurred the boundary between national and Community law and the two have become fundamentally entwined with one another. (This also raises the interesting possibility that the meaning of 'Community' law varies significantly in different national contexts.)

Perhaps ironically, the most dramatic period of legal transformation was one during which processes of political and economic integration were widely perceived as failing. Most of the core principles structuring the Community legal order were set in place during the 1960s and 1970s, when Europe was widely perceived as suffering from political and economic 'Euro-sclerosis'. During this period the existence of the national veto over new European legislation appeared to be deeply entrenched. The veto seemed to prevent the Community from reacting rapidly to changing circumstances. While political scientists stressed the limits to integration rooted in the self-protection of national states, legal analysts, by contrast, foresaw an ever-deepening Community of law.

At least until the mid-1980s political and legal analyses of European integration seemed relatively isolated from one another, with each providing a quite different prognosis for further integration. Yet political and legal changes were interacting in profound, if barely noticed ways. Paradoxically, the national veto also made it difficult for member states to control the ECJ during this period. The Court was allowed considerable autonomy, since changes in legislation to 'correct' a judicial interpretation unpopular with one or more member states required the support of all. De Gaulle's intervention to entrench the national veto is usually regarded as a high point in the defence of national sovereignty. But it may have created the very conditions within which a comparatively powerful supranational legal structure could be forged. This is the real irony of the national legislative veto.

2.2   Politics and law in the development of the Community legal order

At the time of the Treaty of Rome, Community law was usually regarded as a form of international law, albeit of a distinctive type. By the late 1960s, however, the ECJ itself described Community law as a new legal order, neither international nor national in character. And by the time of the Maastricht and Amsterdam Treaties in the 1990s, the role of the Court featured prominently in political debate. Although relatively neglected and unnoticed outside specialist legal circles in the 1960s and 1970s, the part played by the ECJ in the construction and operation of the EU became a matter of controversy during the 1980s and 1990s. Until the 1990s, specialists in Community law were almost without exception strongly supportive of the integration process. Academic Community lawyers taught the rising generation of legal practitioners and provided an interpretative commentary on the developing body of Community law.

Their strong normative support for (legal) integration did not simply reflect the successes of 'legal integration' in Europe – it also contributed to and helped to legitimate those successes. Political analysts finally woke up to the role of the ECJ during the 1990s.

Both the conventional account given by legal scholars of the Community and most political science analyses seem mesmerized by the astonishing 'successes' of the Court in the construction of a 'constitutional' legal order from conventional international treaties. Depending on the individual author's normative stance on integration, this emphasis on the Court as an actor usually results in it being portrayed as either a 'hero' or a 'villain'. The construction of a new legal order is indeed remarkable. It marks out the Community pillar of the EU as a distinctive kind of political and legal order not found in other international organizations. Nevertheless, the contribution of the Court of Justice should not be overplayed. Properly contextualized, the Court should be seen as one actor within a complex set of structures. The story of the development of the 'supremacy' of Community law over conflicting provisions of national law therefore needs to be told with some care.

2.3 Supremacy and direct effect: judicial activism and the ECJ

Textbook discussions of European Community law focus on 'direct effect' and supremacy as its twin foundational principles. The ECJ developed both 'direct effect' and supremacy in its case law. Neither notion was present in the Treaty of Rome. Directly effective Community rules can be relied upon as such by individuals in their own national legal systems, whether or not they have been (adequately) implemented by the member state in question. This characteristic of Community law distinguishes it from conventional international law which usually requires national incorporation before it can be used directly (see also Chapter 3). Moreover, if national legislation is not necessary for European rules to be effective within a member state, then the possibility of a conflict between European and national law exists. The principle of supremacy means that in the event of such a conflict, European law prevails over national law. As a matter of logic, then, there is a close relationship between direct effect and supremacy.

Direct effect and supremacy are also closely interrelated historically. The Court initially stated both notions in the mid-1960s (direct effect in the 1963 *Van Gend* case, and supremacy in the 1964 *Costa* v. *ENEL* case – see Box 4.1). The Commission's Legal Service, several member states and even the Advocate-General in *Van Gend* all argued that direct effect and supremacy could not be separated (Stein, 1981; Wincott, 1995). Nevertheless, the Court proceeded incrementally, initially testing the issue of direct effect. Prior to *Van Gend* a number of national protests against the notion of direct effect were registered; after the decision was taken these protests seemed to evaporate. Only then did the Court take the decision on supremacy.

Box 4.1 Direct effect and supremacy cases

For the most part, when we discuss the decisions taken by the Court of Justice here we are concerned with their 'constitutional' implications, not the substantive subject matter with which they deal. Often the substantive issue at stake may seem obscure while some cases deal with national positions that seem almost inane.

Van Gend case (1963)

The groundbreaking *Van Gend* case falls into the first category. It was concerned with the introduction of an increased tax on ureaformaldehyde in the Netherlands. The charge was thought to have an equivalent effect to an increase in customs duty, and could be illegal under the terms of the EEC's Customs Union. The 'constitutional' question here concerned whether the Community Treaty provision introducing the Customs Union could have a direct effect within Dutch national law. Continuing interest in the case today results from the development of the idea of direct effect, not a concern with Customs Union law on trading in ureaformaldehyde.

Costa case (1964)

The *Costa* case, in which the Court introduced the principle of the supremacy of Community law, was substantively concerned with a rather small electricity bill owed by Mr Costa to the Italian monopoly electricity supplier.

Direct effect and preliminary references

It is important to emphasize that direct effect is not a simple and uniform principle. Direct effect has taken a number of distinct forms in different contexts. The initial *Van Gend* decision meant that some provisions of the Treaty of Rome were directly effective. Only later, in the 1970s, did the Court argue that some directives (probably the most important form of secondary legislation in the EC) could be directly effective, rather than requiring incorporation into national law. This move proved highly controversial in several member states since it transformed the legal character of the European Community, in principle dramatically restricting the degree of freedom available to the member states in the implementation of Community secondary law.

Nevertheless, the direct effectiveness of treaty provisions is more comprehensive than that of directives. Treaty provisions have 'horizontal' and 'vertical' direct effects (they regulate relationships between individuals as well as those between the individuals and the state), while directives have only vertical direct effects (they can only regulate relationships between individuals and the state). In the 1980s and 1990s the Court made a number of additional moves intended to improve the effectiveness of directives. Underlying these moves was an attempt to increase the pressure on member states to implement directives as promptly and fully as possible. Thus 'direct effect' might best be regarded as a technique for ensuring that European law is adequately implemented and enforced in all member states.

Clearly, the ECJ was the central actor in all these developments, which were based on judgements it made. However, the transformation of European law was not simply a matter of these judgements. It also involved changes in the ways in which cases came before the Court and in the relationships between the ECJ and the courts of the member states. As we noted earlier (Section 2.1), initially it was thought that the main litigants in the EC legal system would be the various Community institutions and the member states. The Commission was expected to have the key role in ensuring that Community law was adequately implemented within the member states. The Commission was expected to use the ECJ to bring recalcitrant states into line and individuals were to have very limited direct access to the Court.

You will also recall (from Section 2.1) that to some extent these procedures have been overshadowed by a seemingly innocuous provision of the treaty – Article 234 – which allows national courts to make 'preliminary references' to the ECJ. In other words, national courts can ask the ECJ to interpret the Community law dimension of a case. This procedure has become a means by which individuals have indirect access to the Court and Community law. Taken together with 'direct effect', preliminary references have made individuals potentially influential within the European legal system as 'enforcers' of Community law.

Article 10 (formerly 5) of the Treaty of Rome requires that member states co-operate fully in processes of integration, and in combination with the preliminary reference procedure this has helped to draw national courts into the European legal system. In a sense, national courts are now also 'European' courts and consequently the 'European legal system' has expanded in scope dramatically. As was suggested above, one could not have expected a single, centrally located Court to successfully 'control' developments across the whole territory of the EU. Rather, the scope of Community law may have been increased by the 'Europeanization' of national courts and national law. By the same token, however, the uniformity of European law may also be called into question if various national courts take different views of the same provision of Community law. Of course, from another point of view, the potential for cross-fertilization between Community law and the national legal systems might be a source for a dynamic and creative process of co-evolution.

The supremacy issue

The question of the supremacy of Community law appeared to be resolved during the 1980s (when the German Constitutional Court accepted that Community law contained adequate provisions protecting fundamental human rights – see Wincott, 1994, for a discussion). At least as far as the day-to-day operation of the Community is concerned, this resolution renders Community law supreme over conflicting provisions of national law. More recently, the issue of supremacy has been partially re-opened, at least as a matter of principle: even if Community law is supreme in its own domain (and national laws supreme in their domains), the crucial question of 'competence over competences' remains unanswered. That is to say, who is to decide when and if national courts and the ECJ disagree about the extent of their respective jurisdictions?

Again, the German Constitutional Court was the ECJ's main interlocutor (or challenger) on this matter. During the process of ratifying the Maastricht Treaty a case, *Herr Brunner*, was brought before the German Constitutional Court asking about the constitutional acceptability of the Treaty in Germany (Herdegen, 1994). Although this Court did not find that the Treaty posed practical constitutional difficulties for the Federal Republic, it did raise important normative issues. First, the German Constitutional Court explicitly rejected the *general* supremacy of Community law, strongly emphasizing the idea that the EU was a union of the *peoples* (rather than a people) of Europe. Thus, the German Constitutional Court claimed that the member states remained the 'masters of the Treaty', being particularly concerned to establish that the ECJ alone did not have the competence to decide the extent of its own jurisdiction. The relationship between the ECJ and the German Constitutional Court was not depicted in hierarchical terms, instead it was presented as a relationship of equals, each with its own area of competence.

Legal pluralism: beyond the sovereign state?

It is important to make a distinction between the part played by the ECJ in the construction of the European legal order and its contribution to the development of a range of particular policy areas. Clearly the Court did play a central role in the former process (although even here it was by no means unconstrained). But it has also made important contributions to particular policy areas, sometimes seemingly setting the path for sub-sequent policy evolution and often unsettling established policies. However, its role in relation to the development of individual policies has usually been discontinuous and it has not generally been in a position to fashion the fine detail of a policy. For the most part it would be misleading to cast the Court in autonomous terms, as either hero or villain, as far as detailed policy development is concerned.

More generally as well, a simple narrative about the emergence and supremacy of Community law under the auspices of an activist Court conceals important characteristics of the EU. Whether the role of the ECJ is applauded or derided, an emphasis on its autonomous construction of a Community legal order gives too much emphasis to the Court as an agent and risks ignoring the structural context(s) within which it operates. Moreover, the narrative distracts attention from the question of 'legal pluralism' and the possibility that the EU may be an important cause or manifestation of the move to a world 'beyond the sovereign state'. The idea of legal pluralism questions the identification of the state and the law. There were legal systems in operation before the rise of modern states – merchant law and Church law, for example – and even within modern states not all law has been fully subsumed under state-based law. Some analysts argue that the Community legal system may have developed in the context of, and further encouraged the development of, a politics beyond sovereignty.

An increasingly influential strand in legal theory is concerned with moving beyond the assumption that state law is the paradigmatic form for law. From this perspective, questions of supremacy become less central to the understanding of Community law, and instead the emphasis is placed on the interaction between Community and national law, the two tending to be seen as co-evolving. This is particularly true for those using 'civic' conceptions of the political community (that is, definitions of the political community not in terms of an ethnically or nationally defined 'people' but in terms of the shared civil and political rights individuals may have). Some downplay the possibility of a conflict emerging that determines the 'supreme' source of legal authority. Civic, rather than ethnic, conceptions of political community are usually associated with theories of law 'beyond the sovereign state' (MacCormick, 1993, 1997, 1999). The apparently ethnic or national conception of a plurality of European political communities adopted by the German Constitutional Court and its lack of interest in – if not outright hostility to – civic alternatives may be difficult to accommodate within this approach (MacCormick, 1995).

2.4   The strategic context of the ECJ

How, then, did Community law and the role of the ECJ develop? In addressing this question, I seek to steer a path between two alternative approaches. The first one sees the ECJ as using its power to interpret the provisions of the founding Treaties in order to create a legal system that is now completely binding on states and individuals within the EU. Whether this development is evaluated in positive or negative terms normatively, the ECJ is seen as an autonomous actor in shaping Community law (Burley and Mattli, 1993; Neil, 1995). Textbook narratives of the development of the doctrines of direct effect and supremacy lend themselves to this interpretation and we have already begun to notice some of the problems inherent in it. A second approach argues that Community law is under the control of the member states acting intergovernmentally, that the ECJ is merely the legal instrument by which they accomplish some of their collectively agreed policies. Here, the ECJ is little more than an agent carrying out the wishes of its principals, the member states (Moravcsik, 1995). Against both of these positions, I seek to show that the development of Community law has been a more delicate and contingent construction. It is nevertheless a defining feature of the EU as a political system. My approach places considerable emphasis on the range of different *contexts* within which the ECJ has operated.

We can begin our consideration of the contextual features of the ECJ and of Community law by asking the question: How can a Court operate without having its rulings ultimately backed up by the coercive power of the state? This issue is particularly pertinent for those analysts who characterize the EU as a form of regulatory state (Majone, 1996), where the idea seems to be – if only implicitly – that a new non-coercive form of post-sovereign state is emerging in Europe. In this context, questions about the relationship between the law, the state and coercion that many had thought settled are once again on the agenda.

If its role is to be understood properly, the Court needs to be placed in its strategic context and not simply celebrated or deplored as an actor. This context is enormously complex and its precise specification is difficult as it is made up of a variety of overlapping elements. These include (see Wincott, 2000, for a more detailed discussion):

- the executives of the member states
- the other EU institutions such as the Commission and the European Parliament
- the various systems of national law in the member states
- the emergence of Community law itself
- actors within the civil societies of the member states, particularly litigants
- the transformation of the EU itself through the enlargement of its membership.

The relationship between unity and diversity, tendencies towards convergence and divergence and issues of identity all play themselves out in the relations between distinct national legal systems, patterns of similarity and difference in European legal tradition(s) and 'Community' law.

The role of member state executives

The role played by member state executives has been the focus of much attention from political scientists, particularly those seeking to show that the Court has been an agent subordinate to the intergovernmental control of the member states acting in the European Council and the Council of Ministers. Liberal intergovernmentalist analysts such as Moravcsik (1993, 1995) have argued that even an apparently autonomous, supranational agency like the ECJ can be effectively constrained by its political masters; the Court may function as the agent of these 'principals' by anticipating their preferences and treating them as parameters in its decision making.

However, this is by no means a foregone conclusion. The point of principal–agent relationships is that principals (here, member states) cannot fully control what their agents (in this case, the ECJ) do – there would be little point in establishing an agency that was wholly controlled by its principals. In the context of Community law and the role of the ECJ, it is not clear that the member states, or even their national executives, can be treated as unitary agents with a consistent set of preferences. Different departments within a national executive may take quite different approaches to the development of Community law. The functional structure of the Council of Ministers may mean that departmental ministers gain a fair degree of autonomy for their European activity vis-à-vis their national colleagues. Moreover, as noted above, reversing an unwanted development of Community law by the ECJ requires unanimity among the member states, thereby reversing the usual effect of the national veto.

The role of EU institutions

Another aspect of the Court's strategic context is provided by the other institutions of the EU, the Commission and the Parliament. In general, but not in all specific instances, these institutions have helped the Court to develop the Community legal system. For example, the initial idea that Community law could be directly effective and supreme over national law came from the Commission's Legal Service, not the Court itself. Sometimes 'contextual' changes in the other institutions allow the Court to develop its own position. For example, the ECJ had to convince the German Constitutional Court that Community law contained adequate protection for fundamental rights before the German Court was prepared to accept the supremacy principle. During the 1970s the German Court had claimed that these rights could not be protected unless the Community became more democratic. Arguably, the introduction of direct elections for the European Parliament in 1979 was a precondition for the subsequent acceptance of the supremacy principle by the German Constitutional Court.

Placing the developing role of the ECJ in the context of these other actors throws some doubt on any simple emphasis on the independent agency of the Court. Key contributions have been made to the development of the Community legal order by other institutions. Moreover, the evolution of the legal order cannot be isolated from other facets of the general development of the EU. If political and analytical perspectives that grant too much autonomy to the Court cannot be sustained, neither can those that treat it as an agent largely controlled by its member state principals. We have already seen that the 'principals' in this relationship may be rather more complex than the framework usually allows. The 'agents' to which principals have delegated power are also rather complex. If we accept the rather stark contrast that is sometimes drawn between intergovernmental and supranational institutions within the Community, then the Court, the Commission and the Parliament might be expected often to act in support of one another with the effect of increasing their autonomy from the member states.

The role of European law

'European law' is the usual phrase used to describe the Community legal order. While in one sense this shorthand phrase is not strictly accurate, it may actually reveal some very important features of the system. Even in principle, 'Community law' is not itself a complete, self-sufficient system. Instead, as we have seen, it relies on national ('European') courts and legal systems in a number of ways and these latter are part of the European legal system, one result being that Community law rests on national systems of enforcement and coercion. We have seen, then, that there is considerable potential for diversity within Community law as it is applied across the territory of the EU. The interaction of Community law with various national legal systems may even produce sufficient diversity to challenge the assertion that a single Community legal system exists.

On the other hand, we tend to assume that the internal legal system of each sovereign state is autonomous, that each system operates according to its own internal logic. However, a consideration of the historical emergence and development of the various national legal systems in Europe points in a rather different direction. Such an analysis shows complex patterns of interaction among the various national systems as they developed over time, whether as the result of invasion and imposition, or through processes of learning and emulation across borders. In the light of this history, it is at least possible that the Court has found important sources of inspiration and support in the *common* elements of European law (for a general discussion of these issues see Zimmermann, 1996). Moreover, the ECJ acts in a fashion somewhat akin to a common law court, effectively establishing precedents on which it builds later. This 'common law' approach may help the Court to draw support from any deep common tradition that does exist.

Community law

Community law itself is also part of the Court's strategic context, as the previous analogy between common law and Community law suggests. As the Court itself is one of the most important 'authors' of Community law, it may seem strange to treat this law as part of the ECJ's strategic or structural context. Moreover, the Court is not strictly speaking 'bound' by precedent. On a number of occasions it has reversed a position that had previously appeared to be well established. Nevertheless, there is a sense in which the already established body of Community law partially binds the Court *and* makes the further development of new law possible. Community law both constrains the Court and makes its activity possible.

The social context

The Court itself, other actors and the complex system of European law are all set in a wider social, political and economic context, and too often this is overlooked in both political and legal accounts of the development of Community law. Yet without a broader contextualization of the Court's role many key influences on Community legal and policy development would be overlooked. For example, a number of cases that developed key aspects of the Community legal system during the 1970s were concerned with aspects of Community policy on sex equality (see Box 4.2).

Box 4.2   Sex equality and the ECJ

For a variety of historical reasons that had little or no connection with the movement for women's equality, some basis for sex equality existed in the Treaty of Rome. (In any event, 'second wave' feminism is usually dated from the 1960s, well after the negotiation of the Treaty of Rome.) Notwithstanding the strong Treaty base for sex equality, little or no progress was made with the implementation of this policy in the course of the 1960s and it was only when activist lawyers and/or feminist litigants began to use Community rules to pursue their own concerns that cases concerning sex equality began to come before the Court. It is, of course, quite possible that the Court would have developed the Community's legal architecture in cases concerned with other issues had these equality cases not been brought before it. Nevertheless, effectively the Court may have 'borrowed' some of the moral authority of a rising social, political and economic movement and redeployed it for another purpose. In other words, it may have been more difficult for member states to oppose the gradual trans-formation of the Community legal system if they had appeared to be opposing the rights of women at the same time.

However, if the Court was 'radical' in the early sex equality cases, this radicalism was more evident in relation to the established character of Community law than it was in relation to the content of its judgements. Indeed, there is some evidence that the ECJ was so frightened or confused by the agenda of sex equality that it was not able (or did not want) to grasp fully the opportunity it provided for the further development of Community law (see Kilpatrick, 1998). More recently, evidence of disillusion with the Court and Community law among feminists has mounted. After a long period during which some reform-minded feminists attempted to use Community law to ameli-orate the position of women, some are turning away from it. This disillusion may reflect a realization that the Court's main concern has always been with the development of its own legal system, rather than with the socio-economic position of women.

The role of enlargement

Past and future changes to the membership of the EC, the enlargements, also alter the context for the development of Community law and within which the Court operates. For example, it is often argued that the English common law system might interact with the ECJ in a manner quite distinct from the patterns of interaction established between the Court and the original six member states. The latter all have legal systems based on written civil codes, an approach dating from the Napoleonic era. The enlargement that brought the UK into the Community may have altered the legal dynamics of European (dis)integration for this reason, among others. Similarly, the forthcoming enlargements may pose significant challenges to the development of Community law, which have been largely overlooked by political and legal analysts.

The most obvious problem arises from the sheer organizational difficulty that the ECJ will face (together with the Court of First Instance) in dealing with the increase in size of the EU. There is already a substantial backlog of cases waiting to come before the ECJ and it is hard to imagine the Court continuing to consider the full range of cases that it has been able to in the past. If it reduces the range of cases it considers, then presumably new 'European' level courts will need to be created in order to take over some substantive areas that are at present covered by the ECJ. The planned enlargement to include several Central and Eastern European countries and Turkey will also mount a profound challenge to the Community's legal system. Of course, with each new member state the number of potential cross-border interactions escalates dramatically (as each new state could enter a dispute with every existing state). Moreover, economic differences between the existing states and the new applicants may mean that we should expect a comparatively high level of disagreement about whether, for example, trading and competition rules in the single market are being followed fairly.

From the point of view of diversity in Community law, the challenges facing the Court appear still more daunting. First, it is not certain that the national system in each of the applicant states is as robust as might be hoped. As the Community legal order partly depends on the efficacy of national legal systems, this poses a major problem for the Court. Moreover, a serious breakdown in Community law within a number of member states might lead to a retrenchment of its effectiveness elsewhere. Second, even if this 'doomsday' scenario does not develop, the new states inevitably increase the diversity of national legal traditions that need to be accommodated within Community law. Beyond a certain point, the wide variety of legal systems of member states will make impossible the kinds of mutually supportive legal co-evolution that may previously have been a (largely hidden) source of support for Community law.

2.5 Community law and the EU as a regulatory order

There is an important sense in which 'law' and 'politics' are distinct spheres of activity, with their boundaries policed by well-entrenched academic disciplines and powerful professions, particularly in the case of the law. Yet many of the most interesting patterns of structural change and transformation may result from the interaction between these two spheres. Traditional professional and disciplinary boundaries may make these patterns of change difficult to recognize. Interactions between the political and legal spheres may be relatively direct or indirect. On the one hand, some legal decisions have (and perhaps are intended to have) clear and direct impacts on the legislative process. Thus, for example, the Court directly influenced the regulation of mergers through its decision in the *Philip Morris* case that extended its jurisdiction in this area. In doing so, the ECJ helped to unblock a legislative process that had been stymied since the mid-1970s (although clearly other contextual changes had also occurred during this period).

On the other hand, we cannot only consider the direct impact of particular legal decisions on the political process. To do so would be to ignore the general transformation of the EU that resulted from the development of a comparatively effective supranational legal order. An influential strand in the analysis of the EU identifies it as a regulatory order – or perhaps even a regulatory state (see Majone, 1996). This perspective stresses the strict budgetary constraints under which the EU operates, where the limited size of the budget reflects the weakness of the autonomous coercive and extractive capacities of the EU as compared with the member states (see Cram, 1993; also Chapter 8). The comparatively small size of its budget has meant that the EU has had little scope to develop redistributive policies. Additionally, the early development of a costly form of agricultural policy meant that a large proportion of the EU budget came to be committed to this sector, thereby reducing the space for further redistribution.

The small size of its budget was effectively a structural constraint on EU policy innovation. If policy took the form of regulation, rather than redistribution, then it imposed smaller costs on the EU budget and this is what has made the EU into a distinctive 'regulatory order', according to some analysts. At the very least, regulatory policies have bulked comparatively large within the EU's overall policy profile. However, such analyses of the EU's structural biases sometimes pay insufficient attention to the resources required by regulatory policy. While redistribution can provide direct incentives to influence the behaviour of social actors, regulatory policies generally attempt to set a framework to encourage mutually beneficial co-operation. Sanctions are required to police the boundaries of these frameworks for co-operation and to manage collective action problems of various kinds. In other words, the emergence of the EU as a regulatory order is logically predicated upon the development of a distinctively effective form of non-state law. In addition, the emergence of a regulatory order also begs important questions about the account-ability and legitimacy of this new kind of law (see the Conclusion to this chapter and Chapter 7).

Where it is considered at all, the contribution of the law to the development of the European regulatory order is usually reduced to the impact of a few 'landmark' cases. Particular attention is usually paid to the *Cassis de Dijon* case of 1979 (see Box 4.3), which is sometimes credited with introducing the notion of mutual recognition. This notion, the idea that a good or service legally produced and marketed in one member state should be accepted in all, is a key part of the so-called 'new approach to harmonization' that formed the basis of the internal, single market programme. In fact, the most radical elements present in the *Cassis* decision had already been established in the earlier *Dassonville* case (1974). In other words, it was not the *Cassis* case itself, but the manner in which it was taken up by the Commission, the member states and big business in Europe that was crucial to the development of the internal market.

Box 4.3 Mutual recognition case

Cassis de Dijon is a French blackcurrant liqueur that is used with white wine to make kir. How did it come to be associated with an ECJ decision that provided an important impetus for the development of the single market?

Cassis de Dijon case (1979)

German regulations created various categories of alcoholic drinks partly on the basis of the amount of alcohol in each one. They sought to ban the marketing of cassis as a 'spirit' on the grounds that it contained too little alcohol and, surprisingly, that this might cause harm to German drinkers. The 'reasoning' of the German authorities seems to have been that cassis drinkers might gain an unrealistic idea of their ability to consume spirits and consequently cause themselves harm by drinking similar quantities of whisky or vodka. The German authorities may have adopted this bizarre stance in order to try to defend their position on the public health grounds, on which Community rules are relatively flexible. The ECJ treated it as little more than an attempt to protect German producers of alcoholic drinks from French competition.

However, as we have seen, key changes did occur in the Community legal order between 1974 and the early 1980s. By the latter date, the Community law was widely regarded as a robust 'constitutional' legal order and its role in enforcing Community secondary legislation had become much more significant. As a consequence of this increasingly robust character, Community law had become a 'resource' for other actors to use within the integration process. Thus, the development of a 'constitutionalized' legal order was both a logical prerequisite for the emergence of a regulatory order in the EU, and a vital component of the political process that constructed the internal market.

In explaining the relations between the development of the Community legal order and the idea of the EU as a regulatory order we should be careful not to fall into overly functionalist modes of analysis. Functionalist accounts of the emergence of the EU's regulatory order argue, first, that it developed because it maximized or enhanced the efficiency of the European economy, and second, that this increase in efficiency provides a basis for legitimating the emerging regulatory order. Both of these claims can be questioned in the light of the analysis presented above. In the first place, functionalist accounts are in danger of suggesting that because one of the effects of the development of a legally-based regulatory order is greater economic efficiency, then it is efficiency which explains why the legal order developed. But this is to explain something in terms of its effects. Moreover, such an approach downplays the importance of the particular historical sequences and contexts through which outcomes are produced. Functionalist analyses in effect assume that change occurs (a legal order is created) independently of the intentions of the actors concerned, *because* the consequences of the change are necessary for the operation of a particular system (the single market).

In addition, although the regulatory approach argues that markets require economic and social regulation, and that this regulation involves more than the regulation of free markets, there is a presumption that a regulatory order can establish its own legitimacy. From this perspective, legitimacy is established by means of the 'independence' of regulatory agencies and their technical competence in promoting efficiency. It may be appropriate to argue that a particular agency, say, the European Central Bank, should be independent and judged on its technical merits. It is quite another thing to say that an entire political system – the regulatory order of the EU – can be justified in terms of technical efficiency criteria. This is to judge a system merely by its outputs. But what about the 'input' side – who makes decisions and on what basis? What about questions of accountability and democracy? The problem of democracy in the EU cannot be finessed by pointing to the efficiency of European policy outcomes (see Chapter 7 for a full discussion of democracy and accountability in the EU).

Summary

- Many observers described the EU as suffering from 'Euro-sclerosis', characterized by a lack of political integration because of the national veto. Nevertheless, the Community legal order developed dramatically as the ECJ was able to promulgate the doctrines of the direct effect and supremacy of European law in relation to the national laws of the member states. This involved not only an active role by the ECJ itself but also the growing integration of national legal systems and courts with Community law; that is, the Europeanization of national law.

- Without ignoring the active role played by the ECJ in this process, this development needs to be seen in its wider context, in the roles played by member state governments, other EU institutions, national legal systems, Community law itself, private actors in member states, and the process of enlargement.

- This constitutionalization of the European legal system, its increasingly robust character and its overall legitimacy in the eyes of key players has become a resource that actors can use in the overall process of economic and political integration. As such, the framework of European or Community law has played a central role in the development of the regulatory policies of the EU in the Community pillar, since market regulation presupposes a workable legal framework.

3   Europe and the administration of 'law and order'

Currently, the question of whether the EU should develop its role in policing and the military is much debated. If these roles do develop they would probably increase the EU's coercive capacity significantly. However, it is crucial to remember that policing and internal security, military and foreign policy are all located in the non-Community pillars in the Union (for a discussion of the Common Foreign and Security Policy in the second pillar, see Chapter 10). The 'supranational' institutions, such as the Commission and especially the ECJ, do not have a major role in these areas, if they have any role at all. The Treaty of Maastricht placed Justice and Home Affairs (JHA) in the 'third pillar' of the EU, covering policies on asylum and immigration, police and customs co-operation and judicial co-operation. An 'intergovernmental' process applied to these policies; in other words, the member states, acting unanimously, dominate the policy process. The role of the Commission is much more limited in these areas than it is within the Community pillar. More pertinent for our purposes here, JHA policies fell outside the jurisdiction of the Court.

However, the Maastricht Treaty also provided a 'bridge' from this third pillar to the Community pillar. This 'bridge' would allow the member states to move particular policies into the EC itself. And just a few years later the Treaty of Amsterdam did indeed move several JHA policies into the Community pillar. Even so, the legislative and particularly the judicial rules governing these pillars remain distinct. In other words, the full 'Community method' does not apply to JHA. In relation to judicial procedures, only a strictly limited set of senior national courts is able to send 'preliminary references' to the ECJ, for example. In this respect, the member states appear to have learned from the previous experience of preliminary references in the Community pillar. Under EC law lower national courts often referred sensitive issues to the ECJ directly, perhaps as a way of finessing the authority of national courts above them and effectively setting a particular judicial interpretation in stone.

3.1 European integration and the emergence of the 'law and order' agenda

A 'law and order' agenda has emerged 'around' the Community pillar of the EU. Usually dated from the mid-1970s, the development of European co-operation on matters of law and order and eventual emergence of JHA is an interesting case study of the integration process. An analysis of the development of co-operative policy making in this area can help to establish the sorts of opportunities and pressures that lead to integration in Europe. When the Treaty of Rome was signed issues of law and order fell well beyond the imagined scope of the EU. Yet the habits of intensive co-operation (regular meetings of senior members of the various national governments) eventually provided the opportunity for European-level discussion of these issues. Other aspects of European integration and changes in the EU's external context created pressures for co-operation and/or convergence over matters of 'law and order'.

Issues of JHA, of law and order and internal security, lie at the heart of the power and authority of the (nation) state. The history of co-operation over JHA therefore tells us a good deal about the reluctance of the member states (or at least some of them) to relinquish their authority over these matters. As with other processes of integration and disintegration in Europe, the future of JHA remains essentially open – it has not yet been finally determined. Moreover, the factors that do eventually determine it may not lie in its internal policy dynamics. A key issue here lies in the degree of influence and authority granted to supranational institutions in relation to JHA.

Since the Treaty of Maastricht, and particularly as a result of the provisions of the Treaty of Amsterdam, several JHA policies have been moved from their traditional (and intergovernmental) location in the third pillar into the Community pillar. At first glance this movement – known as *communautarization* – would appear to confirm the argument that the process of European integration is long and slow, but is still an inexorable process of accumulation of powers by supranational institutions. And so it may be. Yet the peculiarities of the JHA policies that have been subject to *communautarization* mean that we should also consider another possibility. The injection into the Community pillar of what have traditionally been nationally distinctive and generally less robust 'European' areas of policy and judicial procedures may gradually infect and weaken the established body of Community policy. In other words, while from the point of view of policy on JHA the *communautarization* of particular policies may appear to be a 'strengthening' of their supranational characteristics, they remain considerably less *communautaire* than existing policies. The risks of this sort of 'infection' may be greater if other pressures for the dilution of the 'Community method' also exist.

The 'TREVI' group (see Box 4.4), established in 1975, is usually regarded as the first manifestation of a 'European' presence in relation to law and order. It grew up alongside 'European Political Co-operation' that was largely concerned with the co-ordination of the foreign policies of the member states (see Chapter 10). TREVI was created partly in reaction to a perceived upsurge in international terrorism and extremism during the 1970s, but was also an outgrowth of the habit of continual contact and negotiation among the member states. The TREVI group was concerned with some of the most sensitive matters of internal and cross-border security and was therefore rather secretive. (It does not, of course, compromise national sovereignty if security services come together in secret to discuss matters of common interest, so long as each retains its independence of action.)

In the 1980s some, but not all, of the member states deepened their co-operation in law and order under the umbrella of the Schengen Agreements (see Box 4.4). Schengen was mainly concerned with the removal of borders within the EU and the common policies necessary to maintain internal security as national systems were dismantled. It was an 'intergovernmental' agreement among its signatories. These agreements are usually viewed as a concomitant of the economic free movement of persons, required by the internal market. Thus Schengen might be viewed as a 'spillover' from economic integration into matters of internal security. In particular, the construction of the internal market meant that a series of traditional national barriers to free movement were destroyed, and as a consequence many traditional restraints on criminal activity were also removed. Of course, the fact that a number of members (Denmark, Ireland, the UK) did not initially sign the Schengen Agreements suggests that at least in this case 'spillover' should be viewed as a pressure, not as an inexorable process. More recently, while Ireland and the UK have remained largely outside the Schengen process, Iceland and Norway – not members of the EU – have associate membership, due to their close integration in a Passport Union with the Nordic countries (Finland and Sweden) that are members of the EU.

Since the Maastricht Treaty, JHA has covered such matters as asylum and immigration policy, police and customs collaboration, and judicial co-operation on civil and criminal law. The rationale for much of the co-operation was still essentially a result of its connection to economic integration. Although these policies existed outside the Community pillar, their development initially remained closely connected to the economic integration within it, rather than simply following a logic of their own. After Maastricht, the creation of procedures and organizations to develop policy in JHA began and a new internal dynamic may have been created.

Box 4.4 JHA development – TREVI and the Schengen agreements

The earliest manifestation of co-operation in Justice and Home Affairs was the Terrorisme, Radicalisme, Extrémisme, Violence Internationale (TREVI) group set up in 1975–1976. It remained the main forum for intergovernmental co-operation on issues of internal security in the EC until after the Maastricht Treaty. After Maastricht, TREVI was largely rolled into the new policy framework of JHA.

From the start TREVI was concerned with combating drug trafficking, organized crime and terrorism, as well as moves to co-ordinate national immigration and asylum policies. Until the mid-1980s the agenda for TREVI was largely ad hoc, driven by events or crises. After the Commission's White Paper on the completion of the internal market, the TREVI agenda became more focused and coherent. The move towards a deeper internal market also provoked differences among the member states on the scale of policies appropriate and necessary to achieve the free movement of people. Free movement is, of course, a core objective of the internal market to which all member states are committed in principle.

However, several member states wished to dismantle internal border controls within Europe completely, while others wanted to keep their traditional checks in place. As a result the Benelux countries, together with Germany and France, signed an agreement in Schengen on 14 June 1985. In this 'Schengen Agreement' the signatories decided that they would remove border controls but develop closer co-operation in matters of internal security and stricter and more co-ordinated external border controls. Progress among the original 'Schengen' countries was not as rapid as had been hoped initially. After an implementing agreement was signed in June 1990, first Italy (November 1990), then Spain and Portugal (June 1991) and then Greece (November 1992) joined the Schengen group. None the less, the date for the total abolition of border controls was postponed several times from the initial date of 1 January 1990 and was only fully achieved in 1994.

Many aspects of the inter-state co-operation initially developed through TREVI or Schengen have now been incorporated into the Union through JHA policy. For example, under the Amsterdam Treaty the Schengen Secretariat (of some 60 people) has been incorporated into the Council Secretariat (the small, but increasingly important body that services the Council as a whole). In formal terms JHA policy is made by the Council of Ministers in the particular form of the Council of Justice and Home Affairs Ministers. In common with other 'Councils' this body is supported by the Committee of Permanent Representatives (Coreper) made up of bureaucrats organized in national groups and owing loyalty to the state governments.

JHA policy making does retain some distinct elements. Most of the work to support the JHA Council is done by a special Committee. Initially this Committee was generally referred to as the K.4 Committee after the provision of the Maastricht Treaty that created it. Subsequently, as the Treaty was reformed and renumbered it began to be known as the K.8 Committee. Under the consolidated Treaty the provision regulating the Committee is now Article 36.

In organizational terms, the JHA Council, composed of national ministers for Justice and Home Affairs, was the key actor in the third pillar and is the final decision-making body. It is supported by the same system of national bureaucrats – the Committee of Permanent Representatives (or Coreper) – that services the Council of Ministers in the Community pillar. Both these bodies are essentially made up of representatives of the member states. The Commission does have a role in this third pillar, but it is a secondary one, much weaker than that which it plays in the Community pillar itself. The right of policy initiative formally rests solely with the Commission in the Community pillar, but it is shared with each and every member state in the third pillar of JHA. The K.4 Committee (now K.8 or '36' – see Box 4.4), named after the Article of the Treaty which governs its activity, sits below Coreper in the JHA hierarchy and includes Commission representatives as well as high-ranking officials from the member states. This Committee co-ordinates the activities of three steering groups, each of which oversees a number of technical working groups that develop policies. There is a steering group for Asylum and Immigration policy, one for Police and Customs Co-operation and a final group for Judicial Co-operation.

If, under the Maastricht Treaty, the role of the Commission in JHA was limited, the Parliament and the Court of Justice were in even weaker positions. Formally, the Council was required to consult with the Parliament on all JHA matters, but in practice the Parliament found itself playing a very limited role indeed, often lacking even basic information. The Court was wholly excluded from JHA policy. Article L (TEU) kept Justice and Home Affairs entirely outside its jurisdiction. However, as we noted above, Article K.9 of the Treaty allowed particular provisions of JHA to be moved from the third pillar into the Community itself. This provision, together with the established practices of co-operation under the Schengen agreements, largely set the tone for the development of JHA policy after Maastricht.

During this initial phase of JHA policy development, a broad distinction was made between those issues that might be transferred into the Community pillar and those that would not be transferred, at least in the short term. Policy concerned with asylum, immigration and external borders fell into the first category, while police, customs and judicial co-operation policy fell into the second one. We have seen that one of the earliest forms of 'European' co-operation in this broad area concerned policing (under TREVI), yet this area remains jealously guarded by the member states. This clearly illustrates that the degree of supranational authority is no simple function of the length of time that co-operation has existed within a particular policy field. Equally, however, the ambitious post-Maastricht agenda for the creation of the European Police Office (EUROPOL) suggests that the member states can envisage intensive and institutionalized co-operation without subjecting it to control by the supranational institutions.

Frustration with JHA provision emerged very rapidly after the Maastricht Treaty came into force, since the JHA policy process was considered inefficient, as well as opaque and undemocratic. The inefficiency of this process was partly a consequence of the traditionally 'international' character of its policy instruments, with 'International Conventions' apparently the major instrument available. Not only was the negotiation of these conventions extremely lengthy, but the fact that they needed to be ratified in each member state further extended the period of time it took for JHA policy to come into force. Nor was the policy process transparent. Perhaps due to the sensitivity of the subject matter with which it dealt, it was largely conducted in secret. In any case, because the policy was an intergovernmental one it was not subject to the usual checks and balances at the supranational level (imperfect though they may be). However, the secrecy surrounding much of the policy process also meant that national mechanisms of accountability may have been attenuated as well, potentially weakening democracy at the national level without any compensatory strengthening of it at the supranational one.

3.2   External dynamics of JHA integration

Although there was considerable consensus that JHA required reform, there was little agreement over the character of the necessary reforms. Nevertheless, given that the Maastricht Treaty itself mandated that a further Intergovernmental Conference (IGC) be called to clarify and tidy its provisions, it became clear that the status quo would not stand unaltered. When seeking an explanation of the reforms undertaken by the Amsterdam Treaty, negotiated through the 1996–1997 IGC, it would be misleading to focus exclusively on discontent with the internal characteristics of the JHA policy process. Other changes also influenced the process, of which the most significant were those set in train by the collapse of the Soviet Union and the 'Eastern bloc'. Many have argued that the Cold War context decisively shaped the foundation and purposes of the EU (see Chapters 2 and 3). It is certainly the case that the crumbling of these state socialist regimes and the end of the Cold War changed the EU's external environment fundamentally (see Chapters 9 and 10).

Some changes to the external context are becoming largely internalized within the EU itself; others remain more 'outside', while continuing to have an impact upon it. Even in this latter case, however, the perception of the external context and its construction into a motivation for a responsive internal policy change are important processes. For example, there is a widespread perception that organized crime has been on the increase, particularly since the collapse of the Soviet bloc. Organized criminal activity originating in Russia spills out beyond its borders and is perceived to have a significant impact within the EU, whether directly, for example in the case of drugs, or indirectly, as when money is laundered through the banking systems of European countries. This perceived increase in transnational or international criminal activity has been used to motivate a somewhat frenzied bout of co-operative or integrative activity.

Together with a number of other factors, the end of the Cold War has also contributed to an apparent increase in the levels of asylum seeking. These influences on the development of JHA policy have been more 'internalized' within the EU than is the case with the threat of organized crime. The 'weaker' boundaries of the new regimes in Central and Eastern Europe may have allowed an increasing number of members of minority groups to leave to seek asylum. Moreover, the EU's involvement in the Kosovo war may have increased the sense of obligation felt by the governments of member states to take in larger numbers of refugees than they might otherwise have done. The pressure for a common response to the movement of these refugees across national borders may also have been stronger in these circumstances. Of course, the perception that the EU faces a 'threat' from a large number of asylum seekers, some of whom it may be felt are actually economic migrants, has other roots as well. Indeed, it sometimes appears that this supposed 'threat' owes a good deal to perceived difficulties in relation to internal minorities. Whatever the reality, the removal or weakening of internal borders may have added to this pressure. There has been much discussion of the process of asylum seekers engaging in 'jurisdiction shopping' (moving from one jurisdiction to another looking for a country that will accept them). If such 'shopping' does occur, the lowering of the barriers to movement within the EU can only have facilitated it.

Finally, the process of EU enlargement itself is partly a product of the end of the Cold War. This is clearly true in the case of countries in Central Europe, but is also true for others as well. The successful applications from Sweden and Austria, both neutral countries, were partly made in the light of changes in Russia. Moreover, the massive increase in the total number of member states will so change the character of the Union that it makes the inclusion of other countries somewhat easier. A case in point is the change in the EU's position on Turkey, long an applicant for membership. These Turkish approaches were kept on hold for more than twenty years, but in a much wider Union, with substantial variation in economic, political, social and cultural traditions, the inclusion of Turkey seems much less problematic.

However, there is considerable disquiet among the existing member states about the adequacy of the national judicial and policing systems of some applicant states. This disquiet has created another set of pressures for the development of common EU policies. To begin with, if existing common policies are well developed, then it may be easier to help the new member states to 'improve' their domestic systems. Common policies also make it much easier for the existing states to create conditions that have to be met before the applicant states can achieve full membership. And finally, if policy is set before enlargement, it is likely too that the existing member states will construct it in their own interests. Policy constructed after enlargement will also bear the influence of the new members.

3.3   The future for JHA

The Treaty of Amsterdam introduced a number of important changes to the structure of JHA. Essentially, a number of policies were moved from the JHA pillar into the Community pillar, albeit with slightly unusual and limited features compared to most Community policies. In relation to the role of the Court of Justice, the most significant unusual feature is that the right to make preliminary references is restricted to national courts of last instance. Moreover, for the first five years the member states share the formal right of initiative with the Commission in these policy areas and decisions are to be made by unanimous agreement of the member states. Asylum, immigration and external border policy as well as judicial co-operation on matters of civil law have been moved into the Community. On the other hand, several states have secured special status in relation to these provisions. In general, they do not apply to the UK and Ireland, although either of these states can 'opt-in' to any policy developed in these areas. Denmark has a general 'opt-out' from these policies. Thus, as we suggested above, the structure of the Community pillar itself has become still more complex and differentiated as a consequence of these provisions.

Police co-operation and judicial co-operation on matters of criminal law remain within the third pillar, but even here the ECJ has some role under the provisions of the Amsterdam Treaty. The Court can review the legality of third pillar decisions and it can also settle disputes between member states concerned with the application of third-pillar policies. This last power may prove interesting. However, a similar role of the Court within the Community itself has lain largely dormant (probably because the politics of member states taking one another to Court would be highly charged). Such disputes are usually resolved through the mediation of the Commission and ultimately the Commission itself has had the power to take a recalcitrant member state to Court for policy matters falling under the Community pillar. This possibility does not seem to exist in the third pillar.

A great deal, then, is currently happening in the area of JHA. As a consequence, it is too soon for the structure of the EU's policies in the area of JHA to be fully assessed. In addition, in the context of further moves towards co-operation or integration on these subjects, there are serious questions relating to the protection of civil and democratic liberties that need to be addressed. In this context, future historians may come to see the Action Plan announced in December 1998 – developing the idea of an 'Area of Freedom, Security and Justice' – as a key moment in the development of this policy sphere. This idea may give EU policies in the areas of JHA a distinct and autonomous foundation, rather than relying on the traditional justification that they are necessary for the complete success of the European market. Nevertheless, in the current conjuncture at least two possibilities seem open for the future of policy development in JHA. On the one hand, these policies may continue to be incorporated within the Community method, either gradually or perhaps in a flurry of activity reminiscent of internal market policy in the period leading up to the Single European Act (SEA). On the other hand, some policies may not develop in a *communautaire* manner, and so remain intergovernmental in form as a consequence of the sensitivities of the member states. Indeed, it is even possible, as we have noted, that the introduction of a higher degree of member state control *within* the Community pillar may result in pressure growing for a more general dilution of the supranational character of this pillar.

Summary

- JHA policy developed in the third, intergovernmental pillar of the EU, outside the more supranational framework in the Community pillar. This has limited the role of the ECJ, and other EU institutions such as the Commission and the Parliament, in policy making in this area. However, the Maastricht Treaty provided a 'bridge' by which policies could cross from the third to the first pillar.

- The kinds of economic integration carried out under the Community pillar, particularly the removal of national border controls, resulted in the emergence of a European 'law and order' agenda around the Community pillar.

- External pressures on the EU – asylum seeking and immigration, organized criminal activity based in the former socialist states and the diversity of the national legal systems in the applicant states for enlargement – have also created pressures to develop common policies in the field of JHA.

- The result has been complex. On the one hand, there has been pressure to move some aspects of JHA policy from the third (intergovernmental) pillar into the Community pillar (the Amsterdam Treaty for example). On the other, the migration of JHA issues into the Community pillar has made decision making on these issues in this latter pillar more complicated and somewhat less supranational than had been the norm for other areas of policy such as the single market.

- Thus, although JHA co-operation began life as an adjunct to economic integration and was organized outside the Community pillar, since Maastricht new procedures and organizations to handle policy in this area have been developed and, while the logic of economic integration and external events exerts important pressures, JHA policy may have developed a logic of its own. If this is so, it remains to be seen what its effect will have on the Community pillar itself.

4 Conclusion

At least two stories can be told about the future of the EU. One is a story of a deepening Union; here, policies initially established by the member states, using forms over which they seem to have control, gradually slip from their grasp. There is certainly a good deal in current patterns of JHA policy development that seems to support such a view. In this story, the Community legal order is sometimes seen as a partly hidden but nevertheless fundamental factor of cohesion within the Union. The second story is one of fragmentation and, perhaps, disintegration. In it, the 'glue' provided by Community law may not be strong enough to hold the EU together. This chapter has tried to offer a subtler narrative.

Having provided some background information on the development of Community law in the first pillar and on JHA policy in the third pillar of the EU, I want to return to the issue of 'what sort of polity is the EU?' Can it be understood within the traditional framework, one that distinguishes national domestic politics and law from international relations? This chapter has argued that, for those who believe that the EU cannot be understood within this traditional framework, the European Community legal system is – or should be – at the heart of their arguments.

Initially, European Community law was usually regarded as a form of international law, albeit of a distinctive type. By the late 1960s, however, Community law had developed into a more binding form of law, as the ECJ itself declared. This new legal order was neither international nor national in character. In a similar way, many analysts who may pay little attention to Community law argue that the EU is a distinctive (or *sui generis*) type of polity. A special term – 'supranationalism' – was coined to describe the distinctive features of the earliest institutions of European integration. The Treaty of Paris (1951), which created the European Coal and Steel Community, called the High Authority (a precursor of the European Commission) 'supranational'. Although the word has not been used since as a *legal* term (and indeed was cut out of the ECSC Treaty in 1965), it remains widely used as a description of some EU institutions and, sometimes, of the overall character of the EU. Nevertheless, the precise meaning of 'supranationalism' remains unclear. More generally, it is easier to claim that the EU is distinctive than it is to define it precisely. This difficulty is encapsulated in an influential characterization of the EU, that it is 'stronger than a mere international organization, weaker than a state' (Keohane and Hoffman, 1990, p.279).

To be sure, not everyone agrees that the EU is distinctive. 'Inter-governmentalists' argue that it is a particularly wide-ranging and success-ful international regime. In other words, the member states remain the primary motive force behind developments in the EU, which in turn remains under their control. Others argue that the EU is developing (or has developed) into a new European state of some sort. Eurosceptics fear the development of a European 'super-state'. A few Euro-enthusiasts look forward to the creation of a Eurostate, often arguing that statehood is the only route to a European polity that is adequately democratic.

Debates about the 'state-like' qualities of the EU are often rather confused: first, because the term *federalism* is used in different ways; and second, because the notion of the *state* is rarely defined. Particularly in the UK, 'federalism' is used to refer to the EU's state-like qualities, but in principle it might be associated with the defence of the powers of the member states. Technically, a federation is a polity; that is, a political system, divided between two territorially defined levels of government, where political authority for a particular policy area might be assigned either to the centre or to the constituent parts, or could be exercised by the two concurrently. According to this definition, the EU has long had federal characteristics. From this perspective its distinguishing characteristic might be the lack of clarity about the policies controlled by each level of government. Indeed, some of those sceptical about the gradual accretion of powers at the 'European' level argue that the creation of a clear (federal) constitution might be one way of halting a perceived 'drift to Brussels'.

According to traditional definitions, states are a particular kind of polity, one in which the state's ability to use violence legitimately (both internally and internationally) is its core characteristic. In some defi-nitions the state has a monopoly of legitimate violence. The EU institutions, as such, have little or no ability to use violence. While they may develop this capacity in the future, for the moment the EU must rely on the co-operation of the member states if it needs to use force. Of course, there may be much more to 'the state' than its coercive power; nevertheless, the absence of this capacity at the European level is important. (It certainly means that the EU is not a federal *state*.)

Some analysts argue that the EU has developed into a 'regulatory state': namely, that it has state-like qualities in the areas of economic and social regulation. These analysts focus on the comparatively rapid growth of regulatory policies since the 1970s (in contrast to the limited develop-ment of redistributive policies). The idea that the EU is an emerging regulatory state assumes that regulation requires only weak coercive powers, as compared with the redistributive welfare policies of traditional states. The latter require strong powers of compulsion to extract large-scale taxes, or economic policies based on state direction and expropria-tion, as in the nationalization of industries for example. Furthermore, 'regulatory' analyses suggest that EU regulation is at the cutting edge of the political evolution of Europe from Keynesian welfare statism towards a market-oriented, regulatory state.

The 4th Chamber of the European Court of Justice: judges at work on the *Volkswagen AG/Wolfsburg Germany v. EU Commission* case (July 2000).

Most accounts of the European 'regulatory state' suggest that it developed because it was the most efficient possibility. However, this chapter has argued that regulatory policies cannot be sustained in the absence of an effective legal system: if a European regulatory state has emerged, it has done so only on the basis of the development of the Community legal system. This point takes us to the heart of the conundrum. Ultimately, state legal systems are backed by the use of force – courts sentence people to fines and, if necessary, to gaol – and it is this coercive capacity that distinguishes national from international law. Yet we have seen that the European institutions do not (yet) have a powerful capacity to use force. The Community legal system may evolve into something quite novel: a new, non-coercive but binding form of law. Or it may, ultimately, rely on the coercive capacities of the national legal systems with which it is entwined; in which case, EU regulation depends on the coercive systems of the member states so fundamentally that any European regulatory state must be, and remain, an amalgam of European and national elements.

References

Burley, A.M. and Mattli, W. (1993) 'Europe before the Court: a political theory of legal integration', *International Organization*, vol.47, no.1.

Cram, L. (1993) 'Calling the tune without paying the piper? Social policy regulation: the role of the Commission in European Union social policy', *Policy and Politics*, vol.21.

Herdegen, M. (1994) 'Maastricht and the German constitutional court: constitutional restraint for an "ever closer Union"', *Common Market Law Review*, vol.31.

Keohane, R. and Hoffmann, S. (1990) 'Conclusion: community politics and institutional change' in Wallace, W. (ed.) *The Dynamics of European Integration*, London, RIIA/Pinter.

Kilpatrick, C. (1998) 'Community or communities of courts in European Integration? Sex equality dialogues between the UK courts and the ECJ', *European Law Journal*, vol.4.

MacCormick, N. (1993) 'Beyond the sovereign state', *Modern Law Review*, vol.56.

MacCormick, N. (1995) 'The Maastricht-Urteil: sovereignty now', *European Law Journal*, vol.1.

MacCormick, N. (1997) 'Democracy, subsidiarity and citizenship in the context of the European Union', *Law and Philosophy*, vol.16.

MacCormick, N. (1999) *Questioning Sovereignty: Law, State and Nation in the European Commonwealth*, Oxford, Oxford University Press.

Majone, G. (1996) *Regulating Europe*, London, Routledge.

Moravcsik, A. (1993) 'Preferences and power in the European community: a liberal intergovernmentalist approach', *Journal of Common Market Studies*, vol.31, no.4.

Moravcsik, A. (1995) 'Liberal intergovernmentalism and integration: a rejoinder', *Journal of Common Market Studies*, vol.33, no.4.

Neil P. (1995) *The European Court of Justice*, London, European Policy Forum.

Stein, E. (1981) 'Lawyers, judges and the making of a transnational constitution', *American Journal of International Law*, vol.75, no.1.

Wincott, D. (1994) 'Human rights, democracy and the role of the Court of Justice in European integration', *Democratization*, vol.1, no.4.

Wincott, D. (1995) 'The role of law or the rule of the Court of Justice? Judicial politics in the European Community', *Journal of European Public Policy*, vol.2, no.4.

Wincott, D. (2000) 'A community of law? "European" law and judicial politics: the Court of Justice and beyond', *Government and Opposition*, vol.35, no.1.

Zimmermann, R. (1996) 'Savigny's legacy: legal history, comparative law and the emergence of a European legal science', *Law Quarterly Review*, vol.112, no.4.

Further reading

Dehousse, R. (1998) *The European Court of Justice*, London, Macmillan.

MacCormick, N. (1999) *Questioning Sovereignty: Law, State and Nation in the European Commonwealth*, Oxford, Oxford University Press.

Weiler, J. (1999) *The Constitution of Europe*, Cambridge, Cambridge University Press (especially Chapter 2).

Chapter 5
The re-forging of European political traditions

David Scott Bell

1 Introduction

If the process of European integration is to draw upon widespread political support and participation by the citizens of the European Union, how can this come about? One possible answer is through a common European political culture that transcends the different national cultures of the member states. The concept of 'political culture' is notoriously difficult to define and measure but in general it refers to the meanings and values that people attach to politics.

We begin this chapter with a brief look at the basic concept of political culture and ask how it applies to contemporary Europe, whether there is such a thing as a 'European political culture' and how the idea of a European political culture relates to the political cultures of the nation states of Europe. Section 2 then considers some elements of European political culture, what aspects are 'European' and what features are 'national'. We also examine how the modernization of Europe under the impact of nation state building and the industrial revolution gave rise to the modern party traditions that can be found in contemporary Europe.

How are political cultures manifested within political systems? There are several dimensions that might be relevant in this context. What meanings and values do people attach to the political system itself and its associated framework of civil and political rights? How do they view questions of political participation and representation? How do they evaluate the outputs of the political process? While all of these are important questions, we will focus our discussion on one particular dimension, namely, how the political demands of the people are expressed and channelled within the political system. That is, how are political parties and party systems organized? Parties and party systems are not the only means by which political demands are expressed and channelled, but they are the principal mechanisms in the member states of the EU.

Thus, the main question for this chapter (which we examine in section 3) is: What are the European party traditions and how do they interact with the process of European integration? Section 3 looks at the main party traditions that developed in modern Europe during the nineteenth and twentieth centuries and which continue to operate today. This will involve a necessarily selective survey of the main families: secular conservatism, Christian democracy, liberalism, the extreme right, social-ism and social democracy, communism, as well as more recent groupings such as the Greens and regional parties.

This leads us to consider (in section 4) the role of the parties and what they do in the European Parliament within a supranational framework. In other words, how do the party traditions manifest themselves at a European level, and do they support or hinder the integration process?

We conclude by asking what impact the process of integration has had on the stability or otherwise of the party traditions in Europe. All these questions are still open and, because integration is a process, not an end result, the contemporary position has to be impermanent and liable to change in both a positive and negative direction.

1.1   What is 'political culture'?

In its broadest sense, 'political culture' is the orientation people have to politics and political institutions, the traditions and style in which politics is conducted. In other words, it is what people believe about politics and how they value political action and it is, of course, a constituent and interacting part of the general culture of a society. Thus people's values, expectations, memories, history, norms and their views of political actors and events constitute the 'political culture'. This is a very broad definition and to go further in refining it is to introduce complications and enter a debate which (while necessary in other contexts) is not directly relevant here. Most observers have contended that political culture does play a part in influencing action, although some (notably Marxists) have regarded political culture as something imposed by the ruling interests. But all these observers argue that what people expect of the political system, what they demand of it as well as what they value, will condition how people behave in political situations.

In other words, what matters in politics is not simply the events but the way they are interpreted, and that is a matter of their political culture, of the prior dispositions of the politicians and people involved. These dispositions might not be rational in any sense of that term. Each political culture will have its own dynamics and politicians themselves will react in a way consonant with the culture into which they are socialized. (This challenges one of the rational choice assumptions some analysts make, by starting from the viewpoint that political actors (people and politicians) are social: their goals as well as their mind sets are not merely individual ones.)

There are, of course, variables outside political culture itself. It is very tempting to attribute the resilience or collapse of societies to something in the political culture, and this is frequently done by both analysts and journalists. However, outside events can hit a society and change it completely without any internal movement. In such cases, it is the political culture that changes in response to other factors. For example, the Eastern bloc became communist very largely as a result of the victorious march of the Red Army at the end of the Second World War. Sovietization then went ahead behind the Red Army's 'Iron Curtain' despite the wishes, and contrary to the pre-existing 'culture', of the occupied societies. There was an accompanying attempt to impose a new 'communist political culture', but it would be wrong to attribute the transformation of these societies into communist regimes to the working of some deep-seated political culture. Indeed, with the fall of communism in Eastern Europe, many are now claiming to rediscover their 'European political culture'.

These questions of causality are, however, intricate and can only be raised here; they cannot be fully addressed within the remit of this short review. There remains an academic and popular assumption that what people think, how they view the world and how they value it, is of paramount importance. Beyond that there is no consensus. Extremes exist on both sides: those who deny any causal role to political culture and those who attribute to ideas the sole shaping momentum in human affairs. As yet, there is no rigorous discussion of the links between the two, the nature of their interaction, which would enable a judgement regarding the weight of political culture relative to other factors.

This chapter will explore one particular aspect of political culture, the *party political traditions*, which are the dynamic in domestic party systems and which operate at European level as well. These are identifiable and comparable cross-national currents of opinion (or developed ideologies) manifest in such forums as the European Parliament (EP). Some of the most important of these (notably the Christian democrats) are not found in the United Kingdom, but the others will be familiar to most observers of the British political scene. There is also a *national* dimension to the party traditions and this orients the representatives of different party families to the EU in various – not always compatible – ways. All the same, the EU can be expected to rely on party political activity to mobilize voters and work in the EP for similar objectives to those of the national movements (see Chapter 7 for a discussion of the work of the EP).

2 European political culture and the party traditions

We have considered what political culture is, but what is 'European political culture'? Where and what is Europe? Europe is not even a geographical expression. Europe has a centre but no periphery. Turkey, for example, was the original 'sick man of Europe' and at various times Russia and the UK have been excluded from Europe or included in it by writers. On one reading, 'Europe' stretches from Vancouver to Vladivostok; on another, it is the core of the six continental states, Italy, Germany, France, Belgium, the Netherlands and Luxembourg that signed the Treaties of Paris (1951) and Rome (1957). One way around this problem of definition is to use an operational one: to include as 'European' those countries which participate actively in the European states system. This would mean that societies move in and out of Europe, and a state (like nineteenth-century Russia) can turn outward away from the continent (Zetterholm, 1994).

2.1 The emergence of a European political culture

When it comes to specifying the *content* of European culture, things are more complex. One view is that European states have interacted with a particular intensity since the Roman Empire and have exchanged ideas to the extent that it makes some sense to talk of 'European' traditions in art, literature and music, but not of national traditions. The rise of the nation state and the recasting of history in national frameworks has obscured somewhat these European interconnections. On close examination, writers regarded as 'national' can often be found to have plumbed the depths of European thought and been influenced by the cross-currents. One example is the European religious interchanges. Here, for instance, the Catholic universalism did not disappear and led people in widely separated countries to look to Rome, but also included are Protestant circuits passing through Switzerland, Scandinavia, Germany and the Netherlands and linking up the national Churches and theologies of the north of Europe.

Likewise, political developments were rarely hermetically sealed in national compartments. One example is the development of human rights, which grew up in Europe from contributions by many societies before reaching their dramatic expression in the French Revolution. This cross-fertilization could be repeated in other political movements, and none of the great contemporary political traditions (socialism, Christian democracy, liberalism, environmentalism and so on) can be said to be the exclusive development of one society. Europe has always been more like a marble cake than a layer cake, with European societies emerging from a 'mediaevalism' in which societies ran themselves through overlapping and conflicting units of government and in which there was no sovereign power (see Chapter 3). Hence, the political traditions of 'Europe' (however defined) are both very diverse and found in most, if not all, national societies. Europe, for example, has been described as a 'city culture', one in which the outlook changes between major conurbations and within existing state boundaries. It may be that what is characteristic of Europe is not a single aspect but, on the contrary, the astonishing variety within such a (relatively) small area.

An objection to this cross-fertilization view is that 'Europe' is an abstruse idea and that people's loyalties are to the nation and the nation state. It is evident that 'Europe' has not eclipsed the nation as the principal focus of political community, but at the same time there are multiple loyalties in politics even if that fact has been occluded by the patriotism of the twentieth century. 'Europe' has become one of a number of loyalties of which the modern political community is composed. A 'nested set' of loyalties is not new. In the Cold War, people could be seen as 'Westerners' (to some extent still are) and would have regarded themselves as 'Western' while simultaneously have seen themselves as 'European', 'British', Welsh or Scottish or English, and perhaps also belonging to a region ('Yorkshire') and a city or trade union. These loyalties might conflict and there might well be tensions, but it is possible (normal, even) to live with a series of identities. 'Europe' in the contemporary world is another of these dimensions.

2.2   National perspectives on Europe

Although there are differences between social groups in their attitudes to Europe (with the young and educated responding most positively), it is notable that these are modest compared with the differences between states (Reif and Inglehart, 1991). Thus, the principal reality of the modern European state system has been the nation state. Since the Middle Ages the creation of the nation state has been the dominant political reality on the 'Old Continent'. Europe in this sense is a community of states. These nation states were the shapers of political culture and they were jealous of anything that challenged their dominance in the political arena. Any movement or ideology that had cross-national pretensions and ties was regarded with suspicion: communism, of course, but also Catholicism. National cultures and national histories became the norm in Europe during the nineteenth century and were equated with modernity in politics (at least until the two World Wars).

Nevertheless, the national perspectives on Europe differed. National orientations to Europe are indicative of the outlook of the political forces in each country and national differences are present throughout the institutions of the Union. For some states Europe was an opportunity, for others it was a restriction, and others linked Europe to their decline. States for which Europe was an opportunity start with the Federal Republic of Germany. German political leaders and the public saw Europe as a way of returning to play a role in the European system. Germany has, of course, been a post-war success story in political and economic terms. Europe played a part in that process and in fact made German re-emergence possible where no other institutions were available.

For Spain, the European Community was a way to modernization. Since the Spanish 'generation of '98' (the liberal intelligentsia formed by the end of the Spanish empire in the Americas after 1898), Europe had been seen as a model of political stability and human rights and had been a focus for the rejection of Spanish 'exceptionalism'. This outlook was rejected by the Franco regime which emphasized 'Hispanidad' and Spanish national difference, but it was kept alive by some of the most eminent of thinkers (including leading liberal thinkers like Ortega y Gasset) and re-emerged after Franco's death. Spain therefore embraced Europe in a positive way and not just as a rejection of the Franco regime. A similar point could be made about Italy where, during Mussolini's time, Europeanism and the Resistance became associated. Again, some of the leading spirits of the Italian anti-fascist movement were strong Europeans (these include the political philosophers Croce and Count Szforza, as well as the Christian democrats around Dom Sturzo and socialists like Spinelli).

Other societies were less positive, but Britain is one of the laggards. For the UK and Portugal the commitment to Europe came after the end of the imperial adventure. Both Britain and Portugal had been imperial societies over many generations and had invested themselves in the colonizer's role, seeing themselves as world empires (not regional powers). For each of these, the end was rapid and disillusioning: losing an empire but not finding a role. For them, Europe was the only option – and one embraced less than wholeheartedly and not without reservations. They ceased to be world powers and found themselves on the edge of a political community that they had little option but to join. In a different context, Sweden had defined itself as neutral in the Cold War, the main conflict of the post-war period; afterwards, Sweden found itself without a role in contemporary politics and turned to Europe to supply that.

In the case of the small states of Europe the original Europeanism of the nineteenth-century nationalists was once again revived. Many nineteenth-century nationalists saw no contradiction between being Europeans and being nationalists. They thought of Europeanism and nationalism as complementary and necessary adjuncts (the Italian Mazzini, for example, took this view). This was for the very pragmatic reason that the framework provided by Europe would enable national cultures to evolve and grow without threat. For many of the smaller states, Europe has been a way of playing a role, exerting an influence they could not otherwise aspire to, and of developing their own state. Europe from that perspective is not a threat but an opportunity.

2.3   Social cleavages and the development of party traditions

So far we have argued that there is a sense in which it is possible to speak of a European political culture, but that this has been overlain by different national outlooks on the project of European integration. The framework for analysis of the ideas, values and theories which make up European political culture is based on the clashes that took place within European societies after the onset of the 'dual revolution' of modernity (see, for example, Hobsbawm, 1962). The first of these was the national revolution, which set in train the process of state building; the second was the industrial revolution, which transformed social and economic relations. Lipset and Rokkan (1967) took up this insight to produce a schema for analysing the major European political families. It has since been used in a wide variety of contexts. In this view, social changes in nineteenth- and twentieth-century Europe created 'cleavages' in society and around these divisions new social groups and powerful social forces expressed their different interests, such that these divisions in turn became political movements based on deep-rooted political traditions. Political parties and the traditions they seek to embody thus evolved as a consequence of the revolutions and the basic divisions they generated in society.

In Europe these were 'revolutions' of nation building and industrialization, because they broke up the old traditional societies to create the class and interest alignments characteristic of post-war Europe. According to Lipset and Rokkan, four such cleavages were especially important:

- first, there was the antagonism between centralizing states and peripheral élites and groups in society;

- second, there were conflicts over secular and religious outlooks on life;

- third, there were economic conflicts between industrial and agricultural interests; and

- fourth, there were social and economic antagonisms between employees and employers.

The typology of Lipset and Rokkan, then, produces eight types of social groupings although only seven continued as real functioning parties (agrarian interests have been subsumed into other parties and traditions). Thus, the origins of party families are to be found in the cleavages created by the modernization of Europe and the choices made by élites and social groups in response to them. The responses and alliances forged in the wake of the nation-building and industrial revolutions, Lipset and Rokkan argued, are the main part of the explanation for the party systems of Western Europe. There was, in this view, a historical sequence to these divisions in European societies. Political parties, which grew out of these political clashes, were able to survive and express their interests, and these traditions persist to the present day.

More specifically, the basic cleavages are as follows.

- There are two arising from the process of state building. These are the resistance to the central state of regional interests and of the Church, which was displaced in the nineteenth century from its dominant position.

- There are two derived from the industrial revolution. These are the dramatic clash between the workforce and business interests, as well as the less evident clash between landed interests and industry. This division is better known as the protection versus free trade division, which split the parties in the UK but which is manifest elsewhere in Europe in different forms.

Not all the cleavages are evident in all societies as many are overcome or reconciled in the political process and the theoretical possibility of all the divisions giving rise to parties in one country was nowhere realized.

These patterns are the basis for subsequent refinements of the idea of political traditions, so a brief exposition of them is appropriate here. Of these divisions the oldest is the 'national revolution' which entailed centre versus periphery clashes. As the state itself grew in authority after the end of the Middle Ages, the power of the central government was increased. As the modern nation state was created it changed the relations of the existing social coalitions and broke up many of them. Different societies had, of course, different problems, but there was generally in European states an attempt to impose a national language (and the marginalization of the minorities) and at the same time the state's relation to the Church had to be reworked. These processes took place within the nation state framework but there were variations in the solutions found by the central state to these challenges of modernity.

After the French Revolution (1789) there was a second series of changes, which were associated with the development of modern nationalism within the state's boundaries. There were conflicts between Church and state and this was particularly so in Catholic Europe where the development of the modern nation displaced the Church. Battles were fought over the whole field of policy making, but they were particularly intense in education where the Church has always had a major (often preponderant) influence in Europe.

However, to this cleavage was added the third in the sequence brought about by the development of the market economy and the industrial revolution. One aspect of this was the divergence of interests between town and country (seen in such issues as protection versus free trade), but the other was the continuation of rural interests as a prevailing source of political cleavage in society (particularly in Scandinavia).

Finally, there was the conflict between the owner and the mass working class of the new society. Socialist parties developed in Europe during the second part of the nineteenth century and the Russian Revolution introduced the communist dimension. Communism was significant because it was a supranational force and challenged the authority of the state within its boundaries with its commitment to the Soviet Union's international communist revolution.

Summary

- We have seen that as a result of a long history of interaction among the societies and states of Europe it is possible to speak of a European culture and to identify traditions that are common across the variety of European states.

- Nevertheless, the principal political reality of modern Europe has been the nation state and there are important national differences toward the project of European integration that continue to overlie the common European political traditions.

- The common family of European political traditions is embodied in the political parties and party systems of the member states and these derived from a series of cleavages created by the modernizing revolutions of nation building and industrialization.

3   The party traditions

The classification of Lipset and Rokkan remains the starting point for much contemporary theorizing but it has been improved upon. There is a general acknowledgement that political expression differs across Europe and not all countries developed the same way, and consequently that the political outlooks are not the same everywhere. But we can say that there is a European family of political parties. However, other classifications have tried to allow for more recent changes in party cultures (the emergence of the 'New Left', feminism, the Greens, and so on) while retaining the basic historical structure derived from the epochal struggles of the past. For example, Von Beyme (1985), using the same cleavages, and noting the same clashes, provides the developmental sequence of: liberals; conservatives; socialist parties; agrarian parties; regional parties; Christian parties; communist parties; extreme right, fascist/Nazi parties; protest parties; and ecology parties. Protest and agrarian parties are anomalies and do not sit easily inside a pan-European typology and therefore will not be examined here. The other party families will be reviewed as will their place in the EP (in section 4).

Von Beyme's sequence starts with the liberal and conservative duality. This was a struggle between the rising new liberal politics and the defenders of the *ancien régime*, and typically became a clash between the monarchists and parliamentarians. Later, with the industrial revolution, came the mass parties of the left and in particular the emergence of socialism as a reaction against the excesses of industrialization (the agrarian parties also opposed the industrial system). Regional parties opposed the centralization of the nation states and Christian parties reacted to the secularization of the state and society. After the Russian

Revolution (1917) came the communist parties, and these and the fascist parties moved against the Western liberal systems. In many post-war European countries there were protest parties campaigning on issues such as high tax and bureaucracy and there were also, by the late 1980s, ecological movements expressing new concerns about the environment.

Perhaps, unsurprisingly, the best place to start the discussion here is with the standard left/right division in Europe and to examine the parties in that range (see Table 5.1). However, this is a somewhat uncertain exercise and issues are rarely so simple. At the turn of the twenty-first century the two dominant groups in Europe, and consequently in the EP, are the socialist parties and the Christian democratic parties, but there are also secular conservatives, liberals, the extreme right, communists, Greens and regionalists. These families also have orientations to the European issue (though with national exceptions), and it is possible to relate them to the EU (see section 4 below). Therefore, we will consider each in turn, with the exception of the regional parties, which are not easy to classify as left or right and are treated as a whole.

Table 5.1 Left and right in Europe since 1954: percentage of votes cast in national elections

	1950s	*1960s*	*1970s*	*1980s*	*1990s*
The Left					
Social Democrats	33.6	32.1	31.8	30.7	29.9
Communists	7.9	7.3	7.5	5.4	3.5
New Left	–	1.1	1.6	2.6	1.8
Greens	–	–	–	2.3	4.8
Total Left	41.5	40.5	40.9	41.0	40.0
The Right					
Christian Democrats	20.7	20.1	19.1	18.3	14.5
Conservatives	17.7	19.1	18.2	19.5	18.2
Liberals	8.7	9.8	9.6	10.3	10.1
Agrarian	6.6	6.9	6.7	5.4	6.4
Extreme Right	1.0	0.5	1.6	2.2	6.3
Total Right	54.7	56.4	55.2	55.7	55.5

The Guardian, Peter Mair, 21 February 2000

Secular conservatism

There is a division within European conservatism between the 'secular' conservatives and the Christian democrats. This is not a clear divide, and at the extremes the left of Christian democracy shades into socialism and the right into the secular conservatives. The secular conservatives are a rival to the Christian democrats and tend to be weak where the Christian democrats are strong, but in a number of countries – like the UK – they have been the dominant party in modern politics.

Conservatism is a diffuse movement, which is usually traced back to the reaction to the French Revolution (and Edmund Burke, its first theoretician). It is often referred to as a temperament and as a pragmatic stance, refusing to endorse any ideology. Conservatives did not want to go back to the old days, and restore the *ancien régime,* but they often resisted change. All the same, the national parties have very different starting points and very different traditions and values to 'conserve'. They have also fluctuated in their attitude to key issues such as state intervention and the welfare state and have reacted to other trends in a flexible manner. Most of the conservative parties in the north of Europe had a Christian background and this has been traced in their politics, but they are 'secular' and do not, unlike Christian democrats, refer back to founding Christian doctrine.

These are conservative national parties, with a consequent emphasis on national interest that conditions their outlook on European integration. For these free-market parties, the European project is primarily economic and the main object is the freeing up of markets to competition; by the same token, they are suspicious of the bureaucracy of the EU and favour the state's rights and sovereignty. Thus, the process in Europe of sectoral and technocratic integration through the agricultural market and development of common policies is viewed with scepticism, and the regulations and institutions are at times regarded as excessive (and, at other times, useless and expensive). One of the themes of these parties is the excessive authority of bureaucrats and their demand is for a reduction of central power and an increase in political control through the nation state (not the Commission). Emblematic of this outlook is the Bruges Group, with which British Prime Minister Margaret Thatcher was closely associated. It was created to promote the free market and fight the bureaucratization and over-regulation of the integration process promoted (as they see it) by socialists and their trade union allies. For the most part, the secular conservatives, who were fiercely anti-communist, also saw Europe as a prop of the Atlantic Alliance in the Cold War. They are equally wary of a decoupling from the USA in post-wall (post-communist) Europe.

Christian democracy

Christian democracy is one of the big European political forces. In the EP its European People's Party (EPP) is, with the socialists, one of the big two. In 1999, after the elections of that year, the conservatives became the biggest group and the French Christian Democrat Nicole Fontaine became the president of the Parliament. Yet Christian democracy is not a tradition that has aroused much interest in the English-speaking world, although it was very influential in post-war Europe and should not be confused with 'fundamentalist' politics (which is more American than European).

Religion in Europe is a better guide to people's voting than class and this means that the Catholic population is on the centre right and right of the political spectrum. Christian democracy has old roots, which are deep in the Catholic areas of Europe and which slowly extended over the nineteenth century despite the Church–state clash in many societies which made Catholic political activity suspect. At the end of the nineteenth century the Church, at the prompting of Pope Leo XIII, advocated involvement in modern politics, but added a concern for social reform. Problems within the Church itself and with the secular authorities prevented a rapid expansion of Catholic parties, although networks were constructed and trade unions were founded. In the early twentieth century there were attempts to apply the Catholic inspiration to political life, which had some small success (Hanley, 1994).

After the Second World War the Christian democratic parties emerged as mass organizations, notably in the ECSC 'six', but also in Austria where the Austrian People's Party emerged from the dictatorship and became a dominant party. In the mid-1940s, at the crucial time for the founding of European institutions, there were big Christian democratic parties in the original six: Germany, France, Italy, the Netherlands, Belgium and Luxembourg. The West German Chancellor Konrad Adenauer, the French Foreign Minister Robert Schuman, and the Italian Premier Alcide de Gasperi, were Christian democrats and their determination to consolidate the peace was the motive force of the new organization in the 1940s and early 1950s. In the Netherlands, the Christian Democrats were in government longer than the Communist Party in the former Soviet Union. No other political family has been quite so closely identified with Europe, and Christian democracy has been at ease with the construction of Europe. It still includes its 'federalists' and this became a 'Christian democratic' cause in countries where those parties maintained a presence.

The EPP statutes refer to 'federal integration' and to a 'United States of Europe', terms that are not acceptable to all conservatives. In fact Catholicism was willing to look for ways to overcome the deficiencies of the state system in Europe, which had caused two wars and divided the Catholic community. In this respect they were similar to the socialists in their willingness to seek or go beyond the normal inter-state rivalries to attenuate the clashes inherent in state rivalry. They also saw the building of European institutions as something more than an economic enterprise destined to ensure growth and higher living standards in the Old Continent; they saw it as an endeavour that would consolidate peace, freedom and justice. Europe was a model for co-operation and peace, which could be extended to societies elsewhere in the world. It is a vision of integration that rejects the socialist and free-market conceptions and claims to see Europe as the enabling of individual development but bolstered by the doctrine of 'subsidiarity'.

Christian democracy is inspired by the teachings of the Catholic Church on social and economic matters and has a moral outlook on political life, which is evident in their programmes. The Christian democrats are not limited to a secular vision of political life and see their vocation as going beyond material well-being to the creation of community and the articulation and practice of certain broad 'Christian' values (like, they say, justice and peace). A community in the ideal form would allow people to express themselves and freely participate at different levels. They are parties that are avowedly 'catch-all', rejecting any notion of the limitation of politics to class or national interests, and they reject confrontation. Christian democrats in Belgium and the Netherlands still have strong unions and have sought to promote union issues in Europe and to 'promote the idea of Europe in the working class' (in the words of the Luxembourg Christian Democrat and former President of the European Commission Jacques Santer). These networks distinguish the Christian democrats from the secular conservatives and make them more enthusiastic for social welfare reforms in Europe than other conservatives. Church and Church-linked organizations are means of social ascent for many Christian democrat politicians. In the Cold War, however, the Christian democrats were anti-communist and pro-Atlantic (pro-NATO).

Christian democracy itself was, however, profoundly marked by the need to find some way – a working peace – to resolve the conflicts which had made the European state system prone to catastrophic collapses. They were more at ease than secular conservatives with cross-border collaboration and the imposition of limits to state sovereignty and their embrace of democratic politics made 'Europe' a core commitment for them. This movement also supported the ideas then being proposed for European integration leading to a close confederation (proposed by the influential neo-Thomist, Catholic philosopher Jacques Maritain, among others) as a solution to the problem of European international relations. There is therefore an idealistic and pacific aspect to Christian democratic Europeanism and 'Europe' is an issue they have come to see as their own.

Liberalism

Liberalism is one of the main currents of political tradition in western Europe. It was the great radical force of the nineteenth century, when it stood against privilege and hierarchy and mobilized ordinary people. However, the main thrusts of liberalism (like constitutional monarchy and religious toleration) have been incorporated into the political mainstream and become a general property of political parties to the extent that commentators have questioned the identity of liberalism itself. Thus, few major political families would question the centrality of liberal ideas and, irrespective of any nuances in appreciation, the disputes within liberalism itself are as wide as between, say, the social democrats and the liberal parties (Kirchner, 1988).

At its origins, liberalism supported parliamentary government and the wider franchise with also, in most cases, a constitution guaranteeing human rights. In contemporary liberalism, freedom and human rights are the chief concerns. This was framed in opposition to aristocracy and to absolute monarchy in many countries and it is from that antithesis that the radical reputation springs. There was a more advanced wing to liberalism, which tried to push the extension of the franchise very early and very fast and to abolish property qualifications. On the continent the radical liberals were sometimes republicans, and where Catholicism was strong they encountered the Church and were anti-clerical. Anti-clericalism only began to disappear from liberal parties after the Second World War and it lingered on in some as (in Italy) demands mounted for reform of the divorce and abortion laws.

In economic policy the liberals were the promoters of the free market and of the rights of private property. They differed in the extent to which they were devoted to economic doctrines of free trade and the minimal state; for instance, the French Radical Party was one of the supporters of protectionist policies (which departed from free trade). The continental liberal parties were supported by small property holders and small farmers (many still reflect the farming interest), classes which were conservative about property rights and not the most dynamic sectors of their economy. They were, however, prepared to envisage nationalization of utilities and state intervention in the economy in many countries while at the same time relinquishing their commitment to private ownership and small firms. Liberal individualism made it difficult for the liberal parties to develop welfare programmes and, as a result, the socialists undercut them in this matter. In contemporary liberalism the left/right split in the family is confirmed by the emphasis which some (the Belgians and Dutch) give to classical liberalism as compared to the social welfare emphasis of others (in the UK, Sweden and Norway). It is a split that the liberals never really overcame and which is still evident in the European party. As Lord notes, the result is that the liberals are fairly well grouped together on the left of the Christian democrats on personal freedom, but are scattered and on the right on economic matters (Lord, 1998). However, they all support environmental issues and welfare although the extent of the significance they give to the latter varies.

The liberal parties were the major centre parties in Europe at the turn of the nineteenth century but were unable to maintain that position. As new challenges arose the liberals were torn between left and right wings and (as mentioned) they also lost their distinctiveness and there were losses to the conservatives and to the socialists. Liberals were vulnerable to both appeals and their dominant position in the political systems straddling the centre began to diminish. In the 1920s the fortunes of the liberals went into sharp decline and by the end of the Second World War they were almost all small, though significant, parties in their respective systems. Subsequently their share of the vote has fluctuated around a low level of ten to twenty per cent or so and, although their demise was widely predicted, liberal parties have remained significant and largely middle-class parties, and they have been able to update their appeal and use new issues.

The Liberal International was founded in 1947 and the transnational European Liberal Democrats Party was founded at a convention in 1976 as a response to the increasing need to establish a European organization. They were involved at the heart of the European integration process from the outset. As with other political families, the liberals have had doubts about Europe; some feared that the pace of integration was liable to divide Europe into trade blocks rather than unite it; and others were suspicious of the 'clerical Christian Democrat domination' of the new institutions. Mostly, however, while maintaining their Atlantic connection, the liberals have pressed for more co-operation and a wider membership.

Extreme right

There has, in recent decades, been a resurgence of the extreme right, which has been reflected in European institutions, although the integration process was led by many of the former Resistance leaders and has been defined in contradistinction to the Nazi/fascist project. However, the extreme right is a long-standing feature of European politics. Leaving aside the exact relationship between the contemporary extreme right and the pre-war fascists, the current right wing is a heterogeneous group with a variety of appeals. The bigger parties do not claim a fascist background and so have a populist and updated approach. The current extreme right parties include the Republikaner in Germany, the Front National in France, the Austrian Freiheitliche Partei and the Danish and Norwegian Progress Parties.

In the 1920s and 1930s the extreme right developed in reaction to the insurrectional challenge from the socialists and (above all) communists and they were a presence in virtually every European state, but were genuine mass movements in only Germany and Italy. After the War there were right-wing protest parties (like the French 'Poujadists') and tax and sectional 'flash' parties, but the only persistent party was the Italian Movimento Sociale Italiano – MSI. (MSI was refounded as Alleanza Nationale in 1994.) But all these parties had roots in a much older tradition of right-wing policies which started with the reaction to the Enlightenment and the French Revolution in the eighteenth century.

However, the extreme right has renewed its programme; it is not composed only of Vichy or Franco nostalgics and has used the parliamentary system to good effect to promote its own values. These values are not the extreme anti-parliamentarianism of the 1920s and 1930s (or of the nineteenth century) and the extreme right have astutely used elections to promote themselves as a new form of politics. They have caught the tide of disillusion with mainstream politics in the face of recession and unemployment, as well as problems with corruption and party funding scandals that have come to light in many countries. Nevertheless, they still remain opposed to the 'bourgeois' politics and 'capitalist' economics which they so reviled in the early nineteenth century, even if such opposition is now subtler. Their targets are still the socialist institutions of the welfare state and the liberal politics of the free market and they are in favour of firm discipline in the state through tougher laws and a crackdown on crime and immigration (the two are, for them, linked). But they also reject the systems of rights which liberal politics has developed and have hoped to see a restoration of hierarchy and order, though not in the old-fashioned 'corporatist' sense of the term. They have also promoted the issues of lower taxation, the cutting down of bureaucracy and red tape and protectionism, and this contradictory combination is difficult to fit into a neo-liberal outlook.

These extreme right-wing parties are above all nationalist parties and they claim a hyper-patriotism in the confrontation with the weakening of national identities in the modern world through such forces as 'globalization', immigration and – inevitably – European integration. The nationalist stance might seem to preclude any European engagement, yet the position which most have adopted is one of a quasi-Gaullist approval for a Europe of nation states with opposition to (as they depict it) an integrated Europe on the way to a federal unity. This means that they are able to combine a right-wing Europeanism with a defence of the national interest and portray themselves as in the best position to defend their country's interests: 'Germany first, then Europe' as the Republikaner Party stated in 1989. Europe in their view is the old civilization threatened by the ideologies from outside and by invading alien cultures (Gaffney, 1996).

Social democracy/socialism

Socialism, or social democracy, has an old history in Europe and the parties belonging to the Second International have long pedigrees. This diverse movement started as a reaction to the early stirrings of the industrial revolution and the parties recruited strongly among the new industrial working class of the nineteenth century, so that by the early twentieth century they were a presence in most European states. They had been formed with the aim of effecting practical improvements in the condition of the ordinary worker but, unlike the reformist parties, they held the view that they were the harbingers of a new and better society. They also believed in the solidarity of workers across the continent and an international society of working people, and the Second International was founded in 1899. For most of the continental parties this view was based on Marxist philosophy. Most parties, therefore, at some time in the past, had a revolutionary outlook and believed that the existing industrial ('bourgeois') society would be overthrown and replaced with a more just and equal one. Their demands for workers' representation went alongside the global trend to extend the franchise in Europe and their efforts in this direction were generally successful. Their initial exclusion from the parliamentary system was significant for many of the parties on continental Europe.

On the continent this revolutionary vision began to weaken in the late nineteenth century when the predictions made by Marx were not fulfilled (living standards rose and welfare reforms began) and the practical advantages of engagement with the parliamentary system became evident. They dropped their commitment to revolution and they became reform parties working with unions to extend health, education and the welfare system. They also dropped their internationalist outlook when it came to the great crisis of the First World War, and socialist parties participated in the war effort (only the extreme wings refused support). By the 1920s most had entered governments and most had consolidated very close links with the trade unions.

After the First World War the Second International parties reacted against Lenin's coup in Russia and, completing their evolution, turned against revolutionary violence and supported the parliamentary systems. They became the main props of the 'bourgeois' parliaments in which they were involved and they saw the socialist aim and the parliamentary system as being co-extensive: defending one was defending the other. They also took from the First World War experience of the industrial states the view that the state could run and develop industry more humanely and efficiently than the free market. Nationalization of major industries (collective ownership) would, it was assumed, cure the ills which the market produced and, although not all parties agreed in their condemnation of private property or the extent of nationalization, it was a general socialist platform. Nationalization of industry became a key demand (Sweden is by no means the minor exception here) and associated with planning for industrial development.

It was the Depression which provided the next test for the European socialists. Confronted by a social disaster in industrial countries, could their vague (though passionate) belief that there had to be a better way be given concrete form? This is where the socialist parties, rejecting the state socialism of the communists, took on their contemporary outlook of Keynesian state intervention to repair the deficiencies of the market and restore full employment. Swedish socialists took on this task first in the 1930s (before Keynes had published) and became the model for other socialist parties of what could be done in keeping with their value system. Swedish socialism also developed the consensus method of government: there was no crisis or upheaval in state and social relations and social reform proceeded through carefully worked out agreements.

At the end of the Second World War it looked as if the socialists' hour had come. There were extensions of the welfare state, government planning and nationalizations, and in Europe exponential growth produced full employment. Socialism was firmly in the Western camp in the Cold War, continuing its argument with communism from the West. Socialists also supported European integration and were pillars of the NATO alliance in the countries of Western Europe. As the fruits of economic growth were spread in society the socialist parties became a natural part of the governing system and unexceptional partners in coalitions, but the socialist programme (in the sense of its aspirations) appeared well on the way to fulfilment.

However, the oil price shock of the 1970s and the subsequent inflation began to call into question the nature of the post-war settlement. Inflation, in particular, proved to be the problem and the growth on which the parties depended to achieve full employment began to slow down. Socialist parties, which had governed, sometimes for long periods, began to be rejected at the polls. To some extent the deterioration was slowed in the 1980s when socialist parties returned to power and were able to restore some growth and restrain inflation, and there were some major successes. But the old confidence that the socialists had solved the problems of production and growth within an open economy and parliamentary system was undermined. The ideology of the free market began to make advances and the massive industrial system of coal and steel, mining, longshore workers and heavy industry began to be replaced. The traditional working class on which the socialists had relied began to change in structure, and new demands emerged for variety and choice and disputing the predominance of the state.

This was the position of the socialist parties in the 1990s and explains something of the continuing diversity and factionalism in the movement. The core values of solidarity and assistance by the state were intact and remained aspirations. But the milieu within which they worked and the society they had adapted to had changed, in some cases out of recognition. More worrying was that, despite the aspiration expressed in party programmes to provide collectively for social welfare, the means to deliver remained problematic. Socialists were back where they were – believing in a better way of managing the system to rid it of its inhumanities – and yet unable to specify how this would be done. It should be remembered, however, that the apparent 'crisis' of socialism is not an electoral failure (the Second International Parties in 1999 were in power or associated with government in thirteen of the fifteen EU states), but the collapse of old certainties. The system of delivering solidarity through the state was no longer felt to be adequate. Collectivism and nationalization have given way – even in socialist-run countries – to privatization and market-oriented solutions to social problems, as the tide turned against state enterprise to the extent that public enterprise came to be regarded as of doubtful utility.

Socialist parties have had a more troubled relationship with Europe than the Christian democratic parties have had although, as much as any party group can lay claim to it, Europe has been a socialist enterprise. The initial project was regarded with suspicion as a conservative, capitalist and clerical organization; what the ordinary worker would get from a market freeing trade and competition rather than increasing security and welfare was – to some – not clear. In the ECSC the socialists feared being trapped in a group of predominantly conservative countries with the big Scandinavian and British parties outside. Even if there was an international outlook, the Europe of the six was not a traditional internationalism; there were also national and patriotic reflexes, which prevented total support for the integration of Europe. These patriotic reflexes had been manifest at the outbreak of the First World War when the movement was unable to delay mobilization and conflict; it re-emerged in the 1930s and again in the 1950s. Some socialist parties missed the bus but others did join the early supporters of the European project. But the social welfare aspect of the ECSC and then the EEC/EU was developed over the years with socialist contributions. This is in line with the view that the new institutions should benefit the whole of society and not just business and that the EU should make a greater redistributive effort (Featherstone, 1988).

To this has been added the recent view, bolstered by the crisis of social democracy in the 1990s, that social democratic policies are no longer deliverable through the nation state. In the current climate, so the argument goes, the global sweep of free markets and the ease, in particular, with which capital can move across the world at the touch of a button, mean that the Keynesian project and the welfare state cannot be insulated within the small nation state. Any society trying to buck the trend would be very rapidly forced to comply through a run on the currency or a movement of industrial production to less well-protected (and less expensive) societies. According to this reasoning, the only way of saving the welfare state is to work at a European level. Europe is big enough and strong enough to defy the world markets, always assuming that the EU can be induced to adopt the right policies and to avoid the neo-liberal approach current in the Western world.

Communism

The states of Western Europe, with American prompting, stood together against the perception of a Soviet threat (see Chapters 2 and 3). Communist parties, supporting the Soviet system, were caught on the wrong side of the divide between a market-oriented, pro-Western and an anti-Soviet institutional process. Not surprisingly, the communist parties in the original six countries of the ECSC opposed European integration from within and the other Western communist parties opposed it from without. They saw the integration of 'capitalist Europe' as inimical to their interests and saw any attempts to extend the domain of the institutions (into defence, for example) as aimed at the Soviet bloc.

Communism is the development of the ancient revolutionary tradition in Western Europe. Contemporary communist parties were founded after the Bolshevik take-over in Russia in 1917 and formed part of the Third (Leninist or Bolshevik) International. These parties had very different national roots but they were quickly brought under the control of the Comintern (the Third or Communist International formed in Moscow in 1919) and became obedient branches of the Society system working in the host country. They were in effect outliers of the communist movement, and their prestige (in the 1930s and 1940s) did gain from their association with 'scientific socialism' and its implementation in the USSR. They also gained legitimacy from the wartime resistance to fascism and Nazi occupation, which was communist influenced in many countries.

However, these communist parties were not supported en masse because of their commitment to the Soviet Union which, by the 1950s and 1960s, was if anything off-putting to potential voters. They exploited the weaknesses in social democratic parties and emphasized a patriotic and welfare-oriented programme, which appealed to the left of the left in these countries. They made very little headway in entering government (some successes were achieved in Portugal and Finland) but they tried to update their appeal by becoming parliamentary parties. This contradicted their totalitarian structures and they found it hard to reconcile their reformist credentials with at the same time remaining loyal to the Soviet system in Eastern Europe. This became increasingly difficult after the invasion and suppression of the free governments in Hungary in 1956, Czechoslovakia in 1968 and then in Poland during the communist struggles against Solidarity in the 1970s and 1980s. Of the big communist parties the Italian and the Spanish had made most progress in freeing themselves from the ties with Moscow before the collapse of the Soviet Union in 1992; others (like the French and Portuguese) had changed very little or had even objected to President Gorbachev's reforms.

When the Soviet Union collapsed, many communist parties simply disbanded. The big Italian communist party dissolved itself and became the Democratic Left, a part of the Second International (though a group remained 'communist'), and recognized that it was the end of a socialist experiment. This substantially reduced the contingent of communist parties in Europe and the question of their survival and continuation as a separate group is constantly under threat.

To some extent the process of ratifying the Maastricht Treaty enabled the remaining communist parties to begin to take this turn. In Spain, Portugal, France and Italy (Refondizione) the parties ran a strongly anti-Maastricht campaign pointing out the dangers, in their view, of further integration and warning of the erosion of national sovereignty were it to go ahead. Thus, in a certain sense, the communist parties turned a page on their Soviet past and returned to their origins as left-wing parties defending the workers' acquisitions and bearing a patriotic banner. They had, however, the continuing problem that they were reduced to small sectors of the European electorate which, though they had once been strong, were declining. These were the heavy industries of the 'rust belt' and the small and marginal farmers in southern Europe, all classes which were diminishing and running down in Western Europe. Moreover, whereas the socialist parties had moved beyond this group the communists had not and showed no signs of being able to do so.

Given their common origins in a recent transnational party the communists in Europe have a similar outlook. They have not constituted a European party federation, but they have remained in contact even though the co-ordinating centre of the Communist International in Prague was disbanded at the end of the 1980s. They agree on their hostility to the free market and – in their view – that there is an alternative and better way (although this is now in the future and not the old Soviet system). Their attention to welfare, union and work issues as well as their voice on Third World and development problems confirm this outlook of idealism, sometimes referred to as 'communist values'. In the EP they form one of the most cohesive groups in the chamber and are well disciplined despite the addition of the more diverse Scandinavian parties with the latest enlargement of the Union.

The root and branch hostility with which the communists had viewed 'capitalist Europe' has long since abated, although they remained vigilant. The communist parties had, by the 1970s, come to agree to participation in the institutions and although they did not embrace the EU they were prepared to go along with it and make what use they could of its institutions. However, it was and remains a point of contention between the social democratic parties and the communists in Europe. The acceptance of the social democratic governments' and parties' outlook on integration (generally supportive to enthusiastic) was necessary before communists could participate in government; where they have had governmental pretensions they have had to remain silent on their anti-Euopeanism.

The fact remains that Europe is not going in their direction. Communists are suspicious of the (increasing, as they see it) market-oriented integration process to the benefit of the multinational companies and the dismantling of social protection inherent in the contemporary free-market trend. At present, the communists do not regard the EU as going in the right direction and they see their national systems as more likely than Europe is to protect their constituencies. They do not reject European integration outright, but they do claim to have an alternative idea of a greater Europe of peoples and countries. In effect, this comes close to a rejection of the current system, but they are not in a position to impose their own view or to construct a coalition that would bring it about. They therefore stand somewhat outside European integration, pressing for changes and acting as a pressure group on the main parties of the left (Lord, 1998; Gaffney, 1996).

Greens

Ecological movements have been seen by many as the first new political culture to emerge in party form since the institution of universal suffrage in the states of Western Europe. The 'post-industrial' societies were viewed as more concerned with the environment, democracy and the quality of life than the traditional occupations where material considerations were uppermost. Most societies in Europe have ecological movements and most have Green parties, although they have made great progress in some countries (like Germany) and rather less in others (like the UK). In the main, they are situated on the left and have an anti-capitalist rhetoric, but there has always been an ambiguity about their exact position and they have an appeal crossing the normal class boundaries (Roots, 1995).

It was in the 1960s that the environment became a politically charged issue. Before then the issue of nature and natural resources had been taken up by a number of pressure groups, but these had no strong political outlook. The environmental disaster of the *Torrey Canyon* oil tanker in 1967 and the problems of nuclear power, which led to demonstrations, reinforced a growing view that the effects of modern manufacture on life and nature were not necessarily benevolent or manageable. In 1979 the first Green was elected to a national parliament (in Switzerland) and that was followed in the 1980s by solid progress: in Belgium in 1981, then Germany and Finland in 1983, Austria in 1986, Sweden in 1988, Eire, Netherlands and Italy in 1989. In the mid-1990s the Greens began to take up ministerial positions, starting with Finland in 1995, followed by Italy, France and Germany in successive years.

The reason why the ecological movement has been seen as the development of a new division in Western Europe is its assimilation to 'post-material' values. These values, identified by Inglehart (1977), do not sit easily in the left/right divide. Post-material values are focused on the quality of life more than on the standard of living. They include: demilitarization and an end to arms sales; the protection of the environment and the conservation of natural resources; the opposition to unrestrained economic growth in Europe; and ending the spoliation of the Third World. In addition to a populist appeal, the ecological movement has been typically decentralized and opposed to traditional forms of organization, based on new class alignments and involved in many new kinds of initiative, protest or direct action.

Ecological movements do not inevitably correlate with the rise of new values in societies and there may be other explanations for their rise. In terms of the classification of European political cultures proposed by Lipset and Rokkan (1967) the ecologists could be seen as an emanation in modern form of the city versus rural dichotomy that was expressed by earlier agrarian parties. The ecologists do express the same antagonism between the free market and the country, but they do so in the form of antithesis between market and environment: unbridled market forces destroy both the environment and social harmony.

Ecology parties have been active at all levels of the European state from the local through the regional to the European Parliamentary stage. They may be particularly well adapted to local, or even micro-level, politics but they have been a presence in European institutions and have developed a view of Europe. However, not all ecology parties have taken the view that Europe is a positive force and some have opposed integration and have adopted more sceptical positions than their national counterparts (Gaffney, 1996). The call for the ratification of the Maastricht Treaty in 1992 found most ecology parties opposing it (though in France they were split) and in some countries the Green parties are more Eurosceptical than is public opinion. Where there is a strong national anti-European undertow the Green parties appear to amplify it (as in Denmark, the UK and Greece), but where there is a generally pro-European outlook the Greens have held similar views to their compatriots.

Europe has figured in the programmes of the ecology parties, yet it has not been a simple relationship and nor has it been a salient one. Europe has been subordinate to the overall objective of the new society of environmentally friendly activity and sustainable growth and this has an anti-European (even anti-Enlightenment) aspect in that the main target is Western-style industrial development and the consumer society. Europe, in this optic, can seem like the embodiment of the free-market project and a paradise for the transnational corporations, which the Greens argue are responsible for many ills. Europe does not present many opportunities for the Green movement and it is not the sort of locally based participative institution that they would be predisposed to favour. There is substantial and widespread criticism of the European integration process from this standpoint by Greens (found in Germany, Belgium,

Denmark and the UK) and parties in Scandinavia and Switzerland were quite strongly opposed to a federal or centralized Europe in which the 'democratic deficit' was large. Swedish, Norwegian and Austrian parties feared a levelling down of environmental standards.

Some ecologists, though, have seen the possibilities for action at a European level and have regarded many issues as being soluble only at a stage above the nation state. Europe, for them, presents positive opportunities, even if the EU's institutions distort the ideal. Their European integration would proceed from the grass roots upward and would be a Europe of territorial minorities and regions (perhaps, for some, self-sufficient). But Europe has a strategic dimension for ecologists: pollution knows no boundaries and the disposal of, say, nuclear waste in one state's territory does not confine the problem to that area. For example, the effects of nuclear spills cannot be confined (as, they say, the accident at the Chernobyl nuclear reactor demonstrated). Other problems, from industrial pollution to agriculture and North/South problems of Third World debt, are similarly best tackled at a European level and go beyond what the nation state can handle. This is true, notably, of the attempts to tame the transnational corporations, which can and do escape the control of the nation state at the moment.

Regional parties

The creation of the European nation states was a determinedly centralizing process and in many cases violently so. In the 'nation-building' of the nineteenth and twentieth centuries the states of Europe incorporated many smaller nationalities, regions and ethnic groups and divided others up. These minorities are now represented by a diversity of political parties whose views on other issues (like the Church or economics) may be poles apart, but which defend their sub-state identity in different ways. Many of the mainstream political families were indifferent to regions or even hostile to regional identities. The late nineteenth century saw the 'Irish problem' as a continuing crisis in UK politics; there were other expressions of political identity which only became widespread forms of political parties in the late twentieth century. There are few common factors in their social structures, although religion and a peripheral position vis-à-vis the capital are significant, and they are not all based on a linguistic difference. Hence, though diverse, they are a significant factor in most of Europe and some are regionally dominant, but they differ in their demands (from devolution to sovereignty) for their region, and they have also had very different effects (from Belgium to France, for example).

Europe is undergoing a process of integration and, as some see it, centralization. This would seem to mean that Europe is inimical to the sub-state nationalists and territorial interests. Many nationalist or regionalist movements have been hostile to European institutions and Europe is also an intergovernmental organization, so that active regionalization by the Commission or Parliament or their action against central metropolitan domination is an implausible development.

However, one of the paradoxes of the building of the new Europe is the opportunity it gives to the smaller nationalities (and states). A 'Europe of the regions' freeing communities from the tutelage of the state is, on the other hand, a well used concept and finds its supporters in all states of the Union. This could be seen as part of a strategy of linking regional forces together for mutual protection against overbearing states or potentially dominant neighbours (the impetus behind regional alliances are various). European integration also deprives the larger states of some of the leverage they might otherwise use against minorities or nationalities.

Summary

- The major party political traditions in Europe are the secular conservatives, Christian democracy, liberalism, the extreme right, the social democrats and the communists. More recent additions include the Greens and the 'regional' parties.

- Although they are embodied in political parties which organize on a *national* basis, the parties and traditions in different countries have enough in common that it makes sense to speak of a *European* family of party traditions.

4   Party traditions in the European Parliament

The party families reviewed above are evident at the European level. Some, like the socialist, liberal and Christian democratic and, of course, communist parties, had started their 'internationals' before the creation of European institutions (and are not purely European), but the integration process forced them to add a European dimension to their activity. In the EP they are all represented in party groups and are a visible force elsewhere in European politics (see Table 5.2 opposite). But there are also groups which appear and disappear, and which do not relate directly to the families as described. However, the rules of the EP place a premium on co-operation and that has meant the swamping of, for example, the Christian democrats in the larger conservative European People's Party (EPP). In addition, the smaller party families in Europe are a feature of the EP (sometimes even when absent from their national parliaments), but they are marginal and struggle to keep a toe-hold in the Parliament, and they can change in composition quite substantially from one election to the next. The political traditions which are typical of old Europe are manifest in the EP itself through the party groups. The seven active political groups, the right and the left and the regionalists, can easily be seen at work.

Table 5.2 Seats in the European Parliament, January 1999

Member state	Party group									Total seats	Citizens per EP seat
	PES	EPP	ELDR	UPE	EUL	G	ERA	IEN	na		
Germany	40	47				12				99	826 000
UK	61	17	3		1	1	2	1	1	87	675 000
France	16	12	1	18	7		13	8	12	87	670 000
Italy	18	37	4	3	5	3	2		15	87	659 000
Spain	22	30	2		9		1			64	613 000
Netherlands	7	9	10	2		1		2		31	500 000
Greece	10	9		2	4					25	420 000
Belgium	6	7	6			2	1		3	25	404 000
Portugal	10	9		3	3					25	396 000
Sweden	7	5	3		3	4				22	400 000
Austria	6	7	1			1			6	21	386 000
Denmark	4	3	5					4		16	331 000
Finland	4	4	5		2	1				16	319 000
Ireland	1	4	1	7		2				15	240 000
Luxembourg	2	2	1				1			6	67 000
Total seats	214	202	42	35	34	27	20	15	37	626	
Per cent	34.2	32.3	6.7	5.6	5.4	4.3	3.2	2.4	5.9	100.0	

Note:
PES = Group of the Party of European Socialists (socialist/social democrat)
EPP = Group of the European People's Party (Christian democrat/conservative)
ELDR = Group of the European Liberal, Democrat and Reform Party (liberal)
UPE = Group Union for Europe (conservative)
EUL = Confederal Group of the European United Left/Nordic Green Left (radical-left)
G = The Green Group in the European Parliament (green)
ERA = Group of the European Radical Alliance (radical liberal/regionalist)
IEN = Group of Independents for a Europe of Nations (anti-European)
na = non-attached members (mostly extreme right)

(http://www.europarl.eu.int/members/en/default.htm)

European Christian democrats had started to collaborate in the Nouvelles Equipes Internationales in 1947, and subsequently their work together was intensified in the Assembly of the European Coal and Steel Community. However, the enlargement of Europe and domestic pressures led to the creation of the EPP by the EEC Christian democrats in 1976 to co-ordinate policy in the EP. Over the years the (initially Christian democratic) EPP has come to dominate the centre right and its hegemonic position has led many secular conservatives to join it to counter the Socialists' influence rather than to remain in their own group (Hix and Lord, 1997).

Secular conservatism is not at ease in the EPP, a group generally well disposed to integration, and secular conservatives are more national in outlook. They might have achieved the dominant position the EPP now occupies had they been united – which they were not. The result has been a spreading out of secular conservatism through the groups in the EP and some are unattached members. In 1992 the British and Danish Conservatives joined the (Christian-democrat dominated) EPP group, as did the Swedish Moderate Samling and the Finnish Kansallinen Kokoomus after the entry of Sweden and Finland into the Community. Spanish conservative leader José-Maria Aznar's renovated Partido Popular also joined the EPP later in an attempt to shake off its reputation (as a post-Franco party of the right) for extreme conservatism and its nationalism. That move left other secular conservative parties in a quandary. These included the members of the Group Community for Europe (UPE) and the former Rassemblement des Démocrates Européens: Forza Italia, neo-Gaullists (RPR), Fianna Fail, Portuguese Christian democrats, and the Greek POLAN. The departure of Berlusconi's Forza Italia had the same effect, further weakening the secular conservative group, but the Christian references remaining in EPP's rhetoric still cause some secular parties to remain outside, although a larger conservatism is possible. Moreover the EPP's watering down of its precepts and its commitment to a free-market and laissez-faire stance has made the re-grouping of the centre right easier.

On the left the situation is similar, with the Party of European Socialists (PES) dominating the moderate centre left, but the parties in it are all members of the Socialist International and there is no equivalent to the Christian democrat/conservative tension (there are, however, others, and it has lacked cohesion in the past). There was a socialist group in the ECSC Assembly which became the PES in 1993 in order to capitalize on their strong position. PES has been the largest group since 1979 and its share of seats in the EP steadily increased from 27.5 per cent in 1979 to 35.5 per cent in 1995. Before 1999 (when the UK electoral system was changed) the PES was dominated by the British and German socialists. However, the PES parties are all from the same political family and are a constant presence in the EP with few fluctuations, and are in a position to exert hegemony on the left in the Parliament.

Although the German and UK liberals had hesitated at the very beginning of European institution building, the ELD (renamed the ELDP in 1985) has been supportive of the integration process. It has wanted to hasten the progress of the Union by extending its functional scope (to bring in ecology and security, for example). ELDP has sought to strengthen the institutions with such measures as more majority voting in the Council and extending the EP's remit. However, European liberals have a bigger influence than their small size (42 seats in 1994) might indicate, because of their position as a balancer in the Strasbourg Assembly. Liberal parties are strongly Atlanticist, pro-NATO, enthusiastically pro-European and some have federal commitments; and at the EP level they stress civil rights, regionalism and democratization of the EU.

In the first direct elections to the European Parliament the MSI took four seats, in 1984 Le Pen's Front National took ten seats and in the 1989 elections the German Republikaner took six seats. A group in the Parliament was formed in 1984 and its composition varied with both the fluctuations in electoral fortunes of the small parties and the numerous fallings out between the members. (There is a continual fracturing and splitting on the extreme right which is as querulous in its way as the extreme left.) These internal recriminations saw the Front National accused of racism and the MSI objecting to the German view of the Tyrol problem and then quitting the group. Le Pen's party had been radicalized by its opposition to the Maastricht Treaty and brought together a broader spectrum of Eurosceptics (including Danish and Dutch MEPs) in the nineteen-strong Europe of the Nations. Co-operation has not been entirely harmonious and it is not cohesive. Upon EU enlargement in 1995, Haider's Austrian Freiheitliche Party might have been expected to join the group, but contemptuously dismissed Le Pen's party and group. It is not surprising that these parties dedicated to national self-expression and autonomy and opposed to integration from different angles should find it difficult to co-operate or to make alliances. They do not moderate their rhetoric and so far have mostly rejected the temptations of office that respectability and compromise might bring them. The exception is the Austrian Freiheitliche Party, which joined a coalition government in 2000, much to the consternation of the governments of the other member states in the EU.

The smaller groups of the communists (with under 5 per cent of seats) and the Greens (with about 4.5 per cent) have only a toe-hold in the Parliament and are more subject to the dips in electoral fortune of their parties than are the bigger groups. The predominantly communist group (United European Left) was subject to disputes between the French and the Italian communists; with the leaving of the Italian party, the group has gained in cohesion and now tries to influence its bigger PES partner by lobbying for issues of concern to it. These have included Third World as well as workers' rights issues in the European market. The Greens are also a small group but they are one of the less cohesive ones (less than the UEL), although that has improved since early existence as the Rainbow group in the 1980s. They organized for the 1979 European elections as the European Co-ordination of Greens and Radicals, and prior to the 1984 elections a meeting was held in Belgium to consolidate this grouping. In 1993, after the Maastricht Treaty, twenty-three Green parties formed the

Federation of European Greens and this had become, by 1999, one of the four main groups in the EP and a significant parliamentary force. Green politics at the European level is a matter of seizing the agenda and using the Parliament for campaigning – which is suited to their style.

The other main party family is the regional movements. Because of their dispersal across the party groups in the EP the regional or sub-state national movements are not a coherent group. In any case their distribution along the whole range of the left/right spectrum (from Vlaams Blok to Sinn Fein) would make co-operation on most matters of daily debate in the Parliament unlikely.

Summary

- The pattern of party representation and organization within the European Parliament is broadly similar to that found at the national level. Despite national differences towards the project of European integration, parties with similar traditions from different countries are generally able to work with one another in the EP.

5   Conclusion

With the exception of the post-war protest parties and the ecologists, the pattern of party families has been stable to the extent that many observers have suggested, following the original lead given by Lipset and Rokkan, that there had been a 'freezing' of party systems in the early to mid-twentieth century. They are all 'modern' in the sense that they all emerged after the French Revolution and as a response to the development of mass politics. It has been the distinctive pattern of politics on the European peninsula that has forged the political traditions described above (though they all have their 'export models', their 'internationals'). The party families of Europe are recognizable cultures and have common referents. This common background makes co-operation in the European institutions possible and, in fact, relatively harmonious.

However, the building of European institutions has been an issue that has divided party families. No political group, however enthusiastic they might be about integration, has been free from divisions over the European issue. Christian democrats include, for example, the sceptical Portuguese Christian Democratic Party, and the socialists also have some notable recalcitrants. Overall, it is the intrusion of distinctive *national* outlooks that is the origin of the division – Britain, Denmark and Portugal being among the sceptics and Germany, Spain and Benelux among the enthusiasts (even this is an oversimplification). Thus, the outlooks of the party families have to be imagined as criss-crossed with fractures, or potential fissures, where Europe is concerned. However, European institution building, one of the major developments of post-war Europe, does not constitute a separate cleavage. There are some parties that have developed around this issue alone (like the UK Independence Party), but generally the national sovereignty problem has been incorporated into the platforms of existing party traditions. 'Europe', and the process of integration within it, exists as an issue of contention or as an issue bringing together the like-minded; it does not itself constitute a new 'revolution' to add to Lipset and Rokkan's historical cleavages.

References

Featherstone, K. (1988) *Socialist Parties and European Integration*, Manchester, Manchester University Press.

Gaffney, J. (ed.) (1996) *Political Parties and the European Union*, London, Routledge.

Hanley, D. (ed.) (1994) *Christian Democracy in Europe*, London, Francis Pinter.

Hix, S. and Lord, C. (1997) *Political Parties in the European Union*, London, Macmillan.

Hobsbawm, E. (1962) *The Age of Revolution, 1789–1848*, London, Weidenfeld and Nicolson.

Inglehart, R. (1977) *The Silent Revolution*, Princeton, NJ, Princeton University Press.

Kirchner, J. (ed.) (1988) *Liberal Parties in Western Europe*, Cambridge, Cambridge University Press.

Lord, C. (ed.) (1998) *Transnational Parties in the European Union*, Aldershot, Dartmouth.

Reif, K. and Inglehart R. (eds) (1991) *Eurobarometer: The Dynamics of European Public Opinion*, London, Macmillan.

Lipset, S.M. and and Lipset, S. (1967) 'Cleavage structures, party systems and voter alignments: an introduction' in Lipset, S.M. and Rokkan, S. (eds) *Party Systems and Voter Alignments*, New York, Free Press.

Roots, C. (ed.) (1995) *The Green Challenge*, London, Routledge.

Von Beyme, K. (1985) *Political Parties in Western Democracies*, Aldershot, Gower.

Zetterholm, S. (ed.) (1994) *National Cultures and European Integration*, Oxford, Berg.

Further reading

Hix, C. and Lord, C. (eds) (1997) *Political Parties in the European Union*, London, Macmillan.

Lord, C. (ed.) (1998) *Transnational Parties in the European Union*, Aldershot, Dartmouth.

Lipset, S.M. and and Lipset, S. (1967) 'Cleavage structures, party systems and voter alignments: an introduction' in Lipset, S.M. and Rokkan, S. (eds) *Party Systems and Voter Alignments*, New York, Free Press (pp.1–64).

Von Beyne, K. (1985) *Political Parties in Western Democracies*, Aldershot, Gower.

Chapter 6
Integration and policy processes in the European Union

Laura Cram

1 Introduction

One of the key questions that preoccupies students of the European Union (EU) is: Who runs the European integration process? How did the new processes and structures of EU politics come about and why did they take the form that they did at the time they emerged? European integration, as described in Chapter 2, has gone through fast and slow periods and has shifted in direction from largely economic integration to include greater social and political integration. The central question – and the one we address in this chapter – remains: Who dictates these changes in pace and direction? Section 2 reviews briefly the key theoretical approaches to the study of European integration, which has been seen by some as a threat to traditional nation states (the supranationalist view) and by others as a means of strengthening the power of nation states (the intergovernmentalist view). Key authors from both schools of thought are introduced, and the relationship between the institutional balance of power within the EU and each view of European integration is explored. We will see that aspects of both supranationalism and inter-governmentalism help to inform our current understanding of what European integration is.

In section 3 a more recent dimension of the debate on the character of governance within the EU is introduced. Many analysts now argue that the debate between supranationalism and intergovernmentalism no longer helps us to understand fully what European integration really is. They argue that we need to spend more time analysing the everyday activities of the national governments, EU institutions (for example, the Commission, the Parliament, the Council of Ministers and the European Court of Justice), big business and national, sub-national, international and European interest groups. The activities of these actors and the policies they produce could tell us a lot about what European integration is and who runs it.

We conclude by considering the scope of European integration. To what extent is European integration limited to events that take place in Brussels or Strasbourg? Students of European integration have begun to consider the impact of the EU on actors in the domestic political context. So, when a national politician brings home a new idea after negotiating with politicians from other EU countries, does this mean that national politics are becoming Europeanized? How clear is the dividing line between national- and EU-level politics? For example, have lobbyists involved in activities at the EU level started to develop a stronger consciousness of the EU or even a sense of attachment to the EU? Do the citizens of the EU increasingly feel they are part of a political community over and above or alongside their national communities?

Before attempting to address these questions, it is useful to start by considering briefly what is meant by the term 'European integration'.

2   What is European integration?

We saw in Chapter 1 that understanding integration is like trying to hit a moving target. Each time we think that we have the process in our sights, it moves on and changes, and we have missed the mark again. European integration has been viewed in a variety of ways: as an end product linked to a specific institutional structure, shaping a new form of politics; as a background condition without which no institutional structure could survive, a pattern of economic, social and cultural interaction between states and societies; and as a process that is ever changing and developing. This section examines each of these in turn.

Some federalist scholars, for example Spinelli (1966), saw European integration as the end product or outcome of collaboration between member states in the European Community and, as such, could be specified in terms of the constitution of a new political order. From this standpoint, the emergence of a European federal state would be an example of European integration, as would a confederal order. A European federal state would involve the transfer of certain key attributes of sovereignty to the European level and a new constitutional definition of the respective authority for the different parts of the EU. In a confederal Europe, the member states would retain more of their sovereign rights, but agree to pool the exercise of their sovereignty for certain common purposes (see Chapter 3). From a federalist standpoint, we have not yet achieved European integration, although (as Chapters 3 and 4 have indicated) a number of steps have been taken in this direction. Many scholars argue that the EU is a confederal order.

Others, such as Deutsch (1967), viewed integration as an essential background condition without which no sense of community could emerge at the EU level. Deutsch argued that the level of community among states was very much a function of the level of interaction and communication between them. Integration would, he argued, emerge as a greater understanding developed between the various EU member states and they learned to share understandings of their problems. Without this shared sense of community any attempt to manufacture a European federal state would be doomed to failure.

Perhaps the most commonly used interpretation of European integration is that it is a dynamic process, resulting in movement towards a new definition of political community. This understanding of integration, promoted initially by Haas (1958), draws upon insights from both federalists (like Spinelli) and from Deutsch. Haas argued that the process of creating new institutions at the EU level (end products) generates a shared learning experience through which a sense of community (an essential background condition) emerges to underpin and support the new institutions. The process through which this takes place is known as European integration.

For our purposes, this last interpretation of European integration as an ongoing process is most useful. This is the interpretation most commonly employed by contemporary students of European integration, since it allows us to recognize the wide range of activities and institutional structures that have emerged at the EU level and the ways in which these change over time. However, we are still left with the question of who controls this process. We could visualize the process as a moving vehicle. Is the driver who has control of the steering wheel the same as the one controlling the accelerator and brake? Is it possible to change drivers, and

European integration – towards a new definition of political community?

what effect would this have on the speed and direction of the vehicle? Remember, too, that a vehicle can be thrust into reverse as well as forward motion. Below, we examine some of the key approaches to European integration that may help us to shed some light on these issues.

2.1   Integration as the building of a supranational political community

In Chapters 1 and 3 we saw that the European nation state only became the exclusive form of political organization in the nineteenth century and that it was not until after the Second World War that these states became stable liberal democracies, and then only in Western Europe. In other words, the liberal-democratic, sovereign nation state is a relatively recent form of political community. It is not inevitable that political communities have to be organized in this fashion. Moreover, we also saw in Chapter 3 that the European nation states and the states system into which they were organized provided the melting pot for the First and Second World Wars. Not surprisingly, then, many in post-war Europe were searching for a new kind of political community and new kinds of relations among nation states.

Writing in the 1950s, Haas made one of the most enduring contributions to the study of European integration. Even today most authors refer back to his work, either in support of or to criticize his arguments. Haas developed an approach to European integration known as neo-functionalism. One of the key contributions of his work on European integration was his argument that the establishment of new supra-national institutions and policies at the EU level might have long-lasting consequences for the ability of national governments to remain in complete control of their activities and maintain the total loyalty of their citizens at home. In particular, Haas argued that the European Commission, which in the founding Treaties had been given the role of acting as the 'motor of integration', would seek to push integration further than the governments of the member states desired.

Haas argued that national governments would be unable to hold back the momentum of integration. Like a runaway vehicle, the integration process would escape their control, and as new members sought to join the EU it would continue to hurtle forward. Haas identified three particular ways in which this might happen, each of which is known as a type of 'spillover'.

- First, he argued that as a policy was created in one area (for example, establishing the right to work in any EU country) a policy would be required in another related area (for example, establishing the right to claim unemployment benefit in any EU country). This is known as technical/functional spillover.

- Second, Haas argued that as individuals, groups and businesses from the various EU countries became aware of the range of activities taking place at the EU level, they would start to focus their energies at the EU level instead of solely at the national level. For example, as women become more aware of the equal opportunities legislation emerging from the EU, they become increasingly likely to lobby at the EU level for more legislation, and might even take their own government to the European Court of Justice for failure to enact EU legislation adequately. It also followed, Haas argued, that as actors begin to feel the benefits of the EU more directly, they might even begin to shift their loyalty to the EU level and away from the national level. This shift in activities and loyalties in response to developments at the EU level is known as political spillover.

- Finally, Haas argued that a process of geographical spillover may also be important, as non-member states may suffer economically through their exclusion from preferential EU markets as well as by losing out on some of the economies of scale that can be achieved by the collaboration of EU members.

Neo-functionalism had its heyday in the early 1960s when European integration seemed unstoppable. The Treaty of Rome (1957) represented a major expansion in the areas in which co-operation could take place between the member states as compared with the functionally limited compass of the ECSC (technical/functional spillover). The European institutions, such as the Commission and the Court, were using their new-found powers to strengthen the process of European integration, as we saw in detail in the case of the ECJ (Chapter 4). More and more actors and interest groups, such as farmers' organizations, became involved in politics at the EU level (political spillover), and more countries were applying to join the EU (geographical spillover; see also Chapter 9).

So what does all this mean for the question of who controls the integration process? By creating supranational institutions, such as the Commission and the Court, national governments could be said to have created competing drivers who might want a turn at the steering wheel of European integration. In addition, as more and more actors become involved at the EU level, it becomes harder for national governments to control the speed and direction of European integration. From this supranationalist standpoint, the new institutions and practices at the EU level appear to undermine the traditional powers of nation states. In this context, Haas defined integration as:

> the process whereby political actors in several distinct national
> settings are persuaded to shift their loyalties, expectations and
> political activities toward a new centre, whose institutions
> possess or demand jurisdiction over pre-existing national states.
> The end result of a process of political integration is a new
> political community, superimposed over the pre-existing ones.
>
> (Haas, 1968, p.16)

2.2   Integration as co-operation to strengthen the nation state

One of the strongest early criticisms of neo-functionalism came from Hoffmann (1966). He argued that Haas had underestimated the staying power of nation states in the international system and hence the ability of national governments to control the integration process. Hoffmann's approach is known as intergovernmentalism. Hoffmann argued that the process of spillover was neither unstoppable nor always a threat to national governments. In fact, Hoffman argued that national governments placed clear limits on the process of spillover and even used it to their advantage. Certain types of co-operation at the EU level are, at best, advantageous and, at worst, neutral for member states. So, for example, co-operation in some areas of agricultural policy prevents unfair competition within Europe. Meanwhile, co-operation in certain areas of communications technology allows for economies of scale and helps EU member states to be more competitive in international markets. Hoffmann argued that national governments allowed the process of spillover to take place in cases like these because it suited them. These examples are what Hoffmann described as areas of 'low' politics concerned with essentially economic and welfare issues. National governments had little to lose but potentially something to gain by allowing spillover to take place, since co-operation was a positive-sum game from which all could benefit.

In contrast, some types of policy that bear directly on the sovereignty of the state are very jealously guarded by national governments, because in these areas states are more concerned about their relative positions vis-à-vis one another. These include, for example, foreign policy, security and defence. Hoffmann called these cases 'high' politics. When it came to matters of high politics, Hoffmann argued that national governments would not allow spillover to take place without careful consideration: integration would be allowed to proceed when it helped to strengthen existing national states, but not when it was likely to threaten vital national interests. From an intergovernmentalist perspective, the supranational institutions implemented and managed the course of integration set by the national governments of the member states, but when legislative or key executive decisions are called for, or when the supranational institutions exceed their brief, national governments are able to take over the wheel again and, if necessary, apply the brake.

Hoffmann also argued that Haas had not paid enough attention to the impact that the international environment or external context had on the pace and direction of European integration. If events in the international environment, such as the oil crisis of 1973/4, were not favourable for European integration then there was little that the EU institutions or national governments could do about it. The integration process could not be explained solely as a battle of wills between national governments and supranational institutions. External factors also had a role to play. As we have seen in Chapters 2 and 3, for example, the Cold War division of Europe and the role of NATO in guaranteeing Western security, were an important part of the wider external context in which the EU developed (see also Chapter 10).

By the end of the 1960s it looked like the neo-functionalist capacity to explain the process of integration was stalling. In 1963 the French President, Charles de Gaulle, vetoed the UK's membership application. This not only halted the process of geographical spillover, it also demonstrated that it was not the Commission but the national governments that remained firmly in the driving seat of European integration. The notion that citizens would transfer their loyalty away from the national level and towards an inefficient body at the supranational level began to seem absurd. Finally, the oil crisis and recession in the early 1970s slowed up progress on specific policies and called even the inevitability of sectoral/functional spillover into question.

Throughout the 1970s and much of the 1980s neo-functionalist explanations of European integration fell out of favour. Not only did national governments appear to be in control, but de Gaulle had also demonstrated the power of member states to slow down and even stop the process of integration in some respects. Thereafter, intergovernmentalism dominated what debate there was on European integration until the late 1980s when the Single European Act (SEA, 1986) marked a renewed effort at European integration. Students of European integration rediscovered the intrigue of this debate, for by the end of the 1980s the situation had again changed dramatically. The SEA came into force in 1987 and launched the high-profile 1992 project, in which all barriers to the completion of a single European market were to be removed by the beginning of January 1992. The launch of the SEA and the 1992 project helped to revitalize the interest of scholars in European integration. The big questions like 'what is integration?' and 'who runs this process?' began to be asked once again.

In some respects, in the late 1980s and early 1990s the debate about European integration mirrored the earlier debate between Haas and Hoffmann. In the supranationalist camp, some of the insights of neo-functionalism are still used by students of European integration today. For example, Sandholtz and Zysman (1989) argue that EU-level institutions and other interests, such as big businesses or lobby groups, seek to steer the process of European integration in directions that not all national governments would choose themselves. Meanwhile, scholars such as Moravcsik (1991; 1993) built upon Hoffmann's intergovernmentalist position and argued that in negotiating the SEA, and later the Treaty on European Union (1992), the key actors were national governments, not supranational institutions.

The EU Parliament building

Summary

We can summarize the discussion so far by a comparison between the perspectives of neo-functionalism and supranationalism, and the intergovernmentalist alternative.

Neo-functionalism/Supranationalism

Supranational EU institutions – the Commission, the ECJ and the European Parliament – have an active role in sponsoring integration, leading to:

- a reorientation of economic and political actors to the European level of policy making, and changes to their loyalty and organization;

- technical/functional, political and geographical spillover driving the process of integration forward, and supranational institutions and Europeanized actors pressing for more integration;

- integration being driven forward and tending to lead to the formation of a new political community superimposed over the old (national) ones.

Intergovernmentalism

The powers of supranational institutions are decided, monitored and regulated by the member states acting intergovernmentally, leading to:

- the governments of member states remaining the dominant actors in the policy-making process;

- governments being able to control the effects of spillover: they may welcome it in areas of 'low' politics (economic and welfare issues), but resist it in areas of 'high' politics (foreign policy, security and defence);

- integration also taking place in a wider international environment, where the EU and the member states are part of a bigger international system which no state or group of states can control.

3 Integration and the EU as a system of governance

Despite the revival of the supranational versus intergovernmental debate in the late 1980s, some analysts have argued that this debate no longer helps us to understand fully the nature of politics and policy in the EU. Indeed, focusing too heavily on major Treaty negotiations and the debate between supranationalism and intergovernmentalism can obscure the fact that a complex system of governance exists at the EU level. An institutional structure has been established, policies are made and put into effect, and a legal structure exists to prevent non-compliance with EU laws. If we focus too heavily on the original debate we miss out on some of the most important developments at the EU level.

This new approach had its origins in the 1970s as European integration seemed to grind to a halt. No major treaty on European integration was signed between 1957 and 1986. It looked as if European integration was going nowhere fast. Not surprisingly, working out who ran European integration became altogether less interesting. However, throughout this period much business continued as usual in the EU policy process. Issues like the Common Agricultural Policy (CAP) still had to be dealt with and bureaucrats, national politicians and interest groups continued to nego- tiate new policies. Scholars such as Wallace et al. (1977) reminded observers of the EU that these everyday policy activities, although less dramatic than major treaty negotiations, still needed to be understood. Indeed, they argued that these low-profile, everyday activities might have important implications for the future of European integration. We still needed to know who or what was driving day-to-day politics, and Wallace et al. argued that examining the negotiations and bargains struck in the EU policy process could tell us much about where power and initiative was located.

An important development in the study of European integration has been this recognition of the importance of the policy process as the focus shifted from politics between the member states to politics *within* the EU. This approach came into its own in the 1990s. Since then, many researchers have produced detailed studies of different EU institutions (for example, the Commission, the Council of Ministers, the Parliament and the Court). Others have focused on decision processes within different policy areas (for example, agricultural policy or social policy). Some specialize in the study of EU law, while others examine the input of different actors (such as big business, environmental groups and farmers' unions). Together, these various studies help us to put together a fuller picture of what happens at the EU level and to develop a clearer understanding of what European integration is and how it changes over time.

Few of these authors would argue that national governments had no role to play in politics within Europe. Similarly, few would argue that national governments had complete control over the policy process. Indeed, today even a number of areas of 'high politics', such as foreign policy and security, have become part of the EU policy machine (see Chapter 10). Most would argue that there are a number of hands on the steering wheel of European integration, not all pulling in the same direction at the same time, but the overall direction of the integration process is a result of the to-ing and fro-ing between the various actors. This image is quite neatly captured in the description by Wallace and Wallace (1996) of EU governance as a pendulum, swinging sometimes towards inter-governmental solutions and sometimes towards supranational solutions but not always in equal measure.

From our perspective, examining the workings of the EU as a system of governance is important for a number of reasons. First, it enables us to see a bit more of the workings of the policy process inside the institutions of the EU, and thus allows us to understand what type of political system we are dealing with. Second, it helps us to identify the diversity of actors available to take control (from supranational and national actors to a whole range of sub-national, European and international actors) and to understand how they might interact with one another to co-determine the shape and speed of integration. Finally, it reminds us that there are many interesting questions still to be asked about the final destination for European integration. Are we heading towards a European state? How democratic or efficient will it be? Will there be any turning back?

3.1   Comparing the EU with other political systems

As we have already established, trying to understand what European integration is and where it is headed is one of the hardest tasks for students of the EU. As Sbragia has stated, the EU is 'neither a state nor an international organization' (1992, p.205). It is tempting just to write it off as unique, to halt any further enquiries and to simply adopt a 'wait and see' attitude. In the meantime, we can try to establish whether supra-national actors or intergovernmental actors are dominating its progress. However, when we examine politics in our own countries we have a whole range of questions we like to ask. We want to know about the accountability and responsibility of the government. We want to know how representative policies are of the public will. We want to know which actors are in the inner circles of the decision-making process and we want to know whether the judicial system is fair and impartial. Given that a whole series of important legislation and policies come out of the EU, should we not be asking how these have come about? That is to say, the outputs of the policy-making process in the EU are comparable to the outcomes of government at the national level and have similar effects for significant aspects of economic and social regulation, so why not ask similar questions about its governance?

One indication of this change of emphasis in the study of the EU was related to the academic frameworks employed. Whereas the debate between neo-functionalism and intergovernmentalism had been seen as a question of *integration* and had been conducted largely by scholars influenced by the discipline of international relations (the study of relations and interactions between states), the study of *governance* and the policy process has been dominated by analysts working in political science. And one of the major tools of political science is the study of comparative politics or comparative government, which involves comparing different political systems (or aspects of such systems) with one another, as well as comparing the same system at different periods over time. The purpose of this exercise is to compare and contrast as a means of learning about both the general and the specific features of such systems. In a sense, comparison in the social sciences serves as a substitute for experimentation – we cannot change some aspect of a political system and see what happens, but we can compare different political systems across space and time.

What comparisons can we apply to the EU as a system of governance? We know that the EU is not a state (like, for example, the UK or Germany), and we know that it is not like most international organizations (for example, the United Nations). We know this because we view the EU in comparison with existing states and international organizations. Repeated comparisons over time can help us to establish whether the EU is moving more in one direction than the other, or if it has begun to shift direction. Examining the EU as a system of governance in a comparative framework also opens up new avenues of enquiry for students of European integration. Instead of focusing just on 'either/or' questions, such as whether the EU is dominated by supranational or intergovernmental actors, we can begin to introduce more subtle questions about the nature of European integration and where it is headed. The comparative method enables us to learn much about the EU, about national states and about other international organizations.

When Sbragia (1992) suggested that we might usefully compare the EU with other federal states, this was not because she thought that the EU had become a federal state or even that this was the direction in which it was headed. Instead, Sbragia argued that if we compared the EU system of governance with an established federal system we would learn much both about the operation of the EU and about the operation of existing federal systems. For example, the Court of Justice of the EU, with its wide-ranging powers, is one of the features that makes the EU different from other international organizations. Does the existence of the Court make the EU more like a state, though? By comparing the Court of Justice of the EU with, for example, the Supreme Court in the USA, we might be able to work out one of the ways in which the EU differs from or is similar to existing federal states, and this type of comparison might also make us ask ourselves questions about the role of the Supreme Court in the USA and the role played by Courts in federal structures more generally. For example, according to the US constitution, the Supreme Court is the final court of appeal for both the federal legal system of the USA as a whole and for the different legal systems of the states of the Union. The ECJ, by contrast, is not a 'Supreme Court' for the EU in this sense, since the EU does not have a constitution as such (although some have spoken of the founding Treaties as a constitutionalization process; see Chapter 4) and since not many matters of national law in the member states can be appealed to the ECJ.

Comparison is not only important in helping us to understand the role played by particular institutions or whether the integration process is moving towards the creation of a state. Comparison allows students of integration to ask complex questions about how democratic the EU is, or even simply how efficient it is as a policy machine. Discussions about the democratic deficit in the EU, for example, abound in the popular press. However, these reports are only meaningful when compared with relevant information from the national level and international level. For example, as Laffan (1999) argues, compared with most international organizations the EU – with its directly elected Parliament and relatively open access for interest groups – appears, if not democratic, then highly accessible. When compared with most national governments, however, the EU lacks many of the safeguards that most citizens take for granted at the national level. Perhaps, though, the fact that we expect the EU to have a democratic structure at all tells us something about how we have begun to see the EU. (See Chapter 7 for a full discussion of democracy and the EU.)

3.2   Examining the EU policy process

In the 1990s, students of the EU began to apply systematically the tools of comparative politics to the study of the EU policy process. This required the breaking down of the policy process into smaller parts or stages. Analysts were no longer happy to accept that the same actors were always in the driving seat of European integration. On closer inspection, the real world of EU policy making began to appear much more complicated than a simple contrast between, or even a mixture of, supranationalism and intergovernmentalism. Students of integration wanted to establish a clear picture of which actors were involved, how they became involved and which were most powerful. They also wanted to know which actors were dominant at which stages of the policy process. For example, if the Commission was a competent agenda setter, was it just as effective at ensuring that implementation of legislation took place at the national level? Similarly, they wanted to know if the same actors dominated in different policy areas. For example, if big business was powerful in discussions on the euro, was it similarly powerful in the area of foreign policy?

Since the times of Haas and Hoffmann, the role of national governments, supranational institutions and economic and political interests in the integration process have preoccupied students of European integration. It is now generally accepted that all of these actors, and others besides, have important roles to play in the policy process. These roles are, in part, dictated by the formal rules of the EU as laid down in the founding

Treaties. So, for example, the Commission has always had a right to make policy proposals. The European Parliament has always had a right to comment on these proposals and increasingly has the power to co-decide with the Council of Ministers (made up of national ministers). The Council of Ministers, meanwhile, has long enjoyed the right to take decisions at the EU level. The Court, of course, is charged with adjudicating and enforcing EU legislation.

Changes in these formal rules have, at different stages, led analysts to conclude (as Wallace and Wallace did) that the European integration pendulum swung between the two extremes of the intergovernmental or the supranational position. So, for example, as the Parliament has gained powers and the Council of Ministers has accepted more proposals on the basis of qualified majority voting (QMV) rather than unanimous voting, it could be said that the swing was towards supranationalism. Conversely, as the European Council (made up of the Heads of State and Government of the member states) has come to dominate high-level agenda setting and as various countries negotiate opt-outs in the Treaties on issues such as Economic and Monetary Union (EMU), it could be said that the swing was towards intergovernmentalism.

However, the formal rules only tell a very small part of the story. For a number of years, scholars have also been analysing the impact of a wider range of actors – such as lobbyists, big business and other international organizations – on the informal aspects of the EU policy process; for instance, individuals and organizations who take up issues through the Court of Justice and local authorities who seek funding from the EU institutions all form part of the EU policy process. Peterson (1995) has tried to make sense of this complex mass by introducing the concept of policy networks. A policy network refers to the range of actors (formal and informal) who coalesce around a particular issue or policy area and who exchange resources and information with one another. In the context of, say, EU agriculture this might include the Commission, the farmers' unions, environmental activists, national farm ministers as well as international trade organizations. Establishing which actors are involved in the negotiation and implementation of particular issues may help us to establish who runs the policy process. However, as we will see below, networks may not remain the same at all stages.

In order to study the policy process as a whole, analysts tend to break it down into different stages. Different analysts draw the precise lines in slightly different ways, but most operate with something like the following:

- first, there is the process of agenda setting and policy formulation;
- second, there is the process of decision making itself; and
- third, there are questions of how policy decisions are implemented and enforced.

We will examine next the range of ways in which various actors have become involved and the key stages, as well as the importance of different policy areas and types. Although there are overlaps between these different categories, they help to simplify the complex system which is the EU policy process. We will see how the various studies help us to clarify what European integration is, what it is not, and who is involved. However, the actors involved at the various stages may vary considerably, not least according to the policy area and the type of policy in question. The diverse studies also serve to remind us that there is no easy answer to the question of who runs the EU policy process.

Agenda setting

Mazey and Richardson (1993) have argued that the best time for a lobbyist to become involved in the EU policy process is before a policy proposal has been drawn up. The most effective lobbying that a group or business can do is to give an idea to a Commission official that can be turned into a proposal for policy. Getting into this position is not easy, yet is undoubtedly helped if the lobbyist is a member of an existing policy network, is known to the official and is known to be trustworthy. Peters (1994) has argued that the Commission has considerable powers at the agenda-setting stage. This is aided partly by its formal right of initiative, but partly too by its position at the centre of a network of actors who not only lobby the Commission but also provide it with privileged access to information. Although the Commission is not able to take the final decision on whether most of its proposals will become law, being able to table ideas is an important power in the policy process.

Other supranational institutions also enjoy agenda-setting power. The increasing attention paid to the Parliament by lobbyists is evidence of its increased powers in the EU policy process. Indeed, the Parliament is increasingly found at the centre of policy networks, such that Tsebelis (1994) argued that with the introduction of the co-operation procedure (which gave the Parliament some limited powers to hold up the decision process) in the SEA (1986), Parliament has enjoyed quite considerable agenda-setting power. Judge et al. (1994) have also argued that tiny ripples generated in the Parliament can turn into waves as their effect on the policy process spreads. With changes in the powers of the Parliament agreed in the Treaty on European Union (1992) and in the Treaty of Amsterdam (1997), the Parliament has been going from strength to strength. The agenda-setting power of the Parliament was strengthened by the introduction in the TEU of co-decision between the Council of Ministers and the Parliament in a number of policy areas (see Chapter 7). The number of areas covered by the co-decision procedure was expanded in the Amsterdam Treaty, and as a result the ability of the Parliament to set the agenda for the EU policy process has increased significantly.

The Court's role in the agenda-setting process has also sometimes been underestimated. As issues come before the Court, it is faced with a choice between simple adjudication and adopting more of a policy-making role. We saw in Chapter 4 that the Court has sometimes taken on this policy-making role. Cases that come before the Court may be used to set the agenda for future policy proposals emerging, for example, from the Commission.

So, the traditional supranational institutions – the Commission, the Parliament and the Court, along with lobbyists from all walks of life – have an important role to play at the agenda-setting stage of the policy process. However, those institutions more associated with the intergovernmental dimension of the EU, such as the Council of Ministers and the European Council, also have a key role to play at the agenda-setting stage. The Council of Ministers will frequently suggest to the Commission an issue that should be placed on the agenda for discussion. The fact that the Council (perhaps along with the Parliament) will take the final decision makes it difficult for the Commission to refuse. Meanwhile, the European Council (which was established in 1974 to represent Heads of State and Government at the EU level) has become more and more involved at the very highest level of agenda setting. As the Presidency of the European Council rotates between the member states every six months, the new President always takes the opportunity to outline what their own country wants to see happen in the EU during its Presidency.

Agenda setting, therefore, is complex. A wide range of actors with formal and informal powers are involved. Some of these actors do not fit easily into the intergovernmental/supranational categories and sometimes actors from both categories are involved. As we shall now see, in different policy areas and for different policy types, different networks of actors may dominate the agenda-setting stage.

Decision making

The main decision-making body of the EU has traditionally been the Council of Ministers. Although the European Council is in many respects its political senior and difficult issues may be referred up to the European Council for discussion, the European Council is not normally able to take legally binding decisions (Hayes-Renshaw, 1999). The power to take legally binding decisions is highly significant: all member states are obliged to adhere to these decisions and, as such, legally binding decisions taken at the EU level have a significant effect on the national politics of EU member states.

At first sight, then, it appears that the decision-making stage is profoundly intergovernmental. National ministers sitting in the Council of Ministers take legally binding decisions. However, as always, the situation is not so simple. First, and least important, the Commission does retain the power to make some decisions without requiring the direct approval of the Council. Second, since the establishment of the TEU (1992) and the Amsterdam Treaty (1997) an increasing range of policies must be co-decided by means of an agreement between the Parliament and the Council. Finally, even in those areas where the Council takes decisions alone, it is now much less common for the national representatives to vote on the basis of unanimity. A unanimous vote allows any national minister to veto a proposal which does not fit its national agenda. However, as the Council votes more and more often on the basis of QMV, it is more difficult for any single government to hold up a decision that goes against its national interest.

When analysing decision making we should not think that all the wider policy networks that are involved at the agenda-setting stage suddenly disappear. Although wider groups of lobbyists are not formally allowed into the decision process, they will have helped to formulate the negotiating positions of the decision makers. So networks of actors at the sub-national, national, European and international level will all have had an indirect impact on the decision that finally emerges from the Council of Ministers.

Implementation

This is perhaps the stage when the wider network of policy interests has the most direct impact on the policy process. In the processes of agenda setting and decision making it is always difficult to establish just how much impact any contribution to the debate had. However, implementation is a particularly difficult stage for the EU institutions to manage. Imagine, for example, trying to implement decisions taken in support of deprived regions in the EU. Institutions are dealing with a considerable amount of money. They are negotiating with fifteen member states and with all of the deprived regions within those fifteen member states. EU officials meet with representatives from local and regional governments and with regional development agencies. In addition, they must deal with the leaders of all of the projects that hope to tackle aspects of regional deprivation. The list could go on.

Contrary to much popular opinion, the Commission is not very large or very well resourced. Policing the implementation of the wide range of programmes and policies is extremely difficult and the Commission relies on national and sub-national actors as well as a wider range of policy actors to help with implementation and with the policing of implementation. Richardson (1996) has called this an 'implementation gap'. At this stage it could be argued that the pendulum is swinging towards intergovernmentalism, but remember that some of the actors in the policy network may still be pushing for supranational solutions to implementation problems.

Enforcement

The enforcement stage of the policy process is, perhaps unsurprisingly, mainly dominated by the Court, which is responsible for ensuring that EU law is applied uniformly throughout the member states. The Commission also has a 'watchdog' role and has a responsibility to ensure that EU legislation is complied with. However, as we saw in the case of implementation, it is very difficult for the supranational actors to carry out these tasks without the support of others. For example, the Court is heavily reliant on national courts, which refer issues up to the European Court of Justice for clarification. Similarly, both the Commission and the Court rely on other actors and the wider public to blow the whistle on member states, local authorities or businesses that fail to comply with EU legislation. Once again, the pendulum swings furiously between the intergovernmental and the supranational forces.

Policy areas and types of policy

So far we have considered the various stages of the policy process and some examples of the various actors involved at these different stages. However, different policy areas and different policy types can affect which actors dominate at different stages of the policy process. Indeed, some elements of Hoffman's 'high' and 'low' politics distinction are still relevant today. For instance, although the Commission is normally very important at the agenda-setting stage, the member states have only allowed it a very limited role in Common Foreign and Security Policy, and hence its agenda-setting powers in this area are very weak. Similarly, the Court does not enjoy the same power of enforcement in this area. So, unlike in the stages of agenda setting and enforcement (where the supranational actors are very important), in this policy area the intergovernmental actors, such as national ministers, are much more powerful.

Meanwhile, the range of actors involved in a policy network is likely to change dramatically according to the policy area or issue in question. This is illustrated in the issue of international trade in bananas, which attracts a wide range of international actors from African and South American producers to the US government and international trade organizations. Here, the additional international dimension makes the supranational/ intergovernmental debate seem hardly relevant.

Similarly, when we are trying to assess which actors are most powerful at which stages of the policy process, it is important to ask what type of policy we are talking about. The EU institutions have the power to take a number of different types of decisions. These range from recommendations and opinions (which are not binding on member states) to decisions, directives and regulations (which have binding legal force). Thus, the Commission might be allowed a little more leeway by the Council when it is formulating a non-binding recommendation than when it is putting forward a proposal for a directive which member states will be forced to comply with. A second distinction between policy types is also relevant here. Some policies redistribute funds between people (such as taxation and expenditure). Others simply make rules and regulations with which citizens must comply (such as health and safety policy). As we will see in the next section, it has always been easier for supranational institutions to get agreement from the Council on regulations than on redistributive policies.

3.3   The rise of the regulatory state

Instead of debating the intergovernmental versus supranational characteristics of the EU, an alternative approach to emerge from the study of
the policy process we have just reviewed is not to ask where the EU is
heading, but what it does now.

From this standpoint, Majone (1996) has argued that the EU performs the
functions of a regulatory state, primarily because of the relatively small
budget (see Chapter 8) to which the EU has access when compared with
the wide range of tasks for which it is responsible. Nation states have the
power to tax and to spend, and this is one of the principal means by
which they relate to their citizens. The government gathers in taxes and is
then responsible for ensuring that the money is spent to the satisfaction
of the voters. If the citizens are not happy with, say, the running of the
health or education service or feel that taxes are too high, they will vote
for another party at the next election. The EU does not enjoy this kind of
direct relationship with the citizens of Europe. Although the Parliament is
directly elected, it does not have the power to tax and spend. In order to
redistribute those funds to which the EU has access, any proposal would
require the agreement of national ministers in the Council. These
ministers will always weigh up what effect such a policy will have on
their relationships with their citizens at home. For example, if a
government is cutting back on social security expenditure at home it
may not be very pleased if an EU policy undermines this objective –
especially if that policy makes the EU more popular than the national
government.

Because of its limited budget and the likely resistance of national
representatives to the development of redistributive policies at the EU
level, the EU has developed mostly regulatory policies, which set out
standards or rules with which member states and other economic and
social actors must comply. These rules and regulations include both
economic and social policies. Economic regulations include, for instance,
rules against unfair competition and rules about our rights to buy and sell
products in any EU country. Social regulations include, for instance,
minimum standards of health and safety and our right to equal treatment
at work regardless of whether we are men or women.

In an influential analysis, Majone argued that the regulatory state of the
EU 'may be less of a state in the traditional sense than a web of networks
of national and supranational regulatory institutions held together by
shared values and objectives, and by a common style of policy making'
(1996, p.276). Nation states traditionally have the power to tax and
spend, to redistribute resources from one group of the population to
another, and hence also attempt to manage the overall direction of
economic growth; a regulatory state focuses on addressing instances of
market failure in the completion of the single market. (We will come back
to the question of the EU as a regulatory order or state in Chapter 11.)

Summary

- An alternative to asking who is in control of the integration process – supranational actors or national governments – is to ask how the EU operates as a political system. The EU produces legislation and policy similar to that of national governments, especially in the field of economic and social regulation, and political actors make demands on it in ways that are similar to the political process within member states. That is to say, the EU functions as a political system; it can be viewed as a form of governance.

- To understand the EU as a system of governance, it is useful to compare it with other kinds of political system – the member states, federal systems like the USA, or international organizations.

- The policy process in the EU is complex: it involves a wide range of actors in agenda setting and decision making, and in the implementation and enforcement of policies. Policy-making processes within the EU vary by policy areas as well as in relation to the type of policy being made.

- The EU functions as a system of governance in which a range of different kinds of actors produce policy outcomes that share the values and objectives of regulating market integration and social integration. These outcomes are arrived at by a common style of policy making. The EU can thus be described as representing the rise of a regulatory state.

4   Conclusion

As the networks of actors involved in EU policy widen and the reach of the EU regulatory state extends, politics at the national level is increasingly affected by developments at the EU level. The presence of the EU has increasingly become a part of the daily lives of EU citizens. This is often called the process of Europeanization. The increasingly high profiles of EU politicians at international summits and in trade negotiations has started to seem normal. National media coverage is often taken up with issues relating to the EU, and in many cases these reports express neither opposition to nor support for the EU; they simply report relevant events and information. Most national daily newspapers now employ a 'Europe' correspondent. To some extent, then, news about the EU has become 'home' news in all of the member states.

What effect does this have on citizens of the EU member states? Individuals are beginning to find unremarkable such things as: the presence of the EU flag among other national flags; EU driving licences and passports; signs indicating the support of EU funding; hearing comments like 'isn't there an EU ruling on that?' in relation to working hours; and going through the EU nationals' channel at customs. It could therefore be argued that membership of the EU has become the norm. Perhaps citizens of the member states are becoming Europeanized, maybe even developing a sense of European identity.

This brings us back finally to the questions with which we began. There is no easy answer to the question: 'What is integration?' We have discussed a variety of ways in which the process of European integration has been viewed: as an end product, as a background condition and as an ongoing process. The way that European integration has been understood has changed considerably over time. Although aspects of the supra-nationalism versus intergovernmentalism debate still persist today, it is generally recognized that the EU policy process is very complex, and that politics and governance operate on a number of different levels. We have also seen that comparing this process with other kinds of political systems helps us to understand what kind of political system the EU represents. Some analysts have, for example, argued that the EU can best be understood as a regulatory state.

We have also seen that no single actor has total control over the EU system itself or the external environment in which it operates. At different stages of the policy process, in different policy areas and depending upon the policy type, different actors are able to have more – or less – influence. The balance of power in the integration process has shifted over time but not just between supranational and inter-governmental actors. Today the EU policy process involves a much wider range of actors, ones that do not slot easily into these categories. Crucially, European integration does not just take place in Brussels and Strasbourg. European integration takes place every day at the national level as a wider range of actors are affected by EU policies and as membership of the EU becomes the norm for citizens of the fifteen member states.

References

Deutsch, K. (1967) *Arms Control and Atlantic Community*, Chichester, Wiley.

Haas, E. (1958) *The Uniting of Europe*, Stanford, CA, Stanford University Press.

Haas, E. (1968, 2nd edn) *The Uniting of Europe*, Stanford, CA, Stanford University Press.

Hayes-Renshaw, F. (1999) 'The European Council and the Council of Ministers' in Cram, L., Dinan, D. and Nugent, N. (eds) *Developments in the European Union*, London, Macmillan.

Hoffman, S. (1966) 'Obstinate or obsolete? The fate of the nation state and the case of Western Europe', *Daedalus*, vol.95, pp.892–908.

Judge, D., Earnshaw, D. and Cowan, N. (1994) 'Ripples or waves: the European Parliament in the European Community policy process', *Journal of European Public Policy*, vol.1, no.1, pp.27–52.

Laffan, B. (1999) 'Democracy in the European Union' in Cram. L., Dinan, D. and Nugent, N. (eds) *Developments in the European Union*, London, Macmillan.

Majone, G. (1996) 'A European regulatory state?' in Richardson, J. (ed.) *European Union: Power and Policy Making*, London, Routledge.

Mazey, S. and Richardson, J. (1993) *Lobbying in the European Community*, Oxford, Oxford University Press.

Moravcsik, A. (1991) 'Negotiating the Single European Act: national interests and conventional statecraft in the European Community', *International Organization*, vol.45, pp.19–56.

Moravcsik, A. (1993) 'Preferences and power in the European Community: a liberal intergovernmentalist approach', *Journal of Common Market Studies*, vol.31, no.4, pp.473–524.

Peters, B. (1994) 'Agenda setting in the European Community', *Journal of European Public Policy*, vol.1, no.1, pp.9–26.

Peterson, J. (1995) 'Decision making in the European Union: towards a framework for analysis', *Journal of European Public Policy*, vol.2, no.1, pp.69–93.

Richardson, J. (1996) 'Eroding EU policies: implementation gaps, cheating and re-steering' in Richardson, J. (ed.) *European Union: Power and Policy Making*, London, Routledge.

Sandholtz, W. and Zysman, J. (1989) '1992: Recasting the European bargain', *World Politics*, vol.42, no.1, pp.95–128.

Sbragia, A. (1992) 'Thinking about the European future: the uses of comparison' in Sbragia, A. (ed.) *Euro-Politics*, Washington, DC, Brookings.

Spinelli, A. (1966) *The Eurocrats: Conflict and Crisis in the European Community*, NY, Johns Hopkins Press.

Tsebelis, G. (1994) 'The power of the European Parliament as a conditional agenda setter', *American Political Science Review*, vol.88, no.1, pp.128–42.

Wallace, H. and Wallace, W. (1996, 3rd edn) 'Politics and policy in the EU: the challenge of governance' in Wallace, H. and Wallace, W. (eds) *Policy-Making in the European Union*, Oxford, Oxford University Press.

Wallace, H., Wallace, W. and Webb, C. (1977) *Policy-Making in the European Communities*, Chichester, John Wiley and Sons.

Further reading

Hix, S. (1999) *The Political System of the European Union*, London, Macmillan.

Richardson, J. (ed.) (1996) *European Union: Power and Policy Making*, London, Routledge.

Rosamond, B. (2000) *Theories of European Integration*, London, Macmillan.

Chapter 7
Democracy and democratization in the European Union

Christopher Lord

1   Introduction

Until recently, asking why it is important to study democracy and the European Union (EU) would probably have provoked the straightforward answer that it is because the EU suffers from a democratic deficit. The idea behind the notion of a 'democratic deficit' is that decisions in the EU are in some ways insufficiently representative of, or accountable to, the nations and people of Europe. But what if it turns out that the EU is not entirely deficient in democratic politics? It would surely be as important to study the half of the bottle that is full as to study the half that is empty. A supranational or multinational attempt to provide democracy beyond the state would, after all, be a strikingly novel challenge to the received wisdom that only states can be democratic.

In any case, the notion of a democratic deficit turns out, on closer inspection, to be one that begs more questions than it answers. In particular, it is unclear whether the deficit should be defined by comparing the Union with the democratic practice in member states or with certain principles of democratic governance. The first amounts to a crude transposition of standards between arenas that takes no account of the EU's unique character as a non-state and multinational political system. The second is more promising, but also more difficult, since it requires two types of test, not one. In addition to core attributes, for which any system must 'test positive' if it is to be labelled democratic, there are other tests that develop only in context (Schmitter and Karl, 1992). These include priorities and trade-offs between the core attributes, add-on standards and, of course, means of institutional realization.

There is, however, a third and even deeper problem with focusing on the idea that European integration is in democratic deficit. How can we be sure that such a deficit exists unless we first ask whether the EU should be a democracy at all? The answer to this question is by no means self-evident. There are many kinds of institution that are justifiably non-democratic, and until recently it was often assumed that the EU was among them (Bellamy and Castiglione, 2000). On the one hand, it was thought to be indirectly controlled by its member states, all of which are themselves democracies. On the other, it appeared to operate within a 'permissive consensus' in which its policy outputs were thought to be too uncontroversial to require any special democratic authority.

Part of the case for the democratization of the Union is that the foregoing conditions no longer hold. By introducing majority procedures to many forms of policy making, and by making supranational institutions more autonomous, successive Treaty changes between 1986 and 1997 have eroded the scope for national democracies to exercise control of decision making at the European level. The notion that the EU need not be democratic since it is not involved in politically contentious allocations of values is also hard to sustain in the post-1986 Union, which distributes values between states, regions, generations, the sexes, socio-economic groups and individuals.

Public bodies that are engaged in controversial decisions about who gets what will often need to make decisions that create losers and demand sacrifices (at least in the short term). Under such conditions they are likely to prevail and be effective only when their *right* to make difficult decisions is widely acknowledged by citizens. We call that right 'political legitimacy', and the question of whether the EU ought to be democratic is largely one of whether its citizenry considers that to be a precondition for it being legitimate (see Beetham and Lord, 1998; Abromeit, 1998).

This chapter will seek to explore a number of questions. In Section 2 I shall consider what democracy means as a political principle and how it can be realized in institutional terms. I shall also examine how democratic principles might be applied to the European Union and at what level – intergovernmental or supranational – they might be institutionalized. Next, I shall ask about the extent to which the EU is democratic in its current form and how its existing democratic features can be developed. In Section 3 I shall consider the democratization of the EU through national institutions, primarily at the intergovernmental level. And in Section 4 I shall look at the democratization of the EU through its own purpose-built supranational institutions. Finally, I shall ask whether the EU could be made more democratic and, in Section 5, briefly consider proposals to strengthen the power of the European Parliament, to directly elect the President of the Commission and to conduct Euro-wide referendums.

2   What is democracy?

To understand why democracy is such a powerful instrument of legitimacy we need to clarify its guiding principles. If democracy is a system of government in which the people rule themselves, it follows that its core attributes can be reduced to two. The first is that the public must be able to control those who make decisions on its behalf, even where it does not directly assume the reins of government; and, second, citizens should exercise such control as equals, since a condition in which some decide on behalf of others is paternalism, not democracy (Beetham, 1994). Pulling these ideas together, Albert Weale defines democracy as a condition in which 'important public decisions on questions of law and policy depend, directly or indirectly, upon public opinion formally expressed by citizens of the community, the vast bulk of whom have equal political rights' (Weale, 1999, p.14).

But what is needed to ensure that policies and laws depend on public opinion? One requirement is that the public should consent to the key office-holders and policy programmes by which they are governed. Another is that decision makers should be representative of the governed, at least in the sense of being institutionally constrained to consider the needs and values of the public. Some also suggest that the decision makers should represent a typical cross-section of society. A third requirement is that the public should have regular opportunities to judge the performance of the governing authority and replace it with another. In sum, public control and political equality are the defining features of democratic rule; and authorization, representation and accountability are the key principles by which it is realized (Weir and Beetham, 1999). Democracy is a powerful instrument of legitimation, first, because a government that is in some sense chosen by the people is necessarily one that enjoys their consent and, second, because the public can be said to have ownership of the political system when there are institutional incentives for decision makers to track the needs and values of citizens, rather than impose preferences of their own.

Yet to study the EU is also to be aware of the dangers of assuming that the relationship between democracy and legitimacy is a simple one. We shall see that some strategies for the democratization of the EU could yield less, not more, legitimacy. To begin to see why, it is worth considering the following two reasons why the construction of a Euro democracy is likely to be an unusually difficult undertaking.

First, consider the size and diversity of the political system. The EU consists of fifteen member states of 373 million inhabitants stretched out across an area from Lisbon to Helsinki. Its membership could yet rise to between 25 and 30 states and a total of more than 500 million inhabitants. A democratic EU would have to institutionalize representative, accountable and responsive government in a very large political unit with boundaries that have yet to be defined. It would also probably encounter resistance to 'one size fits all' solutions, not least because expectations of what it is to be governed democratically may vary across the Union.

And secondly, consider the novelty and unfinished nature of the political system. The 'Weale definition' of democracy presupposes the existence of 'public opinion', 'citizenship' and 'community'. Where there is no sense of common identity, even a democratically impeccable political system may find that many citizens question its right to make collectively binding decisions. This is likely to be a problem for all new political systems. The EU faces two further difficulties: citizen loyalties have already been mobilized around powerful feelings of national identity; and the Union is still incomplete, in both its membership and its institutional configuration, with the result that the citizen is required to identify with something that is indefinite and changeable.

2.1 Institutionalizing democracy

If all of this suggests that democratic institution building should be carefully matched to the peculiarities of the political system, then it is perhaps fortunate that democratic systems can be constructed in a variety of ways. In the discussion that follows, we shall see how a Euro democracy might plausibly be pieced together from combinations along at least four different dimensions of choice.

Direct versus indirect democracy. Direct democracy is where the people take the major decisions of government. The alternative is that the people exercise public control indirectly through appointed representatives.

Consensus versus majoritarian democracy. Majoritarian democracy is where decisions can be taken by a bare majority of the people or their representatives. Its proponents argue that any alternative would amount to minority rule. Consensus democracy is where the aim is to align policies with the preferences of the greatest number of citizens or their representatives, rather than with the preferences of a simple majority (Lijphart, 1984). Its defenders argue that any alternative allows minorities to be excluded and is not really rule by the people as a whole. Examples of consensus democracy include super-majoritarian decision rules (where decisions need the approval of more than 50 per cent), federal systems that parcel out decision making between layers of government, consociational systems that guarantee the participation of many cultural segments in public decisions, and arrangements for the inclusion of opposition parties in some of the tasks of government.

Parliamentary versus presidential democracy. There are two ways in which executive power can be made to depend on the public. Under presidential systems, the chief executive is directly elected by the public. Under parliamentary systems, the government of the day is selected by a popularly elected parliament. The EU has a double-headed executive made up of the Commission, which proposes initiatives, and the Council of Ministers, which takes decisions. Neither is elected at the level of the political system itself, although the Council consists of one minister per national government, elected by his or her member state.

Strategic versus communicative democracy. Strategic models of democracy presuppose that actors have clear and fixed views of their interests. The main goal of democratic institutions is then to find the most efficient means of aggregating individuals' preferences into collective actions, albeit subject to various normative criteria of fairness. Communicative models of democracy hold that preferences must be debated within the political system, either because they are not fully formed prior to a process of discussion, or because group action is so very different from individual action, both actually and morally. A large question for the EU is whether it can move beyond the politics of bargaining between states to a politics of deliberation between groups and citizens (Bellamy and Warleigh, 1998).

2.2 Intergovernmental and supranational approaches

If there are various ways in which the EU might be made democratic, there are also different *levels* at which its democratization could occur. It is useful to distinguish two possibilities. In *intergovernmental* approaches, the EU is democratized through the elected institutions of its member states. Each national democracy has to ratify any change to EU treaties. Most important decisions have to be approved by the Council of Ministers, on which each national government is represented. Those governments are, in turn, accountable to their parliaments and electorates. In *supranational* approaches, entirely new democratic institutions are established at the European level. They are purpose-made for the EU's political system, and they operate with at least some consistency across the Union as a whole. In addition to these two dominant models there are some pressures, particularly in federal member states (Austria, Belgium and Germany), for regions to be given a role as units of representation at the European level. It is, however, essential to note that the intergovernmental and supra-national approaches are separated here only for the purposes of analytical clarity. In practice, many EU decisions are open to the joint influence, even co-determination, of bodies whose claims to be representative are established at different levels: European, national and even sub-national.

Summary

- There is likely to be a strong – but problematical – relationship between the democratization of the EU and the EU's acceptability to its citizens.

- The development of democratic politics beyond the state challenges the outer limits of what has previously been thought possible in institution building. If successful in the case of the EU, it may have even wider implications for the governance of globalization.

- The construction of democratic politics at the European level will be an unusually difficult undertaking. A mixture of care and originality will be needed to find strategies of democratization appropriate to a non-state political system made up of many nationalities.

3 Democratization of the EU through national institutions

One way to democratize the EU through national institutions would be to employ a 'consociational' approach. The notion of consociational democracy was introduced by Arend Lijphart (1977) to describe a form of consensual democracy in which majority rule is replaced by joint decision making based on legislative coalitions, the proportional distribution of executive authority and the presence of veto procedures in the case of important decisions. Lijphart argued that such a system was particularly appropriate for 'plural' societies, in which the main political divisions were vertical cleavages between national, religious or ethnic communities rather than horizontal cleavages of class within a single people. Some have argued that elements of this model are also relevant to the multinational political system of the EU. Under this model, national vetoes would be retained on a number of decisions. There would be no aspiration to create a democratic identity at the European level and the EU would have no competence in areas that bear on the reproduction of national identity, such as education. Collective decisions would be negotiated between democratically elected national élites, with no direct involvement of the public in the political process. To ensure fair bargaining, all national élites would have to be proportionally represented in each EU institution (Chryssochou, 1994; Lijphart, 1997).

Aspects of this model are, indeed, already present in the EU. Matters on which member states (for the most part) retain vetoes include taxation, immigration and asylum, the Common Foreign and Security Policy (second pillar) and Justice and Home Affairs (third pillar). As we have seen, all Treaty changes require the unanimous consent of member states, which are then free to choose their own preferred method of democratic ratification, with some opting for national parliamentary approval and others opting for referendums. In recent years, a 'permanent revolution' of Treaty changes – the Single European Act (1986), the Treaty on European Union (1992), the Amsterdam Treaty (1997) and the Nice Treaty, likely to be concluded at the end of 2000 – together with successive waves of enlargement – Austria, Finland and Sweden in 1995 and the East European countries in the years to come – have turned the politics of ratification into regular tests of public support for the integration process. The TEU, for example, was put to referendum in Denmark, France and Ireland. Austria, Finland, Norway and Sweden held referendums on joining the EU in 1994. The British, Danish and Swedish governments are all committed to holding a referendum before joining Stage 3 of Monetary Union.

As mechanisms of democratic consent, national parliamentary votes and referendums have their strengths and weaknesses. The first may cope better than the second with the objection that Treaty changes are complex packages that cannot be reduced to the 'binary choice' involved in a vote of approval or disapproval. On the other hand, it is arguable that ultimate decisions on the location of political power should be taken by the public itself, not least because EU Treaty changes do not involve a simple transfer of power from national to European level: they also entail a parallel shift within domestic arenas. Executive discretion is increased at the expense of political control by the public or its representatives (Dehousse, 1997). As executives have a substantial presence in national parliaments – to the point at which many are described as 'executive dominated' – the problem with parliamentary ratification of Treaty changes is that it may put national executives in a position to approve extensions to their own powers (Lord, 1999).

Another consociational feature is the proportional representation of nationalities across the range of Union institutions. All governments appoint at least one Commissioner, and there is an assumption that the President of the Commission will be succeeded by someone from another member state. All member states have a seat on the Council and the opportunity to hold its rotating presidency for a period of six months. Both Council and Parliament over-represent smaller member states in a manner that underlines the principle that it is national communities – not just citizens – who should be treated as the units of representation in the EU's political system. Within the Parliament the bureau of each party group contains one representative per national party. Even the Governing Council of the European Central Bank works on the principle 'one national central bank, one vote', in contrast to the US Federal Reserve and the Deutschebundesbank, which do not allow permanent representation to all regional sub-units.

3.1   Beyond consociationalism

One way of going beyond consociationalism, while continuing to rely on national institutions to make EU decisions representative and accountable, is to assume that national élites should not just be left to bargain among themselves at Union level: they should also be subject to continuous supervision by their parliaments and publics. There is already significant potential for national parliaments to exercise influence and control. They can review the negotiating positions of their governments before meetings of the Council of Ministers. They can scrutinize draft legislation, which has to be circulated to each national parliament in its own language at least six weeks before it is voted on in the Council. They also have important discretion in deciding how Union legislation is to be transposed into national law, since directives require member states only to achieve certain results, without specifying the methods to be employed.

The European Affairs Committee (EAC) of the Danish Folketing and the scrutiny committees of the Westminster Parliament are often taken as the leading models of national parliamentary involvement in EU questions. The EAC has seventeen members drawn from senior members of each party represented in the Folketing. The Danish government has to secure the committee's authorization for its negotiating position in the Council of Ministers. Council minutes and agendas are then used to check that the government has, indeed, followed the position of the EAC (Arter, 1996, pp.110–24). In the British case, ministers are not allowed to agree a position in the Council until a legislative proposal has completed the scrutiny process in the House of Commons. Scrutiny committees in the House of Commons and House of Lords now consider around 1,000 documents a year (Norton, 1996, p.96).

3.2 The use of national institutions to democratize the EU

The main argument for making the EU democratic through national representative structures is that, for the overwhelming majority of citizens, national and sub-national identifications are stronger than European ones. Most are, moreover, likely to feel that their national democratic institutions are closer, more visible, more familiar, and more comprehensible.

It might, however, be objected that reliance on national democratic institutions is precluded by those very features of the contemporary Union – majority voting between states and supranational institutions with autonomous powers – that set us off on the search for a strategy to democratize the Union. One way around this is to argue that there are strong structural incentives for majority voting and supranational institutions to be used to increase the efficiency with which national preferences are realized, rather than to replace national preferences with something else (Moravcsik, 1998; Pollack, 1997). Powers may be recalled or revised by subsequent Treaty changes. The Union is, moreover, dependent on the financial and administrative resources of each of its members.

The difficulty, however, is that national democracies may find it difficult to meet all the conditions required for the effective supervision of Union institutions: access to information, opportunities for cross-examination of decision makers and so on. This results in what is known as 'agency loss': the delegated authority will always have significant scope to do its own thing. Indeed, the notion of supervision of the Union by national democratic institutions has to contend with double agency loss: the collective of governments on the Council will have difficulty supervising every act of the Commission; and individual national parliaments will have difficulty supervising the overall operation of the Council, with its powerful socializing effects and its arrangements for delegating decisions to technocratic committees (Hayes-Renshaw and Wallace, 1997). Nor can any national democracy revise or recall Treaty powers without the consent of all the others. Even exit options – from the Union or particular policies – are constrained by the heavy investments that have already been made in adjusting to Europe and the dislocation that would be caused by attempts to break with established policies (Pierson, 1998).

Excessive reliance on the link between Union, national governments, national parliaments and domestic electorates could even de-democratize the member states, rather than democratize the EU.

- Governments may use their privileged access to Union decision making to improve their position relative to domestic democratic actors. They may, for example, confront national parliaments or electorates with *faits accomplis* negotiated at the European level, or shift decisions between the two arenas to where the constraints of opposition are weakest.

- National supervision of EU policy is often realized by networking between functionally equivalent government departments in different member states. But the partial fragmentation of policy making into a series of transgovernmental processes is hard to marry with the notion that governments are chosen and held accountable for overall programmes of government (Dehousse, 1997).

- The issues on which national democratic institutions are elected may not correspond to those that are most salient in the European arena. Voters will, therefore, experience a restriction of choice if there is no mechanism for expressing separate preferences in relation to the two political systems.

- Attempts to make two political systems (national and European) representative and accountable through domestic democratic processes may put the European system under stress. The obvious example is the division and reduced effectiveness of party systems in those member states where the supranational–intergovernmental cleavage cross-cuts the left–right differences that structure domestic politics (Andeweg, 1995).

Summary

- Applying the notion of consociational democracy to the political system of the EU is one means of establishing a consensual basis for European democracy in a predominantly intergovernmental context.

- The democratization of the EU might move beyond this consociational model through the greater scrutiny of national élite decision making in the Union on the part of national parliaments and through popular referendums conducted at the national level.

- The principal strength of making the EU democratic through national representative structures is that, for most people, their national political identities are stronger than their European ones. The main weakness of this, primarily intergovernmental, strategy is that it does not really serve to legitimate the more supranational aspects of the EU.

4 A democratic political system at the European level?

If there are difficulties in using national representative bodies to make the EU democratic, what of the alternative of providing the EU with its own purpose-built democratic institutions? The nearest the contemporary Union comes to this is the European Parliament, which is directly elected every five years by all adult citizens. This raises three closely related questions. How successful are European elections in linking the policy outputs of the Union to the preferences of citizens? How do MEPs organize themselves for the purposes of representation? What powers of public control are exercised by the European Parliament? The following sections examine each of these elements in turn.

4.1 Euro elections

What do Euro elections tell us about the prospects for a Euro democracy? It is possible to imagine a system of European elections that has no relation to member states. All votes could be counted in the one place and all seats allocated centrally. This is not, however, how European elections currently work. Since 1979 each member state has formed a constituency to elect a bloc of MEPs, and each has used its own electoral system to do so.

The absence of a uniform electoral procedure is less of a problem than it was in the first four directly elected parliaments (1979–99), when the left–right balance was significantly distorted by the decision of one member state (the UK) to continue with a plurality system while the rest employed varying forms of proportional representation. Although this difficulty has now been removed, representation in the EP continues to reflect a patchwork of far from uniform voting systems. The relative strength of the liberal and green groups in the last three EPs, for example, has been determined by whether it is the Frei Demokratische Partei (FDP) or the Grüne that has succeeded in clearing the 5 per cent hurdle required for a share in the centrally allocated seats in German elections.

Given that MEPs are elected in national blocs, it is not surprising that voters get to choose between national, and not European, parties. Most accounts follow Karlheinz Reif and Hermann Schmitt in analysing European elections as 'second-order national contests' (Reif and Schmitt, 1980; Franklin, 1996). The principal insight of this theory is that both voters and parties consider competition for power in the national arena to be so much more important than competition for power in the European arena that they use their only opportunity to elect a Union institution to express domestic political preferences. The consequences of second-order voting include the following issues.

- European election campaigns are dominated by national issues. Although political parties get together to issue pan-European manifestos, they dare not make these prominent in their campaigning, since that would mean ignoring the domestic issues that the voters really care about.

- Participation in European elections is lower than in national elections, as most voters consider them less important. In the five elections that have been held since 1979 the difference in turnout has averaged around 20 per cent, although it is closer to 25 per cent if those countries that hold general elections on the same day as European elections are discounted (Hix, 1999).

- The results of European elections are strongly influenced by the domestic political cycle. If they are held immediately before or after a national election they tend to mirror it. If they are held during the mid-term of a national parliament they tend to register an anti-government swing.

- European elections tend to favour small national parties. This is, first, because of mid-term protest votes against sitting governments and, second, because voters in European elections need not feel constrained to plump for parties with a real chance of winning power. The consequence for the EP, however, is that there will be an element of fragmentation in party structures, at least in freshly elected parliaments, before the more centralizing effects of the parliament's party system have had an opportunity to operate (Bardi, 1996).

- European elections tend to favour domestic parties of opposition. In the 1994–99 Parliament, parties of opposition held 61 per cent of the seats and parties of government held 39 per cent of the seats. The unprecedented success of the centre-left in gaining a presence in thirteen out of fifteen governments on the Council of Ministers was counterbalanced in 1999 by the election of the first Parliament since 1973 to be dominated by the centre-right. The likelihood that the EP will provide high levels of representation to national parties that are not a part of the Council of Ministers may be a useful addition to the checks and balances in the Union's political system. But this effect should not be exaggerated, since the EP is constrained in the degree to which it can adopt an oppositional attitude to the Council. Both bodies have to negotiate legislative outcomes to their mutual satisfaction.

- The overall implication of second-order voting is that there is no systematic electoral linkage to the politics of representation or accountability. Electoral outcomes can neither be interpreted as preferences for the prospective development of Union policies over the coming five years (representation) nor taken as comments on the performance of EP or EU over the previous five years (accountability).

European elections might have been expected to have become less second-order in character as the EP acquired more powers of relevance to voters and parties. However, participation has fallen in each election since 1979, even though the last three of those elections (1989, 1994 and

1999) all followed Treaty changes that gave the EP more powers. Indeed, the most precipitous decline of all occurred in June 1999, a mere three months after the EP demonstrated its power to force the resignation of the Commission.

The inverse relationship between the empowerment of the EP and voter participation has led to some questioning of the second-order model. In an extensive survey based on the 1994 elections, Jean Blondel, Richard Sinnott and Palle Svensson found that voters and abstainers differed little in their estimates of EP powers. Their explanation for the low turnout is not that the EP is perceived to be lacking in power. Rather, it is an understandable consequence of a separation of powers: a vote for the legislature only partially determines where power lies in the political system. It is significant in this regard that the US Congress also suffers from low voter participation (Blondel et al., 1999).

4.2   Representation through the European Parliament

Do parties operate as democratic intermediaries at the European level? Although MEPs are elected under national party labels, they serve in the European Parliament in multinational party groups (Hix and Lord, 1997). Table 7.1 (opposite) shows the groups that were formed at the beginning of the present European Parliament, which was elected in June 1999. On the whole the groups are organized along a left–right continuum that corresponds to the main ideological party families found in most member states: socialists, conservatives, Christian democrats, liberals, Greens and the far left and far right. The Union of European Nations, however, attempts to project intergovernmentalist perspectives onto the integration issue, while the Europe of Democracies and Diversities Group takes an overtly eurosceptic stance.

There are strengths and weaknesses in this structure of representation. Although the Euro groups are largely unknown to the public, they do correspond to voter preferences on what is overwhelmingly the most important dimension of political choice in the work of the European Parliament: the left–right spectrum (Thomassen and Schmitt, 1997). But pressure to align along a left–right dimension can sometimes make it difficult for MEPs to represent their voters on the dimension of EU politics concerned with supranational versus intergovernmental approaches to institution building. For example, the British Conservatives, who make up a full 5 per cent of the present EP, are only associate members of the European People's Party. They are in a dilemma: the EPP best fits their views on left–right questions, but its centre of gravity on inter-governmental–supranational issues is far removed from the Conservative Party's largely eurosceptic electorate.

An analysis of how MEPs vote provides an indicator of the representation offered by the party groups in the EP. A striking feature is the frequency with which the main party groups of the centre-right (EPP) and the

Table 7.1   Groups in the European Parliament

LEFT			RIGHT	
Name	**Size**		**Name**	**Size**
Party of European Socialists (PES)	180		European People's Party (EPP)	233
Labour Party	*28*		*Conservative Party*	*36*
SDLP (Northern Ireland)	*2*		*Ulster Unionist*	*1*
Greens/EFA	48		European Liberal and Democratic Party (ELDR)	51
UK Greens	*2*		*Liberal Party*	*10*
Scottish Nationalists	*2*			
Plaid Cymru	*2*			
United European Left (UEL)	18		Union of European Nations (UEN)	18
INDEPENDENT			**EUROSCEPTIC**	
Name	**Size**		**Name**	**Size**
Technical Group of Independents (TGI)	16		Europe of Democracies and Diversities Group (EDD)	16
			UK Independence Party	*3*
Non-attached	8			
Democratic Unionist Party	*1*			

The group affiliations of UK parties are shown in italics.

(adapted from European Parliament, 1999)

centre-left (PES) vote together. Institutional factors constrain MEPs to follow this 'grand coalition' approach to politics. Since it is stipulated in the Treaties that the Parliament can exercise its powers only on a majority of its membership (314 out of the present membership of 626), not just on a majority of the votes cast, winning coalitions will almost always need to include the EPP and PES on the following assumptions: first, that there will always be significant levels of absenteeism (usually around 30 per cent) and, second, that representatives from neighbouring positions on the political spectrum are more likely to form alliances than those who hold polar opposite views (Hix, 1999, pp.79–84).

A common critique is that collaboration between the centre-left and centre-right suspends political competition in the EP, reducing it to a cartel in which MEPs collude to carve up the benefits that accrue from the exercise of parliamentary powers. The long-term cost, according to this view, is the absence of the contestation that would highlight public awareness of the choices or cleavages intrinsic to European integration. This factor interacts with the second-order character of Euro elections to constrain the development of a Euro democracy. It is interesting in the light of this critique that the formation of the 1999–2004 Parliament should have been accompanied by what appears to have been a bid to define an alternative to a dominant EPP/PES alignment. A high-profile spat between the two main groups on the election of the President of the new Parliament produced not only an agreement that the EPP and ELDR would support each other's candidates for the presidency of the first and second halves of the Parliament respectively, but also a continuing commitment to co-operation between the groups (Lord, 2000).

Not all assessments of grand-coalition politics in the EP are negative. Closer examination of the figures reveals that EPP/PES alignments are often only one part of a more inclusive consensus, in which several other groups regularly end up voting with the EPP and PES. Institutional mechanisms that constrain actors to build consensus not only across member states but also across party political divisions may also be defensible in the case of a novel and transnational political system. The Union could well run into legitimacy problems if it consistently excludes a mainstream party political family from the benefits of integration. Nor need rules requiring high levels of inter-party consensus on final decisions preclude political competition and contestation at earlier stages of political debate, notably in the committees of the EP that provide the in-depth preparation of decisions.

4.3   The powers of the European Parliament

There are two main ways in which representative bodies can exercise an element of control over executives. One is through the power to appoint or dismiss key office-holders, who then go on to supervise the various bureaucracies that make up a governing authority. The other is through granting or withholding the key resources (finance and legislative authority) that an executive body needs to function effectively. The conventional wisdom is that the European Parliament has only slender powers of executive formation or dismissal. On the other hand, its legislative powers can be impressive. As such, it is often thought to have a closer resemblance to the US Congress than to national parliaments in Western Europe.

The European Parliament: democratic control and accountability?

Powers of executive formation and dismissal

Since the Treaty of Rome (1957) the European Assembly, and then the European Parliament, has had the power to dismiss the Commission. Two conditions for the exercise of this power have operated throughout: first, the Commission is a collegiate body that can only be dismissed as a whole and, second, the MEPs voting for a censure motion must form a 'double majority'. That is, they must secure two-thirds of the votes cast and represent more than half of the Parliament's membership.

Since the TEU (1992) the Parliament has had the further power to confirm or reject the incoming Commission selected by the member states. In 1994 the EP maximized its leverage by unpacking the investiture process into a three-stage obstacle course stretched out over six months. First, a vote was taken on the European Council's choice for the presidency. Individual Commissioners were then invited to 'hearings' with those parliamentary committees that corresponded to their proposed portfolios. Only then was a vote taken on the overall programme and composition of the Commission.

Although the EP came within eighteen votes of rejecting Jacques Santer as President, the 1994 example highlighted important constraints on the EP's powers of confirmation. In the vote on the presidency, national governments seem to have leant on MEPs via national parties, so confirming that a parliament may gain a role in executive formation only at some price to its independence (Hix and Lord, 1996). When it came to the selection of individual Commissioners, the Parliament was critical of five nominees, but the College was eventually confirmed without a single change. A weakness in the EP's position is that member governments are probably better placed to withstand a stalemate in which it is impossible to agree the appointment of a new Commission.

The EP was, however, in a stronger position when it came to confirm the 1999–2004 Commission. The Amsterdam Treaty of 1997 authorized the ambitious multi-stage process the EP had first used in 1994, and increased the EP's scope to bargain over the shape of the new Commission by giving the incoming Commission President the power to reject national nominations to other places in the College. Some MEPs suggested this power should be used to block a nominee who failed to win its confidence or, more radically, to align the party political balance of the Commission with the results of European elections. In the event, the EP did not press its reservations about any candidate Commissioner to the point of rejection, and the Commission was eventually formed with a slight preponderance of nominees from the centre-left, even though European elections had favoured the centre-right.

A further factor that potentially strengthened the role of the EP in the investiture of the Prodi Commission was that it had demonstrated its power to force the resignation of its predecessor in March 1999: the more the EP is capable of removing a Commission, the more care will need to be taken in aligning its composition or programme with parliamentary opinion. Until the 1990s it was thought not only that the EP would be unlikely ever to secure the double majority needed for a censure but also that dismissal was a 'nuclear option'. That is, the power of dismissal would be made ineffective by the drastic consequences of its use, not least for an EP with an interest in a strong Commission capable of pressing supranational perspectives on the Council. It was even unclear what would happen if member governments re-appointed the same Commission, thus forcing the EP into a stand-off that would paralyse Union decision making.

Yet signs of parliamentary assertiveness began to appear long before the censure of the Santer Commission. Martin Westlake (1994) suggests that the threat of censure may be effective even if the probability of it happening is low. A censure motion can be tabled with the support of only 10 per cent of the Parliament's membership, and its own absence of electoral legitimacy only sharpens the Commission's sensitivity to any move that questions its credibility. In February 1997 the EP introduced the novelty of a 'conditional vote of censure' at the same time as setting up a special committee of enquiry to look into the BSE crisis. Given that the vote had the support of 422 out of 519 voting members, the EP signalled its capacity to move on to a full censure in the event of the Commission failing to respond to the Parliamentary Committee of Enquiry. When the threat was finally lifted in November 1997, the Parliament claimed a series of concessions: new legislation on food hygiene, a reorganization of the Commission to reduce conflicts of interest between those responsible for consumer and producer interests, and support in the Intergovernmental Conference (IGC) for an expanded role for the Parliament in the protection of human health (Westlake, 1997).

The resignation of the Santer Commission saw a further refinement to the censure procedure that was of enormous significance: a quasi-judicial stage was added as Commission and Parliament agreed that an independent committee should investigate allegations that had been made against individual Commissioners. This had three effects. First, it involved the implicit formulation of standards of good governance specific to the EU arena, against which Commissioners were then to be judged. Second, it facilitated the process of double majority formation in the EP, which had previously been thought a barrier to the power of parliamentary censure. Without an investigative process to prove allegations, the EP had struggled to find a majority within and across its party groups. In contrast, parliamentary support for censure became a foregone conclusion once the independent committee published its report. Neither MEPs nor the Parliament as a whole would have been able to maintain public credibility without voting for dismissal. The Santer Commission, accordingly, resigned before a formal vote of the EP was even taken. The third effect was that the investigative process made the censure process non-partisan in nature at the same time as it facilitated majority formation. The power of dismissal was not exercised from any particular political point of view. The eventual outcome was a consensus for dismissal across party groups. Indeed, the Commission resigned the moment it was clear from meetings of the EP's Conference of Presidents (party leaders) that a censure motion would be supported throughout the Parliament.

Legislative powers of the European Parliament

As we have seen, a representative body can control a process of government by granting or withholding resources, as well as by appointing and dismissing office-holders. The EP's powers over the EU's budget are constrained, since only a small proportion of funding commitments can ever be varied at any one time. On the other hand, the EP's powers over the EU's legislation may offer significant scope for control. This is for various reasons. First, rule making, rather than the redistribution of financial resources, is the main business of the EU (see Chapter 4 and Majone, 1996). Second, the EP does not have to follow the orders of a government organized in its midst, and this gives it more freedom than national parliaments to legislate as it feels fit. Third, the EP's legislative powers provide the one point within the EU's political system at which a representative body has some hold over both parts of the EU's two-headed executive, that is, the Commission and Council. Fourth, most of the economic, social and environmental policies of the Union (the first pillar) either give the EP a final say (with the Council) or allow it a role in structuring the choices faced by the Commission and Council. Simplifying things greatly, the EP's legislative powers are as follows.

- The EP gives its opinion on Commission proposals before they reach the Council, which may decide to adopt some of the Parliament's views. Where the *Consultation Procedure* applies, the Council can move directly to legislate once it has adopted its response to the Commission and Parliament. Otherwise, the Council issues a 'common position' – a

Box 7.1   Democracy and the European Central Bank

On 1 January 1999 eleven member states transferred control of important areas of their economic policy to the European Central Bank (ECB). Although this can be seen as a straightforward decision to trade off an element of democratic control for the benefits of low inflation, an alternative perspective is that the delegation of tasks to independent agencies might be justifiable from a democratic point of view, and that serious consideration should even be given to a greater use of the EU to create more bodies like the ECB. Systems in which public control can be exercised 'from beyond any one point on the political spectrum' (Majone, 1996) may be needed where there are dangers of majorities exploiting minorities, of majorities being able to fix the conditions under which they are elected, or where the attainment of widely held political preferences is likely to be frustrated by majoritarian systems.

A key requirement is that independent agencies should be set up under precise mandates, and there should be credible mechanisms to ensure they deliver their objectives. They should, at the minimum, be required to meet transparency requirements, such as providing full public explanations for their decisions. Judicial challenge, loss of public credibility, contractual penalties, or revision or recall of mandate (by a non-majoritarian procedure) would then be among the means of enforcing public control.

The revision or recall of the ECB's statute would be difficult, since all member states would need to agree and ratify any change. The dismissal of key office-holders for non-performance would also be problematic, since a majority of the ECB's board consists of national central bank governors appointed by the member states. On the other hand, it may be possible for representative bodies to play on the importance of market credibility to the ECB, to ensure that it is punished in some way for failure to give convincing explanations for decisions taken. The TEU, accordingly, establishes a structured dialogue between the EP and ECB. The Parliament receives nominations to the Executive Board of the ECB; it holds a three-monthly hearing with the ECB President; and it can summon the ECB to an unscheduled meeting to explain a particular decision or outcome (Levitt and Lord, 2000). The Parliament's intention is that these procedures should be cumulative, with subsequent hearings being used to examine forecasts and targets laid down in previous ones (European Parliament, 1998).

statement of its initial position – and the legislative game moves on through the following stages.

- In the case of the *Co-operation Procedure* the EP can go on to propose further amendments once the Council has made its own 'common position' clear. If these are accepted by the Commission, a qualified majority of the Council is all that is needed to accept the Parliament's amendments, but a unanimous vote is needed to reject them. In other words, it is procedurally easier for the Council to agree with the Parliament than it is for it to reject its amendments (Tsebelis, 1994).

- In the case of the *Co-decision Procedure* the Parliament has the right to reject legislation outright as well as to propose amendments in the manner already described. If the Council does not accept all the amendments proposed by the EP, a conciliation committee is convened between representatives of the two bodies. If either Council or Parliament rejects the outcome of conciliation, the legislation lapses. Co-decision is thus a form of bicameralism in which legislative authority is shared between a Council, which is indirectly representative of the public through their member states, and a Parliament, which is directly representative through European and national parties.

Summary

- We have seen that elections to the European Parliament operate as 'second-order national contests', that is, their outcomes reflect primarily the national or domestic concerns of voters rather than judgements about matters European, and that the EP cannot therefore really be said to be authorized by public opinion in Europe.

- However, we have also seen that, although MEPs are elected under national party labels in essentially 'second-order national contests', they operate in the EP in multinational party groups. And although these party groups tend to operate as grand coalitions for legislative purposes, they are organized along familiar political lines and perform an important representative function.

- The powers of the European Parliament are limited in relation to the 'double executive' of the EU, the Commission and the Council, but they are more extensive in the legislative sphere and they have grown over time. On some (mainly Community-pillar) issues the EP has the power of co-decision with the Council.

5   The further democratization of the EU

In the last section we saw that the European Parliament is approaching full legislative co-decision in relation to many first-pillar matters. It has also shown itself capable of dismissing the Commission. There are, however, two deficiencies in this formula. The first is that there are important forms of collective decision making at the European level that cannot be controlled through the EP's powers of law making or through its relationship with the Commission. In particular, this applies to the Common Foreign and Security Policy (second pillar) and Justice and Home Affairs (third pillar). Paul Magnette (1998) has described the EU as a 'semi-parliamentary regime', in which the development of sophisticated practices of representative politics in some issue areas coexists with their near absence from others. Worse, there is some scope for executive bodies to move the management of issues between arenas in a manner that minimizes their exposure to parliamentary control. The EP has complained about the migration of decision making from the Council of Ministers to the European Council, and the scope that 'comitology' (ad hoc committees of national and European officials together with some non-governmental organizations) offers for the real detail of legislation to be hammered out in secretive committees. The second deficiency in parliamentarianism as currently practised at the Union level is, of course, the absence of a credible electoral link. This means that the EP may have powers, but it has little claim to exercise those powers on behalf of the public.

5.1 Strengthening the powers of the EP

One response, at least to the second problem, might be to give the European Parliament the power to choose the Commission or its President. This, it is argued, would give parties and voters an added incentive to structure competition and choice around Union issues. It is, however, important to understand the likely limitations of this proposal. It would be difficult for the EP to follow the model characteristic of most national parliaments, where a simple majority gets to form an executive, which then has to maintain majority support in the representative body on a continuing basis. This would mean accepting a Commission based on a restricted number of partisan viewpoints. It would also require the EP to organize stable majorities capable of supporting an executive in office for sufficient time for it to deliver the programme on which it was elected. This might be neither practical nor desirable. The groups in the EP are capable of respectable levels of cohesion (Attinà, 1990), but it seems unlikely that multinational parties (consisting of upwards of 20 national parties) could ever achieve the same unity as their mono-national equivalents. In the absence, moreover, of any obligation to support a government in office, the EP is able to put together legislative coalitions on a case-by-case basis, with the implication, important in a transnational polity of uncertain legitimation, that those who lose on some issues often have a good prospect of winning on others. A further point is that as long as there is no governing power that needs to organize support for itself in the legislature, the EP is able to exercise its powers with a freedom from executive domination that is often the envy of national parliaments.

5.2   Democratization through a directly elected executive

I have already distinguished between presidential and parliamentary forms of democracy. If the indirect election of an EU executive by the EP seems neither practical nor desirable, an alternative might be to allow all adult citizens the opportunity to elect the Commission or its President (Bogdanor, 1986). This process might be accompanied by some combination of the following refinements.

- Procedures for candidate selection could be designed either to stimulate interest in the contest or to require those in search of nomination to build coalitions from across a wide range of member states. The possibilities include US-style primaries or an obligation to seek the endorsement of MPs, MEPs or political parties from several member states (Hix and Lord, 1997).

- Campaigning arrangements might be designed to arouse debate on European issues and mobilize voters around choices relevant to the EU. The former Irish Prime Minister, John Bruton, once suggested that candidates for the Commission presidency might be required to take part in televised debates in each member state (EPP Conference, Brussels, April 1995).

- The voting mechanism for the final election of the Commission or its presidency could be designed to require either high levels of general support or, once again, a wide coalition from across member states. A two-round, French-style election, for example, would mean that the eventual winner would end up with at least 50 per cent of the final votes cast. Another possibility might be to have a direct popular election of the Commission President immediately followed by an electoral college in which MPs and MEPs cast votes for individual Commissioners in direct proportion to the popular vote received by their parties in the first round of voting for the presidency. This would ensure that the Commission continued to be recruited from politicians with a range of party political and national backgrounds, so counterbalancing the effects of electing a President from just one party family.

The advantage of a directly elected chief executive is that there would be a single office-holder of strategic importance whom the electorate could hold accountable for the performance of the EU. The most obvious question to ask, however, is whether national publics or member states are yet prepared to invest so much democratic legitimacy in the hands of one supranationally elected office-holder. This difficulty might be lessened to the extent that it continued to be necessary for the Commission to function within a complex balance of powers in which final decisions remained with member states. What would be more difficult to sustain in the event of direct election is the claim that the Commission is an apolitical and technocratic body. In practice, the Commission has already made the transition from non-party to multi-party organization. Yet politicians who are elected and subject to re-election can be expected to behave very differently from those who are not.

5.3 Democratization through referendum

The reader may have noticed that the discussion of the two preceding options rapidly turned to how they might be reconciled with the continued use of consensus politics to ensure a multi-state and multi-party pattern of representation in Union policy making. Neither option would remove the need for the Union to consult extensively with private organized interests or involve member governments and policy networks in implementation. Where, however, there is little alternative to government by consensus, and a correspondingly restricted scope for political competition, it may be important to give citizens opportunities to contest élite deals concluded in their name.

It has, for example, been proposed that the EU should adopt Swiss-style referendums. These allow laws to be challenged by being put to popular vote, on the collection of a certain number of signatures. The advantage, it is argued, of creating a democracy based on the possibility of contestation is that it gives the public some sense that it can control and reverse decisions, while avoiding the difficulties of constructing the institutions and procedures needed for a democracy based on political aggregation: first-order elections, programmatic political parties and competitive party government. Referendum questions could be put to the public at the same time as European elections, so providing an incentive for those competing for the EP to address issues at the European level and increasing the incentive for participation on both the plebiscitary and parliamentary votes.

Summary

- Among the possible options for the further democratization of the EU, three have attracted significant attention:
    - strengthening the powers of the EP
    - directly electing the President of the Commission
    - introducing Euro-wide referendums.

- The first and second options run into the problem that they would have to coexist with the maintenance of the multinational, multi-party character of EU democracy.

- The third option provides a means of involving citizens, not just political élites, in the consensual democracy of the Union.

6 Conclusion

This chapter has attempted to answer three questions. Should the EU be democratic? Is it democratic in its current form? Can it be made more democratic? The first question was presented as one about the legitimacy or public acceptability of Union power. In answering the second question it became apparent that the contemporary Union runs together two different kinds of democratic practice, which have been labelled 'intergovernmental' and 'supranational'. Neither approach is likely to be satisfactory on its own, since the Union has probably outstripped public control by individual national democracies without, so far, creating the preconditions for a fully developed democracy of its own. Yet the attempt to combine them creates tensions as well as complementarities. In particular, this manifests itself in the argument that the EU is better at representation than accountability. Its very success in allowing so many perspectives to be represented in decision making – via national governments, economic/functional interests and parties in the EP – creates a complex form of consensus politics, in which it can be difficult to determine precisely who should be accountable for what (Lord, 1999). It is these problems that I have attempted to address through the third question and an examination of the options for further democratization.

References

Abromeit, H. (1998) *Democracy in Europe: Legitimizing Politics in a Non-State Polity*, Oxford, Berghahn Books.

Andeweg, R. (1995) 'The reshaping of national party systems', *West European Politics*, vol.18, no.3, pp.58–78.

Arter, D. (1996) 'The Folketing and Denmark's European policy: the case of an authorizing assembly' in Norton, P. (ed.) *National Parliaments and the European Union*, London, Frank Cass.

Attinà, F. (1990) 'The voting behaviour of the European Parliament members and the problem of the Europarties', *European Journal of Political Research*, vol.18, no.3, pp.557–79.

Bardi, L. (1996) 'Transnational trends in European parties and the 1994 elections to the European Parliament', *Party Politics*, vol.2, no.1, pp.99–114.

Beetham, D. (1994) *Defining and Measuring Democracy*, London, Sage.

Beetham, D. and Lord, C. (1998) *Legitimacy and the European Union*, London, Longman.

Bellamy, R. and Castiglione, D. (2000) 'The uses of democracy: reflections on the European democratic deficit' in Eriksen, E. and Fossum, J. (eds)

Democracy in the European Union: Integrational Through Deliberation, London, Routledge.

Bellamy, R. and Warleigh, A. (1998) 'From an ethics of integration to an ethics of participation: citizenship and the future of the European Union', *Millennium*, vol.27, pp.447–70.

Blondel, J., Sinnott, R. and Svensson, P. (1999) *People and Parliament in the European Union*, Oxford, Oxford University Press.

Bogdanor, V. (1986) 'The future of the European Community: two models of democracy', *Government and Opposition*, vol.22, no.2, pp.344–70.

Chryssochou, D. (1994) 'Democracy and symbiosis in the European Union: towards a confederal consociation?', *West European Politics*, vol.17, no.4, pp.1–14.

Dehousse, R. (1997) 'European integration and the nation state' in Rhodes, M., Heywood, P. and Wright, V. (eds) *Developments in West European Politics*, London, Macmillan.

European Parliament (1998) 'Resolution on democratic accountability in the third phase of EMU' (the Randzio–Plath Report), Brussels, European Parliament.

European Parliament (1999) *Session News, 13–17 December 1999*, Brussels, European Parliament (PE.280.788).

Franklin, M. (1996) 'European elections and the European voter' in Richardson, J. (ed.) *European Union: Power and Policy Making*, London, Routledge.

Hayes-Renshaw, F. and Wallace, H. (1997) *The Council of Ministers*, London, Macmillan.

Hix, S. (1999) *The Political System of the European Union*, London, Macmillan.

Hix, S. and Lord, C. (1996) 'The making of a president: the European Parliament and the confirmation of Jacques Santer as President of the Commission', *Government and Opposition*, vol.31, no.1, pp.62–76.

Hix, S. and Lord, C. (1997) *Political Parties in the European Union*, London, Macmillan.

Levitt, M. and Lord, C. (2000) *The Political Economy of Monetary Union*, London, Macmillan.

Lijphart, A. (1977) *Democracy in Plural Societies*, New Haven, CT, Yale University Press.

Lijphart, A. (1984) *Democracies: Patterns of Majoritarian and Consensus Government in Twenty-One Countries*, New Haven, CT, Yale University Press.

Lijphart, A. (1997) 'The puzzle of Indian democracy: a consociational interpretation', *American Political Science Review*, vol.90, no.2, pp.256–68.

Lord, C. (1999) *Democracy in the European Union*, Sheffield, Sheffield University Press.

Lord, C. (2000) 'Le nouveau Parlement Européen' in Grunberg, G., Perrineau, P. and Ysmal, C. (eds) *Le Vote des Quinze: Les Élections de Juin 1999*, Paris, Presses de la Fondation Nationale des Sciences Politiques.

Magnette, P. (1998) 'L'Union européenne: un régime semi-parlementaire' in Delwit P., De Waele, J.-M. and Magnette, P. (eds) *A Quoi Sert le Parlement Européen?*, Brussels, Éditions Complexe.

Majone, G. (1996) 'Regulatory legitimacy' in Majone, G. *Regulating Europe*, London, Routledge.

Moravcsik, A. (1998) *The Choice for Europe: Social Purpose and State Power from Messina to Maastricht*, London, UCL Press.

Norton, P. (1996) 'The United Kingdom, political conflict, parliamentary scrutiny' in Norton. P. (ed.) *National Parliaments and the European Union*, London, Frank Cass.

Pierson, P. (1998) 'The path to European integration: a historical institutional analysis' in Sandholtz, W. and Stone Sweet, A. (eds) *European Integration and Supranational Governance*, Oxford, Oxford University Press.

Pollack, M. (1997) 'Delegation, agency and agenda setting in the European Community', *International Organization*, vol.51, no.1, pp.99–134.

Reif, K and Schmitt, H. (1980) 'Nine second-order national elections: a conceptual framework for the analysis of European election results', *European Journal of Political Research*, vol.8, no.1, pp.3–45.

Schmitter, P. and Karl, T. (1992) 'The types of democracy emerging in Southern and Eastern Europe and in South and Central America' in Volten, P. (ed.) *Bound to Change: Consolidating Democracy in East Central Europe*, New York, Institute for East–West Studies.

Thomassen, J. and Schmitt, H. (1997) 'Policy representation', *European Journal of Political Research*, vol.32, pp.165–84.

Tsebelis, G. (1994) 'The power of the European Parliament as a conditional agenda setter', *American Political Science Review*, vol.88, no.1, pp.128–42.

Weale, A. (1999) *Democracy*, London, Macmillan.

Weir, S. and Beetham, D. (1999) *Political Power and Democratic Control in Britain: The Democratic Audit of the United Kingdom*, London, Routledge.

Westlake, M. (1994) *A Modern Guide to the European Parliament*, London, Pinter.

Westlake, M. (1997) 'Mad cows and Englishmen: the institutional consequence of the BSE crisis', *Journal of Common Market Studies*, vol.35, pp.11–37.

Further reading

Beetham, D. and Lord, C. (1998) *Legitimacy and the European Union*, London, Longman.

Lord, C. (1999) *Democracy in the European Union*, Sheffield, Sheffield University Press.

Siedentop, L. (2000) *Democracy in Europe*, Harmondsworth, Penguin.

Chapter 8
Finance and budgetary processes in the European Union

Brigid Laffan

1 Introduction

In the early hours of the morning on 25 March 1999, after twenty hours of continuous negotiations, Europe's political leaders reached agreement on the size of the European Union budget for the period 2000–2006. The Heads of Government endured a sleepless night and spent this length of time in their busy political schedules on the EU budget because it matters. Budgetary negotiations are legendary for their duration and the wheeling and dealing that goes on. Battles about money in the EU have been highly contested and contentious. This chapter traces why the EU budget matters so much and analyses what the politics of the budget teaches us about the governance of the European Union. The EU budget is a relatively small budget, much smaller than national budgets, as a proportion of European wealth. Yet throughout the member states and in developing countries where the EU budget is dispersed, the budget provides benefits and contributes to thousands of projects in Europe's towns and cities, thereby bringing the reach of EU policy into Europe's regions and localities.

Section 2 asks why we should study the budget. What might an investigation of the EU budget tell us about the way in which the EU is governed? Once we have established the importance of studying the EU budget, Section 3 looks at its history. How has the EU gained and spent its resources and how has its budget evolved over time? Section 4 analyses the decision-making processes by which EU budgets are agreed and considers the roles of the various institutions that manage EU monies. We shall see that these apparently arcane questions turn out to be extremely important because they illustrate some of the most contested features of governance in the EU: who determines who gets what, and how, in the EU? Section 5 examines the decisions on the future of the budget taken at Berlin in March 1999 and relates these to the prospective enlargement of the EU. Finally, these issues are drawn together to consider what we can learn about the governance of the EU as a whole from a study of EU finance and budgetary matters.

2   Why study the EU budget?

The EU budget is a highly specialized field, full of Euro jargon, but it provides considerable insight into the kind of political order that is evolving in the EU and into how Europe is governed. The development of the power to tax and spend went hand in hand with the evolution of the modern state and, especially, of 'big government' in the twentieth century. In all political systems, public finances are significant both politically and economically. Politically, budgets represent choices to allocate and distribute monies collected by taxes to groups and organizations in society. Economically, budgets are about the allocation of scarce resources. Given the size of modern budgets, public finances have a major impact on national economies and on the flow of public benefits to individuals and groups in society. Budgets represent a major element of public power and are a means through which public power can moderate or shape the effects of market forces.

Economists identify three major functions performed by budgets.

1   Allocation
    Public monies are used to produce social goods that cannot be provided through the market system. Generally speaking, markets are efficient at producing private goods but not social goods. To function efficiently, market systems must be complemented by a capacity to produce a range of collective social goods; for example, defence, a framework of law, a stable currency, education and basic welfare provision.

2   Distribution/redistribution
    In all modern political systems, a high proportion of public finance is used to redistribute monies from one section or category of the population to another. Taken together, the tax and welfare systems are the main instruments of (re)distribution; for example, taxing those in work to provide benefits to the unemployed.

3   Stabilization
    In modern economies, public budgets are used as instruments of macro-economic management to achieve such goals as higher employment, lower inflation and economic growth. Governments may seek to 'stabilize' levels of output and employment by running budget deficits when there is a shortfall in aggregate demand, financed by surpluses from good times.

All three of these budgetary functions – allocation, distribution and stabilization – are performed by the budgets of national governments. The EU budget, however, is not like a national budget. It does not fulfil the full range of tasks allocated to national budgets for two reasons. First, the size of the EU budget is capped at 1.27 per cent of the Union's gross national product (GNP). In 1998 the EU budget was 1.15 per cent of the Union's GNP. As a consequence of this small size and because very little of its expenditure is discretionary, the EU budget cannot perform an economic stabilization function. Second, the 1998 EU budget amounted to just 2.4 per cent of national public expenditure in the member states. The small size of this figure is significant because it means that European national budgets, rather than the EU budget, remain the chief instruments of allocation and distribution – the power to tax and spend in Europe has remained primarily a national function. What does this tell us about governance in the Union?

The small size of the EU budget highlights a key feature of governance in the EU: namely, that it relies largely on regulation or law as the main instrument of public power, not the getting and spending of money. EU governance is governance with a slender purse. The power of the Union relies heavily on its ability to formulate, implement and enforce a formidable corpus of law, the *acquis communautaire*. These laws enable economic actors to manufacture, distribute and market their goods and services in a relatively open market. The dominance of law in the Union has led some analysts, such as Majone (1996), to the conclusion that the EU is a 'regulatory state', rather than a state in the classical sense.

There is a number of reasons why regulation should be the pivotal instrument of public power in the Union. First, regulation is relatively cheap for the regulators: the cost of compliance falls on the organizations and firms that must conform to the regulations. Second, although regulations are formulated at the level of the EU as a whole, it is the member states that are primarily responsible for enforcing the *acquis*. Regulation by law thus ensures that there is robust EU governance without a large public purse.

Despite the importance of regulation in the governance of the Union, the EU budget has not developed on the margins; it has become central to economic and political integration. The budget has grown considerably since 1973 when Denmark, Ireland and the UK joined the Union, as can be seen from Table 8.1.

Table 8.1   The EU budget in 1973 and 1998*

	1973	1998
Total EU budget (billion euro)	19.00	85.00
EU budget as a percentage of Union GDP	0.53	1.14
EU budget per capita (euro)	18.30	228.20

* 1998 prices

In practice, the regulation of ever wider and deeper market integration has called for an expanding budgetary capacity. The volume of EU expenditure has risen significantly because of functional pressures from market integration and because there were actors in the Union actively looking for a larger budget.

The EU budget performs a number of critical functions that maintain and deepen the integration process.

- The budget has instruments that impact on the lives of a particular social group and on specific regions in the Union. The two important budgetary instruments that distribute and redistribute income are the common agricultural policy (CAP) and the structural funds. (In Section 3 we shall see that the development of the CAP went hand in hand with pressures for a specific revenue base of the EU budget.)

- EU social expenditure through the structural funds and the anti-poverty programmes are directed towards those people in European society who are socially and economically excluded. Migrant workers, the disabled, unemployed youth and some categories of women benefit from EU-financed social programmes. The structural funds now include an element of the agricultural budget, the European Regional Development Fund, the European Social Fund, and the Financial Instrument for Fisheries Guidance.

- The EU budget plays a minor role in allocation through its expenditure on research and development, environmental projects, student exchanges and the trans-European networks (the European-wide infrastructure, known as the TENs). The purpose of the budget in these areas is to animate activities within the member states, to develop 'best practice' and to assist in the diffusion of policies throughout the territory of the Union. Programmes such as student exchange and the exchange of language teachers, young workers and cultural projects are intended to build up a shared social and cultural space in Europe.

- The EU budget has a growing international role through the external policies and commitments of the Union. The Union's budget extends throughout Europe's cities, regions and rural communities, and beyond these to the developing world and Central and Eastern Europe.

When analysing the EU budget we should be mindful that, although it is much smaller than national budgets, it is larger than those usually found in international organizations and it has an autonomous resource base (discussed in Section 3). It supplements and complements national budgetary expenditure on the one hand, and market integration on the other. The existence and development of the EU budget have ensured that market integration has gone beyond negative integration, such as getting rid of barriers to economic exchange. From the beginning, the political forces and institutional actors driving the process of integration wanted more than a free-trade area. While giving priority to market integration and hence regulation, they also wanted to create a social space that was not dominated simply by market outcomes. Of course, they did not want to replicate the powers and instruments of the member states, but they did want to establish a robust system of governance at the EU level.

Summary

- Budgets are an important aspect of public power in modern political systems, and this part of governance has remained primarily at the national level despite the growth of the EU budget.

- Because of its small size compared with national budgets the EU budget does not perform all of the public finance functions – allocation, distribution and stabilization – associated with national budgets.

- Nevertheless, EU governance is not purely regulatory, and the budget plays an important role in complementing and supplementing law-based market integration.

3 A short history of the EU budget

All budgets consist of two parts – revenue and expenditure. In order to spend effectively, budgets must have a stable and predictable resource base. The EU budget – unlike national budgets – is required to balance; the EU is not allowed to run deficit budgets or borrow to fund current expenditure. Looking at the evolution of the EU budget will enable us to see how the Union amassed budgetary resources and what it spends its money on. We shall also discover that there was a move from a highly conflictual budgetary process towards a more institutionalized pattern of budget making. The history of the budget can be divided into three distinct phases.

- *A formative period*, 1952–1969, in which the foundations of the Union's budget were established.

- *A period of crisis*, 1970–1986, involving continuous budgetary conflict and two significant budget treaties.

- *A period of consolidation*, 1987–1999, characterized by both an expansion of the size of the budget and the adoption of new rules and institutions for making and managing the budget.

These major phases are set out in Table 8.2 (overleaf) and discussed in the sections that follow.

Jacques Delors, President of the European Commission from 1985 to 1994.

Table 8.2 Major phases in the development of the EU budget

1952–1969	1970–1986	1987–1999
Paris Treaty (1951) instigating European Coal and Steel Community levies (1952)	*Luxembourg Treaty (1970)* 'own resources'	*Delors 1 (1988)* Financial Perspective 1988–1992; Multi-Annual Financial Perspective
Rome Treaty (1957) establishing EEC, European Investment Bank and European Social Fund	*Brussels Treaty (1975)* EP Budgetary Power	Inter-Institutional Agreement on Budgetary Matters (1988)
European Development Fund (1959)	Financial Mechanism (1975)	*Delors 2 (1992)* Financial Perspective 1993–1999
European Agricultural Guidance and Guarantee Fund (1962)	European Regional Development Fund (1975)	Cohesion Fund (1993)
	Lomé Convention (1975)	*Berlin (1999)* Financial Perspective 2000–2006
	UK budget rebates (1980)	
	Fontainebleau Budgetary Agreement (1984)	

3.1 The formation of the budget, 1952–1969

The evolution of the financial resources of the Union can be traced right back to the European Coal and Steel Community (ECSC), which came into operation in 1952. The Paris Treaty (signed in 1951), in establishing the ECSC, made provision for an autonomous budgetary resource by giving the High Authority (later, the Commission) the power to impose levies on the coal and steel industries to finance its activities. The Treaty of Rome (1957), establishing the European Economic Community (EEC), marked another stage in the formation of the financial resources of the Community, since it made provision for two financial instruments: the European Social Fund (ESF) and the European Investment Bank (EIB).

The ESF was set up in 1960 as a fund to support training, retraining and the mobility of labour. The emphasis was on assisting workers to adjust to the economic costs of market integration. The ESF was the first of what were later called the 'structural funds'. The EIB was designed to offer loans on beneficial credit terms to the member states for economic development. In addition to the two financial instruments, the Treaty of Rome made provision for two policies that had financial implications. First, the inclusion of provision for a common agricultural policy (the CAP) in the Treaty had a profound and lasting impact on the finances of the Union. In the post-war period, public subvention of agriculture was widespread in Europe. The transfer of responsibility for agriculture to the EU level implied that national support was being replaced by European support, and that a mechanism would have to be found to finance this sector at a European level. Financial solidarity, meaning that there would have to be common financing of agricultural support, became one of the key principles of the CAP. The European Agricultural Guidance and Guarantee Fund (EAGGF) was set up as the financial instrument for the CAP in 1962. The Treaty of Rome contained provision for another financial instrument, the European Development Fund (EDF), and the first EDF was set up in 1959 to finance development policies in the overseas territories, especially French territories, of the member states.

The financial capacity of the Union that emerged in the formative period was to have a deep impact on the finances of the Union, since it established the pattern of who would benefit from the EU's financial largesse. In all member states, the farming communities emerged as major beneficiaries when national support for farm incomes was replaced by EU support. The CAP led to a transfer of income from the consumers to the producers of food in Europe, and from taxpayers to farmers. It also, in effect, established member state beneficiaries: the states set to benefit were those with large agricultural sectors. The foundation for an EU role in assisting in economic adjustment was established with the ESF and EIB. The EDF provided the foundations for an EU role in development cooperation. (However, unlike agricultural support, the EDF never became part of the EU budget as such, and remained an intergovernmental arrangement between the member states.)

Compared with what was to follow, the financing of the budget in the formative period was relatively unproblematic.

3.2   Budgetary crisis and conflict, 1970–1986

The second phase in the development of the finances of the Union saw major changes in the revenue base and in the decision-making processes associated with the budget. In addition, during this period the budget became a matter of 'high politics' due to the continuous conflict over its distributional consequences. The period began, however, with a major strengthening of EU finances as a result of the 1970 Budget Treaty, known as the Luxembourg Treaty. This Treaty introduced a new revenue base for the budget, known as 'own resources', with effect from 1971. The term 'own resources', still widely used in discussions on the budget, referred to a revenue source independent of the member states. The treaty established three 'own resources':

- custom duties on all imports into the Union

- agricultural levies on agricultural imports into the Union

- up to 1 per cent of the value-added tax (VAT) collected in the member states.

The 1970 Treaty was followed in 1975 by another important budget treaty, the Brussels Treaty, which gave the 'power of the purse' (discussed in detail in Section 4 below) to the European Parliament.

The 1970 Treaty was concluded before the first enlargement of the Union and was designed to fix the budgetary rules before the UK joined. It could be regarded as a successful attempt to predetermine the gains and losses before enlargement, and was the price that France extracted before it would agree to enlargement negotiations. As a consequence of this, from the outset of its membership the UK was disadvantaged by the pattern of EU expenditure and the revenue base. Once in the Union, the UK Labour government renegotiated the terms of accession and got agreement in 1975 (at the Dublin European Council) to a complex Financial Mechanism that would allow for rebates in the case of heavy gross contributions. The mechanism proved ineffective and in 1978 the UK found itself to be the second largest contributor despite being one of the less prosperous member states. This anomaly placed the question of budgetary *equity* firmly on the EU's agenda. From 1979 onwards, the new British Prime Minister, Margaret Thatcher, demanded a system of rebates to reduce the budgetary burden on the UK. And it took until 1984 to resolve the UK budgetary problem.

The UK-related conflict was exacerbated by the Union's growing revenue problem. By the end of the 1970s the system of 'own resources' was inadequate to enable the Union to meet its financial commitments and to allow it to respond to new demands for financial expenditure. By 1982, the VAT take-up rate reached 0.92 per cent (from a 1 per cent upper limit) and was virtually breached the next year. The pattern of expenditure, with over 70 per cent of the budget going to agriculture in 1979, meant that other policies such as regional programmes were squeezed of resources. By this stage, the price support mechanisms of the CAP were leading to serious over-production with the appearance of 'butter mountains' and 'wine lakes'.

The two major budgetary problems – the question of UK contributions and the inadequacy of the revenue base – came to a head in 1984 at the Fontainebleau European Council under the chairmanship of President Mitterrand. The member states all wanted to reduce the tensions caused by the budgetary crisis so that they could turn their attention to treaty reform and the internal market programme. The UK pursued reform of the CAP and a reduction in its contributions by focusing attention on the distributional consequences of budgetary decisions. It finally won the argument on equity grounds in 1984 when a rebate mechanism was established on a long-term basis.

Although emphasis must be placed on the budgetary crisis during this period, the financial instruments of the Union expanded in a number of important directions. In 1975 the European Regional Development Fund (ERDF) was established as a fund designed to help Europe's poorer regions catch up with 'core' Europe. A host of new policy fields opened up, including environment, fisheries, research and development, and education, all of which were accompanied by spending programmes. The reach of the Union's spending programmes expanded, as did the number of people and regions benefiting from EU largesse. Functional pressures from market integration and demands for an EU role in a variety of policy areas led to an expansion of expenditure programmes, and once a new expenditure programme was established it immediately attracted the interest of public and private groups that could benefit. In this way the reach of EU governance expanded well beyond the central governments of the member states into Europe's regions and civil society.

3.3   Institutionalizing the budget, 1987–1999

The resurgence of formal integration with the Single European Act (1987) was a major turning point for the EU and its finances. The President of the Commission, Jacques Delors, made a direct connection between the single market and the budget. The Commission published two sets of proposals – *Making a Success of the Single Act* and the *Report on the Financing of the Community Budget* (1987) – that instituted an ambitious package of budgetary reform and expansion. The Commission proposed, first, the establishment of a five-year multi-annual financial perspective for the Union (1988–1992), and second, a sizeable increase in the overall size of the budget and in the volume of money going to the less developed parts of the Union (see Section 4.2 below). These reforms were copper-bottomed by a legal system of budgetary discipline to control agricultural expenditure. The Commission felt sufficiently confident of the changed political climate in the Union to adopt a radical approach to budgetary reform. Agreement to what is commonly known as the 'Delors 1' plan was reached under the German presidency in February 1988.

The agreement provided the Union with a stable budgetary environment for the next five years, doubled the amount of money going to the poorer regions in the Union (those known as objective one regions, the most eligible for assistance under the structural funds), and established a regulatory basis for budgetary discipline. On the revenue side, the Delors 1 agreement created a ceiling of 1.3 per cent of Union GNP for commitment appropriations and 1.2 per cent for payment appropriations by 1992. In addition to the three 'own resources' established in 1970, the Union was allocated a fourth resource, based on a topping-up of the revenue available from the other resources related to GNP. Apart from the Budget Treaties (1970 and 1975), the Delors 1 financial package was the most significant budgetary agreement in the history of the Union.

The Delors 1 Agreement in 1988 was followed by what was known as the 'Delors 2' agreement in December 1992. The Commission continued the strategy developed for Delors 1 by publishing its budgetary proposals – *From Single Act to Maastricht and Beyond: The Means to Match our Ambitions* and *The Community's Finances Between Now and 1997* – within days of the signing of the Treaty on European Union (TEU). The proposals represented a consolidation of (rather than a radical departure from) the approach adopted under Delors 1, and included a further commitment to cohesion spending (a new Cohesion Fund), a significant increase in monies allocated to external funding and the continuation of budgetary control for agricultural expenditure. The Cohesion Fund was established by the Maastricht Treaty, and linked to the project of Economic and Monetary Union; it was aimed at improving the growth performance of the four poorest members, Greece, Ireland, Portugal and Spain.

The proposals included a new budget ceiling of 1.37 per cent of GNP. The negotiations of the Delors 2 package were even more difficult than those for Delors 1 for a number of reasons. To begin with, Delors 1 had transformed the budgetary position of many member states making them 'net contributors' to the Union budget. Next, Germany was coping internally with the budgetary consequences of unification. And finally, the European economies began to experience an economic downturn in 1992, which made many states unwilling to agree to sizeable budgetary increases.

The outcome in December 1992 was not as close to the Commission's proposals as was the agreement on the first multi-annual package in 1988. On this occasion the member states agreed to a seven-year financial package (1993–1999) with a GNP ceiling of 1.27 per cent. Additional monies were found for external expenditure arising from the budgetary demands of countries in East Central Europe. The Union's cohesion policy was further refined with additional money for spending on Europe's poorer regions. The presence of a 'net contributors' club began to make itself felt in the budgetary politics of the Union.

The period 1988 to 1999 was a critical period in the development of EU finances to the extent that the Union found the capacity to regularize and institutionalize budgetary negotiations. Consequently, distributional bargaining among the member states about budgetary matters was contained within new 'rules of the game'. This illustrates and highlights an important feature of EU governance: namely, the manner in which devices are found to enable the member states to contain their differences and to alter the terms of bargaining so that every state can buy into negotiated outcomes. As in this instance, these devices usually involve strengthening the predictability of the decision-making process, regulating behaviour with new rules, and embedding both the newly institutionalized processes and rules in a norm relating to how business should be conducted. The new budgetary rules established the principle of multi-annual financial planning by category of expenditure, thereby stabilizing the budgetary process (see Table 8.3).

Table 8.3   The multi-annual financial perspectives

Delors 1 1988–1992	Delors 2 1993–1999	Berlin 2000–2006
Agreed at Brussels European Council, February 1988	Agreed at Edinburgh European Council, December 1992	Agreed at Berlin European Council, March 1999

This period was also characterized by a redefinition of the Union's budget priorities with a significant increase in the amount of money going to Europe's poorer regions and stronger control over agricultural expenditure. All of the other spending programmes introduced at the beginning of the 1980s, such as the environment, research and development, and educational exchange, received additional finance during this period. Finally, the 1990s saw a doubling of external spending, largely as a result of the collapse of communism in Eastern Europe and the former Soviet Union.

Summary

- The history of the EU budget began with a formative period when the Union was founded, and in which the budget was relatively small and budget making was uncontentious. This phase established some of the basic areas on which the EU budget would be spent.

- As the membership of the EU expanded and as the pressures on the budget increased, budget making became more subject to conflict and political crisis. Arguments over an equitable arrangement and, in particular, disputes about the UK contribution to the finances of the EU, paralysed decision making for a while.

- Stability returned to the budgetary process in the late 1980s with the development of multi-annual financial packages and new procedures and rules for budget making and management.

4 Making and managing the EU budget

Decision making in the EU involves many actors and institutions. The governments of member states interact with one another and with the institutions of the EU itself – the European Commission, the European Parliament and the European Court of Justice. A closer look at how the EU budget is drawn up and then managed will allow us to see some of the complexities of decision making in the Union. At the outset, a distinction must be made between the negotiations on the 'history-making' budgetary decisions – Delors 1, Delors 2 and the Agenda 2000 agreement – and those on the annual budgetary cycle. The macro-negotiations characteristic of the 'history-making' agreements are considered in the two sections immediately following (Sections 4.1 and 4.2). Management instruments became necessary to cope with the ever increasing volume and complexity of budgetary lines, and external and internal auditing controls to strengthen accountability; these are discussed in the later parts of Section 4. Section 5 takes the story on into the future and looks at how special features were incorporated into the financial perspective of Agenda 2000 in order to accommodate EU enlargement.

4.1 Making the budget: macro-negotiations and financial perspectives

The 'history-making' decisions are characterized by structured negotiations across a range of issues, culminating in a decision of the European Council. In all three macro-negotiations, the European Council established the broad parameters for the negotiations and the timetable. Indeed, the European Council provided the source of leadership. Moreover, the final agreement was always achieved by intensive negotiations among the Heads of Government in the European Council, with a critical role played by the country holding the presidency. The work of the Council was prepared by the General Affairs Council of Foreign Ministers, the Eco-Fin Ministers (Finance Ministers) on the financial aspects of the packages and the inevitable marathon Agricultural Councils. The history-making decisions included agreement on the future financial perspective (the overall amount of money and the distribution across different categories of expenditure), and reform of the structural funds and agricultural expenditure. The agreements were crafted by detailed technical negotiations in addition to high-level political negotiations. For all three macro-negotiations, the formal negotiating hierarchy in the Council was augmented by special high-level groups of national civil servants that were designed to enhance the negotiating capacity of the system given the complexity and technical nature of the major financial negotiations.

These budgetary deals provide us with considerable insight into how the EU is governed. In the first place, all three budgetary deals highlight the negotiating capacity of the Union and its ability to get agreement on wide-ranging 'package deals' of major importance to the member states. Second, the history-making budgetary decisions underline the growing importance of the heads of state and government in the governance of the Union. Only the chief political office holders in the member states have the political authority to reach agreement on complex and wide-ranging package deals. Third, major budget agreements demonstrate the importance of constructing package deals in the negotiating processes of the Union. Package deals enable the Union to construct agreement by ensuring that all states benefit or can be seen to benefit – that there is something there for everyone to take home to their domestic publics and parliaments. And finally, budget negotiations show how public policy making in the EU is an admixture of highly technical negotiations and high-level politics; the technical specialists prepare the ground for high-level political agreement.

4.2   The annual budget cycle

The financial perspectives provide the broad parameters for the annual budgetary cycle, a cycle that is established by treaty and adapted by agreement among the three institutions – the European Commission, the Council of Ministers and the European Parliament – engaged in setting the annual budget (see Table 8.4 overleaf). The Commission plays a key role in budgetary decision making as it is responsible under the 1970 Treaty for preparing and proposing the *Preliminary Draft Budget* (PDB) each year. This is the task of the Budget Commissioner and the Budget Directorate (formerly known as DG19). The Budget Commissioner does not have the status or powers associated with national Finance Ministers, although the status of this portfolio has increased with the growing size of the budget. The PDB is a massive document running to some 1,500 pages of text that is then passed to the Budgetary Authority for its consideration.

Following the 1970 and 1975 Budget Treaties, the Budgetary Authority consists of the Council of Ministers and the European Parliament (EP), acting in tandem. A key constitutional development in EU finances was the granting of financial powers to the EP. The Parliament was given the final say on items of expenditure defined as 'non-compulsory' expenditure, the right to reject the budget in its entirety and the sole right to discharge the budget each year. The Council, on the other hand, has the final say over 'compulsory expenditure'. ('Compulsory Expenditure' refers to items necessarily arising from the treaties; 'Non-Compulsory Expenditure' is regarded as not arising directly from the treaties.)

Table 8.4   The annual budget cycle

Commission
(Budget Commissioner and Budget Directorate)

Preliminary Draft Budget (PDB)
(Prepared by the Commission in its Budget Service by April)

Budgetary Authority

Council of Ministers ***(Budget Committee)***	***European parliament*** ***(Budget Committee)***
(Ad hoc consultation about Compulsory Expenditure)	
First Reading (July) – establishment of PDB by qualified majority voting (QMV)	
	First Reading (October) – amendments to Non-Compulsory Expenditure, – modifications to Compulsory Expenditure
Second Reading (November) – final decision on Compulsory Expenditure, – position on Non-Compulsory Expenditure by QMV	
	Second Reading (December) – final decision on Non-Compulsory Expenditure can be adopted or rejected by absolute majority and three-fifths of votes expressed

The Budget Council is made up of junior ministers from national finance ministries, who – working from the basis of the Commission's proposals – establish the PDB by July each year. The Council's Budget Committee, consisting of the budgetary attachés from the national finance ministries seconded to the Permanent Representations in Brussels, carries out the homework. This Budget Committee is responsible for getting as much agreement as possible for the PDB and prepares the discussions further up the hierarchy. A distinguishing feature of the Budget Council and the Budget Committee was the willingness to reach decisions by qualified majority voting (QMV), notwithstanding the veto. In its second reading of the Draft Budget, the Budget Committee takes indicative votes although formal voting only takes place in the Council. The use of QMV allowed the Budget Council to reach agreement on a budget consisting of over 1,000 individual budget lines. Once the Budget Council has agreed a Draft Budget, it is passed to the other arm of the Budgetary Authority, the European Parliament.

The Parliament's Budget Committee is the nerve-centre for the management of the budgetary process in the EP. The chair of its Budget Committee is regarded as a privileged position in the hierarchy and MEPs vie with each other to act as *rapporteurs* for the annual budget. The *rapporteur* together with the chair of the committee liaise with the Parliament's sectoral committees and with the Commission and Council. All sectoral committees draw up reports for the EP Budget Committee. However, the final report is the responsibility of the Budget Committee. There is considerable horse-trading and informal bargaining among the political groups and the specialized committees. The Commission's services, the member states and the various lobbies keep in close contact with the relevant committees and the Budget Committee while the EP's response is worked out. The Budget Committee's report and its proposed amendments are then put to a plenary session of the EP. Discipline in the political groups and in the specialized committees ensures that the amendments supported by the Budget Committee are approved by the plenary with relatively few exceptions. The Parliament's amendments and modifications are sent back to the Council for its second reading.

Before the Council responds to the EP's amendments and modifications, a conciliation committee is held between the two arms of the Budgetary Authority so that the EP and the Council can establish what the outstanding issues are. The pattern is for the Council to reject the majority of parliamentary amendments. Following a second reading by the Council, the budget is then sent back to the EP for its second reading. The EP usually restores cuts made by the Council where it has authority to do so and, since 1984, the EP has passed all budgets at its December session.

Agreement to a multi-annual financial perspective increased the predictability of the budgetary process and reduced the endemic conflict (see Box 8.1) between the Council and the EP on budgetary matters. The decision-making processes on budgetary matters in the Union follow a

Box 8.1   Conflict and Inter-Institutional Agreements (IIA)

The arcane distinction between 'compulsory' and 'non-compulsory' expenditure has been the source of continuing conflict between the two arms of the Budget Authority. Inevitably, the division of budgetary responsibility between the Council and the EP, with an uneven distribution of power, was going to lead to budgetary conflict. During the late 1970s and early 1980s, there was in fact endemic conflict between the two institutions. The EP, lacking significant legislative powers, was intent on using its budgetary powers to enhance its power position in the Union. The Council, on the other hand, was determined to protect its power and did not want the EP's budgetary power to spill over into the legislative field. The endemic nature of the conflict led to many actions brought before the European Court of Justice by the Commission, Council, and the member states acting independently. The conflict was finally tamed in 1988 by an Inter-Institutional Agreement (IIA) as part of the 1988 Delors 1 package. Since then, all new financial perspectives are accompanied by an IIA that establishes the ground rules for relations between the three institutions involved in budgetary decision making.

predetermined pattern based on the multi-annual financial perspective, the stuff of high politics, and the annual budgetary cycle. The Commission plays a central role in both levels of decision making as it is responsible for drafting the proposals for the macro-negotiations and for the Draft Budget. Whereas the Council of Ministers, particularly the European Council of the Heads of Government, is the ultimate locus of decision making on the future financial perspective, the Council and Parliament are jointly responsible for the annual budget. Gradually, conflict between the two arms of the Budgetary Authority was replaced by relative budgetary calm although there are still some conflictual issues between the EP and the Council. As with all budgetary processes, those responsible for budgetary decision making have to prioritize the competing claims of the spending programmes and their advocates.

4.3   Expansion: the case for stronger financial management

It was in the 1990s that the focus in the Union switched from budgetary decision making to budgetary management. The Union's budget of 85 billion euro, consisting of thousands of individual budgetary lines and involving some 400,000 individual authorizations of expenditure each year, presents those responsible for financial management with a formidable challenge. Figure 8.1 shows the growth of EU expenditure from 1958 to 2000.

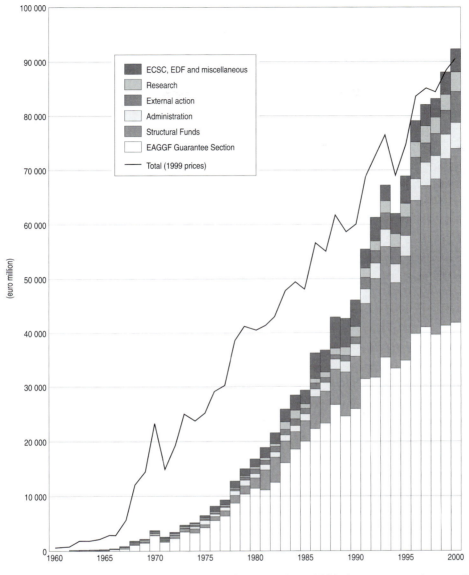

Figure 8.1 Community expenditure from 1958 to 2000 (at current prices and 1999 prices)

(European Commission, 1999, p.32)

The management challenge is exacerbated by the fact that the EU budget is spent by public and private agencies in the member states and throughout the world. The Union's external expenditure is spent in remote corners of the globe. In the early years of the Union, the limited size of the budget meant that financial management did not have a high priority. However, the creation of 'own resources' in 1970 required a strengthening of accountability at EU level. This led to the establishment of an external auditor, the European Court of Auditors, in 1977. Even then, the salience of budgetary management remained relatively muted. The growth in the size of the budget as a consequence of the major budgetary agreement in 1988 and growing publicity about fraud brought the management of the Union's finances to the fore. There are now two dimensions to auditing in the Union: external audit by the Court of Auditors; and internal audit in the Commission and the other institutions.

4.4   External audit and the Court of Auditors

The Court of Auditors was established by the 1975 Budget Treaty to replace the European Audit Board, a part-time auditing body. The Court began its work in 1977 and was faced with having to establish its authority in the Union's institutional landscape. The work of the Court is organized on the basis of an annual programme set within a multi-annual framework of four years. Until the TEU (1992), the Annual Report published in autumn each year was the main product of its work. The Report contains detailed analysis of all areas of EU expenditure and draws attention to problems of financial management. The institutions are allowed a right of reply to the observations of the Court in each annual report. The Report is presented to the EP by the President of the Court of Auditors and receives extensive media coverage in the member states. All reports issued by the Court of Auditors address weaknesses in the Union's systems of financial management and many of the same observations are made each year.

The Court has gradually assumed a more central role in the Union as the importance of sound financial management has become increasingly salient to the Union's political agenda. The 'net contributors' club wanted to be sure that their contributions to the budget were well spent. The Court's relations with the Commission have been particularly difficult, whereas the EP regards the Court as an ally. The TEU elevated the Court to the status of a full institution. This raised its authority so that it now has the same status as the institutions it audits. In return for its new status, the Court was given an additional responsibility – the Statement of Assurance. In effect this means that the Court must now satisfy itself that the financial accounts of the institutions are reliable. If not, the Court can fail to give an assurance or may give a partial assurance.

4.5   Internal audit in the Commission

The main responsibility for internal audit in the Commission falls to what was formerly known as DG20 Financial Control. In addition, all of the services have budget units, which differ in size and responsibility. The number of staff assigned to financial control has not increased in line with the growing size of the budget. The key principle of financial control in the Commission is the need for prior approval of expenditure; this is known as a 'visa' and can be granted only by the Financial Controller in DG20. Paradoxically, the system of prior approval has the effect of reducing the spending departments' sense of responsibility for ongoing financial management. In 1995, the outgoing Budget Commissioner, Peter Schmidhuber, drafted a memo – the 'Schmidhuber testimonial' – for his successor on financial management in the Commission. Schmidhuber trenchantly argued that financial management in the Commission was weak, highlighting the following specific weaknesses:

- the Commission services were more concerned with the content of policy than they were with financial management
- budget planning needed to be strengthened
- the implementation of the budget led to the spending of commitments just before the financial year-end
- there was an over-reliance on the financial controller to detect problems of financial management
- there was inadequate evaluation of programmes.

The testimonial concluded that 'the principle of sound financial management stated in Article 2 of the Financial Regulation and stressed repeatedly by the Court of Auditors is not acknowledged as a general maxim in the Commission'.

The testimonial was taken seriously by the new Commission when it took office in 1995. The President of the Commission, Jacques Santer, immediately requested his new Budget Commissioner to submit a report on how financial management might be reinforced in the Commission. This led to a reform project, *2000 – Sound and Efficient Management*, that had as its stated aim 'a substantial and lasting reform of the financial management culture of the Commission'. Over the next four years the Commission began the slow and tortuous process of enhancing the role of budget units in the services and of updating the procedures for financial management. It is thus somewhat paradoxical that although the Santer Commission recognized the problem of financial management and was attempting to address it, the entire Commission had to resign in March 1999 as a result of a damning report from a group of independent experts. This group began its work as a result of the EP's decision not to give the Commission a 'discharge' for the 1996 budget.

4.6 The discharge procedure

The Budgetary Control Committee of the EP is the central node in the annual discharge procedure. Under the Treaty, the EP has the power to grant or refuse the Commission a discharge for its implementation of the budget. In some years the discharge procedure goes relatively smoothly, whereas in other years there is considerable conflict between the Commission and the EP. The problem relating to the discharge of the 1996 budget surfaced in March 1998: the Budget Control Committee recommended that the EP delay granting a discharge of the 1996 budget in protest against poor financial management in the Commission, following yet another critical report by the Court of Auditors. The discharge issue then became embroiled in allegations of fraud against a number of individual Commissioners. A motion of censure against the Commission, tabled by the Europe of the Nations Group, was rejected by 293 votes to 232 in January 1999, but a related resolution on financial management – combating fraud and demanding better management of the EU budget – was passed. The price the EP extracted in January 1999 was the establishment of a Committee of Independent Experts with a remit to establish to what extent the Commission as a body, or Commissioners individually, bore specific responsibility for recent examples of fraud, mismanagement or nepotism raised in parliamentary discussions.

The publication on 15 March 1999 of the first report of the Committee of Independent Experts, entitled *Allegations Regarding Fraud, Mismanagement and Nepotism in the European Commission*, heralded the end of the Santer Commission. The report was political dynamite. It concluded that there was a loss of control by the political authorities over the administration of the Commission, that in some instances (notably in relation to tourism) the Commission had delayed action, and that there were cases of favouritism by some Commissioners. In one of its most damning comments, the Committee found that there was a 'growing reluctance among members of the hierarchy to acknowledge their responsibility. It is becoming difficult to find anyone who has even the slightest sense of responsibility'. The findings and the tone of the report left the Commission with no option but to resign, as it would have faced a motion of censure from the EP at its next plenary. The conflict over financial management that culminated in the resignation of the Commission in March 1999 was a classical parliamentary–executive clash in the best traditions of parliamentary accountability. The EP exercised its growing power in the Union's institutional landscape to highlight its role of holding the Commission accountable.

4.7   Combating fraud

Fraud against the financial interests of the Union became a topical issue towards the end of the 1980s and has remained on the agenda. The UK House of Lords began to take an interest in the issue and published a number of highly regarded reports. It is impossible to determine with any degree of accuracy just how much fraud is perpetrated against the EU budget and whether financial irregularity in the EU is greater than at national level. The EU budget appears vulnerable to fraud in a number of important respects:

- the transit system is particularly open to fraud because of the ease with which transit documents can be forged
- the complex rules of the CAP leave it open to irregularities

- the structural funds are dispersed widely within the member states, involving many layers of government and private agencies
- there have been instances of fraud within the Commission service itself.

The Commission's Annual Reports, *Fighting EU Fraud*, offer numerous examples of the kinds of fraud that can be perpetrated against the financial interests of the Union (see Box 8.2). In 1996 the European Parliament set up an inquiry into the EU's transit system. The ensuing report, which was published in 1997, highlighted the gap in public authority as a result of the single market programme. The report concluded that: 'Goods cross borders, criminals cross borders, profits from illegal activities cross borders, public authority stops at borders.' The Committee went on to highlight the need for yet further improvement in co-operation among customs authorities and enhanced legal co-operation.

Box 8.2   Fraud in the EU

Fraud against the EU budget has included the diversion of a consignment of refined sugar that was destined for Croatia and Slovenia ending up on the Italian market without the payment of import levies. Another example was a shipment of milk powder from Rotterdam that was destined for Algeria ending up in Emden in Germany. The exporters collected ECU 15 million in export subsidies. Fraud has also been detected in the operation of the Structural Funds through claims for projects that were never completed or for training courses that were never held.

(Laffan, 1997)

Measures designed to limit fraud and to protect the financial interests of the Union were strengthened in the 1990s. The TEU included a provision that commits the member states to protect the financial interests of the Union as they would their own public finances. In addition, the Commission signed formal agreements with the member states establishing national responsibility for overseeing the main budgetary programmes. The Commission established the *Unite de Coordination pour la Lutte Antifraude* (UCLAF) in 1988 in response to repeated requests from the EP. For many years UCLAF was regarded as essentially a symbolic commitment to combating fraud, having little real power. In response to the resignation of the Santer Commission, the new Commission President, Romano Prodi, decided to establish a new anti-fraud office, the *Office pour la Lutte Antifraude* (OLAF). Unlike UCLAF, it will not report to the Secretary General of the Commission but is controlled by a Board of Management.

The appointment of the Prodi Commission in September 1999 heightened the political commitment to Commission reform. Prodi appointed a Vice-President for reform (Neil Kinnock), with responsibility for overseeing an ambitious programme of change in the Commission.

The appointment of the new commission coincided with the publication of the second report of the Committee of Independent Experts, *Reform of the Commission – Analysis of Current Practice and Proposals for Tackling Mismanagement, Irregularities and Fraud* (published on 10 September 1999). The tone of the new Commission was set from the outset, with agreement on a new Code of Conduct for Commissioners and a Code of Ethics for Commission officials. This has been followed by changes in appointments to cabinets and in senior appointments in the Commission services. Kinnock has indicated that upgrading financial control forms a central part of the reform blueprint. He has suggested that the Commission establishes an internal audit service and that responsibility for financial control should be delegated to individual departments. A key challenge facing the Commission is to enhance its capacity for management, especially in the light of enlargement. Financial management forms an important element in the Commission's modernization programme.

Summary

- Since the late 1980s, budget making can be divided into the big multi-annual package deals struck between Heads of Government of the member states, on the one hand, and the detailed annual budget cycle, on the other. Both have become institutionalized through agreement among member states and EU institutions about rules and procedures.

- At the same time as the process of budget making has become more predictable and consensual, the management of the expanding budget has become increasingly important and open to public scrutiny. The concern of the 'net contributors' that monies be properly used, public exposure of fraud against the EU, and rivalry between the EP and the Commission over the control and accountability of expenditure, have all been important.

- Matters came to a head in 1999 when concern about the management of EU finances prompted the resignation of the President of the Commission and all the commissioners.

5   The future of the budget – Agenda 2000

The multi-annual budgetary regime established by the Delors 1 agreement in 1988 faced its sternest test in the search for a budgetary agreement for the period 2000–2006. The 'shadow of enlargement' and the clamour of the 'net contributors' club raised the prospect of a return to zero-sum bargaining on EU finances. The member states were faced with a trade-off between their collective interest in avoiding a return to the budgetary battles of the past and their individual interest in protecting their receipts from the budget, notwithstanding enlargement. Each enlargement shifted budgetary priorities and altered the costs and benefits to individual member states. Enlargement to Eastern and Central Europe and beyond could not be accommodated without restructuring a number of policy regimes and without a larger pool of financial resources. Just how far the restructuring should go was the challenge facing the member states and EU institutions in the Agenda 2000 negotiations. The existing 'net contributors' and the beneficiaries from the budget faced difficult choices about budgetary reform. The Commission, very much aware of the competing concerns of the member states and the applicants, had the task of crafting the broad outlines of a budgetary framework for the period 2000–2006.

5.1 Framing the proposals

Within the Commission, a high-level inter-service task force led by Carlo Trojan, the Secretary General, was given the task of framing the package. The Commission sought to reassure the member states that the costs of enlargement could be absorbed and contained. A key Commission priority was to maintain a multi-annual financial perspective and a regularized budgetary process. Its proposal – *Agenda 2000: For a Stronger and Wider Union* – was published in July 1997 following the conclusion of the Inter-Governmental Conference (IGC) at Amsterdam.

The proposals set out a framework for the reform of the CAP, structural policy and the future financing of the Union. Unlike the Delors Commission, Santer adopted a cautious position by arguing that the present resource ceiling of 1.27 per cent of GNP did not need to be increased, thereby avoiding national parliamentary ratification. The Commission's proposals amounted to an extensive legislative package that would set the framework for the key policy areas to 2006. The Cardiff European Council (June 1998) set March 1999 as the deadline for agreement on the package. (The use of deadlines and a calendar technique is a common feature of EU decision making and governance.) The stakes were very high for each of the member states, for EU institutions and for those states waiting for a seat at the table. The key question was whether or not the integrative negotiations of the previous two package deals could be sustained, or would the negotiations 'unleash a bruising debate on burden sharing, reminiscent of the debilitating battle fought by Baroness Thatcher, which brought most other decision making to a standstill for several years' (*Financial Times*, 20 October 1998).

The Commission's proposals in March 1998 established the boundaries of the subsequent negotiations. A key feature of the Commission's proposals was that, unlike Delors 1 and 2, structural spending would cease to grow as a proportion of the EU budget; it was capped at the 1999 figure of 0.46 per cent of EU GNP. Consequently, existing objective one regions would bear the brunt of the reductions as a proportion of structural fund monies was set aside for the applicants. On agriculture, the Commission sought to build on the policy line adopted by MacSharry in 1992, with further reductions in price supports and an increase in compensation payments to farmers. All of these proposals were designed to ensure that the Union could afford enlargement and that the EU budget would not have to be significantly increased.

5.2 Negotiating the new deal

Once the Commission's proposals were on the table, the Council was the arena for negotiating the deal. Given the complexity and interconnectedness of the dossiers, the formal Council framework was augmented by a number of additional high-level groups of national and EU civil servants. The General Affairs Council had the co-ordinating role in the negotiations, but it was clear from the beginning that the striking of a deal would fall to the Heads of Government in a European Council. The Eco-Fin Council had the task of preparing the financial aspects of the future financial perspective. The Agricultural Council dealt with the CAP reforms. In addition to the three Councils, a plethora of committees prepared the work at political level. Two Presidencies, Austria (second half of 1998) and Germany (first half of 1999) acted as the 'managers' of the negotiations, working to a timetable established by the European Council. The negotiations were divided into three chapters, each chapter involving a number of legislative proposals: the future financial perspective, the structural funds and the reform of the CAP. All of the participants accepted that the final deal, if negotiable, would go to the European Council, scheduled by the German presidency for 25–26 March 1999.

The member states were deeply divided about the desired outcome at Berlin because the terms of agreement would have an important impact on their budgetary position. During the life of the Delors 2 package, a vocal 'net contributors' club emerged in the Union, a club that was led by Germany, determined to reduce its payments to the EU budget. In 1988 and 1992, Chancellor Kohl was willing to act as paymaster in order to achieve agreement. German contributions rose from 4 billion euro in net contributions in 1987 to 11.5 billion euro in 1995. The Netherlands, finding itself moving from the 'net beneficiary' club to the 'net contributors' club in the 1990s, supported the German position. Austria and Sweden, two newcomers, were also part of the growing number of states concerned about the financial burden of the EU budget. The UK found itself in a distinctive position in that it was not at one with the other 'net contributors' because it sought to protect its rebate. In order to placate the 'net contributors' club, the Commission promised to produce a report on the 'own resources' system of budgetary revenue by October 1998.

The 'net contributors' club was faced with a coalition of countries led by Spain that were beneficiaries of the Cohesion Fund. The attitude of the Spanish government was that it was unlikely to benefit economically from enlargement, and it was thus unwilling to pay for the costs of enlargement by suffering a reduction in its receipts from the budget. The

Aznar government was adamant that it would not accept a reduction in Cohesion Fund monies. Greece and Portugal supported the Spanish line although in a less strident manner. The fourth cohesion country, Ireland, was attempting to minimize the loss of structural funding as high economic growth lifted it above the objective one eligibility criteria.

There was a third group of countries that might be termed the minor 'net contributors', countries that bore a relatively light budgetary burden, notably, France, Italy, Belgium and Denmark. The two larger states, France and Italy, were expected to carry a heavier burden. The key cleavage between north and south was augmented by additional cleavages on CAP reform and on the question of a generalized rebate mechanism.

The negotiations did not begin to gain momentum until October 1998 when the Commission published its report on 'own resources'. The report did not contain formal proposals for changing the resource base of the budget; rather the Commission sought to provide a reasonably objective account of the position of each member state in terms of contributions to and receipts from the budget. The Commission had serious reservations about making calculations of the relative budgetary positions of the member states, but felt that the false figures being used by states in the Agenda 2000 negotiations had to be addressed. (The Commission often plays the role in EU governance of providing an objective account of relative gains and losses from the Union's policy regimes.)

The Commission report identified Germany's role as the paymaster of the Union, followed by Sweden, Austria, the Netherlands and the UK. France and Italy emerged as relatively minor contributors. The Commission suggested that if the member states were concerned about burden sharing, a simple solution would be to reduce EAGGF (agricultural) subvention from 100 per cent to 75 per cent. In other words, financing the CAP could be partly renationalized. The German government reacted enthusiastically to the proposal and that in turn brought it into direct conflict with the French government, determined to protect its privileged position in relation to farm expenditure.

The German presidency that took over the chair in the first half of 1999, under its new Chancellor Gerhard Schröder, had the task of delivering agreement by March 1999. The government was immediately confronted by the tension between its role as President of the Council and its strong national position on Agenda 2000. The German presidency established a very intensive negotiating calendar with continuous meetings on the dossiers at different levels in the Council hierarchy. The more radical proposals for a partial renationalization of CAP payments and a generalized corrective mechanism failed to gain support. Attention turned to budgetary stabilization as the means of containing or reducing what the 'net contributors' considered as excessive contributions. For the most ardent proponents of stabilization – Germany, Austria, the Netherlands and Sweden – stabilization meant keeping increases in the budget in line with inflation. This was not acceptable to the cohesion countries, particularly Spain.

The German presidency was at odds with its two large partners in the final phase of the negotiations. The conflict with France about CAP reform threatened to break the well established axis between these two countries on agriculture. The German election weakened the agricultural voice in German politics and enabled the German government to be more radical in terms of CAP reform. France was under considerable pressure to make some concessions on agriculture. The debate with the UK centred on the rebate mechanism established in 1984. The Commission's own resources report underlined the fact that the UK rebate was no longer as justified, although the UK was determined to protect its rebate from the outset and simply never budged from its position that the issue was non-negotiable.

Notwithstanding deep conflict and their differing priorities, the fifteen member states managed to conclude a new budgetary 'package deal' on 25 March 1999. The agreement hammered out in the early hours of the morning in Berlin fell well short of the budgetary figures proposed by the Commission. It represented a consolidation of the financial resources of the Union rather than a major expansion. The 'net contributors' managed to achieve a stabilization of the budget, although they would have preferred an even smaller budget, and the cohesion countries will continue to benefit from structural spending in the years ahead. The Berlin agreement was a classical EU package deal in which the parties to the negotiations reached agreement under the shadow of enlargement, the resignation of the Commission and the outbreak of war in Kosovo.

Summary

- Negotiations over the Agenda 2000 multi-annual package were marked by significant conflicts between coalitions of member states over the net gains and losses arising from enlargement in the context of a limited expansion of the budget.

- Nevertheless, the new rules and procedures survived a strong test to their effectiveness and durability, and the successful outcome showed that the budget-making process had become part of the *acquis* of the EU.

6   Finance and governance

What can a study of EU finance and budgetary processes tell us about EU governance? We noted above that the EU budget is only a small proportion of the GNP of the Union and is dwarfed by the public expenditure of the member states. Budgetary power remains a predominantly national competence within the EU. Accordingly, EU governance relies heavily on regulation and law making as its main instrument of public power. This is why the EU is often portrayed as a 'regulatory state'. However, this is a somewhat limited view of EU governance if taken in isolation. Notwithstanding its size, we have seen that the budget is of considerable importance to the EU and that it has occupied a great deal of the time and political effort of the member states and the EU's institutions.

The budget has supported and complemented the processes of economic and political integration in several ways. To begin with, budgetary resources have helped different social groups and regions in Europe to adjust to wider and deeper market integration, thereby enhancing the ability of the EU to modernize the poorer parts of the Union. Next, the budget has promoted the development of a unified social and cultural space within the EU by supporting mobility grants, student exchanges and inter-regional and cross-national co-operation. The budget has also been a mechanism that enables the EU to act externally with a foreign policy, spending resources in non-EU countries, within Europe and beyond. The development of the budget and agreement to a set of autonomous financial resources was dependent from the outset on a conception of the EU as more than an arena of market integration. Ideas and political beliefs about EU governance went beyond the creation of a market order by means of negative integration. There was agreement that the EU had a role in assisting groups or regions to adjust to the chill winds of market integration and economic competition.

6.1 Expanding the reach of the EU budget

Politically speaking, the budget has functioned as a means of gaining support for wider package deals around changes to the treaties that constitute the EU. And the budget has been an important instrument by which the Commission has been able to expand the reach of EU-level governance as a whole, providing resources to attract governments, regions, cities and groups in civil society into the Brussels policy-making arena and networks. The EU amassed additional budgetary resources in an incremental fashion with the establishment of new policy instruments. Since 1988, major episodes of treaty change have been accompanied by budgetary deals. For example, the Delors 1 package was essential to the internal market project.

At the same time, a historical analysis of EU budgetary priorities illustrates the difficulty that the Union has faced in attempting to reform the original budgetary bargain, particularly on agriculture. Although farmers are fewer in number in contemporary Europe, they have managed to protect their privileged position in relation to the budget, largely through the auspices of the CAP member states, especially France. That said, the EU has agreed new budgetary instruments and new priorities. The most significant additional priority was the growing importance of the structural funds, designed to help Europe's lagging regions catch up economically with core Europe. Another additional budgetary priority has been the growing EU expenditure in developing countries. The Union has built up a formidable range of external budgetary programmes that give it much of its presence in the international system. Together with trade, aid forms the second component of the Union's international reach.

6.2   Stabilizing the process and new 'rules of the game'

The gradual expansion in the size of the budget and its range of policy instruments was also accompanied by the search for a stable and institutionalized budgetary process. A considerable amount of political capital in EU governance is expended in the search for 'rules of the game' that both the member states and the EU institutions can agree to. Devices have had to be fashioned to contain the political disputes about budgetary resources and expenditure and to manage the inter-institutional conflict that resulted from the 1970 and 1975 Budget Treaties.

1988 was a critical juncture in these respects because, in what was a history-making budgetary decision, the member states agreed to new budgetary rules and processes that combined a large package deal, a multi-annual financial perspective and an inter-institutional agreement between the three budgetary institutions – the Commission, the Parliament and the Council. This underlines the importance of agreement on decision rules in EU governance and the effective use of a calendar technique. These large budgetary negotiations also underline another characteristic of EU governance: namely, the combination of technical negotiations at committee level and the 'high politics' of member state summitry.

The increased salience of financial management arising from the growing size of the EU budget, particularly after 1988, raised concerns about the capacity of the EU system to manage and not just to make policy. These were heightened and reached the public domain following extensive newspaper coverage of incidences of fraud against the financial interests of the Union. Those countries contributing to the EU budget wanted to ensure that their money was spent wisely and well. A financial management culture characterized by a consideration of 'value for money' and accountability began to take root. Debates about the new public management of government at national level were replicated in relation to the EU. The Court of Auditors and the EP were to the fore in highlighting the issue of financial management.

The Commission, as the administrator of the budget, was clearly challenged by the focus on financial management. Notwithstanding internal efforts to alter the Commission's management culture, according to the EP not enough had changed by January 1999. The Parliament, in a battle with the executive, forced the entire college of Commissioners to resign in March 1999, following the damning report of the 'Three Wise Men'. The appointment by the new Commission President, Prodi, of Vice-

President Kinnock as the Commissioner responsible for Commission reform underlines the degree to which management has become such a salient feature of the debate on EU governance. Although the focus is on the Commission, the member states who implement 80 per cent of the EU budget will also have to enhance their capacities for managing EU money. The legal obligations on the member states with regard to the budget have been greatly strengthened.

Summary

- The overall size of the budget has resulted in a reliance on regulatory governance, but the budget is still of great import.

- From the start, economic and political integration has not been the only goal. Support for poorer regions and for social and cultural integration in the EU, and support for countries outside the EU, has been an objective of the Union. The budget has enabled the Commission to extend the reach of EU governance across the economies and societies of the member states as well as beyond the borders of the Union.

- In regard to financial matters, EU governance is now characterized by more stable and institutionalized budgetary processes and by greater public accountability and stricter financial management.

7 Conclusion

The outcome of the Berlin Agenda 2000 negotiations in March 1999 demonstrate that a multi-annual financial perspective contained within a large package deal is part of the budgetary *acquis*. Notwithstanding the deep distributional conflicts among the member states on the main issues in the negotiations, the heads of government managed to hammer out a package that they could all agree to. The package essentially protected the status quo, although there is some shift in priorities, with designated financing for the applicants before and after they join the Union. By the same token, the absence of sizeable budgetary increases to accompany enlargement to the East underlines the limited consensus there is in the Union on public finance as an instrument of EU governance.

We shall have to wait to see if political and functional pressures arising from the single currency and enlargement will alter the balance of power in budgetary matters. Even if they do, the EU is not going to replicate the public finances of a nation state. Rather, it will continue to deploy public finance as a complement to national budgetary resources, as a support for political integration and as a supplement to market integration.

References

Laffan, B. (1997) *The Finances of the Union*, London, Macmillan.

Majone, G. (1996) *Regulating Europe*, London, Routledge.

Further reading

Hix, S. (1999) *The Political System of the European Union*, London, Macmillan (Chapter 9).

Laffan, B. (1997) *The Finances of the Union*, London, Macmillan.

Nugent, N. (1999) *The Government and Politics of the European Union*, London, Macmillan (Chapter 14).

Chapter 9
The enlargement of the European Union

Paul Lewis

1   Introduction

The claims of the EU to be a *European* Union have meant that it has, in principle, been ready to accept new members and develop as an association of as many European states as have demonstrated their willingness and asserted their right to join. With the disappearance of the Iron Curtain in 1989 the possibility of the formation of a yet broader and more complete European Union emerged. Enlargement was built into the original concept of the European Community formed in the 1950s, but only in the 1990s was it possible for it to unveil the prospect of a Union that encompassed the majority of European nations. Soon after the end of the Cold War division of Europe it became apparent that the process of enlargement would be one of the central issues – even the key development within the European Union as a whole – for the foreseeable future (Mayhew, 1998, p.xv). Together with Economic and Monetary Union, enlargement was the biggest item on the EU agenda for most of the 1990s. By the end of the decade questions of democratic legitimacy in terms of growing popular dissatisfaction with 'Brussels' and all that this entailed had also become a major issue (Dinan, 1999, pp.159–60), but enlargement remained one of the three greatest challenges involved in future EU development. It is still – with EMU and further democratization – one of the most demanding tasks to be grappled with at the outset of a new century. How it will be tackled and the success of the outcome are matters of critical importance for the development and future success of the European Union.

This chapter begins by setting the context for the contemporary phase of enlargement by looking at its role in the development of the EU, and raises some questions about its future institutional shape (Section 2). The EU has been both broadened and deepened by the enlargements to date, but the scale of the potential enlargements will now necessitate extensive reform – a recasting – of the EU itself. In Section 3 we take a closer look at the role that enlargement has played in the overall development of the

Union, and consider the formal attitude of the EU towards expansion, the nature of the process and some of its political and institutional consequences. Section 4 discusses the prospects for enlargement that confronted the EU with the end of the Cold War division of Europe and suggests that the scale and scope of the challenges for the Union are of a different order from past expansions. Not only are there many more potential entrants than before but they all have very different economic, political and even cultural backgrounds from the existing EU-15. Finally, Section 5 asks how the EU will cope with these challenges and discusses the kinds of institutional and policy reforms that might be required to accommodate the new entrants.

2 Enlargement and the contemporary EU

Since the signature of the treaty on the European Coal and Steel Community (ECSC) which formed the original community in 1951, the EU has grown from an original membership of six to one of nine (in 1973), twelve (from 1981 to 1986) and fifteen (in 1995). Figure 9.1 illustrates these enlargement stages. So far, therefore, the EU has been formed and grown in the following ways:

- it was originally founded in 1951 as the ECSC by Belgium, France, West Germany, Italy, Luxembourg and the Netherlands;
- its membership rose to nine in 1973, with Britain, Denmark and Ireland joining;
- to ten in 1981 with the accession of Greece;
- to twelve in 1986 with Portugal and Spain joining;
- to fifteen in 1995 – Austria, Finland and Sweden being the new members.

The process of enlargement has accompanied the gradual development and strengthening of the EU as an institution. But (as pointed out in Chapter 2) there has been no 'remorseless logic behind the widening, deepening EU'. Nothing, even in retrospect, has been clearly inevitable and the process of European integration has been an erratic one. In broad terms, though, enlargement can be judged to have strengthened the EU as an institution as well as having extended its borders. It has enhanced the structure and role of the EU in both economic and political terms. The Union has derived specific gains from each phase of the enlargement process, and each extension of EU borders has influenced the character and identity of the EU in different – and broadly positive – ways (Baun, 1999, p.283). Different phases of enlargement were followed by distinctive forms of Community deepening in terms of the formulation of common regional and environmental policies, the use of structural funds as a means of equalizing Community resources, as well as the strength-

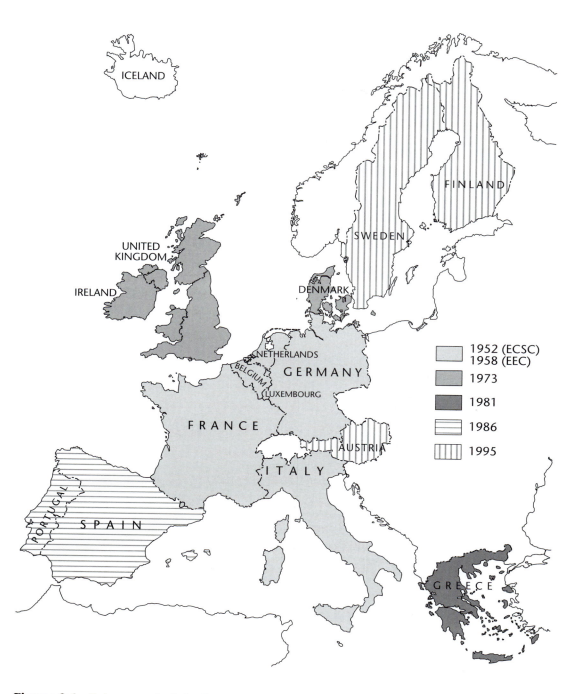

Figure 9.1 Enlargement of the European Union

ening of plans for economic and monetary union (Avery and Cameron, 1998, p.175).

Nevertheless, the progressive expansion of the EU has placed increasing strain on Community structures and the way its institutions function. Throughout the process of EU growth and continuous development, they have remained, in essence, structures devised for a community of six in the 1950s. Following the announcement of plans for yet further enlargement at the end of 1999, former President Jacques Delors thus pointed to the distinctive problems facing the EU in terms of sustaining the drive for closer European integration during the critical phase of contemporary enlargement. Lessons could be derived in this area from previous enlargements and there were, he stated, risks of diluting the whole European project and undermining efforts for integration if plans for admitting as many as twelve new members were not thought through properly (*The European Voice*, Brussels, 20–26 January 2000).

2.1   Enlargement on the contemporary plane

The growth of the original EC/EU from six to fifteen members involved the accession of nine states over forty-four years and took place in a context of gradual and multi-phased evolution; at least five of the nine new states were relatively highly developed in economic terms and all had economies that had modernized and taken shape within a capitalist framework; most had a lengthy record of well-established democracy and only three had recent experience of political authoritarianism. None of these enlargements were easy, and some involved major battles and controversy. But by the late 1990s, eleven further applicant countries were deemed eligible for membership by the EU, ten of whom (the exception being Cyprus) were former communist countries in Central and Eastern Europe. In 1999 Malta and – more tentatively – Turkey were added to the list. The enlargement that now faced the EU (see Figure 9.2) was of a far different order from that seen during its early history. The accession of Britain, Denmark and Ireland had indeed raised the number of member states by 50 per cent, but the prospect of thirteen new states joining involves the near doubling of EU membership.

Some indication of the costs of integrating post-communist economies with the West on an all-round basis is given by the relatively limited experience of German reunification throughout the 1990s. The results were not wholly encouraging in terms of annual costs through the decade of approximately $100 billion, roughly the equivalent of the entire EU budget for one year (*The Observer*, 21 March 1999). Even with spending at this level, unemployment in eastern Germany has remained high, the impact of social dislocation by no means fully dealt with, and sentiments of political dissatisfaction sometimes dangerously antagonistic. The burden this placed on the German economy imposed a significant brake

Figure 9.2   Existing and potential accession states

on the country's growth and had a major influence on recessionary tendencies within the European economy as a whole.

On the verge of this more far-reaching phase of EU enlargement the economic contrasts between existing and potential members are also striking. The ten former communist applicants have a per capita GDP less than one-third of the EU average; 22 per cent of their labour force is employed in agriculture, compared to 5 per cent in current member states during the late 1990s; and expansion from 15 to 26 members would more than double the EU population eligible for assistance provided through the Structural Funds (Baun, 1999, pp.271–2). The political context is equally problematic: lengthy communist experience has placed the democratic credentials of many applicants under close scrutiny, the human rights status of Turkey and the treatment of its Kurdish minority is highly questionable, while Cyprus remains a divided island and a source of continuing friction between Greece and Turkey.

Enlargement has been a permanent feature of the EU's experience, but the expansion of EU borders at the outset of the twenty-first century thus emerges as a process of a different order. The large number of new states cannot be accepted into the EU without changing its nature in a fundamental way, in both economic and political terms. Even if the new states, or at least some of them, can be regarded as credible democracies and will not bring about a change in the political character of the EU as a whole in that respect, the demands of integrating such a large number of new members and developing new mechanisms of integration and government will surely involve a political transformation of a highly significant kind.

2.2   Enlargement and models of EU development

The steady growth of the EU has involved an uneasy compromise between principles of intergovernmentalism and supranationalism. Early enlargements could be mixed or neutral in terms of their implications for the path of development followed in this respect. The enlargement of the community from six to nine in 1973, in which Britain was the major new member, strengthened intergovernmental tendencies. But subsequent changes tended to push the Union along the supranational path, particularly in the light of the latest accessions in 1995 which involved the membership of states with well-developed economies and strengthened the move to more integrated development in the form of economic and monetary union (although Sweden, for one, was very sceptical about the prospect of stronger economic integration at the beginning). The influence of the supranational model is likely to become that much stronger as the movement to incorporate a large number of new members accelerates in the foreseeable future. Some member states (particularly Britain) have consistently argued for the 'widening' of the EU precisely to prevent its further 'deepening'. In the current situation this increasingly appears to be a false dichotomy and quite the reverse is likely to be true of any forthcoming enlargement, although the possibility of greater differentiation in terms of kinds of EU membership (known as the issue of 'variable geometry') may further complicate this particular argument.

In general terms, the institutional consequences of enlargement now seem to point in one direction. For example, the gradual strengthening of the principle of qualified majority voting (QMV) in the Council of Ministers is likely to increase as a large number of small Central and East European countries get closer to acquiring membership. Similarly, the nature of the European Commission cannot fail to change as the number of member states approaches and promises to exceed the number of commissioners themselves (twenty at present and certainly not likely to be increased). At any rate, proposals for institutional reform are now part of the enlargement agenda (see sections 3.5 and 5.1). While, then, it is suggested in Chapter 2 that 'the more supranational its procedures, the more integrated the EU', this can be reformulated to cast a slightly different light on the consequences of future enlargement: the more integrated that Europe becomes, the more supranational the European Union. If, too, as argued in Chapter 3, the realities of political decision making 'are increasingly supranational and not just intergovernmental', this tendency will become yet stronger as the number of EU members rises from fifteen to twenty-one or twenty-eight or even more. The past history of enlargement has been very much one cast in an intergovernmental framework and, as will soon become apparent, the terms on which new members have been accepted into the community have been bitterly contested by the governments of all states involved. Previous discussions and the conflicts involved in past enlargements did not bring questions of 'supranational' development into play, but this does not necessarily mean that they can be kept off the agendas produced by the process of further enlargement.

Progressive enlargement and the institutional development of the community overall have thus meant that the EU has grown in organizational density and increased in complexity. The further 'stretching' of EU institutions and procedures is just not feasible. After earlier enlargements each new member could simply appoint a new commissioner or two, send a judge to the European Court of Justice, and elect members to the European Parliament. The sheer arithmetic of the prospective enlargement to come involves change of a qualitatively different character. Any major enlargement is likely to mean that the EU will have to recast itself and consider issues of fundamental reform far more seriously than it has done so far.

Summary

- Enlargement has been a permanent feature of the development of the EU, broadening its membership and on balance strengthening its economic and political role in the governance of Europe.

- Previous enlargements have had no clear impact on the balance between the intergovernmental and supranational features of the EU. The first expansion (Britain, Denmark and Ireland) probably strengthened intergovernmentalism, while the most recent additions (Austria, Finland and Sweden) contributed towards more integrated development.

- However, future enlargements are difficult to envisage in the absence of significant institutional reform of decision making within the EU, perhaps amounting to a major recasting of the Union in a more supranational direction.

3 The history of EU enlargement

EU members have differed in their views of enlargement, the vision they have had of developing EU structures and the degree of enthusiasm with which they have anticipated the accession of some or all prospective members. It is, however, a process that has been regarded as more or less inevitable in the long term, and the objective of a united Europe was one that lay at the heart of the post-war European project, even though national interests often seemed to take precedence over a broader European commitment.

3.1 EU commitment to enlargement

The six countries that formed the original European Economic Community in 1957 already saw themselves as forerunners of a more inclusive association and representative of a broader Europe. A commitment to extending that community to other states that could reasonably claim a European identity was present from the outset and effectively part of its founding constitution. The Cold War division both of Germany and of the continent as a whole was, in particular, always deplored by the states of the free West and the eventual union of both was anticipated at some unforeseen date in the future (although this did not mean that when a plausible timetable eventually emerged for this it was universally welcomed). The Union Treaty of 1992 thus echoes the Treaty of Rome, which established the EEC in 1957, in affirming that: 'Any European State may apply to become a Member of the Union'.

The clarity of this position, though, has always been qualified by the fact that neither the EU nor any of its predecessors has pronounced on a geographical definition of Europe. Indeed, only by avoiding attempts at precise definition has the possibility of forming any 'Europe' been sustained at all. At times this vagueness has led to the longer established members of the Union tending to assume that European integration was synonymous with western European integration and a process centring on the River Rhine, regarding enlargement as a distant concern with little more than ritual significance. In the mid 1980s, for example, it was necessary for the report of the Dooge Committee on EC institutional reform to begin with the affirmation that the Community has 'not lost sight of the fact that it represents only a part of Europe' (Dinan, 1999, p.185).

Even more than the accession of the Mediterranean states during the 1980s, though, the prospect of substantial enlargement to the east that emerged in 1989 was perceived as being as much a threat to the interests of existing EC members as a promise of enhanced European unity. (The accession of the developed countries of the European Free Trade Association (EFTA) during the 1990s was never viewed in this light as it did not impose any additional costs.) It was ironic, though hardly surprising, that recent arrivals like Spain and Portugal were among the most vociferous opponents of proposals to give the more advanced east-central European countries liberalized access to EU markets in the early 1990s. A more generous mood of European unity finally prevailed, however, and the prospect of more substantial enlargement became firmly established on the EU agenda, although completion of the process promised to be lengthy, complex and hard fought by all involved. EU enlargement in general has been considerably more fraught and contentious than it seems in retrospect, and the process of expansion has by no means been a straightforward one.

3.2   Conditions for enlargement

Commitment to the principle of enlargement has not meant, firstly, that all European applicants could automatically become members. The obvious initial condition for membership was a willingness to join, and this was conspicuously lacking in the case of the UK in the early post-war days when Britain saw its role as primarily a global rather than a European one, and its position defined more by relations with the USA and a still extensive empire than by links with European neighbours. But membership of the EC became increasingly attractive to both Britain and other European states, and the 'pull' of the European Union has grown increasingly stronger. The motivation to join the EU has become more compelling as the Union has developed more dynamic institutions and expanded into a wider range of activities.

The motives of more recent applicants have been summarized under the following areas (Jones, 1996, pp.275–6):

- guaranteed access to EU markets and the boost given to intra-EU trade;
- insider participation and influence over the Union's decision-making processes;
- fear of marginalization and isolation from major European developments;
- access to resource transfers and benefits enjoyed by the less wealthy members;

- better prospects of investment – at least on the basis of Spanish and Portuguese experience;

- removal of Cold War prohibitions on entry for neutrals as well as east European states;

- lack of alternatives to EU membership after COMECON and the shrinkage of EFTA;

- panic over the 'closing door' and fear of being left at the end of a long queue.

In terms of the current post-communist applicants a general, and rather ill-defined, desire for 'security' in material and political as well as military terms has also been very important. The major distinctions with respect to objectives, membership and sphere of operations between the EU and NATO were not fully appreciated. The main objective was to get as firmly anchored into Western structures as soon as possible. Accompanying this were equally general (although undoubtedly strong and sincerely held) aspirations of a more cultural nature for a 'return to Europe' and the adoption of the fully 'modern' lifestyles exemplified by the developed West. Powerful and compelling as these motivations have been in the Central and East European context, they may also mean that the prospective EU members 'may increasingly be joining for the "wrong" reasons: their motivation is not positive – they lack the desire to pursue the vision of Europe of the (more federalist) existing members – but is essentially negative – they simply do not want to be left out' (Croft et al., 1999, p.66).

In the early stages, too, the political and economic conditions of EU membership were not always clearly specified, although the terms of accession for Greece, Portugal and Spain after periods of authoritarian rule made it clear that both a certain level of free-market economic develop-ment and a democratic orientation was required. Before then, the approach taken was very much ad hoc which, it was later realized, could lead to some faulty judgements. It came to be generally recognized that it was a mistake to conclude an association agreement in 1963 with Turkey which virtually promised eventual entry to the Community (Jones, 1996, p.280). The conditions for joining the EU were initially understood to be primarily economic, although political requirements were at least implicit in the process. While not spelled out very firmly, they were clearly present in the changing view taken of Spain and Portugal after the end of dictatorship in the 1970s. On some occasions political considerations were more prominent, as when the Council of Ministers overrode the Commission's negative opinion on Greece's application based on its assessment of overall Greek economic backwardness and the need for an unlimited period of transition before a final decision was taken (Nugent, 1999, pp.29–30).

On a basis of accepting new members that combines economic and political considerations, therefore, the EU has grown in size over the years, but suffered a short-term reduction in average GDP following all accessions apart from that of the former EFTA members in 1995 (Table 9.1).

Table 9.1   The impact of successive enlargements

EU member states	Area	Percentage increase in:			Average per capita GDP: EC6 = 100
		Population	Total GDP	Per capita GDP	
From 6 to 9	31	32	24	−6	94
From 9 to 10	9	4	2	−2	92
From 10 to 12	34	16	9	−8	85
From 12 to 15	17	6	8	+1	86

(Ardy, 1999, p.109)

By the time that the Central and East European States were in a position to contemplate membership, and under the considerably greater pressure exerted by the wide range of post-communist applicants, the conditions for accession were more precisely defined. The conditions of membership for the countries of Central and Eastern Europe were spelled out by the European Council in Copenhagen during 1993, and these have since come to be regarded as having more general application. Later changes fleshed out the previously accepted position by clarifying that this concerned European states which accepted the principles of liberty, democracy, respect for human rights and fundamental freedoms, and the rule of law (Avery and Cameron, 1998, p.23). The European Council summed up the criteria in three main areas:

- the stability of institutions guaranteeing democracy, the rule of law, human rights, and respect for and protection of minorities;
- the existence of a market economy, as well as the capacity to cope with competitive pressures and market forces within the EU;
- an ability to take on the obligations of membership, including adherence to the aims of political, economic and monetary union.

3.3   Consequences of enlargement

The successive enlargements have considerably strengthened the structure and role of the EU in both economic and political terms. They have lent conviction to its claim to be a more fully constituted European body, a status that is further strengthened by the positive approach taken to the critical challenge of eastern enlargement and the steps taken to involve at least the more developed of the post-communist countries in EU processes. Enlargement has, therefore, facilitated the overall coherence of the region in both economic and political terms, and the Union has derived particular gains from each phase of the process which has affected the character and identity of the EU in different ways (Baun, 1999, p.283). These involve a range of factors. The admission of Britain, Denmark and Ireland added a more sceptical and pragmatic dimension to the group of founding members, strengthened transatlantic links and introduced elements that sometimes resisted the growing pull of pan-European integration. The enlargements of the 1980s enhanced its Mediterranean aspect and made it a more agricultural – and generally poorer – entity (although the most obvious consequence was the accelerated development of the modestly endowed new entrants). The accession of Sweden, Finland and Austria counterbalanced the southern expansion and opened perspectives on strengthened links with Eastern Europe. They also gave some impetus to social-democratic traditions within the EU, and heightened the prominence of liberal and market tendencies associated with the former European Free Trade Area (EFTA).

Generalization about the specific effects of EU enlargement should, nevertheless, not be taken too far. The EU and its predecessors have evolved over several decades in a rapidly changing global context and the distinctive influences cannot be clearly separated. The effects of accession have also been rather different in cases that might appear, at first glance, to be relatively similar. Greece, for example, did not prosper much overall from membership apart from the direct support it received from EU agencies. Between 1981 and 1990 real GDP grew by only 1.7 per cent per annum, inflation stood at around 18–20 per cent, and its public sector borrowing requirement rose to 20 per cent of GDP by 1990. By that stage it took Portugal's place as the poorest member of the community. In 1981 Greek per capita GDP had been 58 per cent of the EC average; by 1990 it stood at 51 per cent. A harsh economic climate at the time of accession, inappropriate domestic policy and the tempting capacity to compensate for national weakness by reliance on EU subsidies all played a part in the relatively poor Greek performance. An underlying ambivalence to Western Europe, strong traditions of ethnic nationalism and a sharply divided social structure also contributed to the problems encountered in building a path of socio-economic development close to that embodied in the prevailing EU model.

The results of the first decade of Spanish and Portuguese membership were far more positive and at odds with a number of more pessimistic expectations. EC membership 'not only accelerated economic growth and structural change, but also brought tangible welfare gains to most of their inhabitants and "progressive" changes in thinking, attitudes, institutions and practice' (Bideleux, 1996, pp.134, 149). In this context it may not be an exaggeration to suggest that these experiences represent different models of accession, and that the Greek and Iberian paths of development may be replicated in different aspects of the east European enlargement, both positively and negatively, in political as well as economic aspects.

3.4 Conflicts and tensions in the enlargement process

All enlargements have been lengthy and complex processes, and fourteen distinct stages between application and accession can be identified (Avery and Cameron, 1998, pp.24–5). Some accessions have been relatively rapid (less than three years in the case of Finland), but others slower and considerably more cumbersome. Those of Denmark, Ireland and the UK took more than eleven years (including the failed first attempts to join); they still took more than five years if just the single successful application is considered. Of some relevance to contemporary applicants, whose economic levels are less advanced and whose democratic background is more problematic, is the case of Spain whose accession also took more than eight years.

The process of enlargement has not been a smooth one or, indeed, a one-way process. Norway was accepted as a member both in 1973 and for accession in 1995, but national referendums failed to confirm the accession. Switzerland began the process of accession in 1992, but this too was abandoned due to lack of popular support. Iceland had also considered joining in 1973, but decided its interests were best pursued outside the Union. Greenland, too, had joined the EC in 1973 as a dependency of Denmark. In 1979 it gained its autonomy, and in 1985 it left the Community, the first and – so far – only territory to do so.

EU enlargement has, therefore, not been an inevitable process for all potential members, nor has it been a status universally desired. Existing members often resisted the accession of new members, at least in the short term or not before 'the conditions were right' (a diplomatic euphemism for 'never'?). EU bodies themselves might be divided over such cases, as noted in the case of Greece. National interests have played a large part in pre-accession negotiations, and acrimonious conflicts over accession conditions have often been involved. Building on Britain's early refusal to contemplate any close European partnership, French President de Gaulle consistently refused British overtures and vetoed the possibility of entry when later governments adopted a different attitude from that of Churchill and the post-war Labour government. Only after de Gaulle's retirement was Britain able to join in 1973, in the company of Denmark and Ireland, two countries with strong links to the British economy.

In the context of a later enlargement involving a relatively small country, the prospect of Portuguese accession seemed to cause fewer problems than that of Spain, but this was not always apparent at the time. Under Prime Minister Margaret Thatcher, Britain supported Portugal as a traditional ally with the general intention of creating a wider and weaker Community. President Giscard d'Estaing blocked accession procedures for both Spain and Portugal to protect the interests of French agriculture and maximize political support among peasant farmers, a major constituency in the 1981 presidential elections. Only after Mitterand's election to the French presidency in May 1981 did negotiations begin to move forward again. Even then, the treatment of issues concerning textiles, fisheries and the free movement of labour was a source of major dissension – conflicts that had by no means fully subsided twenty years later (Dinan, 1999, pp.105–6).

The accession of the three EFTA members (Austria, Finland and Sweden) in 1995 was considerably faster and apparently a lot smoother, but this was largely because the countries concerned had already adopted much of the body of EU laws and rules (the *acquis communautaire*) and were members of the European Economic Area, whose construction had been completed by EFTA and the EU in 1991. The *acquis* is of considerable importance in the accession process; it comprises the extensive body of EU legislation, all treaties it has entered into, and the case law it has built up over the years (Avery and Cameron, 1998, p.32). But some issues in the development of the EEA were bitterly fought, particularly those arising between Scandinavia and the Iberian countries over fishing rights, as well as others concerning heavy truck transit through Austria and Switzerland, and Spanish demands for increased subsidies from EFTA members. Further battles were fought in the more focused accession negotiations that followed, particularly on the terrain of agriculture, environmental policy, fishing and energy policy. Norway was understandably reluctant to grant EU access to its extensive resources in the latter two areas and, despite the accession agreements being satisfactorily brought to an end, the differences of interest made an important contribution to the refusal of the Norwegian electorate to confirm accession. Even greater conflicts of interest were perceived when the possibility of substantial enlargement to the east of the EU arose.

3.5 Institutional outcomes of enlargement

Enlargement has generally played a positive role in the overall development of the EU, the strengthening of its structures, as well as the evolution and growth of its individual members (although in this respect the post-accession fate of Greece may be rated relatively negatively in comparison to the more positive developments in Spain and Portugal). Equally, however, the development of the remaining countries outside the EU (Switzerland, Norway and Iceland) cannot be evaluated negatively, they have hardly suffered by remaining outside its structures. The case of the Central and East European countries is rather different, but they did not remain outside the EU as a result of national choice and a whole range of other factors entered into their failure to prosper during the post-war period. As well as individual member nation states, the EU itself has developed in a number of important ways throughout its now lengthy existence and the sequence of enlargements. But the relationship between the process of enlargement and the institutional development of the EU has not been an easy one.

The sequence of enlargements has placed increasing pressure on institutional arrangements devised several decades ago for just six members (Baun, 1999, p.280–1). The decision-making processes had worked quite satisfactorily for a few states that had recently combined to pursue a commonly agreed purpose. These processes had become far less effective as time wore on, new members joined, a whole range of unforeseen issues emerged to be tackled and the overall purpose of the Union became less certain. Major aspects of reform that have been proposed concern reductions in the size of the Commission, the re-weighting of votes in the Council, and the extended use of QMV. Key policy areas and aspects of EU activity that account for the largest part of Union expenditure were also crying out for attention – particularly when the accession of less developed agricultural countries was at issue and economic disparities within the EU were set to rise dramatically. The Common Agricultural Policy and structural policies required serious attention, particularly as overall expenditure was not set to rise. The view prevailed that, as presented in Commission proposals for the 2000–2006 period, eastern enlargement could be managed within the budgetary limits set at the Edinburgh Council held in 1992 (it proved politically impossible for any of the major players to mount a serious challenge to this proposal).

Attempts at institutional reform have been involved in several of the key phases of enlargement but the demands of change have (increasingly) not been fully confronted. A Commission report on 'The Challenge of Enlargement' published in 1992 expressed the clear view that institutional reform to tackle the issues outlined above was necessary if a larger EU was to operate effectively, but the following years saw little practical progress in such reform. The Treaty on European Union that emerged in February 1992 after the conference at Maastricht (held in 1991) proved to be remarkably difficult to ratify in a number of member countries, was quite vague in many matters of detail, and already permitted opt-outs in some key areas for Denmark and the UK. It can be seen as a defensive device to 'deepen' the EU before the major process of 'widening' was really broached in terms of the Central and East European enlargement but, while formulating a broad agenda for EU institutional development, it is not one whose provisions have yet been carried out (Croft et al., 1999, p.67).

Issues of reform were again high on the agenda at the Intergovernmental Conference (IGC) that opened in March 1996 and ran into 1997, concluding in Amsterdam during June. A Reflection Group was established in July 1995 to begin the formal debate over the reform of the institutional system that was to be conducted during the IGC. An initial report identified the main issues as the size of the Commission and the Parliament, and the reform of the voting system in the Council of Ministers. The Treaty concluded at Amsterdam, however, failed to come to any agreement on the basic issues and settled only some of the less important points. The powers of the European Parliament were somewhat enlarged and the scope of QMV was widened, but no major initiatives were launched. With regard to the key areas, the most that was agreed was that a further IGC on institutional reform has to be convened 'at least one year before the membership of the EU exceeds twenty'. To this extent the Amsterdam Treaty had to be regarded as a significant failure (Dinan, 1999, p.182).

Enlargement has increasingly exacerbated the weaknesses and acknowledged shortcomings in EU structure, but has at the same time made it more difficult to find solutions for them. The initial agenda for the next IGC, which opened in February 2000, was therefore deliberately restricted to three main items left unresolved by the Amsterdam Treaty:

the re-weighting of votes in the Council, limiting the number of European Commissioners in an enlarged Union, and extending QMV (*The European Voice*, Brussels, 10–16 February 2000). Almost inevitably, it seemed, the diverse interests of EU members would cause the agenda to be lengthened, but the nearing of the date when decisions on enlargement will finally have to be taken should mean that agreement will be that much easier to reach.

Summary

- The history of EU enlargement is one of the contrasts and diverging processes indicated in the main themes of EU development.

- A broad *consensus* has existed in the EU with regard to the desirability of enlargement and the principle of uniting Europe as a whole through this means. This has always been accompanied by bitter *conflicts* between the different member states about the acceptability of different potential members and the conditions they should meet before being accepted.

- A drive towards *unity* has clearly made great progress within the EU in terms of gradually strengthening processes of intergovernmental co-operation and possible signs of supranational development. The logic of enlargement points to the growth of unity and further integration. However, great *diversity* still exists in Europe as a whole; further integration will need to take due account of the strong elements of diversity that remain and institutions need to be evolved that take account of national and regional differences.

- The principle of *inclusion* has clearly prevailed throughout the lengthy period of EU development and the sequence of enlargements. Paradoxically, the degree of inclusiveness that has been achieved was premised until 1989 by the *exclusion* of at least half of Europe from formal union. Even since that date not all European countries are considered to be viable applicants for EU membership and some remain excluded from formal plans for continuing enlargement.

4   The contemporary process of enlargement

The process of enlargement that confronted the EU with the end of the Cold War division of Europe was of a different kind from those which had previously taken place. Previous enlargements were all comparable in terms of the level of economic development and political background of the applicants, whereas the future challenge to the existing EU that took shape during the 1990s was distinctive in terms of:

- the sheer number of applicants,
- the size of the economic gap between the applicants and existing members,
- the distinctive political background of the applicants and uncertainty about their contemporary status,
- the degree of institutional change that would be required of existing EU arrangements.

The prospective enlargement that took shape during the 1990s was, therefore, the first in which the burden of adjustment was to be borne not just by the new members but also by the existing EU in terms of the need to change existing procedures and undertake significant internal reform (Baun, 1999, p.280).

4.1   Mixed responses to the removal of the Iron Curtain

Initial responses to the accelerating pace of change in Eastern Europe during the late 1980s were mixed. In view of the lengthy restriction of processes of 'European' integration in the West of the continent and the manifold uncertainties that surrounded the unprecedented changes that were under way in the East, early EU responses were surprisingly positive. In July 1989 the Commission, on behalf of Western Europe, accepted responsibility for co-ordinating aid to Poland and Hungary, the countries furthest forward in terms of political change. Five months later, in December 1989, the EU launched its PHARE programme (Poland–Hungary: Actions for Economic Restructuring) which became the main framework for co-ordinating assistance, first to the two countries mentioned, then in July 1990 to Bulgaria, Czechoslovakia, East Germany and Yugoslavia, and in October 1991 to the Baltic states. It channelled 500 million euros to the East in 1990 and double that amount in 1992. It soon encompassed the European post-communist area as a whole and, in association with the European Bank for Reconstruction and Development (EBRD) proposed by President Mitterand and established in 1990, became the main agent of change facilitating the transformation of the east European economies along free-market lines.

The political responses were, in some ways, more mixed and the process of establishing new relations between the EU and the newly liberated countries less steady. The emerging prospects for a more extensive EU were closely linked with the controversial issue of German unification (they were imaginatively and cleverly linked by Chancellor Kohl in a speech to the German parliament on 28 November 1989). Prime Minister Margaret Thatcher and President Mitterand were both particularly sceptical about Kohl's proposals for a united Germany, although Mitterand at least soon came to share Kohl's vision. As the Commission moved forward to build on the PHARE programme, too, these initiatives also provoked conflict among existing EU members. Early trade and co-operation agreements with some east European countries had been signed in 1988 and 1989, and in 1990 the Commission proposed that new 'European agreements' should be concluded with the more advanced countries of Czechoslovakia, Hungary and Poland (the 'Visegrad' group – named after the Hungarian location where a co-operation agreement was concluded).

The negotiations to complete the agreements were lengthy, and attempts to liberalize mutual market access were often resisted as existing EU members sought to protect domestic industries and national economic interests. Steel, agriculture and textiles were particular objects of contention, and France, Portugal and Spain were particularly active in the defence of national interests. A demonstration by French farmers against the opening up of EC markets for Central and East European produce prompted Commission President Jacques Delors to complain that it made no sense to shed tears of joy for a united Europe one moment and then to block the sale of eastern products the next (Dinan, 1999, pp.188–9).

4.2   Agreement on new conditions for enlargement

European agreements with Czechoslovakia, Hungary and Poland were finally signed in December 1991, and went beyond the basic economic accord to include an acknowledgement that membership of the EC was the final objective of all three countries. This, however, brought little stability into a rapidly changing situation. If, as some had seemed to hope, the European agreements would provide some satisfaction for east European aspirations and delay application for EU membership this was not what happened. The eyes of most east European governments were firmly set on full integration with Europe, if only as a long-term goal. Many in Eastern Europe, as well as in the USA, were critical of the limited trade concessions granted by the EU and of the Union's general reluctance to clarify the conditions that had to be satisfied before new members could be accepted from the post-communist world. Most east European governments were eager to get on with the process, as were some Western governments – although, as with the British, this was often in order to weaken the process of EU integration and make it more difficult to construct powerful institutions rather than to strengthen the European association overall.

The Commission responded to the growing pressure, and in June 1992 spelled out the factors that would be involved in deciding whether new applications would be viewed positively or not. Intense negotiations over the ratification of the Treaty on European Union were proceeding at the same time, so progress on east European enlargement was relatively slow. It was not until the Copenhagen summit in June 1993 that a decision on the accession criteria was taken, after which the 'Copenhagen criteria' (spelled out in the last section) became established as the basis on which formal accession processes could begin. The evolution of a coherent and positive attitude of the EU towards potential applicants in Eastern Europe had, hardly surprisingly, already taken several years. A common positive view had to be established and basic criteria set in place before the accession process could begin in formal terms. The submission of an application is the very first stage by which an eventual accession process gets under way – and it was clear from the lengthy preparatory period that acceptance of all or any of the current thirteen applicants would not be a rapid process.

The first applications from the post-communist countries came directly after the Copenhagen meeting of the European Council that gave the green light to go ahead. Hungary and Poland applied in March and April 1994 respectively, and the others followed in 1995 and 1996. Other potential applicants remained in an official ante-chamber, although several other countries outside post-communist Eastern Europe had been accepted as possible members by the end of the decade. Russia and other former Soviet countries, with the significant exception of the Baltic states, were not offered European agreements and remained outside the circle of potential members. An informal dividing line seems to have been drawn across the 'new Europe' in this sense, although the basis for the differentiation has not been spelled out. Turkey had also applied as far back as 1987, but remained blocked from 1989 to 1999. Cyprus, too, applied in 1990, but after a favourable judgement in 1993 found its progress very slow. Malta also applied in 1990, but suspended the process as government policy changed. By the end of 1999, though, all had been accepted as potential members and valid applicants.

Once formal applications had been made the thirteen other stages of accession all had to be confronted. Concrete preparations got under way after the Essen meeting of the European Council in December 1994 with the drafting of detailed plans for the participation of Central and East European countries in the single market. The White Paper on the subject published soon after contained guidelines for engagement in the single market by each economic sector, and applicants were faced with a daunting range of complicated tasks – particularly daunting because their overall level of economic development was strikingly low (see Table 9.2), lengthy post-war experience under a Soviet-style system had provided them with little expertise or knowledge of modern market economies, and the quality of administration was also generally quite poor. The tasks were squarely faced and specific requirements met with considerable dedication, showing a degree of practical commitment that followed from the general eastern enthusiasm for the European cause and eventual EU membership. The action was carried forward as the European Commission investigated conditions in the applicant countries and evaluated their state of readiness to join the Union.

Table 9.2 Indicators of Central and East European economies and the European Union in 1995

	Population, m.	Gross Domestic Product:			Purchasing power as % of EU 15
		Billion ECU	% of EU 15	ECU per cap.	
Poland	38.6	90.2	1.4	2 360	3
Romania	22.7	27.3	0.4	1 200	2.
Czech Rep	10.3	36.1	0.6	3 490	5.
Hungary	10.2	33.4	0.5	3 340	3
Bulgaria	8.4	9.9	0.2	1 180	2
Slovakia	5.4	13.3	0.2	2 470	4
Lithuania	3.7	3.5	0.1	930	2
Latvia	2.5	3.4	0.1	1 370	1
Slovenia	2.0	14.2	0.2	7 240	5
Estonia	1.5	2.8	(0.04)	3 340	2
CEE – 10*	105.3	234.0	3.6	2 220	3
EU – 15	371.6	6441.5	100.0	17 260	10

[*CEE-10 refers to ten states in Central and East Europe: Poland, Hungary, Czech Republic, Slovakia, Estonia, Slovenia, Latvia, Lithuania, Romania and Bulgaria.

(Ardy, 1999, p.108)

4.3 Agenda 2000 and the decision on membership negotiations

Formal Commission 'Opinions' on the applicants were prepared and delivered in July 1997, the outcome being the decision that membership negotiations should begin with five post-communist countries plus Cyprus (Avery and Cameron, 1998, p.43). Objective economic and political judgements were of prime importance in identifying the leading candidates for membership. Nevertheless, more pragmatic considerations also came into play as proposals were formulated for Estonia and Slovenia to combine with Hungary, Poland and the Czech Republic to form an advanced group of east European applicants ready for fast-track accession negotiations. The case of the first two countries was strongly promoted by the Scandinavians (for Estonia) and Austria (for Slovenia), but there was also a clear inclination to extend the group beyond the obvious three so as not merely to duplicate the process of NATO enlargement. The relationship between the EU and NATO, and their parallel though differently conceived projects for enlargements, is a complex one that cannot be explored here. It is certainly possible, though, that the

European Commission had its own reasons to push its recommendations for enlargement beyond that of NATO (Smith, 1999, p.56). The decision to open negotiations with as many as five countries certainly carried a stronger promise of regional stability and co-ordinated development than the more restricted choice made by NATO.

The opinions and report on the impact of enlargement were published as a general statement, *Agenda 2000*, which comprised a collection of official views and guidelines that dominated discussion of the issue for the rest of the decade. The general conclusions about the applicants' suitability for EU membership fell into the following three main categories (Dinan, 1999, p.193).

- Democracy and the rule of law: constitutional and institutional arrangements were judged to be adequate, and all countries apart from Slovakia had put them into practice.

- Functioning market economy, competitive pressures and market forces: good progress had been made by all applicants, but much remained to be done in terms of structural reform, improvements in the banking and financial sector, and in social security.

- The *acquis communautaire*: all had begun to incorporate the extensive *acquis* into national law, but much still had to be done. The weak basis of the Central and East European States (CEES) in terms of a very limited administrative and judicial capacity made the process that much more demanding and time-consuming for new applicants.

Apart from the opinions expressed on the specific countries applying for membership, *Agenda 2000* also identified the principal questions that arose for all applicants hoping to progress through the enlargement process to eventual membership. The areas they covered (Avery and Cameron, 1998, pp.107–13) are summarized in the points below.

- *Agriculture*, where certain price gaps could be identified between applicant countries and the existing EU (prices were cheaper in the former), although they were expected to diminish in the near future. Quotas and transitional arrangements would be needed to maintain stability in the medium term and, in particular, to moderate the impact accession would have on processing industries and the consumer market. This was an area of critical importance, if only because of the sheer size of the farm sector (see Table 9.3).

The euro in the marketplace

Table 9.3 Agriculture in Central and Eastern Europe and the European Union in 1995

	Agriculture as: percentage of employment	Value added to national economy
Romania	34.4	20.5
Poland	26.9	7.6
Lithuania	23.8	9.3
Bulgaria	23.2	13.9
CEE – 10	22.5	8.6
EU – 15	5.3	2.4

(Ardy, 1999, p.116)

- *Cohesion Policy*, in terms of which the commitment of the EU to economic and social cohesion meant that new members would progressively benefit from co-financing under continuing structural policies. Applicants should take full advantage of pre-accession assistance in order to benefit fully from these provisions. This was also of great importance because structural funds accounted, with agriculture, for by far the largest part of EU expenditure (29.3 and 52.0 per cent respectively in 1995). As the overall cost of the EU budget was not intended to rise for existing member states (remaining limited to 1.27 per cent of national GDP) and the projected increase was limited to that expected from normal processes of economic growth, outgoings for existing recipients were planned to fall between 1999 and 2006 as new members joined. The relative sums involved were not large in terms of the needs of countries negotiating for membership, but any reductions for existing recipients would certainly be keenly felt (Table 9.4).

Table 9.4 *Agenda 2000* expenditure on structural operations (in ECU billion)

	1999	2000	2001	2002	2003	2004	2005	2006
EU – 15	34.3	34.2	35.0	34.2	33.2	32.1	31.1	30.2
New members	–	0.0	0.0	3.6	5.6	7.6	9.6	11.7
Pre-accession aid	–	1.0	1.0	1.0	1.0	1.0	1.0	1.0

(Ardy, 1999, p.112)

- *Implementation of the Single Market*, which is crucially important because it offers a major potential for growth and new jobs. Potential problems in the areas of agriculture and labour mobility should not be used to prevent full implementation or as excuses for protectionism.

- *Environmental Standards*, a major concern during enlargement and a primary focus of attention for the current applicants; 'massive investment' will be needed, which will require close co-ordination with EU agencies.

- *Transport*, another very important area for investment. Substantial EU support should be available for planned trans-European networks (TENs).

- *Nuclear Safety*, where the continuing use of plant based on some variants of Soviet technology raises particular anxiety. Supervision and safety upgrading will be sufficient for some plant, but closures are being envisaged in Bulgaria, Lithuania and Slovakia.

- *Freedom, Security and Justice*, where major reforms and substantial training will be needed; institution building during the pre-accession period will be of 'utmost importance'.

- *Border Disputes* should be resolved before accession and not imported into the EU. In the event of continuing conflict, candidate countries should 'submit unconditionally to compulsory jurisdiction'. Cyprus is likely to be a particularly sensitive case in this respect.

- *Application of Community Rules Prior to Accession*, an important dimension which should take precedence over other international or domestic agreements.

The accession process was launched in a more concrete way with meetings of the foreign ministers of all eleven countries concerned during March 1998. Bilateral governmental conferences then carried the process forward in terms of detailed accession negotiations with the six main candidates accorded priority at this stage (Avery and Cameron, 1998, p.135). The first stage involved an analytical review of the *acquis* conducted by officials of the European Commission and representatives of the governments of the applicant countries, in effect a screening process that was due to last until July 1999. Running in parallel was the substantive bilateral negotiation that began in November 1998, and initially concerned seven of the thirty-one chapters or specific issue areas that had already been covered in the screening process. As late as March 1999, though, the principle negotiators of some central European governments were still of the opinion that the substantive issues had yet to be raised and that effective negotiations were only just about to commence. Central European representatives were still complaining the following year that negotiations over key issues like agriculture, regional policy, and the free movement of people were being held up by the failure of the Commission and EU governments to define their position on these highly sensitive questions (*The European Voice*, Brussels, 23–29 March 2000).

What this implied for the date of any eventual accession was unclear, although one general principle that could be accepted was that any date originally proposed for accession was soon likely to be set back. President Chirac and Chancellor Kohl had both mentioned the year 2000 during the early phase of negotiations, but even at the time this was a date set in the context of political rhetoric rather than a formal EU target. By the end of the 1990s, 2002 was often seen as the year of the first new accession and financial proposals in *Agenda 2000* also assume that some countries will join in that year (Avery and Cameron, 1998, pp.41, 177). By early 2000, though, 2003 was accepted as the target date for the first accession. But this, too, may soon appear to be prematurely set and the only certainty appears to be that further slippage is not just likely but probably inevitable. Moreover, the extent of the current enlargement process became that much larger in October 1999 with the announcement of the European Commission that all countries which had lodged an application to join should now be judged ready to join the accession process (although this was cast in somewhat more qualified and preparatory terms for Turkey). This position was confirmed at the Helsinki conference held in December 1999.

In total this meant that thirteen countries now had practical prospects of EU membership, and negotiations with five more Central and East European States (Bulgaria, Latvia, Lithuania, Romania and Slovakia) thus began in March 2000. This raised a number of important and increasingly sensitive questions about the status of the first-wave accession countries identified in 1997. The opening negotiations on a broader Central and East European front were accompanied by the reassurance that even those now just beginning could catch up and join as quickly as some of those in the first wave. This, however, provoked further anxiety on the part of the more advanced central European states that the complexity of the whole process could now be used as an excuse to delay the accession of all countries or hold back the membership of particularly problematic cases. Broadly speaking, the dominant view propounded in the Spring of 2000 was that the vanguard of first-wave countries identified in 1997 was still likely to join as a group before the other applicants, but there was no shortage of alternative voices to be heard expressing different views on this critical question.

4.4   The Mediterranean dimension

Much of the content of *Agenda 2000*, and the debate on enlargement throughout the 1990s, was concerned with the prospects and outcome of EU membership of the former communist countries of Central and Eastern Europe. They provided by far the greatest challenge to the EU in terms of extending the boundaries of the existing Union and were, for the most part, clearly engaged in a major process of 'Europeanization', which involved both radical economic transformation and fundamental political reform. Even then, extensive parts of Eastern Europe (former Soviet countries and parts of the Balkans) had not filed an application for EU membership and, of those that had, only the five more developed countries received priority attention in the late 1990s. This limited selection already presented the EU with an enormous task of enlargement. For the time being, potential members outside the Central and East European region posed far less of a problem. In terms of the other possible area of EU enlargement, the south and broadly constituted Mediterranean area, only Cyprus received much attention. Its economic situation created few problems, as its population at some 734,000 (1994) was very small and around half that even of Estonia, the other small country identified for rapid accession negotiations in 1997. Much of its economy was quite well developed and closely integrated with that of Greece.

The problems likely to crop up in relation to Cyprus essentially concerned the island's divided status between Greece and Turkey, which sharply reflected the wide-ranging historical antagonism between those two countries themselves. This had an economic dimension, as average annual income in the Turkish-dominated north was about 3600 euro, approximately one-third of that of the Greek south. The main challenge, though, was to achieve some form of agreement between the hostile ethnic communities, as integration with the Union without a basic political settlement was quite inconceivable. This in turn involved consideration of Turkey's fractious relations with Greece and the prolonged stand-off in relations between Turkey and the EU as a whole. The potential problems of integrating Cyprus undoubtedly sharpened the EU focus on the country, but a general improvement in relations followed reconsideration of Turkey's status after its participation during 1999 as a NATO member in the war on Serbia and improved relations with Greece after the earthquake the same year. The more favourable EU view of Turkish accession culminated in the statement on the issue made at the Helsinki conference (December 1999), although it was still distanced from the twelve other applicants.

Turkey's new status raised considerable problems of a broadly 'east European' nature in terms of its level of economic development, which was reflected in a GDP per capita less than all fast-track Central and East European applicants and even below that of some former communist countries not considered for EU membership. A ranking of all EU members and potential members in terms of general readiness for accession placed Turkey at 27 in a list of 28, just above Bulgaria (*Economist*, 18 December 1999). The stability of Turkish democracy, its record on human rights and treatment of the Kurdish minority (which has involved major military operations) also raise searching political questions. In addition, unlike Cyprus and Malta (the other small and less problematic Mediterranean candidate for membership confirmed in 1999), it is a large country with 59 million inhabitants in 1995. Another aspect to note is Turkey's European status and the general 'Europeanness' of its identity that is also needed to make it a viable applicant for EU membership. Few seem to have regarded this as any obstacle to EU membership, and there appears to be broad public acceptance of a European *cultural* area relatively open to influence and mutual exchange both to the east and to the south of a traditionally conceived geographical Europe. Israel, whose existence as a state was largely premised on the fate of Europe's Jews during the 1940s, has also credibly identified itself as a part of a 'European community' and responded directly to such internal EU developments as those concerning the participation of Jorge Haider's Freedom Party in the Austrian government. It is by no means inconceivable that other Mediterranean countries might develop an equivalent European identity in years to come.

Summary

- The end of the Cold War division of Europe and the fall of communism presented the EU with a major challenge that was quite unlike the previous expansions that had marked its development. The potential new members were much less developed economically than the EU-15, had only recently adopted liberal-democratic political systems, and comprised a range of different cultures and national outlooks. The potential entry of new members from Central and Eastern Europe also raised the prospects for aspiring members in the Mediterranean.

- After much negotiation and political bargaining, by 1993 the EU was able to agree the 'Copenhagen criteria' which set out the terms of accession for future members. And by the end of 1999, the Commission declared that thirteen applicant states – Poland, Hungary, the Czech Republic, Estonia, Slovenia, Slovakia, Latvia, Lithuania, Romania, Bulgaria, Cyprus, Malta and Turkey – were ready to join the accession process and were, therefore, potential future members of the Union.

- The entry of all or some of these countries into the Union is bound to change it in fundamental ways, since their membership will profoundly transform its economic, political and cultural character. The likely changes to the nature of the EU will also be institutional as it is hard to see how a Union of 25–30 members can be governed in the same way as a Union of 15.

5   Enlargement: facing new challenges

The sheer number of current applicants and their poor socio-economic status compared to the current EU average member mean that the EU is faced with an enlargement process that will be the most challenging yet – and which it simply has to handle with a visible degree of success if it is to maintain its own identity and authority as an effective international (if not supranational) union. Apart from the long-term challenge of bringing all actual and potential candidates for membership into an effective union, the problems involved in preparing for the admission of just five or even fewer new members may prove to be difficult or even impossible to meet (Phinnemore, 1999, pp.73–4). Extensive reform is necessary in both institutions and policies. In the first area, measures will have to be taken to extend QMV and to review the distribution of votes in the Council of Ministers. The size and overall structure of the Council and European Parliament will have to be changed, while current procedures for rotating the presidency of the Council among member countries are unlikely to be appropriate in a larger EU.

5.1   A more flexible EU?

One important variant of institutional reform, and in many ways a substitute for it, has often been reflected in the various proposals for a more flexible EU and in the idea of structural differentiation. It has been a perspective that opened up with seeming inevitability whenever serious proposals for deepening the EU were on the agenda, and it also appears as one solution to the very considerable problems associated with contemporary proposals for enlargement. 'Variable geometry' gained increasing credibility as a scenario during the 1990s, but there was little inclination to explore its practical possibilities. Early plans for Economic and Monetary Union presented in 1991 raised the distinct possibility of a two-speed Europe, although they were not favourably received in an atmosphere that continued to look towards effective European integration. The idea of a 'hard-core' Europe was again launched in 1994, this time referring to as few as five member states (the original six minus Italy), but such proposals were again sidelined in favour of more inclusive conceptions of European development. Arguments for integrated European development seemed, indeed, to be strengthened by the electoral victory of the British Labour Party in 1997, which appeared to promise a new departure in European relations, and by the surprisingly large number of states that entered into formal monetary union in January 1999.

The continuing existence of a distinct 'Euroland' separate from the EU as a whole, and in particular the strong resistance of many British decision makers to full Economic and Monetary Union, nevertheless suggests that flexibility is still very much on the agenda. The principle is widely discussed but the actual models on offer are rarely spelled out. In practical terms a whole range of possibilities exists which indicate not just a considerable choice in questions of variable geometry, but also the extensive differentiation in terms of past and present EU practice:

1 A single-speed EU in which every member participates fully at every stage in every policy; this has not generally been the case since 1973, as progressive enlargements have meant that some transitional arrangements generally applied to one or more members at any one time, while the various economic and monetary policies pursued since the 1970s were also multi-speed in their original conception.

2 A single-tier EU in which each member state pursues the same group of policies, the situation until 1992 when the UK and Denmark gained certain opt-outs from the Treaty on European Union (i.e. Maastricht).

3   A multi-speed EU where each member is formally included in every policy but in practice is implementing them at a different speed; this reflects the current situation in the EU.

4   A multi-tier EU (or one of concentric circles) where all members do not pursue all policies; EU members are not just progressing at different speeds, but are effectively aiming for different destinations.

5   Similar to (4) above, but the EU is composed more of intersecting 'Olympic rings' in which there are a number of 'hard cores' representing a greater variety of degrees of commitment to Union policies.

6   A Europe *à la carte* or a Europe with a range of opt-outs available to every country, which would effectively mean a disunited Europe or Europe without order.

The most contentious scenarios are numbers 4 to 6, which raise fundamental difficulties with regard to the operation of key EU institutions (especially the European Parliament) and its major decision-making procedures. However, while (5) and (6) might raise insuperable problems of operationalization, the model represented by (4) might well offer a viable solution to the problems that the contemporary enlargement process raises (Croft et al., 1999, pp.81–2). Nevertheless, while this solution may be acceptable to the British government (and seemed to become firmly entrenched in the late 1990s with continuing British refusal to contemplate a fixed schedule for joining Euroland), it is less convincing as a solution to the problems of enlargement. The attraction of the EU to prospective members in the east and south is precisely one of inclusion and a confirmation of full Europeanness, which partial solutions are unable to provide and whose incompleteness will cause more political frustration.

5.2   Policy reform

Policy reform is of critical importance in the major spending areas of agricultural and Structural Fund entitlement. The initial costings of enlargement have been scaled down, but the more modest spending proposals contained in *Agenda 2000* also involve reduced receipts for existing EU members which will prove extremely difficult to secure agreement on. The level of pre-accession costs has also risen since the original estimates were made, and the cost of pre-accession aid already stood at 3.1 billion euro annually in 1999 (*The European Voice*, Brussels, 27 January–2 February 2000). But the climate for reform in the EU as a whole has not been favourable in recent years, as reflected in the limited progress made in the provisions of the Amsterdam Treaty. Public support for further integration has been weak, the position of many national governments has not been strong or conducive to ambitions for the exercise of broader European leadership, while voters remain highly sensitive to public spending plans or proposals for high rates of tax (Ardy, 1999, p.125). As in earlier cases of enlargement, conditions are likely to be vigorously contested. The tensions are graphically outlined by Dinan:

> As the talks progress, applicant countries will fight tenaciously for concessions and derogations in problematic areas such as agriculture, environmental policy, and services. The EU will drive a hard bargain, and the CEES seemingly have little leverage. As it is, some applicants complain that the EU treats them like supplicants and that the accession partnerships are not partnerships at all but an opportunity for the EU to bully the CEES. For its part, the EU tends to see the CEES as excessively demanding and grasping.
>
> (Dinan, 1999, p.199)

Negotiations with Poland on agriculture and the food trade became particularly heated, for example, and all talks on further liberalization were suspended for a time by the EU in April 2000. There was, in the view of EU representatives, little point in continuing the process while Poland showed little inclination to budge over the custom duties it had imposed on food imports following the extensive demonstrations and further direct action during 1999 by peasant farmers (very much on the lines of those seen periodically in France).

This, indeed, was just one example of an increasingly prevalent problem. Central and East European governments were caught between growing pressures from two sides. On the one side, demands from the EU for the removal of subsidies and import restrictions in favour of liberalization and free trade invariably favoured the exporters and producers of the EU economies. On the other were the growing opposition of domestic producers and dissatisfaction in the face of falling incomes and increasing hardship, for which closer EU links bore a major responsibility. Domestic support for EU membership was clearly declining in some Central and East European countries. The proportion of Poles supporting EU membership fell from 64 per cent to 46 per cent between early 1998 and the end of 1999 (having stood at 79 per cent in 1991). In the Czech Republic EU support halved between 1991 and 1996, but recovered to a still markedly unenthusiastic 49 per cent in 1997 (Kucia, 1999, p.145).

5.3   Enlargement and the broader European space

The inclusion of the former captive nations of Eastern Europe has long been one of the EU's most cherished goals and enlargement to include them within a European Union that is truly worthy of the name is a challenge the EU simply cannot afford not to meet. Enlargement in this very real sense becomes a process that will make or break the existing Union. Previous enlargements have generally had a significant impact on integration processes and were associated with different aspects of the deepening of the Union. The first enlargement, for example, was followed by the adoption of common policies in new areas (regional, environmental and technological). The second saw the development of Structural Funds as a mechanism for the transfer of resources to less developed regions. The third phase in the 1990s saw further progress toward EMU and a common foreign policy. In order to produce a European Union that is not just larger but also works effectively and is capable of carrying out the additional tasks that recent union treaties and agreements have imposed, it seems inevitable that the next enlargement will have to be accompanied by significant institutional reforms that introduce a qualitative change in the nature of its structures and the way it carries out its various responsibilities. To this extent, successful enlargement is likely to strengthen supranational tendencies over the existing and well-established patterns of EU intergovernmentalism.

As a basis for such a transformation, the prospect of membership itself can be seen as a major factor enhancing regional integration and the accession process as a form of European governance even before the CEES join the Union. The end of the Cold War and the dismantling of the Iron Curtain transformed the boundaries of Europe in senses that were more than physical. The dubious claim of the pre-1989 EC to represent Europe as a whole became even less convincing, but the reconstituted EU that emerged after Maastricht was soon able to reassert its authority on a new basis. The representation of the EU as a community of political and cultural values reinforced the incentives for membership on the part of the newly liberated Central and East European States, while the porous nature of the boundary that now emerged between the EU and the broader Europe increasingly gave the Union the capacity to govern beyond the territories it formally controlled. In the sense that EU influence was not limited to the exercise of formal authority but was increasingly able to shape the development of norms and values that condition the actions of its members, it was able to present itself as a basis for 'soft governance' throughout a broader European space (Friis and Murphy, 1999, pp.214, 217).

This framework for the exercise of semi-formal authority has not been limited to countries involved in accession negotiations and having the prospect of being involved in them in the near future. In July 1999, just after the end of the Kosovo war, a Stability Pact was launched for the whole of the Balkan region of south-east Europe. Initially presented as a kind of Marshall Plan for the whole region, it had little immediate concrete impact and was soon viewed with considerable scepticism (*The European Voice*, Brussels, 20–26 January 2000). In broad terms, it provided the framework for an agenda of development and a linkage-structure with the EU rather than a source of funds or material assistance. But it, too, soon began to develop a capacity for governance with the initiation of Stabilization and Association agreements with most countries of the region. Although not directly linked with negotiations for EU membership, the agreements nevertheless involved the drawing up of joint action plans with representatives of the Union and, in comparison with the more advanced states of central Europe and the Baltic region, actually gave the participating countries 'clearer guidelines as to where the reforms must be going and what they have to implement' (Radio Free Europe/Radio Liberty Newsline, Prague, 20 April 2000). This seemed to give the EU an equivalent capacity (if not one actually greater) for governance of countries not necessarily directly engaged in accession negotiations, with somewhat lower costs.

There is little reason, therefore, to regard the formal process of enlargement and associated changes within the broader European space as imposing a major burden on the EU. Significant overall gains from enlargement to include the CEES currently concerned are likely to accrue to the Union as a whole, and these may be summarized under the following headings (Avery and Cameron, 1998, p.176):

- enlargement of the EU's internal market to include more than 100 million additional consumers with rising incomes;

- support for newly liberalized market economies by opening up new markets and stimulating growth in Europe as a whole;

- integration of the countries of Central and Eastern Europe into firmly constituted European structures and the enhancement of overall stability and mutual security;

- more effective co-operation in enhancing justice and the rule of law and counteracting the growing threat of transnational crime, drug trafficking and other threats to civil order;

- higher environmental standards throughout Europe as a whole and the reduction of cross-border pollution.

In the long run, direct economic benefits are likely to be considerably greater for the countries joining the EU, but there are likely to be direct advantages for virtually all countries involved. Detailed calculations for the EU as a whole suggest joint benefits of about 11 billion euro, with most gains for Germany, France and the UK as the largest members. Only Portugal may suffer a direct economic loss, but this is likely to be at a very low level (Mayhew, 1998, p.194). The overall balance of enlargement in these terms, it has been argued, is thus likely to be a broadly positive one, although the model of integration adopted will undoubtedly have an influence on the material outcome.

Summary

- We have seen that the potential future enlargements of the EU are like no other and that they raise basic questions about the institutional governance and policies of the Union. Will the EU need to develop a greater supranational character to cope with an expanded membership or will it move towards a more flexible form of integration in which different countries move at different speeds to different destinations? And if the Union becomes more flexible in terms of institutions and policies, then what does that imply for the overall process of European integration? And finally, how does the process of European expansion relate to the governance of the broader European space beyond even an expanded Union?

- Only the future will tell, but these are some of the questions that the EU will have to answer if it is to maintain its identity and authority as an effective international (if not supranational) union.

6   Conclusion

The process of EU enlargement as discussed in this chapter may be summarized in terms of three major themes: inclusion/exclusion, consensus/conflict and unity/diversity.

There are clearly enhancing tendencies to *inclusion* over *exclusion*. Most particularly this is implied in the decision in 1999 to accept the applications for membership from all who had tendered them and to commence accession negotiation on a broad front. Of note in this regard was the decision taken in the early 1990s to offer the prospect of membership to many of the former communist countries of Central and Eastern Europe that created the vision of a more inclusive Europe – and made it easier to overcome the long-lasting ambiguities about relations with Turkey. The extension of membership prospects for some eastern countries nevertheless still excludes other less attractive candidates, notably in parts of the Balkans and the former Soviet Union. As EU relations strengthen with states outside the more western-oriented east-central European core, a firmer line seems to be drawn to exclude those further east from even medium-term prospects of EU membership. Apart from Russia itself and its increasingly authoritarian Belarusan neighbour, this also concerns the more ambiguous cases of Moldova and the Ukraine.

There is continuing *consensus* over the principle of enlargement, although high levels of *conflict* may be anticipated over the negotiation of accession details and the specific conditions of membership. A broad consensus over the principle of englargement derives from the Treaty of Rome (1957) and has been reaffirmed in subsequent Union Treaties. But conflicts arising from the pursuit of national interests within the EU framework and from different perceptions of how the different communities and European associations should develop were present during the earliest stage of EU enlargement. The wide range of inequalities involved in the current programme of enlargement is likely to provide the basis for wide-ranging conflicts and hard-fought negotiations.

There is a general movement to European *unity*, while *diversity* continues in certain areas. The tendency towards European unity is implicit in terms of the growing number of states accepted for EU membership or regarded as having reasonable prospects for becoming candidates. Considerable *diversity* exists in terms of views and expectations of EU development and on the basis of strong contrasts and continuing inequalities within Europe as a whole. EU enlargement over the decades has generally enhanced the movement towards European unity by fostering more intense interaction and greater structural complexity, producing overall a higher level of integration. Growing demands for structural reform make prospects for greater unity, however, increasingly problematic.

References

Ardy, B. (1999) 'Agriculture, structural policy, the budget and eastern enlargement of the European Union' in Henderson, K. (ed.) *Back to Europe: Central and Eastern Europe and the European Union*, London, UCL Press.

Avery, G. and Cameron, F. (1998) *The Enlargement of the European Union*, Sheffield, Sheffield Academic Press.

Baun, M. (1999) 'Enlargement' in Cram, L., Dinan, D. and Nugent, N (eds), *Developments in the European Union*, London, Macmillan.

Bideleux, R. (1996) 'The southern enlargement of the EC: Greece, Portugal and Spain' in Bideleux, R. and Taylor, R. (eds) *European Integration and Disintegration: East and West*, London, Routledge.

Croft, S., Redmond, J., Wyn Rees, G. and Webber, M. (1999) *The Enlargement of Europe,* Manchester, Manchester University Press.

Dinan, D. (1999) *Ever Closer Union: an Introduction to European Integration*, London, Macmillan.

Friis, L. and Murphy, A. (1999) 'The European Union and central and eastern Europe: governance and boundaries', *Journal of Common Market Studies*, vol.37, no.2.

Jones, R.A. (1996) *The Politics and Economics of the European Union: an Introductory Text*, Cheltenham, Edward Elgar.

Kucia, M. (1999) 'Public opinion in central Europe on EU accession: the Czech Republic and Poland', *Journal of Common Market Studies,* vol.37, no.1.

Mayhew, A. (1998) *Recreating Europe: the European Union's Policy Towards Central and Eastern Europe*, Cambridge, Cambridge University Press.

Nugent, N. (1999) *The Government and Politics of the European Union*, London, Macmillan.

Phinnemore, D. (1999), 'The challenge of EU enlargement: EU and CEE perspectives' in Henderson, K. (ed.) *Back to Europe: Central and Eastern Europe and the European Union*, London, UCL Press.

Smith, M.A. (1999), 'The NATO factor: a spanner in the works of EU and WEU enlargement' in Henderson, K. (ed.) *Back to Europe: Central and Eastern Europe and the European Union*, London, UCL Press.

Further reading

Avery, G. and Cameron, F. (1998) *The Enlargement of the European Union*, Sheffield, Sheffield Academic Press.

Croft, S., Redmond, J., Wyn Rees, G. and Webber, M. (1999) *The Enlargement of Europe*, Manchester, Manchester University Press.

Henderson, K. (ed.) (1999) *Back to Europe: Central and Eastern Europe and the European Union*, London, UCL Press.

Manning, M. (ed.) (1999) *Pushing Back the Boundaries: the European Union and Central and Eastern Europe*, Manchester, Manchester University Press.

Chapter 10
European foreign and security policy

Michael Smith

1 Introduction

By the end of the 1990s it appeared that an accelerating process of institutionalization and policy making in foreign and security policy was taking place within the European Union (EU) in response to its increasing role and importance in areas previously defined as 'high politics' and traditionally the prerogative of member states and the North Atlantic Treaty Organization (NATO). Where did the movement toward a European foreign and security policy come from, how has a common foreign and security policy been institutionalized within the EU, and how are these developments linked with broader processes of change, co-operation and conflict within post-Cold War Europe? Are these trends transforming the EU into the rough equivalent of a state, with its own foreign policy and defence establishment?

The origins of the European integration project in the 1940s were inextricably entangled with considerations of security and foreign policy. The formation of the European Coal and Steel Community and the European Economic Community were events of a profound political significance, and at the heart of both was the desire to establish a new kind of 'security community' in Western Europe (see Chapters 2 and 3). French and German leaders, in particular, were clear that European integration was about the stabilization of the continent, and about the ways in which their national competition could be muted within a collective enterprise. Since the 1950s the growing membership, economic weight and political influence of the EEC and then the EU have inexorably meant that foreign and security policy issues have remained central to the 'European project'. The enlargement of the EU in the early twenty-first century will mean that it has a common border with Russia, and it already has an established and growing set of security concerns around the Mediterranean. The EU is and has been seen by all concerned as a central feature of European foreign and security policy in the post-Cold War era.

The idea of a 'European foreign policy' to go alongside the growing economic integration of Western Europe has not surprisingly been on the agenda for a long time, and it is important to recognize that many supporters of integration have seen this as an integral part of 'political union' from the outset. But there has been a persistent gap between the aspiration of some EU member states for a common European foreign and security policy and the reality of complex and messy national interests, compounded by the influence of external actors and organizations such as NATO and the USA.

1.1   Evolution and issues

As early as 1952 there was a proposal to establish a European Defence Community, with national units subordinated to international command in a kind of 'European army'; a proposal that would have implied not only a type of European foreign policy but also a defence establishment to carry it out. The proposed European Defence Community did not come about, and the Treaty of Rome (1957), which established the European Economic Community (EEC), took no steps toward its revival. This is not to say that the EEC did not have a 'foreign policy' dimension, but it was centred almost exclusively around external trade policy and, during the 1960s, the beginnings of a policy of aid to developing countries (many of them ex-colonies of the French in particular). The growing 'weight' of the EEC in international economic relations, and the need to deal with important international partners and rivals such as the USA, meant that it could not avoid the need to construct external policies. But there was a 'gap' between this growing economic 'foreign policy' and the politics of diplomacy and security, which for Western European countries were predominantly organized around the North Atlantic Treaty Organization (NATO). Faced with a somewhat speculative *European* foreign and security policy project and the reality of *transatlantic* defence co-ordination in NATO, most member states not unnaturally chose NATO. So the apparent impetus behind a European foreign and security policy in the early 1950s did not lead to significant developments, in terms of institutions or policy, for at least twenty years. In the early 1960s there was another abortive proposal to establish mechanisms of foreign policy co-operation between the members of the EEC (the Fouchet Plan), and by the late 1960s there were the beginnings of a process of diplomatic co-ordination that became known as European Political Co-operation (EPC), but it was not until the Maastricht Treaty of 1992 that a Common Foreign and Security Policy (CFSP) was formally incorporated into what by then had become the EU, as the second of the so-called 'three pillars'.

The Maastricht Treaty, in hindsight, can be seen as the validation of a long historical process, which by the end of the 1990s had produced not only the building blocks of a common foreign policy but also the first element of a common security and defence policy. This process was also a reflection of changes in the nature and implications of 'security' itself, which during the 1990s came to encompass a wide range of economic and social concerns. As an illustration, the Finnish presidency of the EU, which took place in the second half of 1999, centred in important ways on the definition and elaboration of foreign and security policy in its broadest meaning. In November 1999 a meeting of justice and interior ministers in Tampere set out the framework for an area of security in the 'societal' sense, dealing with matters of immigration, asylum, visas and the like, and centred in the 'third pillar' of the EU: Justice and Home Affairs (see Chapter 4). At the close of the Finnish presidency, the Helsinki European Council not only confirmed the developments in the CFSP but also installed detailed procedures for crisis management and humanitarian intervention by the EU based on the creation of a 60,000-strong Rapid Reaction Force.

This type of extension of the 'European project' raises some fundamental questions about how Europe is 'governed'. To what extent can the EU be an independent actor in security and foreign policy? To what extent do the member states maintain control over what the EU might do, and over their own national security and foreign policies? What happens when the EU comes into collision with other institutions, such as the North Atlantic Treaty Organization (NATO)? And to what extent can the EU hope to 'manage' European security when confronted by the kinds of crisis and conflict that have erupted in the post-Cold War era? One commentator on the foreign and security policy aspects of the EU has drawn attention to a nagging and persistent 'capability–expectations gap', emerging from the mismatch between what the European institutions might do, or what their supporters might like them to do, and the harsh reality of persistent under-achievement (Hill, 1993; 1998).

Here, as elsewhere, we are evidently confronted with a set of paradoxes. The EU, a powerful set of institutions, exists alongside or in competition with other powerful institutions, particularly the member states but also other international bodies such as NATO and the Organization for Security and Co-operation in Europe (OSCE). States have traditionally been concerned with national security and with their own national priorities, but they have been prepared to yield some of this autonomy in situations of threat or where collective action seems to promise national benefits. Security, traditionally defined in terms of military security but more recently defined in terms of economic needs or of social stability as well, remains a core concern of states. Security in this broad sense lies at the centre of European order, or what might be termed its 'architecture'. In the post-Cold War era the challenges to national and European security are both less predictable and less controllable than they were at the height of the Cold War, creating both new opportunities and new challenges for the EU and other organizations. Can the EU's institutions cope with the tensions that result, and can they hope to 'govern' security both for EU member states and for the continent as a whole? Attempting to answer these questions will give us a new perspective on the key issue of the relationship between intergovernmentalism and supranationalism in the EU.

This is especially so because in the field of foreign and security policy the challenge of government is distinctive. While the EU can build and has built complex institutions for producing a Common Foreign and Security Policy, these have to find a role in a turbulent and often crisis-torn environment. Sometimes the turbulence and the crises can erupt into full-scale armed conflict, as was the case in the former Yugoslavia during the 1990s. In such a context some central questions are posed for the project of European integration and for the EU. To what extent can the institutions of the EU establish their legitimacy and credibility in such conditions? Is it essential to develop a European defence establishment as a precondition of the EU's effectiveness in managing European security? How far can the EU supplant the essentially national structures that were traditionally the key to maintaining European stability (and also the major cause of its periodic overturning)?

In what follows I shall address these questions by focusing on four areas of analysis. In Section 2 I explore the links between foreign and security policy and 'government', both in general and in the context of the development of European integration during the Cold War. Section 3 reviews the development of foreign and security policy within the EU from the mid-1980s to the end of the 1990s, concentrating on the institutional developments that took place. Once we have considered some of the historical and institutional background, Section 4 investigates the extent to which the EU has become part of the European foreign and security policy 'architecture' and has overcome two of the tensions mentioned above: the tension between European and national priorities and the tension between the EU and other security institutions in Europe. Section 5 examines the EU's role in the former Yugoslavia to illustrate and test the more general arguments about institutions and policy making, and to evaluate the EU's capacity to manage crisis and conflict in Europe. Finally, the Conclusion (Section 6) reassesses the development of European foreign and security policy and links it with some of the more general themes of 'governing Europe'.

2   Statehood, security and foreign policy

Chapter 3 of this book explored the issues surrounding the notion of sovereignty and its relationship to statehood in Europe. It is not necessary for me to repeat here the general arguments developed there, but it is important to explore their implications for foreign and security policy. Only when we understand the intimate link between statehood, sovereignty, security and foreign policy can we begin to investigate the ways in which and the extent to which the EU has overcome the persistence of national security and foreign policies. This will in turn help us to address the extent to which European integration is bringing about a 'new Europe'.

2.1   Tradition and transformation in foreign and security policy

Since the beginnings of modern sovereign statehood in the seventeenth century the claim to sovereignty has had two components. The first is the claim to internal sovereignty: the ability to control a national territory and to regulate the affairs of the citizens living there. The second claim to sovereignty, and the one most relevant to this chapter, is the claim to external sovereignty: that is to say, the claim to independence and equality in the 'community of states'. At its most ambitious this claim implies that each recognized state is both independent and in principle equal to all the others; such a claim is reflected in the fact that each member of the United Nations (UN) has a single vote in the UN General Assembly. But we know, and it is plain in the everyday practice of world politics, that while all states might in principle be equal, each is different. There are profound inequalities in world politics, and these are reflected at the formal level by the fact that (for example) there are only five permanent members of the UN Security Council (Britain, France, the USA, Russia and China), each with its own veto over Security Council actions.

Because of the claim to sovereignty and the pervasive inequality of states, world politics is an insecure and competitive system. This is a simple statement of a fact that has lain at the heart of issues of war, peace and development since the end of the Middle Ages. The implication of this is that for each state the most vital interest of all is survival, and thus that national security is the paramount concern of government. Alongside this implication, there is another: that if states act in an uncontrolled or irresponsible way, there is a danger of a 'spiral of insecurity' which can lead to war. While war is to be avoided if at all possible, it is a 'contingent liability' of the system, and thus states must prepare for it as fully as possible given their resources. As well as maximizing their own national resources, states can act collectively through alliances, using the power of others to buttress their national security at the cost of some freedom of action. This can stabilize world politics by creating a 'balance of power' in which potentially dominant states are constrained and deterred from expansionist or aggressive actions.

This traditional or realist view of foreign and security policy – state-centric, competitive and insecure – still has powerful resonances. But, increasingly, it has been modified and in some respects challenged by broader conceptions of both foreign policy and the security issue. The growth of global economic and communications systems, and the increasing connectedness of national societies, has meant that foreign policy is no longer a 'secret garden', different from and insulated from the broader political and social processes. It has also meant that all states are less independent than they have ever been before. In economic, social, environmental and other domains, autonomous national action is both less practical and less fruitful than co-operation, either between governments or at the transnational level between non-governmental organizations ranging from large firms to humanitarian pressure groups.

At the same time, the notion of 'security' has been broadened, both for national governments and for other bodies. The traditional focus on military security has had to accommodate an immense variety of groups with the capacity to use force and coercion, from liberation or ethnic movements to transnational criminal groups. Alongside this, the growing awareness of threats and risks that are not directly military, such as economic instability, environmental degradation and large-scale migrations, has created a new and challenging context for foreign and security policies. And in the military sphere itself, the advent of nuclear weapons may have restrained the use of force, at least between states with a nuclear capacity.

2.2   Tradition and transformation in the 'new Europe'

What is the relevance of this discussion to the issue of security and foreign policy in Europe? At one level, the traditional expression of foreign and security policy has shaped the Europe in which we live. The notion of the sovereign state is peculiarly European, and the accompanying idea of the balance of power is one that had its fullest expression in eighteenth- and nineteenth-century Europe. The failures of the balance of power and of 'power politics' in the First and Second World Wars exerted a profound influence on thinking about the development of Europe after 1945, and thus on the initiation and the consolidation of European integration. The belief that European order could be managed or 'governed' through responsible statehood and through the balance of power was discredited, and the establishment of new European institutions was seen as a means of governing European order in a new and more effective way. If relations between member states of the EU were governed more effectively, the European integration project would make a contribution to the more effective governance of European security in the broader sense.

This was in many ways a profound and persuasive line of thinking, but it had to cope with a world in which things were not always amenable to the kind of reason applied by the founding fathers of European integration. In particular, the European institutions did not exist in a vacuum: they were surrounded by the pervasive hostility and frequent confrontations of the Cold War (see Chapters 2 and 3). In many ways, the European integration project became subsumed into the Cold War system; as Alfred Grosser described them, the Western European countries were 'protected but powerless' because of the domination of the United States and its rivalry with the Soviet Union (Grosser, 1979). The proposed European Defence Community of the early 1950s failed, but the North Atlantic Treaty Organization prospered and expanded, taking on the mantle of primary European organization in the field of 'hard security' and adding nuclear weapons to its resources during the late 1950s.

For the member states of the EU this meant a form of 'containment'. The term is often used of the USA's policies toward the Soviet Union, but in effect not only the EU's members but all Western European states were contained by the structures set up by and between the two superpowers during the 1950s and 1960s (DePorte, 1987). This was not without its advantages, since member states were able to devote resources to economic and social provision that they might otherwise have had to devote to defence spending. The Americans were frequently irked by the fact that leading EU member states, such as Germany, were able to indulge in social spending and investment while the US had to support European defence through its own swollen military establishment. The EU could be and was presented by its members as a 'civilian power', with none of the unattractive attributes of the superpowers. As economic success was translated into political and diplomatic influence during the 1960s and 1970s, the tension between this image of the EU and the persistent superpower confrontation was at times acute (Hill, 1989). For example, the Europeans were increasingly critical of the USA's actions in the Middle East and Vietnam, but operated from the position that they could not and would not take responsibility for 'hard security' themselves (while reserving the right to capitalize on any economic opportunities that arose).

These tensions were especially severe during the early 1980s, as the 'second Cold War' resulting from assertive policies in both the USA and the Soviet Union set in. The Reagan administration in the USA took the EU to task for shirking its responsibilities, while the Europeans criticized the Americans for creating an unnecessary atmosphere of crisis and risk. At times it appeared that the crisis between the USA and its partners in Western Europe was more critical than the hostility between Washington and Moscow (Allen and Smith, 1989). Here, it could be argued, was the catalyst that would lead to new European initiatives toward what might be called 'self government' in the security and foreign policy domain. During the early and middle years of the 1980s the member states developed the mechanisms of European Political Co-operation (EPC). They began to develop the security mechanisms of the Western European Union (WEU), which had lain dormant since its establishment in the mid-1950s, and they laid substantial foundations for the development of a Common Foreign and Security Policy in the 1990s (see Section 3).

Did this mean that the EU and its member states had the makings of a collective security and foreign policy by the mid-1980s? What they had was in many ways intangible. The EU had developed strong mechanisms for managing its external relations in the terms of trade policy and related areas. For example, in the Falklands War of 1982, and in relations with South Africa, it had begun to develop the political use of economic weapons, through sanctions of various kinds. It had also developed what might be described as 'habits of co-operation', particularly through EPC, in which the 'club' of member states had learned to trust each other on the whole in many areas of foreign policy. In some areas, such as the Conference on Security and Co-operation in Europe (which met in several guises from 1975 onwards), the member states made a distinctive contribution to the reshaping of Europe, which was eventually to lead to the end of the Cold War itself (Nuttall, 1992). But this set of influences was largely confined to 'soft security' and to diplomatic co-operation. As American policy makers often observed during the 1980s, the member states seemed to believe that the act of agreeing on a declaration was enough: they simply did not have the muscle or the will collectively to sustain and to implement more concrete measures. It was in this context that the 'rebirth' of European security and foreign policy was to take place.

Summary

- The European integration project has always had a strong link to European security, and can be understood partly as a reaction to the damage done by competitive national interests in the First and Second World Wars.

- This link was the focus of tensions, because of the persistent strength of ideas of statehood and sovereignty within the EU itself, and because of the ways in which the EU was 'contained' by the superpowers during the Cold War.

- By the mid-1980s these tensions were severe, and the conditions for a reassessment of foreign and security policy as part of European integration were present.

3 From political co-operation to a foreign and defence policy

Thus far, I have focused on the tensions between European foreign and security policy, the broader 'architecture' of foreign and security policies in Europe and the events of the Cold War. I shall now turn to the ways in which the institutional development of foreign and security policy has taken place since the mid-1990s. I shall seek to identify the key stages through which the institutions developed in the period 1985–99, examining the features of successive rounds of 'bargaining' about foreign and security policy, particularly in the context of three major treaties: the Single European Act of 1985, the Treaty on European Union (TEU – the Maastricht Treaty) of 1991 and the Amsterdam Treaty of 1997. I shall conclude this survey by looking at the developments at the end of the 1990s, which were reflected in two European Councils: Cologne in June 1999 and Helsinki in December 1999. The question to bear in mind throughout is: how have these successive bargains extended the 'government' of the EU into security and foreign policy?

3.1   The Single European Act

The Single European Act of 1985 is most frequently associated with the institutional reforms surrounding the '1992 programme' for the completion of the single market. Not so immediately prominent, but in many respects equally significant, was the fact that the SEA dealt for the first time with foreign and security policy. In doing so, it built on the habits and procedures developed in the framework of European Political Co-operation since the early 1970s. While these had been criticized for substituting 'procedure for policy', and for producing a series of declarations and position papers without any further development of policy, they had undoubtedly contributed to a growing perception not only that the member states should attempt to co-ordinate their positions but that they should do so in the light of distinctive 'European' interests and orientations. In 1981 the so-called London Report had first raised the possibility of a move into security policy, and had started the development of mechanisms for the active consultation and co-ordination of policy positions among the member states. A number of devices had been adopted to try to ensure greater continuity of policy co-ordination; for example, the so-called 'troika', which saw the presidency-in-office in any given half year assisted by both the preceding and the succeeding presidency countries. All of these activities in EPC remained outside the formal treaties; in other words, they were explicitly intergovernmental, with no hint of Community pillar competence or, for that matter, of Commission initiative, although the Commission was associated with the process.

The SEA, for the first time, incorporated EPC into a formal treaty. It did so in a separate part of the Act, Title III, in which even the language used was different from that of the 'Community' parts. Thus Title III looked far more like a traditional diplomatic agreement than did the more 'integrationist' parts of the Act. But the SEA did establish both a set of obligations and commitments and a set of mechanisms for the development of EPC. It committed the member states to consult, and to ensure that EPC policies were 'consistent' with those pursued through the Community, and it established a small secretariat. It also mentioned 'security' in a formal sense, but this usage was carefully limited to the political and economic aspects of security, and the primacy of NATO and the WEU as defence organizations was underlined.

The apparatus through which these commitments were pursued remained explicitly intergovernmental, based on co-operation and consultation between national foreign offices through regular meetings of ministers, backed up by working groups and a network of 'political correspondents'. There was also co-operation between the embassies of member states in third countries, and the beginnings of a secure communications network, again run through co-ordination between the foreign ministries.

To what extent can this be seen as the setting up of an embryonic 'foreign policy'? If one takes the requirements of such a policy as a foreign office, diplomatic representation and a defence policy, for example (as in the case of a state), then clearly this was not the EPC model. What was being established here was a system of diplomatic co-ordination, based on *shared national* interests but not on a definition of a *common European* interest. It was quite possible for member states to act independently of EPC or for their commitments to other bodies, such as NATO, to take precedence over those to EPC. Although there were areas in which EPC produced impressive solidarity, this was mainly at the declaratory level. A 'reflex of consultation' had developed, but this was some way from joint action, let alone a common policy with distinct policy instruments.

3.2   Maastricht: toward a Common Foreign and Security Policy?

The relatively modest advances in EPC under the Single European Act were effectively a ratification of the existing practices and procedures. On the face of it, the same could not be said of the provisions of the Maastricht Treaty, which was agreed in December 1991. The end of the Cold War, and the pressing need to give the EU more substantial diplomatic credentials in the 'new Europe', led to a qualitative shift in the provisions for the Common Foreign and Security Policy (CFSP). Significantly, while the major member states expressed important differences of view on other matters in the Treaty, all (including the UK) agreed that the CFSP was a vital element of the EU's role. As a result, the commitments entered into were of a more far-reaching and material kind than those in the SEA. The key provisions were set out in Article J of the Treaty, which formally proclaimed the establishment of the CFSP and raised the possibility of an eventual progression toward a common defence policy and even a 'common defence' (understood to represent the operational aspects of defence policy). In line with the latter, the Western European Union (WEU) was given a closer relationship with the EU as a potential 'defence arm'. The responsibility for the CFSP remained squarely with the Council of Ministers, within guidelines set by the European Council for Heads of State and Government (see Box 10.1).

Box 10.1   The CFSP after Maastricht

The Common Foreign and Security Policy agreed at the Treaty of Maastricht included a new instrument: the Joint Action. This would, in principle, allow the EU to take a wide range of diplomatic and related initiatives. Qualified Majority Voting (QMV) was established as a possibility in undertaking Joint Actions, but there were many qualifications to its use. In particular, a so-called 'double lock' was established: before QMV could be used in the context of a Joint Action a unanimous vote was required. For the first time, the Commission had a role in this area, albeit a marginal one, and the structures of the Council and EPC working groups were to be merged (they had previously often duplicated each other). The Commission and the Secretariat of the Council of Ministers were to be adapted so as to work better together and to consider CFSP matters.

For practical purposes a national veto would exist, as it had done in EPC (where consensus was the basis for common positions). None the less, the Maastricht provisions represented a substantial change in the basis for foreign and security policies in the EU. Perhaps most importantly, CFSP was placed within a common institutional framework for the Union, thus bringing it much closer to the original Community structures. How far, though, did this move it beyond the stage of 'procedure as a substitute for policy'? As can be seen from Figure 10.1, the administrative structure of the CFSP was fiendishly complicated, involving not only links between the Community pillar and the second pillar (CFSP) but also connections with the European Parliament and the Western European Union (WEU), which had become more closely related to the EU. This raised in a concentrated form a question that had been lurking throughout the development of EPC and the CFSP: could the fluid, secretive and often crisis-ridden nature of foreign policy be enshrined in detail in treaties or flow charts? After all, the constitutions and practices of many if not most national governments give a special place to foreign and security policy, which demands confidentiality and does not produce legislation in the conventional sense. 'National security' can be and has been the excuse for much withholding of information, and the need to act rapidly in crises is counter to any procedures of parliamentary or other consultation.

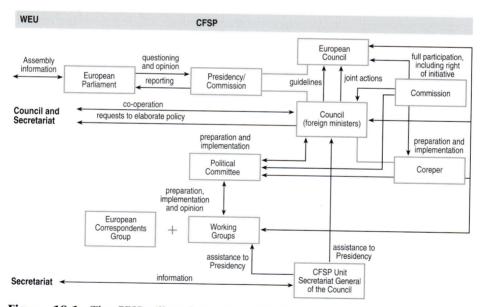

Figure 10.1 The CFSP pillar of the EU and its links with the EC and WEU

(adapted from Edwards and Spence, 1994, p.303)

The CFSP provisions in the Maastricht Treaty, therefore, raised as many questions as they answered. It was not clear who was to pay for the CFSP or how (through the EU budget or otherwise), what the role of the Commission was to be, and where the WEU would sit in relation to NATO and the EU. Not surprisingly, there were many who saw the TEU as representing no real change from the EPC mechanisms, with intergovernmentalism triumphant (see, for example, Box 10.2 for the views of the former British Foreign Secretary in the Major government, Douglas Hurd).

Box 10.2

The key to successful and coherent foreign policy co-operation is persuading your partners of the force of your arguments, not resorting to the procedural means of a vote to overrule their point of view. Experience under EPC shows that intergovernmental co-operation on this basis can work. A policy which all can support, because all agree with it, carries far more weight than one where underlying dissent might all too easily be exposed. Countries are not going to operate successfully a foreign policy measure to which they are strongly opposed. Nor does the effort to reach a consensus hamper decision making in practice. All member states are prepared to work for the greater influence of the Twelve, speaking and acting together on foreign policy issues. While in economic policy conflicting short-term interests of member states need to be reconciled for the greater overall good, our foreign policy interests are far more often than not compatible with each other. There is rarely difficulty in reaching agreed positions, even on such difficult foreign policy issues as China, Russia or nuclear non-proliferation.

(Hurd, 1994, pp.422–3)

Views such as those of Hurd raise a fundamental question of 'government' in the security and foreign policy field: can a treaty such as that agreed at Maastricht really 'establish' a foreign and security policy in an area of political life that is by definition 'ungovernable', since it deals with the competition, crises and conflicts between sovereign entities?

The early record of development under the Maastricht Treaty adds substance to this criticism, but at the same time it created pressure for further 'constitutionalization' of the CFSP. During the first two or three years of its operation, the CFSP mechanism produced a number of Joint Actions (see Box 10.1): for example, observing elections in South Africa or Russia, and establishing a Stability Pact to regulate relations between states in Central and Eastern Europe. But in many respects the operation and the output of the 'machine' remained indistinguishable from that of EPC. The Treaty had explicitly made provision for a review of the CFSP five years after the Maastricht Conference, including a re-examination of the relationship between the EU and the WEU. What had not been foreseen was that the Treaty would not enter into force until November 1993 (because of the lengthy and fraught ratification process in several member states) and that there would be a full-blown war in Yugoslavia between 1991 and 1996.

3.3   The CFSP from Maastricht to Amsterdam

In the light of the argument in the previous section, it is not surprising that one description of the CFSP provisions agreed at Maastricht was 'an unstable compromise' (Forster and Wallace, 1996). The tensions within the Treaty itself, combined with the persistence of different interpretations of the CFSP and a turbulent external environment in the 'new Europe', were bound to create a demand for further changes. As already noted, it was preordained that this demand would be expressed in the form of a further 'constitutional conference', which ended at Amsterdam in June 1997. By that time the CFSP provisions had formally been operating for only four years; in fact, the preparations for the Amsterdam Treaty had begun, in the form of a Reflection Group and then an Intergovernmental Conference, as early as 1995. This meant that the CFSP provisions were being reassessed at the very time they were being 'road tested'. Indeed, some governments – including the British government – held the view that the IGC would only perform a '6,000 mile service' on the CFSP, with a bit of fine-tuning of the existing provision and no more.

Those who wanted a 'minimalist' review of the Treaty were up against those who felt that Maastricht had only started the job of perfecting the CFSP, and that the next IGC should take further major steps. Both camps had little to go on, given the embryonic state of the CFSP itself. But it was clear that the QMV provisions were very difficult to use (and had not, in fact, been used), and that much of the 'policy' still consisted of declarations of the type familiar from EPC. At the same time, the Commission's role had expanded through a new Directorate-General (DG1A), but on a relatively flimsy treaty base. In operational terms, the lack of formal budgetary provision for CFSP, the absence of a collective intelligence and planning capability, and the lack of a 'figurehead' to represent CFSP other than the six-monthly presidencies still posed serious issues of continuity.

While there was considerable agreement on these issues, there was much less agreement on the ways in which the IGC should deal with them. As a result, the lengthy negotiations in 1996 and 1997 saw a clash between those who wanted to install CFSP at the centre of the EU and reduce its intergovernmental limitations and those who wanted to preserve exactly those limitations on the grounds that co-operation among the member states rather than integration along Community lines was the appropriate way forward.

The result, in the Treaty of Amsterdam, was in many ways a perpetuation of the 'unstable compromise' set up at Maastricht (see Box 10.3). Many observers were rather disappointed that the Treaty did not seem to take a decisive step forward, but we should remember that European integration has a history of producing large results from apparently small constitutional changes (as, for example, in the SEA).

Box 10.3   The Treaty of Amsterdam and the CFSP

What were the main features of the Amsterdam provisions? First, the European Council was given a more formal role in establishing 'Common Strategies', although only the Council of Ministers could formally introduce them. Alongside this there was provision both for the extension of QMV and for what was called 'constructive abstention' if some members did not want actively to participate in a particular Joint Action, or for a national veto where a number of states saw an issue as being of vital national interest. The institutional framework was extended with the designation of a 'High Representative' for CFSP who would work with the Commission President and the Council presidency country. At the same time a firmer basis was agreed for both the financial and the intelligence aspects of the CFSP.

Finally, the Amsterdam Treaty made the commitment to a 'common defence policy' and a 'common defence' more tangible. Although it was still clear that member states held the whip hand in this area, the first steps were taken in defining what might become the principles of a common defence. A set of tasks known as the 'Petersburg Tasks' (after the place in which they had been defined within the WEU) was added to the Treaty: these tasks focus on humanitarian intervention, peace-keeping and (subject to members' agreement) the enforcement of decisions by bodies such as the UN. They do not include any hint of a 'security guarantee' among member states, and indeed they refer to the need to recognize the specific character of the policies of some member states (that is, neutrals such as Ireland or Sweden). The Union can, by a unanimous vote, 'avail itself' of the WEU as an instrument of defence policy, and provision is made for the progressive merger and eventual incorporation of the WEU into the Union (again, only by a unanimous vote of the European Council, ratified by all member states).

To many the Amsterdam arrangements appeared to be a 'minimalist' set of results, and this was a source of satisfaction or dissatisfaction according to the stance of the governments concerned. But if we compare the position reached in the Amsterdam Treaty, as summarized in Box 10.3 and Figure 10.2, with the position in the mid-1980s, prior to the SEA, we can see a major set of developments both in principle and (more variably) in procedures and practice. After Amsterdam, it was possible to talk of a common European defence policy, of the incorporation of the WEU into the EU, and of joint action in the military domain, albeit qualified by the 'Petersburg Tasks' and by the need to use the still-separate WEU apparatus.

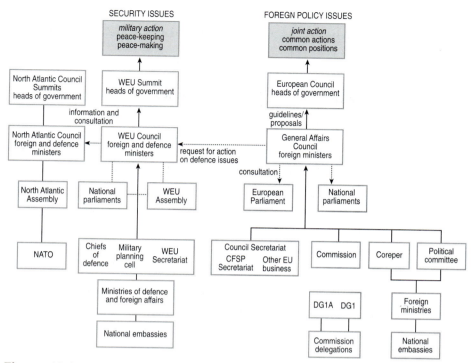

Figure 10.2   CFSP: the tangled web of policy making

(adapted from Forster and Wallace, 2000, p.476)

These successive attempts to institutionalize the CFSP give us an important insight into the ways in which 'government' in the area of foreign and security policy has been extended. Even after Amsterdam it was still not the case that the EU had a 'proper' foreign policy, like that of unified states, but it had developed a process of intense consultation, co-ordination and joint action in an expanding area that now included elements of defence policy. We shall see in Sections 4 and 5 how this has impacted on the policies of member states and of other international organizations, and how it has affected the management of crisis and conflict in the Europe outside the EU, specifically in the former Yugoslavia. At this stage, however, we need to examine the developments of 1998 and 1999, which promised further significant change in the CFSP.

3.4   From Amsterdam to Helsinki

The Amsterdam Treaty entered into force only in early 1999, because of delays to its ratification in France and other member states. By that time, however, the atmosphere for the implementation of the CFSP and defence policy provisions had changed radically (Forster and Wallace, 2000). There were two main reasons for this shift. In December 1998, the French President, Jacques Chirac, and the British Prime Minister, Tony Blair, met in St Malo in France and issued a clarion call for the development of a common defence policy with material military capabilities. This produced an unprecedented declaration of intent that was endorsed by the (Vienna) European Council and was to shape the debate for the next year and beyond. The second factor was an external one: the Kosovo crisis and the bombing campaign of spring and summer 1999 provided a painful reminder that the EU was incapable of undertaking concrete steps to enforce or apply agreements reached through negotiation. The dominant role played by the USA in the diplomacy and the military action surrounding Kosovo was a central factor in giving impetus to the Blair–Chirac proposals and in reducing the opposition of member states who might otherwise have been cautious about moving forward on defence. In addition, the evolution of the defence industries in the EU was increasingly making it possible that a single, integrated supplier of defence equipment could be established, and the British and French industries were central to this process. In a sense, this development brought together the foreign and security policy dimension with the integration process at a more economic level.

The net result of these forces and events was that between late 1998 and late 1999 the Amsterdam provisions were given a major push forward. In April 1999 NATO's Fiftieth Anniversary Summit provided support for the development of a European Security and Defence Identity (ESDI), and in May the members of the WEU decided to work toward the merger of the organization with the EU, greatly accelerating the timetable envisaged at Amsterdam. In June the Cologne Summit of the European Council considered proposals to incorporate large parts of the WEU into the EU, and to give the Council of Ministers the power to make decisions on military crisis management (while retaining the right of member states to opt out). This was backed up by a set of proposals to introduce a defence element into the Council, through the attendance of defence ministers as appropriate, to establish a permanent Political and Security Committee in Brussels, and to set up an EU Military Committee which would make recommendations to the Political and Security Committee. In addition, it was proposed to put in place an EU Military Staff and other intelligence and crisis management bodies. At much the same time, the first 'High Representative' for CFSP was designated. The post went to Javier Solana, who in addition to being a past Foreign Minister of Spain was also the serving Secretary-General of NATO, and thus a highly credible candidate. Before the end of the year he was also designated Secretary-General of the WEU, thus uniting the two principal institutional components of the EU's foreign and security policies.

At the Helsinki European Council in December 1999 the Finnish Presidency produced progress reports on these actions, which were adopted on an interim basis. The Council also adopted a plan for the creation of a 'rapid reaction force' that would amount to 60,000 personnel by 2003, and which could be deployed in the EU-led operations. When this was set alongside the various mechanisms for defence planning, crisis management and military co-ordination set in motion at Cologne, there was the appearance of qualitative change in the EU's security and defence institutions. Although the project of creating a single European defence equipment supplier was moving more slowly, and was qualified by the attractions for some companies of a transatlantic link-up, there was still a sense that this strand of development represented important support for a European defence policy. Whether member states would accept the financial implications of a 'real' defence policy for the EU, in an era when defence budgets had been falling steadily, or welcome the potential reconfiguration of their national defence establishments, was another matter.

Summary

- The period from 1985 to 1999 witnessed a cumulative and in some respects revolutionary advance in the foreign and security policies of the EU, leading to an emerging defence capability.

- The Single European Act introduced foreign policy and security issues into the framework of European Treaties, albeit with considerable limitations and qualifications.

- The Maastricht Treaty incorporated the CFSP into the Treaties, and began to set in place the instruments required to implement it. The CFSP 'on the ground' remained very much at the intergovernmental level, and in many ways the Treaty represented an evolution of the SEA provisions.

- The Treaty of Amsterdam disappointed some 'maximalist' supporters of radical change and new institutional arrangements, but it contained important seeds of further consolidation and set the scene for a more active consideration of defence policy in the EU.

- A major shift in British and French policies in 1998 laid the basis for a significant change in which the elements created at Maastricht and Amsterdam were transported into a new political context. By the end of 1999 it appeared that the Union was on course for a common defence policy and even a military establishment at the European level.

- Viewed from the perspective of the 'internal' institutional development of the CFSP and defence policy, it is clear that foreign and security policies in the EU are increasingly institutionalized and thus 'governed' by rules, conventions and norms.

4 The EU and the architecture of European foreign and security policy

There is no doubt that the processes of institutionalization and 'constitutionalization' described in Section 3 represented a major feature of the European foreign and security policy 'landscape' during the late 1990s and into the new millennium. The EU has developed, expanded and consolidated the structures of the CFSP and (later) of a security and defence policy. But how far has this actually affected the 'architecture' of European foreign and security policies? I argued in Section 2 that foreign and security policies traditionally reflected the claims to sovereignty and the competitive search for security generated by the system of states. Under these circumstances, co-operation between states is expected to reflect calculations of interest and advantage, leading to temporary alliances and 'balancing' policies rather than permanent institutional commitments. We also saw in Section 3 that the project of European integration in part represented a transformation in this traditional conception, and that the 1980s and 1990s witnessed a new set of global and regional forces entering into the equation.

How much and in what ways has the EU's development changed the traditional understanding of foreign policy? Let us look first at the foreign and security policies of states. One way of estimating the EU's impact is to ask how far EPC and the CFSP have displaced the foreign and security policies of member states and reduced their capacity to conduct autonomous policies (Hill, 1996). Here, the answer until the mid-1990s would have been rather negative: the member states resolutely kept the EPC process in the intergovernmental realm, and reserved their rights to conduct independent foreign and security policies even when these were formally incorporated into the Treaties. The 'second pillar' was seen as a distinctive area of the EU, and generated its own distinctive rules and norms, very different from the 'Community method' embodied in the 'first pillar'. The phraseology and the expectations were different; for example, reference was made not to the Community or the Union but to 'the Twelve'. From the mid-1990s onwards it appears that the 'habits' of consultation, and the social learning that had taken place over a period of many years, were increasingly influential. Although there was no sudden step-change, with the establishment of a European 'foreign ministry' or military staff, there was an increasingly powerful expectation that the member states would be constrained both formally and informally by their membership of the EU, and that this would translate into activities outside the EU context. This did not mean that the member states had effectively given up their capacity to formulate and pursue foreign and defence policies. Rather, national policies were increasingly 'Europeanized', and conducted in a context in which the first steps were to consult with EU members and to co-ordinate policies. The possibility of defection had not been eliminated (as we shall see in relation to the break-up of Yugoslavia in Section 5), but the framework for national foreign policy making in the EU was increasingly one in which member states (both large and small, although the smaller with more enthusiasm at times) 'thought European'. The combined effect of the Maastricht and Amsterdam Treaties and of the decisions reached at Cologne and Helsinki in 1999 meant that they could also 'act European'.

I would argue that, in many instances, this means that the foreign and security policies of the member states have not been displaced so much as extended. The process has been one in which the risks of foreign and security policy in post-Cold War Europe have been subject to 'political economies of scale'; that is to say, they have been shared with other member states, and the political and financial costs have been subject to new calculations that are not based simply on national priorities. This does not mean that the risks have disappeared, or that arguments about the allocations of responsibilities and costs have been eliminated. As noted above, it means that they take place in a different institutional and 'social' context, where the making of foreign and security policy increasingly takes the form of a continuous negotiation (Smith, 2000). Nor does it mean that competition between member states or groups of members has been eliminated. There has been a continuous struggle during the past decade for the right to control the process of institutionalization and rule formation in the CFSP and beyond. But this competition is in an increasingly structured arena: structured by the formal treaty commitments embodied in the Maastricht and Amsterdam Treaties and by the learning and experience accumulated over the past two decades.

The implications of these arguments are not restricted to the states of the EU. The process of enlargement proceeded fitfully during the late 1990s, but an important part of the process was the way in which candidates for membership felt constrained to take on what has been called the *acquis politique*: the set of understandings and institutional commitments embodied in the CFSP and related areas. Thus the governments of Poland, Hungary and the Czech Republic (to take only three examples) felt during the late 1990s that their foreign policies should be 'governed' by some sense of compatibility with the evolving CFSP, and this was also encouraged in a series of 'structured dialogues' by the EU itself (Smith, 1999). Other significant international actors, especially the USA, found that the new arrangements and understandings made a difference. During the 1970s and 1980s, American presidents and secretaries of state had periodically enquired about 'who speaks for Europe' in various contexts and had received conflicting answers. This problem had by no means been resolved at the end of the 1990s, but it had taken on a new and arguably more challenging form through the institutional changes and the accumulation of 'Europeanization' (Allen, 1998).

Has the development of CFSP and the EU defence identity displaced the traditional focus on shifting alliances and 'balancing' in national foreign policies? There are two aspects to any answer to this question. First, the 'security architecture' of Europe changed a long time ago from the 'balance of power' demonstrated in the nineteenth and early twentieth centuries. The Cold War, as noted earlier, had institutionalized the East–West divide, creating a 'permanent alliance' in NATO that included the member states, non-members in Europe and non-European countries (the USA and Canada). The EU in this context was a latecomer to the organization of European foreign and security policies, and had to find a place alongside others, such as NATO, that possessed far more military and diplomatic muscle. As a result, when the Cold War ended there were several long-established institutions available for the reconstruction of the 'architecture' (Croft et al., 1999).

NATO spent much of the 1990s 'reinventing' itself as a set of institutions for the post-Cold War era, including a process of enlargement that took in candidate members of the EU itself; and there were those who pointed to the speed with which Poland, Hungary and the Czech Republic were allowed to enter NATO and contrasted it with the apparently grudging nature of the EU enlargement process. NATO and the Organization for Security and Co-operation in Europe provided institutional frameworks broader than those of the EU, and thus arguably a more suitable basis for dealing with the challenges of post-Cold War foreign and security policy. As can be seen from Figure 10.3 (below), by the late 1990s a complex

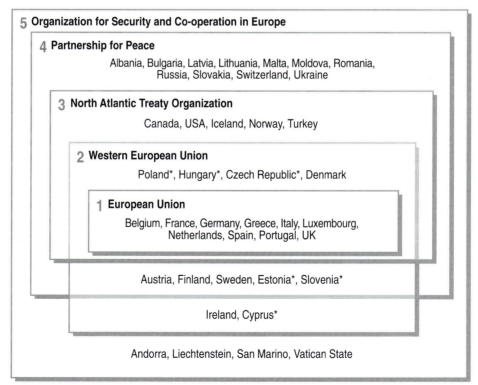

* First wave applicant in EU and/or NATO

Figure 10.3   Europe's security architecture in the late 1990s

(adapted from Keatinge, 1997, p.116)

mosaic of overlapping and complementary or competing institutions had built up, which constituted 'institutional overcrowding' and created the possibility of 'gridlock' in the consideration of foreign and security policy issues.

By the year 2000 the EU had made major strides forward in 'governing' the foreign and security policies of its members, and in influencing those of other important actors, but it is clear that this is a significantly qualified form of 'government'. The CFSP represents a constant tension or 'negotiation' between forces of intergovernmentalism and supra-nationalism, and between the tendencies toward unity and diversity. This leads to what might be described as the 'collective action' problem in the EU itself. Despite the impressive development of institutional frameworks and rules for the co-ordination of foreign and security policies, that is what it remains – co-ordination, not full integration. Because it remains at the level of co-ordination, there are a number of problems: the 'investment' of different members in the process, which will vary and be subject to calculations of national advantage; the pressure to defect when faced with situations in which national advantage can be gained (or risk avoided) by non-compliance with the 'European' position; and the competing attractions of external partners or different institutional commitments.

Summary

The EU has emerged as a major element in the 'security architecture' of post-Cold War Europe through its formal institutionalization and the learning accumulated by its member states. However, this position is subject to considerable qualification, as the result of a number of factors.

- The persistence of national foreign policies, and the limitations on the extent to which the EU can displace them.

- The ways in which the EU process can reflect competition among member state foreign and security policies, and the links between member states and external partners, particularly the USA.

- The existence of well-established institutional competitors in foreign and security policy, such as NATO, with significant resources and with overlapping claims on the loyalties of EU member states.

These factors form an essential part of the background to any consideration of the EU's role in situations of crisis and conflict.

5 The EU and the management of European security

Thus far I have argued that the EU has developed a significant framework for foreign and security policy. At the same time, I have noted that there are distinct 'architectural' limitations on the EU's role, arising from a number of national and international institutional contexts. In this section I shall consider how these assets and limitations interacted in a situation of crisis and conflict: the disintegration of the former Yugoslavia during the 1990s. This is not intended to be an exhaustive history of the former Yugoslavia; rather it is intended to act as a test of some of the ideas I have set out in this chapter, and to show you how you might take your study of this area further by looking at other case studies.

It is clear that the collapse of the Yugoslav Federation during the 1990s started some time earlier, after the death of President Tito in 1980. Throughout the 1980s the increasing economic and political tensions within the multinational federation intensified, only to burst out into the open with the ending of the Cold War. This said, the tangled history of the former Yugoslavia during the 1990s can be divided into three interrelated phases. The first, and the shortest, involved the independence of Croatia and Slovenia, and lasted from 1990 to 91. The second, the war in Bosnia-Herzegovina, lasted from 1991 to 95, and the aftermath persisted into the new century. The third (and not necessarily final) phase centred on the crisis in Kosovo between 1998 and 1999. Each of these phases had its own distinctive characteristics; each created both opportunities and considerable risks for the pursuit of foreign and security policy through the EU.

5.1 Croatia and Slovenia

The declaration of independence by two Yugoslav Republics, Croatia and Slovenia, in mid-1990 was followed by a short but vicious outbreak of fighting. Significantly, both of the defecting republics expressed their wish to join the EU, and this is symbolic of the extent to which it was seen as a model for stability in post-Cold War Europe. Unfortunately, the crisis found the EU involved in a great debate about its own role, and in particular about the development of the CFSP itself. This is an important feature of the situation as it developed during 1990 and 1991: the EU was attempting to achieve the institutional developments dealt with earlier in this chapter at the same time as it was confronting the challenges of new and unexpected crises in Europe. This led to a series of contradictions in the EU position. While the member states were capable of establishing diplomatic unity in general through EPC, they could be detached and fragmented by events on the ground. Thus the Twelve were able to set up a series of diplomatic initiatives, including an international conference on the former Yugoslavia, and they were instrumental in working for ceasefires between combatants on the ground. But in the end they were only capable of words; they had no enforcement power, and thus no capacity to back up their diplomatic efforts with the credible threat of force. They could and did implement economic sanctions, but ultimately this had little impact on combatants who were determined to fight for one reason or another.

This did not prevent the EU from being the target of great expectations, both from within the Union and from external sources. One of the more risky pronouncements about the EU's role was made by the Luxembourg Foreign Minister, Jacques Poos, in July 1991. Fighting had escalated again and Bosnia-Herzegovina was becoming an increasingly pressing issue. In his capacity as President of the Council of Foreign Ministers, Poos declared: 'this is the hour of Europe, not the United States'. By so doing, he not only expressed the belief that the EU could and should take the lead, but also expressed the feeling that this was in contrast to the role of the one remaining superpower. The USA's policies were cautious, not to say paralysed, and the attention was focused largely on the EU. The problem was that not only did the EU have no autonomous foreign or security policy existence, it also contained several members whose interests did not automatically coincide. There was a distinct tension between those who wanted to recognize Croatia and Slovenia as a means to consolidate their independence, and those who wanted to bolster the remainder of Yugoslavia. The Twelve established a Commission to try to develop a formula for recognition, which was due to report in early 1992, but this formal approach was at odds with events on the ground, where the fighting continued. The issue came to head in December 1991, at precisely the time that the CFSP was being negotiated in Maastricht. The German government threatened to recognize Croatia and Slovenia independently, and did so in advance of the findings of the Commission on recognition. This led to recognition by the other member states, despite the fact that Croatia in particular did not fulfil the requirements eventually agreed. As a footnote to this episode, it should be noted that for a long time EU members' policies on recognition were further complicated by the refusal of Greece to recognize the government of the former Yugoslav Republic of Macedonia, a decision that reflected long-standing regional tensions.

It could be argued that this history shows precisely the difficulties that I identified earlier. In terms of *collective* action, the EPC mechanisms were insufficient to overcome the incentives for certain members to defect from a common position and act independently. The lack of the capacity to enforce any agreements reached on the ground meant that the EU or its members were incapable of achieving effective collective action (Crawford, 1996). And the recognition of Croatia and Slovenia threw into stark relief the growing pressures for independence in Bosnia-Herzegovina, thus helping to precipitate the next phase of the conflict.

5.2   Bosnia-Herzegovina

By the spring of 1992 it was increasingly likely that the Twelve would recognize Bosnia-Herzegovina. One of the problems with recognition as a diplomatic tool in this context was that once it had been used it could not be used again, so the Twelve were arguably using up one of their most potent resources at what might turn out to be the early stage of a protracted conflict. Moreover, recognition was akin to taking sides in a conflict and the Twelve still aspired to a mediation role. The Bosnian conflict of 1992–95 turned out to be a severe test of the solidarity among EU members, and a further demonstration of the limitations built into the EPC/CFSP mechanisms (Zucconi, 1996).

One way of presenting the complex events of the period is to chart the ways in which, and the extent to which, the EU and its members were involved. For the Twelve as a collective, the story can be seen as one of progressive marginalization. In the early stages, Brussels was a centre of diplomatic activity and concern, and the EU's negotiators, first Lord Carrington and then Dr David Owen (both former British Foreign Secretaries), were major players in the development of successive peace plans for Bosnia-Herzegovina. The most significant was the Vance–Owen Plan of 1993, which resulted from the efforts of Owen and the UN negotiator, Cyrus Vance. There is considerable argument about whether this was a realistic basis for a peace settlement, but one thing is clear: the implementation of the plan demanded a significant military force, which by implication would have had to have come largely from the USA. Since the USA was less than enthusiastic about the plan for various reasons, it was handicapped from the outset. From the EU point of view, the fate of the plan made it painfully clear that not only did the Union have no capacity to enforce or implement the plan itself, but it also suffered from major divisions among its member states as to how and even whether the plan could be enforced.

From the failure of the Vance–Owen Plan onwards, the EU was in many respects marginalized from the Bosnian conflict. Increasingly, three interconnected processes came to dominate. The first process was what could be described as 'old-style concert diplomacy' in which the major interested powers formed a Contact Group to put forward successive peace proposals. The Group encompassed the USA, Russia, Britain, France, Germany and (eventually) Italy; although its plans drew at least in part on the earlier Vance–Owen Plan, the diplomatic clout it could exert was undoubtedly more direct and by implication more coercive. A second process was the increased involvement and commitment of the USA, not only through the Contact Group but also through bilateral diplomacy both with partners on the ground and with the Russians (who had special links with the Yugoslavia leadership of Milosevic in Serbia). Of all the potential 'peacemakers' the USA had the military might to enforce a settlement and make it credible. Finally, and with spectacular impact in the final part of the conflict, NATO intervened, with US leadership but also with active participation from several leading EU member states, including France and Britain.

As the conflict developed, the EU became subordinated not only to its own member states but also to other participants, particularly the USA, the UN, NATO and the Organization for Security and Co-operation in Europe. This did not mean that the EU position, under the newly ratified CFSP, fell apart. What it did mean was that the EU position remained solid but at a very limited level, expressing the ways in which collective action was constrained not only by institutional boundaries but also by the political and military commitments of member states. In the final settlement negotiations, symbolically conducted in Ohio rather than in any European capital, the EU representative, Carl Bildt (a former Swedish Prime Minister), took only a minor role. In the end, what mattered was the pressure exerted on Serbian leaders by the USA and its chief negotiator, Richard Holbrooke. Several member states drew from this the conclusion that the EU procedures should be radically strengthened, thus feeding the 'maximalist' position in the negotiations leading up to the Amsterdam Treaty. Others drew the conclusion that in post-Cold War European security, there was an emerging 'division of labour' between those who did the fighting (the USA and NATO members) and those who provided the longer term reconstruction and 'peace building' services (largely the EU and the OSCE).

We can see from this admittedly brief outline of the Bosnian episode that several of the points raised earlier are given at least some support. The EU was the object of great expectations in the early stage of the conflict, but these were progressively eroded as the practical incapacity of the EU, both under EPC and the CFSP, became apparent. While the EU could negotiate, it could not do so credibly in a situation where force was pervasive, both as used by those on the ground and eventually as practised by the USA and NATO. As a result, it could be argued that EU member states had incentives to keep their collective action via the EU firmly limited, and to use competing institutional frameworks for the pursuit of their national and collective aims. But two provisos should be entered here. First, there is no doubt that the marginalization of the EU in this conflict created at least some pressure for more ambitious schemes in the context of the Amsterdam Treaty negotiations, and for a serious examination of possible collective action in security policy. Second, it can be argued that the expectations generated with respect to EU action were misplaced in the first place, and that the real substance of the EU's impact on the security situation was to be seen in terms of longer-term reconstruction and peace building. These issues were to re-emerge in the third phase of the conflict.

5.3   Kosovo

It can be, and has been, argued that the Kosovo conflict began in the late 1980s, or even earlier. In 1988 President Milosevic of then-Yugoslavia withdrew the extensive autonomy enjoyed by what everyone agreed was part of Serbia. While the underlying problem was masked to a degree by the conflicts in Croatia and Slovenia, and then Bosnia-Herzegovina, the (at least temporary) settlement of the latter created conditions in which the Kosovo question was bound to come to the fore. This it did in 1998, following an outbreak of internal unrest in Albania in 1996 and 1997 which had also demonstrated the limitations of the EU members' commitment to European security operations. In this case, the Italians had had to lead a 'coalition of the willing' to restore order after what was essentially an eruption of lawlessness rather than an organized civil conflict. Kosovo was of a different class. While it was internationally recognized as part of Serbia, it could be argued that escalating Serb repression of the Albanian majority created a threat to stability in the Balkans as a whole and thus made it a case for active diplomacy and, if necessary, coercion.

Significantly, the diplomatic activity that emerged during late 1998 and 1999 was conducted from the outset within the framework of the Contact Group (Weller, 1999). While the EU had a presence in the Contact Group through the membership of Britain, France and Italy, it was never suggested that the Union itself should be a leading participant as a collective entity. Another important feature of the process was the engagement from the earliest stages of the USA, which had been a reluctant participant in Bosnia but had now become a leading advocate of 'coercive diplomacy'. Thus, when a peace negotiation was established at Rambouillet in France in early 1999, the co-chairs were British Foreign Secretary Robin Cook and French Minister for Foreign Affairs Hubert Védrine; but the most significant diplomatic pressures were arguably those from Washington and (to a lesser extent) Moscow. While the EU through CFSP was undoubtedly a significant influence on the ways in which British and French policies were shaped, there was no evidence of its direct involvement in the diplomatic process that produced a proposed settlement. The context for the proposals was inexorably shaped by, on the one side, the resistance of Milosevic and the Serbs and, on the other, the imminent threat of NATO bombing.

The EU thus appeared to have been marginalized from the start, although this was a somewhat misleading impression. The negotiations took place in the shadow of threats by NATO to bomb Serbia, but all those involved were also aware that there would be a phase of post-conflict stabilization and reconstruction: the same type of 'peace building' in which the EU was already heavily engaged in Bosnia-Herzegovina. Thus from a very early stage, and increasingly as the conflict evolved during the spring of 1999, the EU was active in developing plans for reconstruction. As the conflict continued, the role of the EU's special representative, the Finnish Foreign Minister Martii Ahtisari, also became significant, as he played his part in the negotiations that eventually led to the end of the bombing. The EU was also the – not entirely willing – progenitor of the proposal for a post-conflict 'stability pact' for the Balkans, in which peace-keeping, economic reconstruction and regional co-operation would be overseen in large part by the EU (Friis and Murphy, 2000). Perhaps the most concrete incentive attached to the pact was the promise of EU association agreements for regional states, and by implication the prospect of eventual EU membership. Indeed, the Albanian government in the midst of the bombing declared that, since it had done its bit for Balkan stability, it should be 'fast-tracked' for EU membership.

In the Kosovo conflict, we can again see many of the features that we have placed at the centre of foreign and security policy in the EU and the 'new Europe'. The EU was prevented by institutional constraints and by political factors from taking a major role in the 'coercive diplomacy', let alone the bombing phase of the conflict, although it was noticeable that the solidarity of the member states was maintained in those areas where the EU could act. Individual EU member states, both on national grounds and on the basis of other institutional affiliations (especially NATO membership), were able to play significant roles in the diplomacy and the bombing. When the necessity arose for a post-conflict framework for stabilization and peace building, the EU was a natural focus for activity and responsibility, and this was given added weight by the (admittedly distant) promise of EU membership for regional states in the Balkans.

There is, finally, a further dimension to this story, which I noted earlier in the chapter. One of the key impacts of the Kosovo conflict, added to the earlier lessons of Bosnia-Herzegovina, was on the debate surrounding the CFSP, and in particular on the idea of an EU 'defence identity'. It is no coincidence that the major shift in British policy that led to the St Malo declaration, and thence to the development of major new defence structures for the EU, took place in the run-up to the Kosovo conflict. The perception that the EU suffered from institutional constraints and from consequent deficiencies of member state commitment, and that this could not be allowed to persist, was central to the emerging debate, and the Cologne European Council took place at the climax of the bombing in Kosovo. It was widely believed at that time that continued reliance on the USA as the 'stabilizer' of post-Cold War Europe was unhealthy, and that the role of the EU should not be to displace US military influence but to provide a means by which EU member states and others could act collectively in situations where the Americans were unable or unwilling to lead. The path that then opened up in institutional terms has been outlined in Section 3. The path that opened up in political and security terms was likely to be challenging and risky, placing the EU at the centre of competing pressures and creating a new need for the skills of 'coercive diplomacy' or even the use of force.

Summary

The conflicts that emerged during the 1990s in former Yugoslavia were a formidable test for the foreign and security policy dimensions of the EU. Analysis of the EU's role in the three main phases of the conflicts reveals a number of trends and tendencies.

- First, the onset of the crisis in the former Yugoslavia during the early 1990s coincided with a period of debate and redefinition in the EU, and fed into the Maastricht Treaty and the CFSP.

- Second, crisis diplomacy created incentives for EU member states to defect, or to emphasize competing institutional affiliations as crisis turned to conflict. This was particularly clear in the recognition of Croatia and Slovenia, and later in the Bosnian conflict as the involvement of the USA, the UN and NATO increased.

- Third, while the EU provided a framework for negotiation, it could not provide credibility based on the threat of force or the capacity to implement settlements reached between unwilling participants. This was particularly the case with the Vance–Owen Plan.

- Fourth, the EU became marginalized in terms of the conflicts themselves, but remained an important (if not the most important) component of peace building and post-conflict reconstruction. This was particularly apparent in the implementation of the Dayton Accords and the formation of the Stability Pact for the Balkans after the Kosovo conflict.

- Finally, the debate about an EU 'defence identity' in the late 1990s was powerfully shaped by the perceived failures of the CFSP in Bosnia and particularly in Kosovo. The moves in 1998 and 1999 to create real substance for such a defence dimension were in many respects a direct response to these failures on the part of leading member states, although at the time of writing the longer term development of these moves is uncertain.

6   Conclusion

At the beginning of this chapter, I drew attention both to the uneven history of foreign and security policy as part of the European integration project and to the ways in which it raises distinctive questions about 'governing the Union'. The chapter has dealt in turn with three central aspects of this broad area of enquiry: first, the institutional and 'constitutional' developments surrounding foreign and security policy in the EU; second, the ways in which this relates to the changing 'architecture' of foreign and security policy as expressed in state policies and other international institutions; and finally, the ways in which this developmental process can be thrown into relief by the problems of managing security in post-Cold War Europe, as exemplified in the conflicts in the former Yugoslavia.

I shall not repeat here the conclusions drawn from these three areas of enquiry. Rather, I wish to highlight some of the issues that emerge from the chapter for the 'governing' process in the EU.

- The 'governing' process in foreign and security policy is distinctive, since it places the European integration project in the midst of a wide range of vital national interests, institutional contexts and potential crises.

- Because of this, the institutional frameworks surrounding foreign and security policy in the EU have remained much more inter-governmental in character than those in other areas of European governance.

- The intergovernmental character of European co-operation and the CFSP does not mean that they are simply an expression of traditional (national) foreign policy interests among the member states. Increasingly, the foreign policies of these countries, and of others around the EU, are 'Europeanized' and express a complex interaction between national and European processes.

- There has been a significant move toward the creation of a 'hard' defence capability as a collective enterprise by EU member states, but much remains to be settled. In particular, the budgetary implications and the consequences for national establishments will be a major source of debate for the next five years at least. In this way, the move toward a 'common defence' creates problems of economic and industrial structure that link with the core integration project of the Union.

- In dealing with foreign and security policy there are important questions to be asked about the overall character of European integration and the nature of the EU. First, the extent to which the EU is united in this area has historically lagged behind other areas for a variety of reasons (including national priorities, competing institutions and the influence of external actors such as the USA). Second, the extent to which Europe is governable and the extent to which consensus can be established and maintained in this area are limited by the continued turbulence of the external environment and by the high stakes attached to national security for many EU members. Third, there is an important linkage between the EU and the wider Europe in foreign and security policy, which makes it difficult to resolve problems of inclusion and exclusion procedurally. This means that the EU can both 'govern' outside actors (such as candidate members) and be governed by them (for example, by the USA) in distinctive ways. Finally, the debate on foreign and security policy in the EU, specifically the emergence of an EU defence identity, is inextricably linked with the security dimension of the 'new Europe' in the post-Cold War era, which creates a new dynamic for 'governing' both within and outside the Union.

These conclusions get to the heart of the overall question of governing Europe. They cast a new light on governance as authoritative rule making, and suggest some limitations to it. They place the activity of governments and of national states in a distinctive relationship to the European project, given the association of foreign and security policy with sovereignty, vital national interests and the competitive search for security. And they cast into a challenging light the idea that Europe can be organized through forms of multi-level governance which take account of the diversity of forms of authority and legitimacy. Together, they encompass one of the most dynamic and exciting areas of 'governing the Union' in the early twenty-first century.

References

Allen, D. (1998) 'Who speaks for Europe? The search for an effective and coherent foreign policy' in Peterson, J. and Sjursen, H. (eds) *A Common Foreign Policy for Europe? Competing Visions of the CFSP*, London, Routledge, pp.41–58.

Allen, D. and Smith, M. (1989) 'Western Europe in the Atlantic system of the 1980s: towards a new identity?' in Gill, S. (ed.) *Atlantic Relations Beyond the Reagan Era*, Brighton, Harvester-Wheatsheaf, pp.88–110.

Crawford, B. (1996) 'Explaining defection from international co-operation: Germany's unilateral recognition of Croatia', *World Politics*, vol.48, no.4, pp.482–521.

Croft, S., Redmond, J., Wyn Rees, G. and Webber, M. (1999) *The Enlargement of Europe*, Manchester, Manchester University Press.

DePorte, A. (1987) *Europe Between the Superpowers: The Enduring Balance*, New Haven, CT, Yale University Press (second edition).

Edwards, G. and Spence, D. (1994) *The European Commission*, London, Longman.

Forster, A. and Wallace, W. (1996) 'Common Foreign and Security Policy: a new policy or just a new name?' in Wallace, H. and Wallace, W. (eds) *Policy-Making in the European Union*, Oxford, Oxford University Press, pp.411–35.

Forster, A. and Wallace, W. (2000) 'Common Foreign and Security Policy: from shadow to substance?' in Wallace, H. and Wallace, W. (eds) *Policy-Making in the European Union*, Oxford, Oxford University Press (fourth edition), pp.461–91.

Friis, L. and Murphy, A. (2000) 'Negotiating in a time of crisis: the EU's response to the military conflict in Kosovo', *Journal of European Public Policy*, vol.7, no.5.

Grosser, A. (1979) *The Western Alliance*, London, Macmillan.

Hill, C. (1989) 'European foreign policy: power bloc, civilian model – or flop?' in Rummel, R. (ed.) *The Evolution of an International Actor: Western Europe's New Assertiveness*, Boulder, CO, Lynne Rienner, pp.31–55.

Hill, C. (1993) 'The capability–expectations gap, or conceptualizing Europe's international role', *Journal of Common Market Studies*, vol.31, no.3, September, pp.305–28.

Hill, C. (ed.) (1996) *The Actors in Europe's Foreign Policy*, London, Routledge.

Hill, C. (1998) 'Closing the capabilities–expectations gap?' in Peterson, J. and Sjursen, H. (eds) *A Common Foreign Policy for Europe? Competing Visions of the CFSP*, London, Routledge, pp.18–38.

Hurd, D. (1994) *International Affairs*, vol.70, no.3, July, pp.413–97.

Keatinge, P. (1997) 'Security and defence' in Tonra, B. (ed.) *Amsterdam: What the Treaty Really Means*, Dublin, Institute of European Affairs.

Nuttall, S. (1992) *European Political Co-operation*, Oxford, Oxford University Press.

Smith, K. (1999) *The Making of EU Foreign Policy: The Case of Eastern Europe*, London, Macmillan.

Smith, M. (2000) 'The EU as an international actor' in Richardson, J. (ed.) *European Union: Power and Policy Making*, London, Routledge (second edition).

Weller, M. (1999) 'The Rambouillet conference on Kosovo', *International Affairs*, vol.75, no.2, April, pp.211–52.

Zucconi, M. (1996) 'The EU in the former Yugoslavia' in Chayes, A. and Chayes, A. (eds) *Preventing Conflict in the Post-Communist World: Mobilizing International and Regional Organizations*, Washington, DC, Brookings Institution, pp.237–78.

Further reading

Bretherton, C. and Vogler, J. (1999) *The European Union as a Global Actor*, London, Routledge.

Forster, A. and Wallace, W. (2000) 'Common Foreign and Security Policy' in Wallace, H. and Wallace, W. (eds) *Policy-Making in the European Union*, Oxford, Oxford University Press (fourth edition).

Smith, M. (2000) 'The EU as an international actor' in Richardson, J. (ed.) *European Union: Power and Policy Making*, London, Routledge (second edition).

Chapter 11
Conclusion: What is the European Union?

Simon Bromley

1   Introduction

Chapter 1 posed the question 'What is the European Union?', and it was suggested that there are two difficulties that confront any attempt to answer it. The first of these is that the European Union (EU) represents a 'moving target': it is constantly changing, and any attempt to say what it is must therefore also include some idea of what the process of integration is about. The second problem is that we do not and cannot know where that process is heading or where it will end, or even stabilize. Has the EU developed about as far as it can, or does it have further to go and, if so, where is it going from here? Chapter 1 also argued that studying the EU is particularly interesting for the light it casts on the changing nature of governance in contemporary societies; 'governance' being defined as *the relatively standardized processes and institutions by which purposeful outcomes are produced for any political system*. The other chapters of this book have attempted to cast light on the nature of the EU by exploring different aspects of its governance.

A simple view is that governance within nation states is carried out by governments claiming exclusive and compulsory jurisdiction over their territories. Between states, by contrast, there is no governance, since there is no international or world government. However, such a view is misleading in several important respects and certainly won't work in the context of the EU. In the first place, the governance carried out by governments in liberal-democratic states is conditional because it operates primarily on the basis of legitimacy rather than force or fraud. This means not only that significant spheres of social and economic activity are left ungoverned, or govern themselves, but also that the scope and intensity of government is limited, if also guaranteed, by the fact that it operates according to the constitutional rule of law, derives its authority and purposes from the rights of the people and is subject to democratic contestation through competitive party elections. In this context, it was argued that the *de facto*, informal, self-governing activities of the governed may regulate (that is, govern) the *de jure*, formal rulers of the state just as much as the latter govern the former.

In much the same way, while the relations between states may remain formally anarchic, it does not follow that states interacting with one another cannot establish a consensus over norms of conduct, perhaps through extensive participation in shared institutions like the EU. In such a case the interacting states would not be subordinate to an international government, but they might develop a highly institutionalized degree of informal governance. Moreover, these two points are related, since the economic and social spheres that are to a degree 'privately' governed in liberal-democratic states can and do cross national borders in ways that escape the control of governments. Thus just as governments may share the governance of 'their' societies with the self-governing processes of, say, the economy, so they may also share in the governance of international or transnational economic processes with other states. In relation to the EU, not only is governance shared as between the member states of the EU, it is also negotiated between these states and their increasingly transnational economies and societies.

This is not the place to summarize the specifics of the preceding chapters, since each has already done so in its own terms. The rest of this chapter will attempt, first, to review the debate between the intergovernmental and supranational interpretations of the EU; second, to consider the idea that the EU can be characterized as a new form of governance, a 'regulatory state'; and third, to raise some open questions about the bases of authority and legitimacy in the governance of the contemporary EU. These issues provide the key to the future development of the EU.

2   The EU: intergovernmental or supranational?

Chapter 1 started with two deliberately oversimplified models of the EU, and the subsequent chapters elaborated and commented on these models in various ways. One model considers the EU to be a particularly extensive and intense form of intergovernmental co-operation, in which the purpose-built institutions of the Union – the Commission, the European Court of Justice (ECJ) and the European Parliament (EP) – are seen as having power and authority only by virtue of delegation from the member states and are effectively governed by the Council. In this model, the member states are able to circumscribe, monitor and control the extent of these apparently supranational institutions. Not only does this view maintain that the member states are the dominant actors in the process of European integration but it also contends that co-operation between member states is largely concerned with extending their collective powers to do things that cannot be done individually at the national level. In this view, integration does not so much undermine the power and authority of the member states as reorganize, or 'Europeanize', it in shared or pooled ways, sometimes delegating certain executive tasks to the supranational institutions. This model has the virtue of simplicity but, perhaps because of this, it is hard to square it with a number of salient features of politics in the EU. We shall see, however, that despite its simplicity it captures a fundamental point about the contemporary Union.

The other model, the supranational model, argues that things are considerably more complicated. Supranational accounts see the EU as a new form of supranational governance, as a political system that reaches beyond the nation state in important respects. The role of the Commission, the Parliament and the ECJ (and the associated framework of Community law) are seen as serving a transnational society of economic and other actors operating within and across the territories of the member states. While member states remain important actors in the overall process, this latter view sees them as having to share power and authority with the other institutions that make up the political system of the EU. According to supranationalists, the governance of the EU is a multi-level phenomenon, operating at local, regional, national and supranational levels, and functioning within as well as across the territories of the member states. For this reason, this view is sometimes characterized as the 'multi-level governance' theory of the EU.

Each of these perspectives interprets the dynamics of integration in different ways. Intergovernmental accounts portray the evolution of the EU in terms of a series of inter-state bargains, in which the member states agree to common policies and institutions in some areas but nevertheless retain control of the overall process and remain in charge of the nominally supranational institutions of the EU such as the Commission and the European Court of Justice (Chapter 2). The neo-functionalist theorists of supranationalism and more recent analysts of multi-level governance, by contrast, see the politics of European integration as a reshaping of national politics towards the supranational realm, as ever greater economic and socio-cultural connections among and across states bring about ever deeper co-operation between them (Chapter 6). As a result of the growing functional integration of politics and policy across national borders, and because of the rise of transnational actors pressing for European-level policy, the EU has steadily acquired supranational competence. Governance has, to some extent, migrated from governments to the EU.

Another way of presenting these contrasting models is as follows. For the intergovernmental reading of the EU, the basic components of analysis are still the national political systems of the member states. These interact in complex ways within the institutions of the EU, but this institutional framework is ultimately under the collective authority and control of the governments of the member states. The institutions of the EU itself therefore constitute a 'second-order' political system: one that is based upon the political systems of the member states. According to the supranationalist interpretation, the EU represents a political system in its own terms, a form of governance reaching beyond that of the nation state. In turn, political actors within the member states (for example, local authorities, parties, pressure groups and citizens), as well as the EU institutions and actors that organize across state boundaries (for example, networks of business organizations or trade unions) interact *within* the multi-level structure of the EU and the member states. This complex of national and supranational governance is no longer under the control of the member states, either individually or collectively. Moreover, neither does it derive its authority solely from the national political systems of the member states. It is in part directly legitimated by European-wide elections and legal procedures. The EU therefore constitutes a political system that is superimposed over and above, yet interacting with, the national systems of the member states; it is a *sui generis* (unique, or literally 'of its own kind') form of governance.

We have seen that both of these models capture important aspects of the politics and governance of the EU. More importantly, perhaps, we have seen that each model casts more light on some aspects of the EU than it does on others. Put somewhat crudely, the first, or Community, pillar of the EU is the most supranational in its workings; the second (the Common Foreign and Security Policy) and third (Justice and Home Affairs) pillars remain the most intergovernmental; and the arrangements for Economic and Monetary Union (EMU) represent a mixture of the two. Speaking rather more precisely, Simon Hix has summarized the relevant differences as follows.

> Regulatory and redistributive policies are adopted through *supranational* (quasi-federal) practices: where the Commission has a monopoly on policy initiative; legislation is adopted through bicameral procedures between the Council and the EP, and QMV [qualified majority voting] is often used in the Council; [Community] law is directly effective and supreme over national law and the ECJ has full powers of judicial review and legal adjudication. In contrast, citizen and global policies are mainly adopted through *intergovernmental* procedures: where the Council is the main executive and legislative body; decisions in the Council are usually made by unanimity; the Commission can generate policy ideas but its agenda-setting powers are limited; the EP only has the right to be consulted by the Council; and the powers of judicial review of the ECJ are restricted. On the other hand, macroeconomic policies are adopted through a mix of supranationalism and intergovernmentalism, where the ECB [European Central Bank] is an independent and powerful federal monetary authority ... but the Council of Economic and Finance Ministers (EcoFin) is the collective 'economic government' of EMU, and the EP plays an important scrutiny role but cannot enforce its wishes on the ECB or the Council.

(Hix, 1999, pp.8–9)

We have also noted shifts in the balance between intergovernmentalism and supranationalism over time. Indeed, it is tempting to conclude that there has been an inexorable, if intermittent and uneven, shift toward a strengthening of the supranational elements in the EU.

What began life as an ambitious set of Treaties signed by sovereign nation states under international law has developed into a system with its own, increasingly robust, legal order, such that some analysts now speak of the 'constitutionalization' of the Community legal order (Chapter 4). The European Parliament, which began life as an appointed assembly, now has legislative powers of co-decision with the Council of Ministers on many Community pillar matters (Chapter 7). Political parties, the principal expressions and channels of popular political demands, increasingly operate at both the national *and* the European level (Chapter 5). The Commission's role has steadily expanded and it now lies at the centre of a network of European regulatory agencies, what some have called a European regulatory state, and forms a focal point for lobbying by significant political actors (Chapter 6). The getting and spending of the EU budget is now a highly institutionalized process, even if the major agreements are still decided by the Heads of Government in the European Council (Chapter 8). Most member states have relinquished their national currencies and joined a Euro-wide single currency, overseen by a relatively independent European Central Bank (Chapter 2). Even the second and third pillars of the Community, which relate to external security and internal 'law and order' respectively, have developed forms of institutionalized co-operation, if not much in the way of common policies (Chapters 4 and 10). And the EU is set on a course of major enlargement, which is likely to strengthen its supranational characteristics (Chapter 9).

The steady consolidation and expansion of the EU political system and the increasing salience of its supranational features have led many analysts to become less interested in the question of whether the Union should be characterized as intergovernmental or supranational and more interested in what kind of governance the multi-level system provides. What does this distribution of supranational and intergovernmental elements across the various domains of the EU – the three pillars and EMU – tell us about its character as a system of governance? Remember that we have defined governance as the relatively standardized processes and institutions by which purposeful outcomes are produced for any political system (Chapter 1). We have also argued that the government of the nation state is only one particular form of political system. Political systems can be and have been organized in different ways.

According to Hix, the supranational aspects of the EU and the highly institutionalized nature of its intergovernmental features show that 'the EU is already a fully functioning political system', that 'a highly developed political system can emerge without either the full-blown apparatus of a state or a high level of popular support and mass political participation' (1999, p.364). Similarly, David McKay has argued that since the Treaty on European Union (1992), and with the forthcoming introduction of full Economic and Monetary Union, the EU:

> ... qualifies as a species of federal state. Almost all of the conditions for federalism will then have been met, including the assumption of exclusive powers for the federal government, the acceptance of two levels of citizenship, and a supranational institutional framework, which, in some areas at least, provides for Europe-wide policy making by European politicians and officials rather than what has been called 'intergovernmentalism' or policy making by *ad hoc* meetings of national representatives.
>
> (McKay, 1999, pp.21–2)

Notice, however, that this new kind of 'fully functioning political system' (Hix) or 'federal state' (McKay) is a rather peculiar thing, for as both these authors point out the EU does not have many of the features we normally associate with the state: namely, a territorially organized people, with a government that successfully claims domestic supremacy and external independence, a monopoly over the organized means of violence and a degree of mass or popular legitimacy (Chapters 1 and 3).

As we have seen, the member states retain their sovereignty under international law, even if they have agreed to limit their individual right to exercise it in some areas (Chapter 3); the Community legal order is dependent on recognition by, and the co-operation of, the national legal systems of the member states (Chapter 4); the institutions of the EU do not possess a monopoly over the organized means of violence to maintain internal law and order, or to carry out external military action (Chapters 4 and 10); the power of the EU to tax and spend and the size of its budget are very small in comparison with the fiscal powers of the member states (Chapter 8); notwithstanding the growth in power of the EP and decision making at an EU level, the orientation of political parties and elections remains primarily national (Chapters 5, 6 and 7); and the quasi-federal aspects of the EU are heavily qualified by the fact that both executive and legislative authority are shared between the supranational and intergovernmental aspects of the Union: between the Commission and the still powerful Council for executive decisions and between the Council and the EP for legislative acts (Chapters 2 and 3). That is to say, the EU lacks many of the resources that the governments of the member states continue to rely upon.

Thus we seem to be confronted by a mixed situation. On the one hand, the EU has strong intergovernmental characteristics; but in agreeing to ever wider and deeper co-operation the member states and their governments have *Europeanized* much of their political activity. On the other hand, a significant amount of the co-operation that takes place is organized supranationally, but the supranational institutions lack the political resources available to these governments.

3   Is the EU a regulatory state?

Does it matter? Not necessarily. Just because the form of EU governance is not the same as that of the governments of the member states writ large, we cannot assume that it is unimportant. On the contrary, some have argued that the EU represents a new kind of political system, a kind of *regulatory state*. Moreover, this argument further suggests that the governments of the member states are also being refashioned in a regulatory direction, as governments become less concerned with intervening in the economy to shape a particular distribution of income and wealth or with managing overall economic performance. This position is associated, above all, with the argument of Giandomenico Majone.

> The Union is not, and may never become, a state in the modern
> sense of the concept. It is, at most, a 'regulatory state' since it
> exhibits some of the features of statehood only in the
> important but limited area of economic and social regulation.
> In this area, however, non-majoritarian institutions are the
> preferred instruments of governance everywhere.

(Majone, 1996, p.287)

By 'non-majoritarian institutions' Majone is referring to 'independent regulatory bodies, like independent central banks, courts of law, administrative tribunals or the European Commission', which serve 'as one important means of diffusing power' and which 'may be a more effective form of democratic control than direct accountability to voters or to elected officials' (1996, p.285). Majone develops his argument by distinguishing 'three main functions of government in the socio-economic sphere: income redistribution, macroeconomic stabilization and regulation', arguing that 'in the field of regulatory policy making, European integration has meant "rule creation" – new and generally better rules both at the national and the supranational levels – rather than simply "rule diversion" from one level of government to another' (1996, pp.54 and 59).

The rule creation identified by Majone is primarily oriented to regulating the internal market of the EU, the original 'common market' based on the four freedoms of movement of goods, capital, labour and services as set down in the Treaty of Rome and given new momentum by the Single European Act (1986). This regulation has taken two forms. The first is essentially a 'negative' form of integration carried out under the auspices of the Commission and the ECJ. As Fritz Scharpf has pointed out, the 'nearly invisible power' of judicial law-making by the Commission and the ECJ 'is mainly available against national policy measures that could constitute barriers to the free market' (1999, p.24). The second is positive integration, which 'depends on the agreement of national governments in the Council of Ministers and, increasingly, on the agreement of the European Parliament as well' (Scharpf, 1999, p.50). Given the supranational basis of negative integration, it can and does operate even if it results in outcomes that go against the preferences of a given member state. Positive integration has a stronger intergovernmental basis, although QMV in the Council and the role of the EP give it some supranational aspects, and this means that 'Europe is capable of positive action if, and only if, there is a possibility of *common* gains' (Scharpf, 1999, p.74).

In general, member states have given their support to Treaty-based commitments to negative integration, as well as to particular measures of positive integration in the Council, because they believe that the creation of wider and deeper markets provides net benefits for all, even if not everyone benefits equally all of the time, and because they believe that an EU-wide level playing field is preferable to nationally imposed distortions. (Of course, any given member state would like the others to observe fair play and itself be able to cheat, but this would mean that everyone ends up cheating. Given this prospect, it is better for each member if all play fair and neutral referees – the Commission and the ECJ – observe that the rules are upheld.) In other words, the regulatory activity of the EU, its supranational ability to create rules for the single market, has taken place in what has been called a 'permissive environment'. Regulation, whether in the form of negative or positive integration, has developed against a background in which the results of EU policy making are seen to benefit all and are, to that extent, relatively uncontroversial.

The two points we have just reviewed are obviously connected. That is to say, it is because the *results* of EU governance benefit all and don't create significant 'losers' that it has been able to develop as a 'regulatory state' – it has even been able to construct limited forms of quasi-federal authority – without needing the kinds of *resources* that national governments rely upon. This point is explicitly recognized by Giandomenico Majone. Whereas public decisions about redistribution and stabilization can only be legitimated by democratic contestation, since such decisions inevitably create winners and losers, 'efficiency issues ... may be thought of as positive-sum games where everybody can gain, provided the right solution is discovered' (1996, p.294). In the 'sphere of efficiency issues', Majone concludes, 'the delegation of important policy making powers to independent institutions is democratically justified ... where reliance on expertise and on a problem solving style of decision making is more important than reliance on direct political accountability' (Majone, 1996, p.296).

I shall return to the question of regulatory legitimacy in Section 4. For the moment, simply note that recent developments have called this diagnosis into question, suggesting that the EU is developing a role in areas well beyond the regulation of the internal market. As we have seen, the EU is developing capabilities in relation to fields traditionally reserved to national governments, such as Justice and Home Affairs and the Common Foreign and Security Policy. Moves towards EMU will almost certainly begin to create 'winners' and 'losers' in the EU political system, or lead to further EU-level control over national taxation and spending powers, or both. Enlargement will surely increase the level of political diversity within the EU and complicate ideas of a single European political identity and community, while increasing the need for supranational governance. The EU is now significantly more than a 'regulatory state' in Majone's rather precise sense.

In any case, the intergovernmentalist rejoinder to the idea that the EU constitutes a regulatory state is surely obvious. The EU may remain focused on positive-sum regulatory activities that benefit all, in which case it may not need any more resources for its system of governance, but by the same token it can scarcely be called a 'state'. Or, as the EU develops capabilities and responsibilities in the areas of macroeconomic stabilization and redistribution, to say nothing of internal and external security, it will need to be able to enforce and legitimate decisions that inevitably create 'winners' and 'losers' in the political system. At present, the supranational aspects of the EU can concentrate on regulatory activities on the basis of limited political resources (legitimacy, money and administrative capacity), because the member states continue to provide the other aspects associated with modern citizenship – namely a degree of socio-economic security, internal 'law and order' and external defence – even if they increasingly do this intergovernmentally, in co-operation with one another in the Union.

The transfer of these latter functions to the supranational realms of the EU is difficult to envisage in the absence of considerable strengthening of the resources of the EU political system. The EU would need a greater degree of legitimacy to give authority to its decisions, a larger budget to fund its activities, and an enhanced administrative capacity to implement policy. Such a transfer is already underway in some respects, but whether the corresponding resources will follow only time will tell. One of the foremost advocates of the idea that the EU does indeed constitute a 'fully-functioning' political system has described the situation as follows.

> The end of the permissive consensus, the launch of EMU, and the rise of party political contestation over the EU agenda all mean that EU citizens, rank and file party members and non-governing party élites are starting to take notice of the governing and policy making processes at the European level. The result is increasing restrictions on the freedom of manoeuvre of élites at the EU level. ... If the outcomes were highly redistributive, the EU would either require a greater use of force to impose its policies or a greater level of democratic participation to legitimize redistributive outcomes. Ironically, then, if economic and political integration is to proceed much further, the EU is likely to need a greater state capacity as well as genuine democratic contestation to legitimize this state power.

(Hix, 1999, pp.363–4)

McKay makes essentially the same point in relation to the political implications of Economic and Monetary Union, concluding that 'In sum, it is difficult to identify a scenario where EMU does not also require a degree of political union which is well beyond that operating in the European Union of 1999' (1999, p.182). The alternative is that member states seek to relinquish the traditional responsibilities associated with modern citizenship in the nation state, without transferring them to the supranational elements of the EU. That is, the member states also seek to become essentially regulatory states, disengaged from the wider social responsibilities historically associated with interventionist welfare states. From the intergovernmental standpoint, it is even harder to see how the EU could survive, let alone prosper, if the member states were to attempt this.

Let us attempt to summarize the discussion thus far by going back to some of the general considerations raised in Chapter 1. We can ask the following questions of any system of governance: first, what is the source of authority for the processes and institutions of collective decision making?; second, what is the scope of people's demands on the political system?; third, how are the collective decisions of the system implemented and enforced?; and fourth, how do the results, or 'outputs', of the political system feed back into the demands the people place upon it? Table 11.1 (opposite) compares the nation state and the EU as systems of governance, as political systems, along these four dimensions, as viewed from an intergovernmental perspective.

A supranationalist interpretation might reply that the intergovernmental reading unfairly assumes that the EU can only develop in the image of the nation state. Ben Rosamond, for example, has recently cautioned that: 'The danger for intergovernmentalists is to conclude that because organs of supranational governance have not developed into nation-state-like repositories of power and authority, it follows that there has been no meaningful displacement in the authority of member states' (Rosamond, 2000, p.154). Has Table 11.1 fallen into this trap? Perhaps. In order to balance things up, we need to redraw the picture as it is seen by the analysts of multi-level governance or supranationalism. Table 11.2 gives the other side of the story.

Table 11.1 Comparing the nation state and the EU: the inter-governmental view

	Governance of the nation state	*Governance of the EU*
What is the source of political authority?	Direct: the rights of a self-governing people, with the people defined as members of a national community	Indirect: derived from the governments of the member states
What is the scope of the people's demands on the political system?	Basic civil and political rights; a degree of economic and social welfare; internal law and order; security from external threats	Regulation of economic activity that relates to issues of common concern to the member states, which cannot be handled at a national level and which generally benefit all
How are collective decisions implemented and enforced?	Law and public policy; extensive taxation and public spending; coercion in the last resort	Law and public policy that rely upon the legal, financial and administrative resources of the member states for implementation and enforcement
How important are the outputs of the system for people's political demands?	Political parties offer candidates for public office in competitive elections and are judged on their performance in government	There is no 'government' of the EU that can be held accountable for policy outputs, and inputs are limited to relatively non-contentious issues

Table 11.2   Comparing the nation state and the EU: the supranational or multi-level view

	Governance of the nation state	*Governance of the EU*
What is the source of political authority?	Direct: the rights of a self-governing people, with the people defined as members of a national community; *but* the people regard themselves as having transnational as well as national rights and allegiances	Direct: from the rights of the people of Europe, the people defined as members of a new, transnational community + Indirect: derived from the governments of the member states
What is the scope of the people's demands on the political system?	Basic civil and political rights; a degree of economic and social welfare; internal law and order; security from external threats; *but* none of these can be guaranteed at the national level in a transnational society	Regulation of economic activity that relates to issues of common concern to the member states, which cannot be handled at a national level and which generally benefit all + Basic civil and political rights; a degree of social regulation; growth of common policies for internal and external security
How are collective decisions implemented and enforced?	Law and public policy; extensive taxation and public spending; coercion in the last resort; *but* law, tax and coercion are exercised in accordance with *European* norms	Law and public policy that have supremacy and direct effect over national law, and where the Community legal order is *de facto*, if not *de jure*, a constitution for Europe on some mainly economic matters
How important are the outputs of the system for people's political demands?	Political parties offer candidates for public office in competitive elections and are judged on their performance in government; *but* many of the issues on which governments are judged are not within the control of individual states	Multi-level governance is accountable for policy outputs in different ways at different levels, where control is not exercised from any one point in the system, but the system is under control; growing demands on the system

4   Questions of governance, authority and legitimacy

The differences between the intergovernmental and the supranational views of the EU ultimately turn on some deep theoretical questions, as well as the more empirical and descriptive questions of what the Union is responsible for and how it works. The characterization of the EU as a system of supranational or multi-level governance is certainly useful empirically and descriptively: first, because it points to the fact that there can be governance if not without then at least beyond the reach of governments; and second, because it depicts 'governance as fluid and authority as dispersed, in terms of both domestic politics and transnational relations' (Rosamond, 2000, p.197). But is it, as Rosamond suggests, more a metaphor, a picture of how the EU works, than a theory? Does it offer an explanation of the authority of multi-level governance in the EU that is fundamentally distinct from that supplied by the political systems of the member states? Majone (1996), for one, suggests that it does.

'The main task delegated to regulatory agencies is to correct market failures so as to increase aggregate welfare,' Majone contends, and the search for efficiency enhancing regulations is essentially a matter of finding the 'right solution' to the problem (1996, pp.294–5). Moreover, according to Majone, since efficient market regulation is a *technical* matter, regulation is not really a *political* activity at all but something more akin to a scientific enterprise. And just as we do not expect our scientists to be democratically appointed and removed (we want them to be independent of politicians, if also accountable to the public), so in the regulatory sphere 'independence and accountability can be reconciled by a combination of control mechanisms [legally defined objectives, judicial review, transparency, professionalism] rather than by oversight exercised from any fixed place in the political spectrum ... At that point the problem of regulatory legitimacy will have been largely solved' (1996, p.300).

If this were so, it would be a very important development, especially as Scharpf has argued that 'as a consequence of the supremacy of European law, the four economic freedoms, and the injunctions against distortions of competition, have in fact gained constitutional force *vis-à-vis* the member states' (1999, p.58). In other words, if Majone's analysis is sound, there is a *de facto* economic constitution for Europe, enshrined in the regulatory law of the Community, that limits national autonomy and is legitimated according to technical, not political, criteria.

If the EU's activities were confined to market regulation (which they aren't), there would be two fundamental objections to Majone's case. In the first place, the historical parallel that Majone draws upon is of dubious validity. Majone makes much of the fact that regulatory agencies, independent non-majoritarian institutions, play an important role in the governance of the economy and society of the USA. Indeed, the regulatory agencies in the USA are often referred to as the 'fourth' branch of government, to add to the traditional three specified by the constitution: the executive, the legislature and the judiciary. Majone draws on this experience to defuse the argument that the independence of regulatory agencies – in the case of the EU, the Commission, the ECJ and the ECB – are in some ways undemocratic. But surely the comparison argues precisely the opposite. The fourth branch of the US government, if that is what it is, is just that: the fourth branch of the US *government*. And the US government derives its authority from the US Constitution and ultimately from the people of America. To what degree does the EU have a government, or a constitution, or a people to confer authority?

And secondly, Majone's argument assumes that the choice of market efficiency is not a political question. Surely this is questionable. While it may be argued that there are technical aspects to decisions concerning economic regulation, questions whose status is in some sense 'scientific', Majone is claiming something stronger: that collectively binding decisions about how to promote efficient market economies are not political. This could be true only in a world in which there is one correct theory of how the economy works and of how it can be purposefully governed. That does not seem to reflect the world of contemporary Europe. Furthermore, not only are particular policy choices contested within the context of a market economy (for example, should a Central Bank only follow an inflation target or should it also take account of levels of output and employment?), but the choice of an economic system is also a political decision in need of legitimation.

Majone argues that one can make a sharp distinction between measures that enhance efficiency, and therefore benefit all, and questions of redistribution, which are zero-sum and take resources from some in order to give to others, thereby inevitably creating 'winners' and 'losers'. This may be so in theory, but in practice such a distinction is often hard to draw. In a revealing passage, Majone seems to concede this point.

> A striking feature of the integration process is that all major efficiency-increasing strategies – from the creation of the Common Market to Economic and Monetary Union – were accompanied by *separate* redistributive measures in favour of the poorer member states: the Social Fund, the European Investment Bank, the European Regional Development Fund, the Structural Funds and finally the Cohesion Fund, which the Maastricht Treaty explicitly ties to the adjustments made necessary by monetary union. By this method it has been possible to achieve a remarkable level of economic integration, in which the richer member states are particularly interested, while distributing the benefits so as to induce all the members to participate in such projects.
>
> (Majone, 1996, pp.295–6).

What this demonstrates, surely, is that even measures that are efficiency-enhancing will be supported only if all the parties actually do benefit. It is not enough that improved efficiency leaves the beneficiaries sufficiently better off that they could compensate those who lose out and still gain themselves, they must actually do so. This means that, in practice, efficiency gains will be accompanied by distributional issues. And even if such distributional issues are not zero-sum redistributions (since no one is made worse off), they still involve a *political* process, as the struggles over the EU's budget have amply demonstrated. In fact, if people or states view their welfare in relative rather than absolute terms, that is, if they define their welfare not just by how well they are doing but also by how they are doing relative to others, then even positive-sum distributions are redistributional. For example, EMU might make all member states richer in absolute terms and yet the already rich may gain disproportionately, such that the gap between rich and poor gets wider. In a political *community* that stresses integration, this may be a matter of considerable concern.

For these reasons we should be sceptical of the argument that in so far as it is a 'regulatory state' the EU supplies its own technocratic legitimacy through the notion of market efficiency. For all its empirical and descriptive limitations, then, the enduring insight of the inter-governmentalist position is that the question of the authority of governance mechanisms cannot ultimately be finessed by appeals to non-political criteria, no matter where and how decisions are taken. Changing the level at which decisions are made does not alter the criteria by which they are judged. There can certainly be governance beyond governments, as the EU clearly demonstrates, but there cannot be governance without politics. Intergovernmentalists have been slow to see the reconfiguration of European governance around the EU. But they are not mistaken in believing that if it is to be capable of taking meaningful decisions, then any form of political governance requires legitimacy; it has to find a source of authority and a broadly accepted purpose for the exercise of that power. The EU may represent a movement of governance beyond the governments of the member states, but it does not amount to a move beyond liberal-democratic politics.

The member states that have been building the EU are all liberal democracies. Even if their politics has been Europeanized and their economies and societies have become transnational, their people still expect public power to conform to well established and deeply held norms of political legitimacy. That these points have not been lost on the political élites and social forces that have been building the EU can be seen from the fact that over time there has been a shift 'from the indirect towards the more direct mode of legitimation; from performance as the sole justificatory criterion towards issues of democracy and identity; from inter-European élites to national populations as the addressees of legitimacy claims' (Beetham and Lord, 1998, p.129).

Clearly, a major part of what the EU has been and will continue to be about is its role as a regulatory order (although not, we have suggested, a regulatory 'state') and questions of economic performance and the effects of such regulation, including new areas like the environment and social protection, will remain crucial for the support that the Union can rely upon (see Thompson, 2001, for a fuller discussion of the role of the EU in governing the European economic order). However, the EU has already moved considerably beyond positive-sum regulatory policy making and even the latter cannot be legitimated solely by appeals to 'efficiency'. Accordingly, the questions of whether and how the EU can create a sense of political community at a European level, the degree to which identities and loyalties among the citizens of the EU can be newly imagined in a more 'European' and less 'national' direction, perhaps hold the key to where the EU develops from here (see Guibernau, 2001, for a consideration of diversity and identity in contemporary Europe).

The EU already meets one of the criteria for political legitimacy – governing according to the rule of law – perhaps better than some of its member states. However, this legal order is not yet part of a constitution for the people of Europe (or if it is, they have not been consulted about it and it is confined to being a constitution for a free-market economy). The EU lacks a source of authority in popular sovereignty and it cannot elicit the consent of those it governs in the ways that member states can. Giving more positive effect to these principles at an EU level need not involve replicating the features of the nation state at a European level. But if the EU is to advance significantly beyond its present position it will have to find new ways of legitimating itself to the people and states of Europe.

References

Beetham, D. and Lord, C. (1998) *Legitimacy and the European Union*, London, Longman.

Guibernau, M. (ed.) (2001) *Governing European Diversity*, London, Sage/The Open University.

Hix, S. (1999) *The Political System of the European Union*, London, Macmillan.

Majone, G. (1996) *Regulating Europe*, London, Routledge.

McKay, D. (1999) *Federalism and the European Union*, Oxford, Oxford University Press.

Rosamond, B. (2000) *Theories of European Integration*, London, Macmillan.

Scharpf, F. (1999) *Governing In Europe: Effective and Democratic?*, Oxford, Oxford University Press.

Thompson, G. (ed.) (2001) *Governing the European Economy*, London, Sage/The Open University.

Further reading

Beetham, D. and Lord, C. (1998) *Legitimacy and the European Union*, London, Longman.

Majone, G. (1996) *Regulating Europe*, London, Routledge.

McKay, D. (1999) *Federalism and the European Union*, Oxford, Oxford University Press.

Siedentop, L. (2000) *Democracy in Europe*, Harmondsworth, Penguin.

Appendix
A chronology of the building of the European Union

1948	May	A congress in the Hague, attended by many leading supporters of European co-operation and integration, issues a resolution asserting 'that it is the urgent duty of the nations of Europe to create an economic and political union in order to assure security and social progress'.
1949	April	Treaty establishing North Atlantic Treaty Organization (NATO) signed in Washington by twelve states.
	May	Statute of Council of Europe signed in Strasbourg by ten states.
1950	May	Robert Schuman, the French Foreign Minister, puts forward his proposals to place French and German coal and steel under a common authority.
1951	April	Treaty establishing European Coal and Steel Community (ECSC) signed in Paris by six states: Belgium, France, Germany, Italy, Luxembourg and the Netherlands.
1952	July	ECSC comes into operation.
1955	June	Messina Conference of the foreign ministers of the six ECSC states to discuss further European integration. Spaak Committee established to identify the way forward for European integration.
1956	June	Negotiations formally opened between the six with a view to creating an Economic Community and an Atomic Energy Community.

1957	March	Treaties of Rome signed, establishing the European Economic Community (EEC) and the European Atomic Energy Community (Euratom).
1958	January	EEC and Euratom come into operation.
1959	January	First EEC tariff cuts and increases in quotas.
1960	January	Stockholm Convention establishing the European Free Trade Association (EFTA) signed by Austria, Denmark, Norway, Portugal, Sweden, Switzerland and the UK. EFTA comes into operation in May 1960.
1961	July to August	Ireland, Denmark and UK request negotiations on Community membership.
1962	January	Basic features of Common Agricultural Policy (CAP) agreed.
	July	Norway requests negotiations on Community membership.
1963	January	General de Gaulle announces his veto on UK membership.
1965	April	Signing of Treaty establishing a Single Council and a Single Commission of the European Communities (the Merger Treaty).
	July	France begins a boycott of Community institutions to register its opposition to various proposed supranational developments.
1966	January	Foreign ministers agree to the Luxembourg Compromise. Normal Community processes are resumed.
1967	May	Denmark, Ireland and UK re-apply for Community membership.
	July	1965 Merger Treaty takes effect.
	December	The Council of Ministers fails to reach agreement on the re-opening of membership negotiations with the applicant states because of continued French opposition to UK membership.
1968	July	The Customs Union is completed. All internal duties and quotas are removed and the common external tariff is established.

1969	June	Community re-opens membership negotiations with Denmark, Ireland, Norway and UK.
	July	President Pompidou (who succeeded de Gaulle in April) announces that he does not oppose UK membership in principle.
	December	Hague summit agrees a number of important issues: strengthening Community institutions, enlargement, establishing economic and monetary union by 1980, and developing political co-operation (that is, a common foreign policy).
1972	January	Negotiations between the Community and the four applicant countries concluded. Signing of treaties of accession.
	May	Irish approve Community accession in a referendum.
	September	Norwegians vote against Community accession in a referendum.
	October	Danes approve Community accession in a referendum.
1973	January	Accession of Denmark, Ireland and UK to the Community.
1974	December	Paris summit agrees to the principle of direct elections to the European Parliament and decides to institutionalize summit meetings by establishing the European Council.
1975	March	First meeting of the European Council in Dublin.
	June	Greece applies for Community membership.
1977	March	Portugal applies for Community membership.
	July	Spain applies for Community membership.
1978	October	Community opens accession negotiations with Portugal.
1979	February	Community opens accession negotiations with Spain.
	March	European Monetary System (EMS) comes into operation after a year of high-level negotiations.
	June	First direct elections to the European Parliament.

1981	January	Accession of Greece to the Community.
1985	June	Signing of accession treaties between the Community and Spain and Portugal.
		The Commission publishes its White Paper *Completing the Internal Market*.
	December	Luxembourg European Council meeting agrees the principles of the Single European Act (SEA). The Act confirms the objective of completing the internal market by 1992.
1986	January	Accession of Spain and Portugal to the Community.
1987	June	Turkey applies for Community membership.
	July	SEA comes into force.
1988	June	European Council entrusts to a committee chaired by Jacques Delors the task of studying how the Community might progress to Economic and Monetary Union (EMU).
1989	April	'Delors Committee' presents its report (the Delors Report), which outlines a scheme for a three-stage progression to EMU.
	June	Madrid European Council meeting agrees that Stage 1 of the programme to bring about EMU – the dismantling of internal barriers to the movement of capital – will begin on 1 July 1990.
	July	Austria applies for Community membership.
	December	Commission advises Council of Ministers to reject Turkey's application for Community membership.
		Strasbourg European Council meeting accepts Social Charter and agrees to establish an Intergovernmental Conference (IGC) on EMU at the end of 1990. Both decisions taken by eleven votes to one, with the UK dissenting in each case.

1990	June	Dublin European Council meeting formally agrees that an IGC on political union will be convened.
	July	Cyprus and Malta apply for Community membership.
	October	Unification of Germany; territory of former East Germany becomes part of the Community.
	December	The two IGCs, on EMU and political union, are opened at the Rome summit.
1991	July	Sweden applies for Community membership.
	December	Maastricht European Council meeting agrees to Treaty on European Union. Treaty is based on three pillars: the European Communities, a Common Foreign and Security Policy (CFSP) and co-operation in the fields of Justice and Home Affairs (JHA). The Community pillar includes the strengthening of Community institutions, the extension of the Community's legal policy competence and a timetable for the establishment of EMU and a single currency.
1992	February	Treaty on European Union formally signed at Maastricht by foreign and finance ministers.
	March	Finland applies to join the EU.
	June	In a referendum the Danish reject the TEU by 50.7 per cent to 49.3 per cent.
	September	In a referendum the French endorse the TEU by 51 per cent to 49 per cent.
	November	Norway applies to join the EU.
	December	In a referendum the Swiss vote not to ratify the EEA by 50.3 per cent to 49.7 per cent; Switzerland's application to join the EU is suspended.
		Edinburgh European Council meeting agrees on several key issues, notably Danish opt-outs from the TEU and any future common defence policy, a financial perspective for 1993–99, and the opening of accession negotiations in early 1993 with Austria, Finland, Sweden and Norway.

1993	February	Accession negotiations open with Austria, Finland and Sweden.
	April	Accession negotiations open with Norway.
	May	In a second referendum the Danes vote by 56.8 per cent to 43.2 per cent to ratify the TEU.
	November	TEU comes into force.
1994	January	Stage 2 of EMU: establishment of the European Monetary Institute.
	March	Austria, Finland, Sweden and Norway agree accession terms with the EU.
	April	Hungary and Poland apply for membership of the EU.
	June	In a referendum on accession to the EU, the Austrians vote in favour by 66.4 per cent to 33.6 per cent.
	October	Referendum in Finland on EU membership: vote in favour by 57 per cent to 43 per cent.
	November	Referendum in Sweden on EU membership: vote in favour by 52.2 per cent to 46.9 per cent.
		Referendum in Norway on EU membership: accession rejected by 52.2 per cent to 47.8 per cent.
1995	January	Austria, Finland and Sweden become EU members.
	June	Romania and Slovakia apply to join the EU.
	October	Latvia applies to join the EU.
	November	Estonia applies to join the EU.
	December	Lithuania and Bulgaria apply to join the EU.
1996	January	The Czech Republic and Slovenia apply to join the EU.
1997	June	Amsterdam European Council agrees to the Treaty of Amsterdam. The Treaty fails to provide for the institutional change that enlargement will require, but does contain some strengthening of EU institutions and policies.
	October	Amsterdam Treaty formally signed by EU foreign ministers.

1998	March	Accession negotiations formally opened with Hungary, Poland, the Czech Republic, Slovenia, Estonia and Cyprus.
	May	At a special European Council meeting in Brussels it is agreed that eleven states will participate in the launch of the euro in 1999: France, Germany, Italy, Belgium, Luxembourg, the Netherlands, Ireland, Spain, Portugal, Finland and Austria.
1999	January	Stage 3 of EMU and the euro come into operation.

Adapted and abridged from Nugent, N. (1999) *The Government and Politics of the European Union*, London, Macmillan.

Index

acquis communautaire 29, 234

acquis politique 273

Adenauer, Chancellor Konrad 64, 124

Agenda 2000 212–16, 240–44:
　　Agenda 2000 241, 243, 244, 248
　　For a Stronger and Wider Union 213

agrarian parties 121, 134

Agricultural Council 214

agricultural levies 198

Ahtisari, Martii 280

Albania 280–81

anarchy, definition 10

asylum 99, 101, 102, 103, 105, 257

Austria:
　　budgetary contributions 214, 215
　　finances and 214
　　Freiheitliche Partei (Freedom Party) 127, 139, 245
　　Green party 133
　　joins EU 2, 105, 232, 233
　　People's Party 124
　　presidency 214, 215

authority:
　　definition 10
　　development of 16
　　source of 16

Aznar, José-Maria 138

Balkans: Stability Pact 250–51, 280, 282

Baltic states: EU and 237, 239

bananas, trade in 159

Beetham, David 9

Belarus 252

Belgium:
　　budget and 215
　　Christian Democrat party 124, 125
　　empire 60
　　Green party 133, 135
　　Green/Radical co-ordination 139–40
　　invasions of 46
　　liberal party 126

　　regional parties 135
　　Second World War and 65
　　Treaty of Paris and 1, 2

Berlin Agreement 214, 216, 219

Berlusconi, Silvio 138

Bildt, Carl 279

Blair, Tony 269, 270

Blondel, Jean 176

border controls 34, 101, 102, 105

Bosnia-Herzegovina 277, 278–79

Bruges Group 123

Brunner, Herr, case of 89

Brussels (Merger) Treaty (1965) 2, 32

Brussels Treaty (1975) 198, 218

Bruton, John 185

BSE crisis 180

budget:
　　accountability 207–8, 219
　　Agenda 2000 and 212–16
　　allocation 192
　　annual cycle 203–6
　　CAP and 96, 194, 197, 198, 199
　　compulsory expenditure 203, 206
　　crisis and conflict 197–99
　　decision-making processes 197, 202–6
　　development, phases in 196
　　distribution 192, 197, 200
　　enlargement and 212, 213, 214, 219
　　EP powers and 181
　　expanding 217–18
　　expenditure:
　　　　expansion 199, 217–18
　　　　external 207
　　　　non-compulsory 203, 206
　　financial management 206–8, 209, 218
　　formation of 196–97
　　fraud and 210–12
　　functions 192, 194
　　future of 212–16
　　governance and 193, 195, 216–29
　　history of 195–201
　　importance of 191, 195, 217

institutionalizing 199–201
integration and 193–94, 217
Inter-Institutional Agreements 205
inter-institutional conflict 218
international role 194
multi-annual financial planning
     201, 205, 213
own resources 198, 207, 214, 215
reform of 217, 218–19
size 70, 96, 160, 195, 206
size increase 199, 208
stabilization 192, 193
studying 192–95
Budget Commissioner 203
Budget Council 205
Budget Directorate 203
Budget Treaty (1970) (Luxembourg
   Treaty) 197–98, 218
Budget Treaty (1975) (Brussels
   Treaty) 198, 218
Budgetary Authority 203, 206
Bulgaria: EU and 29, 237, 244
Burke, Edmund 123

Canada 39, 63
Caporaso, J. 15
Carrington, Lord 278
Cassis de Dijon case 97
Central Europe:
     communism and 115
     democracy in 61
     economic development 239, 240
     EU and 105, 237, 238, 251
     responses to fall of Iron Curtain
        237–38
     USSR's domination of 62, 115
Chernobyl nuclear reactor 135
Chirac, President Jacques 243,
   269, 270
Christian democrat parties 115, 122,
   123–25, 136, 138, 140:
     Catholic Church and 124
citizenship 35, 71
Cohesion Fund 200, 214
Cold War:
     beginning of 60
     EU and 17, 260, 274
     European co-operation and 38–39,
        47

NATO and 149
socialist parties and 129
Comintern 131
Committee of Permanent
   Representatives (Coreper) 102, 103
Common Agricultural Policy (CAP):
     budget and 96, 194, 197, 198, 199
     establishment 30
     expenditure, controlling 199, 200
     income transfer and 197
     over-production 198
     reform of 202, 213, 214, 215, 217
Common Foreign and Security
   Policy (CFSP):
     administrative structure 265
     architecture 272–75
     Community pillar and 265
     creation of 2, 256
     enforcement and 159
     European Parliament and 265
     evolution of 256–71
     governing processes and 282–84
     High Representative 270
     independence of EU and 257
     instability of 267
     institutions for 258
     integration and 255, 283
     intergovernmentalism 35, 82, 159,
        275, 283, 290
     Joint Actions 264, 266
     Kosovo and 281
     national policies and 272–73
     origins of 255–56, 261
     policy making 269
     Rapid Reaction Force 257, 270–71
     security challenges and 257
     supranationalism and 275
     tradition and transformation
        259–62
     WEU and 265
     Yugoslavia and 276–82
communautarization 100, 101
communism:
     fall of 17, 61, 115
     fear of 60
     supranationality 120
Communist International 132
communist parties 122, 131–33,
   136, 139
Community pillar:
     Commission 103

creation of 2
Justice and Home Affairs pillar and 99, 100, 103
law and order agenda and 100
as new political and legal order 86
policy and 103
supranational nature 290
confederation 68, 144
conservative parties 122–23, 138
Contact Group 278, 280
Cook, Robin 280
Copenhagen criteria 238
Costa v. ENEL case 86, 87
Council of Europe 5, 74
Council of Ministers:
agenda setting and 157
budget and 203, 206
decision making 157
EP, co-decision with 156
executive powers 14
functions 42, 43
intergovernmental 69
JHA policy and 102
military crisis management 270
origins of 67
policy proposals and 155
Political and Security Committee 270
QMV 43–44, 68, 69, 155, 227
Court of Auditors 208, 210, 218
Court of First Instance: creation of 83
crime 102, 105
Croatia 276–77, 282
customs 99, 101, 103,198:
union 28, 87
Cyprus: EU and 29, 224, 226, 239, 243, 245
Czech Republic:
Common Foreign and Security Policy and 273
EU and 29, 40, 248
Czechoslovakia:
EU and 237, 238
invasion of 39, 132

Delors, Jacques 42, 199, 224, 238
Delors Plan 1 Agreement 199, 200, 212, 213, 217

Delors Plan 2 Agreement 200, 213, 214
democracy:
consociational approach 170–72, 173
definition of 166–68
EU and 165–90
institutionalizing 168–69
legitimation and 167
national institutions and 170–73
referendums and 186
spread of 39–40
Denmark:
budget and 215
ECJ and 77
EMU and 35
Folketing European Affairs Committee 171–72
Green party 134, 135
joins EEC 2, 33, 231, 233
Justice and Home Affairs pillar and 106
monetary union and 28
Progress Party 127
Second World War and 65
Deutsch, K. 144, 145
developing world *see* Third World
Dinan, D. 249
directives 87
Dooge Committee 229
drug trafficking 102, 105

Eastern Europe:
communism and 115
democracy in 61
economic development 239, 240
EU and 105, 237, 238, 251
responses to fall of Iron Curtain 237–38
USSR's domination of 62, 115
see also under names of countries
Eco-Fin Council 214
ecological parties *see* Green parties
Economic and Monetary Union (EMU):
effects of 14–15
federalism and 292
intergovernmentalism and supranationality 290
Maastricht Treaty and 2, 70

national currencies relinquished 14
political implications of 296
two-speed Europe and 247
winners and losers 294–95
economic union 28 *see also previous entry*
ECU 33
European Liberal Democrats Party (ELDP) 139
enlargement:
  agriculture and 241
  applicants, attitudes to 237, 238, 239
  applicants, existing and potential 225
  applicants' motives 229–30
  area increases 231
  budget and 212, 213, 214, 219
  Central and East European states 224, 226, 231, 232, 236–44
  Cohesion Policy and 242
  Cold War and 105
  commitment to 228–29
  conditions for 229–31, 238–39
  conflicts and tensions 232–34, 252
  consensus over 252
  contemporary process 236–46
  costs of 213
  development models and 226–28
  diversity and 252
  economic contrasts and 226
  effects of 231–32
  environmental standards and 242
  Europe and 249–51
  first enlargement 2, 29, 222, 226, 250
  flexibility needed 247–48
  GDP and 230
  history of 222, 228–36
  importance of 221
  institutional consequences and 222, 227, 228, 234–36, 246–47
  Iron Curtain and 221, 228
  Mediterranean dimension 244–46
  NATO and 240–41
  new conditions for 1991 238–39
  nuclear safety and 243
  population increases 231
  problems of 246–52
  reform and 246–49, 250
  second enlargement 29, 33, 222, 250
  Single Market and 24
  speed of accessions 232–33, 243
  third enlargement 29, 222, 250
  threat perception and 229
  transport and 243
  unanimous consent required 29
  unity and 252–53
Estonia: EU and 29, 240
Europe:
  conflict in 1, 46, 50 *see also* First World War; Second World War
  containment of 261
  de-colonization 47–48
  decline of 59–61
  division of 38, 39, 62
  dominance of 58–59
  empires and 58–59
  federal 49–50
  geographical definition and 228–29
  geographically distinct 38, 51
  Green parties 133–35
  identity 45
  nation states, evolution of 54–61
  nation states, loyalty and 117
  national perspectives on 117–18
  nuclear waste 135
  specificity of 47–48
  tradition and transformation in 260–62
  USA and 39, 60, 62–63, 79, 261, 281
  see also following entries
Europe of Democracies and Diversities Group 176
Europe of the Nations 139
European Agricultural Guidance and Guarantee Fund (EAGGF) 197, 215
European Atomic Energy Community: creation 2, 32
European Audit Board 208
European Bank for Reconstruction and Development (EBRD) 237
European Central Bank:
  creation of 35, 70
  democracy and 182
  European Parliament and 182

European Coal and Steel
Community (ECSC):
  budget 196
  Common Assembly 32, 67, 138
  Common Foreign and Security
    Policy and 255
  Council of Ministers 32
  Court of Justice 32, 67
  creation 1, 3, 31
  governance 67
  High Authority 31–32, 67, 196
  members 1, 29
  motivations for joining 65
  socialist parties and 130
  supranational characteristics 31
European Commission:
  agenda setting 156, 157
  budget and 203, 206, 208, 208–9,
    210, 213, 215, 218
  bureaucracy 42
  CFSP and 159
  Commissioners 42
  decision making 157
  enlargement and 227
  executive powers 14
  finances and 199
  fraud and 210–12
  functions 42–43
  governance and 217
  integration and 146
  law and 88, 99, 107, 158
  Legal Service 86, 92
  legislation and 42
  EP, conflict with 209, 210
  policy proposals and 155
  President 42, 171, 180, 185
  reform and 211, 212, 234, 235
  resignation of 43, 179, 180, 183,
    210, 211, 218
  supervision of 172
  supranational 69
  see also Prodi Commission; Santer
    Commission
European Commission for Human
Rights 74
European Communities pillar:
creation of 2
European Convention of Human
Rights (1950) 31
European Council:
  agenda setting 157

Amsterdam Treaty and 268
budget and 202, 205–6
Cardiff meeting 213
Cologne meeting 270, 281
Common Foreign and Security
  Policy and 264
Copenhagen meeting 238–39
decision making and 157
definition 34
directives 67, 76
Dublin meeting 198
EP and 181, 182, 183
Essen meeting 239
Fontainebleau meeting 198
functions 42
Helsinki meeting 29, 257, 270–71
intergovernmental 69
policy proposals and 155
Presidency 34, 157, 179
QMV 71, 157, 268
reform of 234
regulations 67, 71
unanimity 43
Vienna meeting 270
European Council of the Heads of
Government 206
European Court of Auditors 207
European Court of Human Rights
74, 77
European Court of Justice (ECJ):
  Advocates-General 83
  agenda setting and 156, 157
  cases coming to 84
  CFSP and 159
  citizens' rights and 70
  Commission and 92, 107
  community law and 76, 85, 93
  contexts 91
  Council of Ministers and 92
  creation of 67
  development of 90–91
  direct effect 86–90
  EEC Treaty and 75
  enforcement and 77, 158
  European institutions and 92–93
  EP and 92
  EU's uniqueness and 153
  fines 84
  functions 43
  intergovernmental control of 91–92
  judges, home states and 83

jurisdiction, determining 77
Justice and Home Affairs pillar and 99, 103
law and order 82, 99
member state executives and 91–92
member states before 84
national and community law 85
national legal systems and 77
new legal order and 86, 90–91
powers of 77
preliminary references to 84, 88, 100, 106
purposes of 90–91
sex equality and 94
social context 94
strategic context 90–95
supranational 69, 72
supranational policies and 81
supremacy of 86–90
treaties and 77, 84, 88, 90
US Supreme Court and 153–54
European Defence Community 39, 256, 260
European Defence Union 64
European Economic Community (EEC):
    budget 196
    creation of 1
    foreign policy 256
    governance 67
    socialism and 130
European Free Trade Association (EFTA):
    EU and 229, 233–34
    members 32–33
    UK and 32–33
European Investment Bank (EIB) 196, 197
European law see legal system
European Liberal Democrats Party 126
European Monetary System 30, 33
European Parliament (EP):
    agenda setting 156, 157
    Amsterdam Treaty and 2
    budget and 181, 198, 203, 205, 206, 208, 218
    censure motions 180, 181
    Commission, conflict with 209, 210
    Commission's resignation and 43, 176, 179–81, 210, 218

Conference of Presidents 181
Council of Ministers, co-decision with 156
democracy and 174–83
elections 92, 174–76
European Commission and 181–82, 182–83, 184
European Council and 181, 182, 183
executive formation and 179–81
functions 43
legislative powers 181–83, 184, 291
lobbyists and 156
party groups 136, 137, 176, 183, 184
policy proposals and 155
political competition in foiled 177–78
political parties in 136–40, 291, 292
powers of 155, 176, 178–83, 184, 186
representation through 176–78
supranational 69
US Congress and 178
European People's Party (EPP) 123, 124, 136, 138, 176, 178
European Police Office (Europol) 104
European Political Co-operation 256, 261, 263, 264, 265, 272–73
European Recovery Programme (Marshall Plan) 30, 39, 62, 63
European Regional Development Fund (ERDF) 199
European Security and Defence Identity (ESDI) 270
European Social Fund (ESF) 196, 197
European Union (EU):
    agenda setting 156–57
    attractions of membership 229–30
    authority and 300
    characteristics of 30–31
    citizens, relationship with 160
    citizenship of 4
    communist parties and 132–33
    comparisons with other systems 152–54, 161
    consociational approach 170, 171
    constitution for 78
    currencies and 291
    decision making 157–58
    decisions, types of 159

defence identity 283
democracy and 79, 154, 165–90
democratization of 167, 170–73,
     183–86
development 1–2, 27–52, 36
directives 159
distinctiveness of 108–9, 290
East Central Europe and 200
environment changes 79
Europe and 249–51
European security and 276–82
explaining development 1–2, 3, 4,
     36
federalism 109
finance 216–19 *see also* budget
functions of 30–31
GDP 27
governance 3–4, 13–15, 67–72, 79,
     151–61, 216–19, 219, 287, 289
     see also intergovernmental
     model; supranational model
government of 42–44
history of 29–36
institutions 41, 77:
     structure 30
institutions leading to 2
international and 75–78
law and order and 99, 100–4
law's dominance 193
market efficiency and 300–1
member states' governance and 4
Military Committee 270
models of 13–17
as 'moving target' 4–5, 287
mutual recognition 97
nation states and, comparison with
     297, 298
national authority and 299–301
national communities and 171
national institutions and 170–73
nature of 3, 4, 13–17, 46, 81, 108,
     152, 287–303
novelty of 5, 53, 71
opinions 150
policy process 151, 154–59
policy types 159
population 27
powers delegated to 14–15
recommendations 150
redistribution and 96, 130, 159,
     160, 300–1

reform of 234 *see also under*
     European Commission; European
     Council
regulations 159
regulatory policies 160
as regulatory state 109–10, 160–61,
     193, 217, 291, 293–96
renamed as 2
role extended 17
security architecture 273–75
social regulations 160
socialism and 130
sovereignty and 75
state-like qualities 16, 109, 292
states' power and 71–72
supervision of 171–72, 173
trading bloc, world's largest 27
treaties founding 75
uniqueness of 13
violence and 109, 292
WEU and 264, 265, 266, 268, 270
Yugoslavia and 276–82
see also under Common Foreign and
     Security Policy *and under names of*
     bodies of
European Development Fund
     (EDF) 197
Euroscepticism 123, 139, 176, 177
Exchange Rate Mechanism (ERM)
     33, 34

fascist parties 122
federalism:
     EU and 49–50, 69
     integration and 144
     sovereignty and 69
     supranationalism and 78
Federation of European Greens 140
feminism 94
Finer, S. 6
Finland:
     communist party 131
     Green party 133, 134
     joins EU 2, 232, 233
     Kansallinen Kokoomus party
          138
     presidency 257, 270
First World War 37, 57, 59, 60, 61
fishing rights 234

Fontaine, Nicole 123
foreign and security policy: tradition and transformation in 259–62
Fouchet Plan 256
France:
    budget and 215, 216
    CAP and 216, 217
    Christian Democrat party 124
    communist party 132, 139
    de-colonization 47–48
    decline of 61–62
    ECJ and 77
    EDC and 39
    empire 59, 60
    enlargement and 198, 238, 251
    farmers 238, 249
    Germany and 59, 60, 63, 64, 66
    Green party 134
    integration and 65
    National Front 127, 139
    NATO and 66
    Radical Party 126
    regional parties 135
    Revolution 116, 120, 123, 127
    Treaty of Paris and 1, 2
    UK, veto against 33, 66, 149
    USA and 65
    Yugoslavia and 278, 280
Franco, General 61
fraud 210–12
free-trade area 28

Gasperi, Alcide de 124
Gaulle, Charles de 33, 66, 85, 149, 233
General Affairs Council 214
General Agreement on Tariffs and Trade 62, 63
George, Stephen 49
Germany:
    budgetary contributions 214, 215, 216
    Christian Democrat party 124
    Constitutional Court 89, 92
    division of 38, 61, 62
    ECJ and 77
    enlargement and 251
    Europe and 117–18
    European elections and 174
    fascism 57

    finances and 214
    France and 59, 60
    Green party 133, 134, 135
    Maastricht Treaty and 89
    occupation of 61, 62, 64
    power, rise of 59, 60
    presidency 213, 215, 216
    Republikaner Party 127, 128
    reunification 2, 63, 200, 224–25, 237
    Second World War and 60, 65
    Yugoslavia and 278
    see also following entries
Germany, East: EU and 237
Germany, West:
    establishment of 63
    France and 63, 64, 66
    integration and 65
    integration in Europe 63
    NATO and 63, 64, 66
    as post-war problem 66
    rearmament 39, 63–64
    Treaty of Paris and 1, 2
    USA and 62, 63–64
Giscard d'Estaing, Valéry 233
globalization: internationalization 48–51
Gorbachev, President Mikhail 132
governance:
    civil society and 11–12
    definition 6, 10, 291
    economy and 11–12
    expansion of 217
    government and 10, 11–12
    governors and governed, relations between 12, 16–17
    international 12, 17, 287, 288
    laws and 12
    legitimacy 12
    multi-level 79
    nature of 13–17
    structures of 6
    type of 3
    see also intergovernmental model; supranational model *and under* European Union (EU)
government:
    definition 6–7, 10
    governance and 10, 11, 12
    governed, powers of 288
    law and 287

Greece:
    democracy in 61
    economy 200
    EMU and 28, 35
    Green party 134
    joins EEC 2, 33, 230, 232, 233, 234
    military government 61, 230
    NATO joined 63
    POLAN party 138
    Second World War and 65
    Turkey and 245
Green parties 122, 133–35, 139–40
Greenland: joins and leaves EU 233
Grosser, Alfred 260
Guibernau, M. 13

Haas, E. 145, 146–47, 148, 149
Haider, J. 139, 245
Hartley, T. 76
Helsinki conference 244, 245
Hitler, Adolf 60
Hix, Simon 290, 291, 295
Hobbes, Thomas 11, 12
Hoffmann, S. 148, 149
Holbrooke, Richard 279
human rights: development of 116
Hungary:
    Common Foreign and Security
        Policy and 273
    EU and 29, 237, 238, 239, 240
    invasion of 132
Hurd, Douglas 266

Iceland: EU and 233, 234
immigration 99, 101, 102, 103, 257
industrial revolution 119, 120, 121
Inglehart, R. 134
integration:
    budget and 193–94, 217
    Common Foreign and Security
        Policy and 255
    communist parties and 131
    conflict over 35, 40, 44
    conservative parties and 138
    control of 143, 147
    debate over 28, 149
    definition 144–50
    division and 38, 39

    economic 16
    EMU and 35
    fast periods 19
    governance and 151–61
    Green parties and 135
    'high' politics 148
    intergovernmentalism and 149,
        150, 153, 162
    law and order 100
    'low' politics 148
    motives for 45–46
    nation state and 64–66, 148–50
    nation state strengthening and
        148–50
    national self-interest and 49, 50
    negative and positive 44–46
    origins of 1, 4
    pattern of 61–66
    political 16
    political dynamics 70–72
    process of 145–46
    process of not inevitable 44
    shift towards tighter 30, 41, 43–46
    slow periods 19
    social 16
    sovereignty and 45, 49, 50, 148
    'spillover' and 146–47, 148, 149
    stages in 28
    supranationalism and 146–47, 149,
        150, 153, 162
    USA and 65, 66
    war and 37–40, 65
    see also confederation; federalism;
        supranational model
Inter-Governmental Conference 34,
    180, 213, 235
intergovernmental model:
    citizen policies 14
    definition 30, 288
    democracy and 169
    economic stabilization policies 14
    enlargement and 226, 227, 228
    global policies 14
    institutions 42
    integration and 149, 150, 153, 226
    nature of 13–15, 288–89
    organizations exemplifying 13–14
    policy outputs 14
    policy process and 154, 155
    redistributive policies 14
    regulatory policies 14

supranational model and 17, 41,
150, 226, 288–92, 292, 295, 296,
299
veto 41
International Monetary Fund (IMF)
62, 63
Ireland:
budget and 215
economy 200
Fianna Fail 138
Green party 133
joins EEC 2, 33, 231, 233
Israel 245
Italy:
Albania and 280
Alleanza Nationale 127
budget and 215
Christian Democrat party 124
communist party 132, 139
ECJ and 77
empire 60
Europe and 118
fascism 57
Forza Italia 138
Green party 133, 134
liberal party 126
Movimento Sociale Italiano (MSI)
127, 139
Second World War and 65
Treaty of Paris and 1, 2
world wars and 60, 61, 65
Yugoslavia and 278, 280

Japan 59
empire 60
occupation of 61
Judge, D. 156
judicial co-operation 99, 103
Justice and Home Affairs pillar:
Commission and 103
Community method not applying
99–100
Community pillar and 99, 100,
103
Council 102, 103
creation of 2
European Court of Justice and 99,
103, 106
European Parliament and 103
external factors and 104–6

future for 106–8
inefficiency of 104
integration and 100–6
intergovernmental 35
policy making 102–4
reform of 104

K.4 Committee (K.8, '36') 103
Kant, Immanuel 12
Kinnock, Neil 211, 219
Kohl, Chancellor Helmut 214, 237,
243
Korean War 63, 64
Kosovo:
bombing of 105, 270, 280
conflict, origins 279
EU and 270

Laffan, B. 154, 211
Latvia: EU and 29, 244
legal system:
citizens' role 79
description of 83–85
direct effect 86–90
enlargement and 95
importance of 81
intergovernmental and
supranational policies 81
legal pluralism and 89–90
national enforcement of 93
national legislative veto 85
national systems and 93, 95, 292
nature of 108, 110
new legal order and 85–86,
90–91
novelty of 75
as regulatory order 96–98
review of 83–85
role of 93
single market and 81
supremacy over national 76, 86,
87, 90, 92
legitimacy: definition 10 see also
under nation state
Leo XIII, Pope 124
Leviathan state 11, 12
liberal-democratic states:
governors and governed, relations
between 12

governors and governed,
  sovereignty and 73
  legitimacy and 9, 12
Liberal International 126
Liberal parties 122, 125–27, 136
Lijphart, Arend 170
Lindblom, Charles 7, 9
Lipset and Rokkan 119, 121, 134,
  140
Lithuania: EU and 29, 244
Lively, Jack 12
lobbyists 156, 158
Locke, John 12
London Report 261
Lord, C. 126
Luxembourg:
  Christian Democrat party 124, 125
  Second World War and 65
  Treaty of Paris and 1, 2
Luxembourg Compromise 41
Luxembourg Treaty *see* Budget
  Treaty

Maastricht Treaty *see* Treaty on
  European Union
Macedonia 277
McKay, David 291–92, 296
Magnette, Paul 184
Majone, Giandomenico 293, 294,
  299–300
Malta: EU and 29, 224, 239
Mann, M. 5
Maritain, Jacques 125
Marshall Plan *see* European Recovery
  Programme
Marx, Karl 58, 128
Mazey and Richardson 156
Messina Conference 32
Milosovic, Slobodan 278, 279, 280
Milward, Alan 46, 65–66
Mitterand, President François 198,
  233, 237
Moldova 252
monetary union 28, 33, 170
Monnet, Jean 3, 31
Moravcsik, Andrew 49, 65, 149
multi-level governance 289, 291, 298

Mussolini, Benito 60, 118
mutual recognition 97

nation states:
  boundaries 48
  bribery and 8, 9
  characteristics of 54–55
  Church and 120
  definition 7–8, 10, 55–56
  democracy and 57
  dualist 73, 74
  EU and 64–66
  European integration and 65
  evolution 55–57, 120
  exclusive rule 8
  features of European 7–8
  force and 8, 9, 56
  globalization and 48–49
  independence 7, 9
  legal regulation 8
  legitimacy 8, 9
  liberal-constitutional 57
  monist 73, 74
  national identity and 55
  politics in 55
  private sphere 8
  relations between 9, 10–11, 12
  society and 8
  sovereignty 7, 56
  territory and 8
  violence and 109, 110
  see also sovereignty
nationalization 129
NATO (North Atlantic Treaty
  Organization):
  enlargement 274
  European defence and 260, 261
  formation 62, 63
  reform 274
  role of 63
  Yugoslavia and 278
neo-functionalism 147, 148, 149, 150
net contributors club 200, 208, 212,
  213, 214, 215, 216
Netherlands:
  budgetary contributions 214, 215
  Christian Democrat party 124, 125
  Green party 133
  liberal party 126
  Second World War and 65
  Treaty of Paris and 1, 2

Nice Treaty 170
Norway:
    EU and 29, 233, 234
    liberal party 126
    Progress Party 127
    Second World War and 65
Nouvelles Equipes Internationales 138
nuclear power 133

objective one regions 199
oil 129, 148
Organization for Economic
    Co-operation and Development
    (OECD) 63
Organization for Security and
    Co-operation in Europe (OSCE)
    274, 279
Ortega y Gasset, José 118
Owen, David 278

Party of European Socialists (PES)
    138, 139, 177, 178
Pen, Jean La 139
Peters, B. 156
Petersburg Tasks 268
Peterson, J. 155
PHARE programme (Poland–
    Hungary: Actions for Economic
    Restructuring) 237, 238
Philip Morris case 96
pillars, three:
    definition of 2, 81–82
    see also Common Foreign and
        Security Policy pillar;
        Community pillar; Justice and
        Home Affairs pillar
Poland:
    Common Foreign and Security
        Policy and 273
    EU and 29, 237, 238, 239, 240, 248
    Second World War and 60
    Solidarity 132
police 99, 101, 103, 104
political culture:
    Catholics and 124
    definition 113, 114–15
    emergence of 116–17
    party traditions 115, 116–42

variety of 117
political parties:
    left/right division 122, 126
    national dimension 115
    social cleavages and 119–21
politics:
    definition 5, 6, 10
    government and 7
pollution 135
Poos, Jacques 277
Portugal:
    authoritarian government 39, 40,
        61, 230
    budget and 215
    Christian Democrat party 138, 140
    communist party 131, 132
    democracy in 61
    economy 200
    empire 118
    enlargement and 229, 238
    Europe and 118
    joins EEC 2, 33, 230, 232, 233, 234
Second World War and 60, 65
Prodi, Roman: fraud and 211, 218–19
Prodi Commission 180, 211

qualified majority voting (QMV)
    235: 236 see also under Council of
    Ministers; European Council

Rainbow group 139
Rambouillet negotiations 280
Rapid Reaction Force see under
    Common Foreign and Security
    Policy
Reagan, President Ronald 261
recession, 1970s 149
Reeve, Andrew 12
referendums 170
regional parties 121, 122, 135–36,
    140
regulatory agencies 299
Reif and Schmitt 174
Richardson, J. 158
right, extreme parties of 127–28, 139
Romania: EU and 29, 244
Rosamond, B. 299
Runciman, W. 5

Russia:
   crime in 105
   EU and 239, 252
   Europe and 116
   Revolution 57, 59, 120, 121–22,
      129, 131
   Yugoslavia and 278, 280
   see also Union of Soviet Socialist
      Republics

St Malo declaration 270, 281
Sandholtz and Zysman 149
Santer Commission 179, 180, 181,
   209, 210, 211, 213
Santer, Jacques 125, 179, 209
Sbragia, A. 152, 153
Scharf, Fritz 293, 299
Schengen Agreements 101, 102–3
Schmidhuber testimonial 209
Schröder, Chancellor Gerhard 215
Schuman Plan 3, 31
Schuman, Robert 3, 124
Second International 128, 129, 130
Second World War 37–38, 60–61, 65
security: concept of broadened 260
Serbia 278, 279, 280
single currency 28, 34
   beginnings of 35
   see also Economic and Monetary
      Union
Single European Act (1986):
   Commission and 42–43
   Common Foreign and Security
      Policy and 263–64
   Common Market and 2, 34
   EMU and 35
   finances and 199
   integration and 149
single market 28, 34
Sinnot, Richard 176
Skinner, Quentin 56
Slovakia 29, 244
Slovenia 29, 240, 276–77, 282
Smith, Adam 11
socialism: fear of 60
Socialist International 138
socialist parties 120, 121, 122,
   128–31, 132, 136, 140

Solana, Javier 270
sovereignty:
   co-operation and 45
   controlling 56–57
   debate over 41
   definition 73
   democracy and 79
   emergence of 56
   European and 75, 76, 78
   foreign and security policy and
      258, 259, 272
   international law and 73
   law and 57, 73
Spaak, Paul-Henri 32
Spain:
   authoritarian government 39, 40,
      230
   budget and 214–15, 215
   communist party 132
   democracy in 61
   enlargement and 229, 238
   Europe and 118
   joins EEC 2, 33, 230, 232, 233, 234
   NATO joined 63
   Partido Pupular 138
   Second World War and 60, 65
Spinelli, A. 144, 145
Stalin, Josef 59, 60
state:
   definition 10, 55–56
   Hobbes on 11, 12
   see also nation states
statehood: foreign and security
   policy and 258
states *see* nation states
Stone, Alec 15
structural funds:
   budget and 194, 199
   enlargement and 226, 242
   fraud and 211
   importance growing 217–18
   reform of 202
subsidiarity 124
superpowers 60, 62–64
supranational model:
   authority and 16
   definition 30, 68, 289
   democracy and 169
   early institutions and 108
   enlargement and 226, 227, 228

institutions 42, 67–68, 108
integration and 41, 146–47, 149,
  150, 153, 226, 288–92
intergovernmental model and 17,
  41, 150, 226, 292, 295, 296, 299
multi-level view and 298
nature of 15–17, 68–69
policy process and 154
shift towards 30, 41, 43–46, 51, 72,
  226
sovereignty and 72–73
states' acceptance of 71
see also integration
Svensson, Palle 176
Sweden:
  budgetary contributions 214, 215
  economic integration and 226
  EMU and 35
  Europe and 118
  Green party 133
  joins EU 2, 105, 232, 233
  liberal party 126
  Moderate Samling party 138
  socialist party 129
Switzerland:
  EU and 29, 233, 234
  Green party 133, 135

terrorism 102
Thatcher, Margaret 123, 198, 213,
  233, 237
Third International 131
Third World 134, 135, 139, 194, 218
Thompson, G. 13
Three Wise Men 218
trans-European networks (TENs) 194
transnational corporations 134, 135
treaties 73–74, 87, 170, 171 *see also*
  following entries
Treaty of Amsterdam (1997):
  citizens' rights 70
  Common Foreign and Security
    Policy and 78, 267–69
  confederation 70
  effects of 2, 34–35
  failure of 235
  Justice and Home Affairs 78, 99,
    106
  provisions of 268
Treaty of Paris (1951):

budget and 196
ECSC and 1, 31
sex equality and 94
signatories 2
Treaty of Rome (1957):
  budget and 196
  CAP 197
  common market and 34
  customs unions 32
  ECJ and 84, 86, 88
  EEC and 1
  enlargement and 228
  European Atomic Energy
    Community 32
  motivations for signing 65
Treaty of Versailles 37
Treaty of Westminster 74
Treaty on European Union (1992)
  (Maastricht Treaty):
  Cohesion Fund 200
  common currency and 71
  Common Foreign and Security
    Policy and 1, 256–57, 264–66,
    267
  communist parties and 132
  EMU and 1, 34, 78
  enlargement and 228
  EU and 1
  European Central Bank and 78
  European Commission and 179
  European Parliament and 179
  Green parties and 134
  instability of 267
  intergovernmentalism and 149
  Justice and Home Affairs and 1, 103
  pillars and 34, 35, 99
  ratification difficult 235
  revision of 34–35
  right-wing parties and 139
  significance of 34
  single currency and 34, 35
  tensions within 267
TREVI Group 101, 102–3
Trojan, Carlo 213
Tsebelis, G. 156
Turkey:
  economic development 245
  EU and 29, 105, 224, 226, 230, 239,
    244, 252
  Europe and 116
  'Europeanness' and 245

Greece and 245
human rights and 226, 245
Kurdish people and 226, 245
NATO and 63, 245

Ukraine 252
Union of European Nations 176
Union of Soviet Socialist Republics
(USSR):
    collapse of 132
    containing 39, 62–63
    Europe and 38
    industrial development 59
    nuclear bomb tested 64
    Second World War and 60, 62
    see also Russia
United European Left 139
United Kingdom (UK):
    aloofness of 39
    budgetary contributions 198, 199,
      214, 215
    CAP reform and 198–99
    Conservative party 176
    de-colonization 47
    decline of 61–62
    dualist state 74, 76
    ECJ and 77
    empire 59, 60, 63, 118
    EMU and 17, 28, 35, 49
    enlargement and 251
    ERM and 34
    EU and 2, 32, 33, 231, 233
    Europe and 49, 118
    European law 76–77
    European Communities Act (1972)
      76
    European Convention on Human
      Rights 74
    European Court of Human Rights
      and 74
    French veto against entry 33
    Germany and 59, 60
    Green party 133, 134, 135
    House of Lords 210
    Human Rights Act (1998) 74, 77
    Independence party 141
    integration and 65
    joins EEC 2, 33, 231, 233
    Liberal Party 126

Maastricht Social Chapter and 43
monetary union and 28
parliament, EU scrutiny and 171,
    172
rebates for 198, 199, 216
renegotiation 198
Second World War and 65
USA and 49, 63, 229
as world power 63
Yugoslavia and 278, 280
United Nations 62
United States of America (USA):
    Common Foreign and Security
      Policy and 273
    Europe, conflict with 261
    European defence and 261, 273
    European Recovery Programme
      30, 39
    Germany and 59, 60
    power increases 59
    regulatory agencies in 299–300
    Second World War and 60, 62
    West Germany and 62, 63–64
    Yugoslavia and 277, 278, 279, 280

Van Gend case 86, 87
Vance, Cyrus 278
Vance–Owen plan 278, 282
Védrine, Hubert 280

Wallace, Helen 13, 151, 152, 155
Wallace, William 46, 151, 152, 155
wars 1, 37–40, 259
Weale, Albert 167
Weber, Max 55–56
Werner Report (1970) 33
Western European Union (WEU)
    39, 64, 261, 263, 264, 266, 268,
    270
Westlake, Martin 180
World Bank 62, 63

Yugoslavia 237, 266, 273, 276 *see
    also* Balkans Stability pact;
    Bosnia-Herzegovina; Croatia;
    Kosovo; Slovenia

Acknowledgements

Grateful acknowledgement is made to the following sources for permission to reproduce material in this book.

Text

Appendix: Nugent, N. (1999) *The Government and Politics of the European Union*, Macmillan Press Ltd.

Figures

Figures 8.1 and 9.1: Adapted from the Office for Official Publications of the European Communities (1999) *The Community Budget: The Facts in Figures*, © European Communities, 1999; *Figure 10.1:* Nuttall, S. (1994) 'The commission and foreign policy-making' in Edwards, G. and Spence, D. (eds) *The European Commission*, John Harper Publishing; *Figure 10.2:* Forster, A. and Wallace, W. (2000) 'Common foreign and security policy' in Wallace, H. and Wallace, W. (eds) *Policy-Making in the European Union*, fourth edition, Oxford University Press. Reprinted by permission of Oxford University Press; *Figure 10.3:* Keatinge, P. (1997) 'Security and defence' in Tonra, B. (ed.) *Amsterdam: What the Treaty Means*, Institute of European Affairs.

Tables

Table 5.1: Mair, P. (2000) 'Left and right in Europe since 1954', *The Guardian*, 21 February 2000, © Guardian Newspapers Ltd 2000; *Tables 5.2 and 7.1:* Adapted from www.europarl.eu.int/ © European Parliament; *Tables 9.1 and 9.3:* Ardy, B. (1999) 'Agricultural, structural policy, the budget and eastern enlargement of the European Union' in Henderson, K. (ed.) *Back to Europe: Central and Eastern Europe and the European Union*, UCL Press Ltd; *Tables 9.2 and 9.4:* European Commission (1997) 'Agenda 2000: For a stronger and wider Union', *Bulletin of the European Union, Supplement 5–97*, © European Communities, 1997.

Photographs

Pages 3, 33, 84, 145, 179, 195 and 241: © European Commission Audiovisual Library; *page 64:* AGIP/Interfoto Pressebild; *page 110:* PA Photos Ltd; *page 150:* Agence France Presse.